CISCO

Course Booklet

Routing Protocols

ciscopress.com

Cisco | Networking Academy
Mind Wide Open

Routing Protocols Course Booklet

Published by:
Cisco Press
800 East 96th Street
Indianapolis, IN 46240 USA

Printed in the United States of America

First Printing   October 2013

Library of Congress Control Number: 2013944487

ISBN-13: 978-1-58713-321-3

ISBN-10: 1-58713-321-0

Warning and Disclaimer

This book is designed to provide information about Cisco Networking Academy Routing Protocols course. Every effort has been made to make this book as complete and as accurate as possible, but no warranty or fitness is implied.

The information is provided on an "as is" basis. The authors, Cisco Press, and Cisco Systems, Inc. shall have neither liability nor responsibility to any person or entity with respect to any loss or damages arising from the information contained in this book or from the use of the discs or programs that may accompany it.

The opinions expressed in this book belong to the author and are not necessarily those of Cisco Systems, Inc.

Publisher
Paul Boger

Associate Publisher
Dave Dusthimer

Business Operations Manager, Cisco Press
Jan Cornelssen

Executive Editor
Mary Beth Ray

Managing Editor
Sandra Schroeder

Project Editor
Seth Kerney

Editorial Assistant
Vanessa Evans

Cover Designer
Louisa Adair

Interior Designer
Mark Shirar

Composition
Bronkella Publishing, LLC

CISCO.

Trademark Acknowledgments

All terms mentioned in this book that are known to be trademarks or service marks have been appropriately capitalized. Cisco Press or Cisco Systems, Inc., cannot attest to the accuracy of this information. Use of a term in this book should not be regarded as affecting the validity of any trademark or service mark.

Feedback Information

At Cisco Press, our goal is to create in-depth technical books of the highest quality and value. Each book is crafted with care and precision, undergoing rigorous development that involves the unique expertise of members from the professional technical community.

Readers' feedback is a natural continuation of this process. If you have any comments regarding how we could improve the quality of this book, or otherwise alter it to better suit your needs, you can contact us through email at feedback@ciscopress.com. Please make sure to include the book title and ISBN in your message.

We greatly appreciate your assistance.

Contents at a Glance

Contents

Command Syntax Conventions

The conventions used to present command syntax in this book are the same conventions used in the IOS Command Reference. The Command Reference describes these conventions as follows:

- **Boldface** indicates commands and keywords that are entered literally as shown. In actual configuration examples and output (not general command syntax), boldface indicates commands that are manually input by the user (such as a **show** command).

- *Italic* indicates arguments for which you supply actual values.

- Vertical bars (|) separate alternative, mutually exclusive elements.

- Square brackets ([ ]) indicate an optional element.

- Braces ({ }) indicate a required choice.

- Braces within brackets ([{ }]) indicate a required choice within an optional element.

About This Course Booklet

Your Cisco Networking Academy Course Booklet is designed as a study resource you can easily read, highlight, and review on the go, wherever the Internet is not available or practical:

- The text is extracted directly, word-for-word, from the online course so you can highlight important points and take notes in the "Your Chapter Notes" section.

- Headings with the exact page correlations provide a quick reference to the online course for your classroom discussions and exam preparation.

- An icon system directs you to the online curriculum to take full advantage of the images imbedded within the Networking Academy online course interface and reminds you to perform the labs, Class activities, Interactive activities, Packet Tracer activities, and chapter quizzes and exams.

The *Course Booklet* is a basic, economical paper-based resource to help you succeed with the Cisco Networking Academy online course.

Companion Guide

Looking for more than the online curriculum? The Companion Guide is fully aligned to Networking Academy's online course chapters and offers additional book-based pedagogy to reinforce key concepts, enhance student comprehension, and promote retention. Using this full-fledged textbook, students can focus scarce study time, organize review for quizzes and exams, and get the day-to-day reference answers they're looking for.

The Companion Guide also offers instructors additional opportunities to assign take-home reading or vocabulary homework, helping students prepare more for in-class lab work and discussions.

Available in print and all major eBook formats (Book: 9781587133237   eBook: 9780133476323)

Course Introduction

0.0 Welcome to Routing Protocols

0.0.1 Message to the Student

0.0.1.1 Welcome

Welcome to the CCNA Routing and Switching Routing Protocols course. The goal of this course is to introduce you to fundamental networking concepts and technologies. These online course materials will assist you in developing the skills necessary to plan and implement small networks across a range of applications. The specific skills covered in each chapter are described at the start of each chapter.

You can use your smart phone, tablet, laptop, or desktop to access your course, participate in discussions with your instructor, view your grades, read or review text, and practice using interactive media. However, some media are complex and must be viewed on a PC, as well as Packet Tracer activities, quizzes, and exams.

Refer to
Online Course
for Illustration

0.0.1.2 A Global Community

When you participate in the Networking Academy, you are joining a global community linked by common goals and technologies. Schools, colleges, universities, and other entities in over 160 countries participate in the program. A visualization of the global Networking Academy community is available at http://www.academynetspace.com.

Look for the Cisco Networking Academy official site on Facebook© and LinkedIn©. The Facebook site is where you can meet and engage with other Networking Academy students from around the world. The Cisco Networking Academy LinkedIn site connects you with job postings, and you can see how others are effectively communicating their skills.

Refer to
Online Course
for Illustration

0.0.1.3 More Than Just Information

The NetSpace learning environment is an important part of the overall course experience for students and instructors in the Networking Academy. These online course materials include course text and related interactive media, Packet Tracer simulation activities, real equipment labs, remote access labs, and many different types of quizzes. All of these materials provide important feedback to help you assess your progress throughout the course.

The material in this course encompasses a broad range of technologies that facilitate how people work, live, play, and learn by communicating with voice, video, and other data. Networking and the internet affect people differently in different parts of the world. Although we have worked with instructors from around the world to create these materials, it is important that you work with your instructor and fellow students to make the material in this course applicable to your local situation.

Refer to
Online Course
for Illustration

0.0.1.4   How We Teach

E-doing is a design philosophy that applies the principle that people learn best by doing. The curriculum includes embedded, highly interactive e-doing activities to help stimulate learning, increase knowledge retention, and make the whole learning experience much richer – and that makes understanding the content much easier.

Refer to
Online Course
for Illustration

0.0.1.5   Practice Leads to Mastery

In a typical lesson, after learning about a topic for the first time, you will check your understanding with some interactive media items. If there are new commands to learn, you will practice them with the Syntax Checker before using the commands to configure or troubleshoot a network in Packet Tracer, the Networking Academy network simulation tool. Next, you will do practice activities on real equipment in your classroom or accessed remotely over the internet.

Packet Tracer can also provide additional practice any time by creating your own activities or you may want to competitively test your skills with classmates in multi-user games. Packet Tracer skills assessments and skills integration labs give you rich feedback on the skills you are able to demonstrate and are great practice for chapter, checkpoint, and final exams.

Refer to
Online Course
for Illustration

0.0.1.6   Mind Wide Open

An important goal in education is to enrich you, the student, by expanding what you know and can do. It is important to realize, however, that the instructional materials and the instructor can only facilitate the process. You must make the commitment yourself to learn new skills. The following pages share a few suggestions to help you learn and prepare for transitioning your new skills to the workplace.

Refer to
Online Course
for Illustration

0.0.1.7   Engineering Journals

Professionals in the networking field often keep Engineering Journals in which they write down the things they observe and learn such as how to use protocols and commands. Keeping an Engineering Journal creates a reference you can use at work in your ICT job. Writing is one way to reinforce your learning – along with Reading, Seeing, and Practicing.

A sample entry for implementing a technology could include the necessary software commands, the purpose of the commands, command variables, and a topology diagram indicating the context for using the commands to configure the technology.

Refer to
Online Course
for Illustration

0.0.1.8   Explore the World of Networking

Packet Tracer is a networking learning tool that supports a wide range of physical and logical simulations. It also provides visualization tools to help you understand the internal workings of a network.

The pre-made Packet Tracer activities consist of network simulations, games, activities, and challenges that provide a broad range of learning experiences. These tools will help you develop an understanding of how data flows in a network.

Refer to
Online Course
for Illustration

0.0.1.9   Create Your Own Worlds

You can also use Packet Tracer to create your own experiments and networking scenarios. We hope that, over time, you consider using Packet Tracer - not only for experiencing the pre-built activities, but also to become an author, explorer, and experimenter.

The online course materials have embedded Packet Tracer activities that will launch on computers running Windows® operating systems, if Packet Tracer is installed. This integration may also work on other operating systems using Windows emulation.

Refer to
Online Course
for Illustration

0.0.1.10   How Packet Tracer Helps Master Concepts

Educational Games

Packet Tracer Multi-User games enable you or a team to compete with other students to see who can accurately complete a series of networking tasks the fastest. It is an excellent way to practice the skills you are learning in Packet Tracer activities and hands-on labs.

Cisco Aspire is a single-player, standalone strategic simulation game. Players test their networking skills by completing contracts in a virtual city. The Networking Academy Edition is specifically designed to help you prepare for the CCENT certification exam. It also incorporates business and communication skills ICT employers seek in job candidates.

Performance-Based Assessments

The Networking Academy performance-based assessments have you do Packet Tracer activities like you have been doing all along, only now integrated with an online assessment engine that will automatically score your results and provide you with immediate feedback. This feedback helps you to more accurately identify the knowledge and skills you have mastered and where you need more practice. There are also questions on chapter quizzes and exams that use Packet Tracer activities to give you additional feedback on your progress.

Refer to
Online Course
for Illustration

0.0.1.11   Course Overview

As the course title inidcates, the focus of this course is on learning the architecture, components, and operations of routers, and explains the principles of routing and routing protocols. You will do the following:

- describe the purpose, nature, and operations of a router, routing tables, and the route lookup process
- configure and troubleshoot advanced operations of routers and implement RIP, OSPF, and EIGRP routing protocols for IPv4 and IPv6
- understand and describe the purpose and types of access control lists (ACLs)
- configure and verify static routing and default routing
- manage Cisco IOS Software licensing and configuration files

By the end of this course, you will be able to configure and troubleshoot routers and resolve common issues with RIPv1, RIPv2, EIGRP, and OSPF in both IPv4 and IPv6 networks.

Refer to
Online Course
for Illustration

0.1.1.1   Course GUI Tutorial

Your Chapter Notes

Routing Concepts

1.0 Routing Concepts

1.0.1.1 Introduction

Networks allow people to communicate, collaborate, and interact in many ways. Networks are used to access web pages, talk using IP telephones, participate in video conferences, compete in interactive gaming, shop using the Internet, complete online coursework, and more.

At the core of the network is the router. A router connects one network to another network. The router is responsible for the delivery of packets across different networks. The destination of the IP packet might be a web server in another country or an email server on the local area network.

The router uses its routing table to determine the best path to use to forward a packet. It is the responsibility of the routers to deliver those packets in a timely manner. The effectiveness of internetwork communications depends, to a large degree, on the ability of routers to forward packets in the most efficient way possible.

When a host sends a packet to a device on a different IP network, the packet is forwarded to the default gateway because a host device cannot communicate directly with devices outside of the local network. The default gateway is the destination that routes traffic from the local network to devices on remote networks. It is often used to connect a local network to the Internet.

This chapter will also answer the question, "What does a router do with a packet received from one network and destined for another network?" Details of the routing table will be examined including connected, static, and dynamic routes.

Because the router can route packets between networks, devices on different networks can communicate. This chapter will introduce the router, its role in the networks, its main hardware and software components, and the routing process. Exercises which demonstrate how to access the router, configure basic router settings, and verify settings will be provided.

Refer to **Lab Activity** for this chapter

1.0.1.2 Class Activity - Do We Really Need a Map?

Activity - Do We Really Need a Map?

This modeling activity asks you to research travel directions from source to destination. Its purpose is to compare those types of directions to network routing directions.

Scenario

Using the Internet and Google Maps, located at http://maps.google.com, find a route between the capital city of your country and some other distant town or between two places within your own city. Pay close attention to the driving or walking directions Google Maps suggests.

Notice that in many cases, Google Maps suggests more than one route between the two locations you chose. It also allows you to put additional constraints on the route, such as avoiding highways or tolls.

Copy at least two route instructions supplied by Google Maps for this activity. Place your copies into a word processing document and save it for use with the next step.

Open the .pdf accompanying this modeling activity and complete it with a fellow student. Discuss the reflection questions listed on the .pdf and record your answers.

Be prepared to present your answers to the class.

Refer to
Online Course
for Illustration

1.1   Initial Configuration of a Router

1.1.1   Functions of a Router

1.1.1.1   Characteristics of a Network

Networks have had a significant impact on our lives. They have changed the way we live, work, and play.

Networks allow us to communicate, collaborate, and interact in ways we never did before. We use the network in a variety of ways, including web applications, IP telephony, video conferencing, interactive gaming, electronic commerce, education, and more.

As shown in the figure, there are many key structures and performance-related characteristics referred to when discussing networks:

■ **Topology** - There are physical and logical topologies. The physical topology is the arrangement of the cables, network devices, and end systems. It describes how the network devices are actually interconnected with wires and cables. The logical topology is the path over which the data is transferred in a network. It describes how the network devices appear connected to network users.

■ **Speed** - Speed is a measure of the data rate in bits per second (b/s) of a given link in the network.

■ **Cost** - Cost indicates the general expense for purchasing of network components, and installation and maintenance of the network.

■ **Security** - Security indicates how protected the network is, including the information that is transmitted over the network. The subject of security is important, and techniques and practices are constantly evolving. Consider security whenever actions are taken that affect the network.

■ **Availability** - Availability is a measure of the probability that the network is available for use when it is required.

■ **Scalability** - Scalability indicates how easily the network can accommodate more users and data transmission requirements. If a network design is optimized to only meet current requirements, it can be very difficult and expensive to meet new needs when the network grows.

- **Reliability** - Reliability indicates the dependability of the components that make up the network, such as the routers, switches, PCs, and servers. Reliability is often measured as a probability of failure or as the mean time between failures (MTBF).

These characteristics and attributes provide a means to compare different networking solutions.

Note   While the term "speed" is commonly used when referring to the network bandwidth, it is not technically accurate. The actual speed that the bits are transmitted does not vary over the same medium. The difference in bandwidth is due to the number of bits transmitted per second, not how fast they travel over wire or wireless medium.

Refer to
Online Course
for Illustration

1.1.1.2   Why Routing?

How does clicking a link in a web browser return the desired information in mere seconds? Although there are many devices and technologies collaboratively working together to enable this, the primary device is the router. Stated simply, a router connects one network to another network.

Communication between networks would not be possible without a router determining the best path to the destination and forwarding traffic to the next router along that path. The router is responsible for the routing of traffic between networks.

In the animation in the figure, the network topology diagram consists of two hosts, two switches and a Cisco 1841 Integrated Series Router (ISR).

When a packet arrives on a router interface, the router uses its routing table to determine how to reach the destination network. The destination of the IP packet might be a web server in another country or an email server on the local area network. It is the responsibility of routers to deliver those packets efficiently. The effectiveness of internetwork communications depends, to a large degree, on the ability of routers to forward packets in the most efficient way possible.

Refer to
Online Course
for Illustration

1.1.1.3   Routers Are Computers

Most network capable devices (i.e., computers, tablets, and smartphones) require the following components to operate, as shown in Figure 1:

- Central processing unit (CPU)

- Operating system (OS)

- Memory and storage (RAM, ROM, NVRAM, Flash, hard drive)

A router is essentially a specialized computer. It requires a CPU and memory to temporarily and permanently store data to execute operating system instructions, such as system initialization, routing functions, and switching functions.

Note   Cisco devices use the Cisco Internetwork Operating System (IOS) as the system software.

The table in Figure 2 summarizes the types of router memory, the volatility, and examples of what is stored in each.

Routers store data using:

- **Random Access Memory (RAM)** - Provides temporary storage for various applications and processes including the running IOS, the running configuration file, various tables (i.e., IP routing table, Ethernet ARP table) and buffers for packet processing. RAM is referred to as volatile because it loses its contents when power is turned off.

- **Read-Only Memory (ROM)** - Provides permanent storage for bootup instructions, basic diagnostic software and a limited IOS in case the router cannot load the full featured IOS. ROM is firmware and referred to as non-volatile because it does not lose its contents when power is turned off.

- **Non-Volatile Random Access Memory (NVRAM)** - Provides permanent storage for the startup configuration file (startup-config). NVRAM is non-volatile and does not lose its contents when power is turned off.

- **Flash** - Provides permanent storage for the IOS and other system-related files. The IOS is copied from flash into RAM during the bootup process. Flash is non-volatile and does not lose its contents when power is turned off.

Unlike a computer, a router does not have video adapters or sound card adapters. Instead, routers have specialized ports and network interface cards to interconnect devices to other networks. Figure 3 identifies some of these ports and interfaces.

Refer to
Online Course
for Illustration

1.1.1.4 Routers Interconnect Networks

Most users are unaware of the presence of numerous routers on their own network or on the Internet. Users expect to be able to access web pages, send emails, and download music, regardless of whether the server accessed is on their own network or on another network. Networking professionals know that it is the router that is responsible for forwarding packets from network to network, from the original source to the final destination.

A router connects multiple networks, which means that it has multiple interfaces that each belong to a different IP network. When a router receives an IP packet on one interface, it determines which interface to use to forward the packet to the destination. The interface that the router uses to forward the packet may be the final destination, or it may be a network connected to another router that is used to reach the destination network.

In the animation in Figure 1, R1 and R2 are responsible for receiving the packet on one network and forwarding the packet out another network toward the destination network.

Each network that a router connects to typically requires a separate interface. These interfaces are used to connect a combination of both local-area networks (LANs) and wide-area networks (WANs). LANs are commonly Ethernet networks that contain devices, such as PCs, printers, and servers. WANs are used to connect networks over a large geographical area. For example, a WAN connection is commonly used to connect a LAN to the Internet service provider (ISP) network.

Notice that each site in Figure 2 requires the use of a router to interconnect to other sites. Even the Home Office requires a router. In this topology, the router located at the Home Office is a specialized device that performs multiple services for the home network.

Refer to
Online Course
for Illustration

1.1.1.5 Routers Choose Best Paths

The primary functions of a router are to:

■ Determine the best path to send packets

■ Forward packets toward their destination

The router uses its routing table to determine the best path to use to forward a packet. When the router receives a packet, it examines the destination address of the packet and uses the routing table to search for the best path to that network. The routing table also includes the interface to be used to forward packets for each known network. When a match is found, the router encapsulates the packet into the data link frame of the outgoing or exit interface, and the packet is forwarded toward its destination.

It is possible for a router to receive a packet that is encapsulated in one type of data link frame, and to forward the packet out of an interface that uses a different type of data link frame. For example, a router may receive a packet on an Ethernet interface, but must forward the packet out of an interface configured with the Point-to-Point Protocol (PPP). The data link encapsulation depends on the type of interface on the router and the type of medium to which it connects. The different data link technologies that a router can connect to include Ethernet, PPP, Frame Relay, DSL, cable, and wireless (802.11, Bluetooth).

The animation in the figure follows a packet from the source PC to the destination PC. Notice that it is the responsibility of the router to find the destination network in its routing table and forward the packet on toward its destination. In this example, router R1 receives the packet encapsulated in an Ethernet frame. After de-encapsulating the packet, R1 uses the destination IP address of the packet to search its routing table for a matching network address. After a destination network address is found in the routing table, R1 encapsulates the packet inside a PPP frame and forwards the packet to R2. A similar process is performed by R2.

Note Routers use static routes and dynamic routing protocols to learn about remote networks and build their routing tables.

Refer to
Online Course
for Illustration

1.1.1.6 Packet Forwarding Mechanisms

Routers support three packet-forwarding mechanisms:

■ **Process switching** - An older packet forwarding mechanism still available for Cisco routers. When a packet arrives on an interface, it is forwarded to the control plane where the CPU matches the destination address with an entry in its routing table, and then determines the exit interface and forwards the packet. It is important to understand that the router does this for every packet, even if the destination is the same for a stream of packets. This process-switching mechanism is very slow and rarely implemented in modern networks.

■ **Fast switching** - This is a common packet forwarding mechanism which uses a fast-switching cache to store next-hop information. When a packet arrives on an interface, it is forwarded to the control plane where the CPU searches for a match in the fast-switching cache. If it is not there, it is process-switched and forwarded to the exit interface. The flow information for the packet is also stored in the fast-switching cache.

If another packet going to the same destination arrives on an interface, the next-hop information in the cache is re-used without CPU intervention.

■ **Cisco Express Forwarding (CEF)** - CEF is the most recent and preferred Cisco IOS packet-forwarding mechanism. Like fast switching, CEF builds a Forwarding Information Base (FIB), and an adjacency table. However, the table entries are not packet-triggered like fast switching but change-triggered such as when something changes in the network topology. Therefore, when a network has converged, the FIB and adjacency tables contain all the information a router would have to consider when forwarding a packet. The FIB contains pre-computed reverse lookups, next hop information for routes including the interface and Layer 2 information. Cisco Express Forwarding is the fastest forwarding mechanism and the preferred choice on Cisco routers.

Figures 1 to 3 illustrate the differences between the three packet-forwarding mechanisms. Assume that a traffic flow consisting of five packets are all going to the same destination. As shown in Figure 1, with process switching, each packet must be processed by the CPU individually. Contrast this with fast switching, as shown in Figure 2. With fast switching, notice how only the first packet of a flow is process-switched and added to the fast-switching cache. The next four packets are quickly processed based on the information in the fast-switching cache. Finally, in Figure 3, CEF builds the FIB and adjacency tables, after the network has converged. All five packets are quickly processed in the data plane.

A common analogy used to describe the three packet-forwarding mechanisms is as follows:

■ Process switching solves a problem by doing math long hand, even if it is the identical problem.

■ Fast switching solves a problem by doing math long hand one time and remembering the answer for subsequent identical problems.

■ CEF solves every possible problem ahead of time in a spreadsheet.

Refer to **Interactive Graphic** in online course.

1.1.1.7   Activity - Identify Router Components

Refer to **Packet Tracer Activity** for this chapter

1.1.1.8   Packet Tracer - Using Traceroute to Discover the Network

The company you work for has acquired a new branch location. You asked for a topology map of the new location, but apparently one does not exist. However, you have username and password information for the new branch's networking devices and you know the web address for the new branch's server. Therefore, you will verify connectivity and use the `tracert` command to determine the path to the location. You will connect to the edge router of the new location to determine the devices and networks attached. As a part of this process, you will use various `show` commands to gather the necessary information to finish documenting the IP addressing scheme and create a diagram of the topology.

Refer to **Lab Activity** for this chapter

1.1.1.9   Lab - Mapping the Internet

In this lab, you will complete the following objectives:

■ Part 1: Determine Network Connectivity to a Destination Host

■ Part 2: Trace a Route to a Remote Server Using Tracert

Refer to
Online Course
for Illustration

1.1.2 Connect Devices

1.1.2.1 Connect to a Network

Network devices and end users typically connect to a network using a wired Ethernet or wireless connection. Refer to the figure as a sample reference topology. The LANs in the figure serve as an example of how users and network devices could connect to networks.

Home office devices can connect as follows:

- Laptops and tablets connect wirelessly to a home router.

- A network printer connects using an Ethernet cable to the switch port on the home router.

- The home router connects to the service provider cable modem using an Ethernet cable.

- The cable modem connects to the Internet service provider (ISP) network.

The Branch site devices connect as follows:

- Corporate resources (i.e., file servers and printers) connect to Layer 2 switches using Ethernet cables.

- Desktop PCs and voice over IP (VoIP) phones connect to Layer 2 switches using Ethernet cables.

- Laptops and smartphones connect wirelessly to wireless access points (WAPs).

- The WAPs connect to switches using Ethernet cables.

- Layer 2 switches connect to an Ethernet interface on the edge router using Ethernet cables. An edge router is a device that sits at the edge or boundary of a network and routes between that network and another, such as between a LAN and a WAN.

- The edge router connects to a WAN service provider (SP).

- The edge router also connects to an ISP for backup purposes.

The Central site devices connect as follows:

- Desktop PCs and VoIP phones connect to Layer 2 switches using Ethernet cables.

- Layer 2 switches connect redundantly to multilayer Layer 3 switches using Ethernet fiber-optic cables (orange connections).

- Layer 3 multilayer switches connect to an Ethernet interface on the edge router using Ethernet cables.

- The corporate website server is connected using an Ethernet cable to the edge router interface.

- The edge router connects to a WAN SP.

- The edge router also connects to an ISP for backup purposes.

In the Branch and Central LANs, hosts are connected either directly or indirectly (via WAPs) to the network infrastructure using a Layer 2 switch.

Refer to
Online Course
for Illustration

1.1.2.2   Default Gateways

To enable network access, devices must be configured with IP address information to identify the appropriate:

- **IP address** - Identifies a unique host on a local network.

- **Subnet mask** - Identifies with which network subnet the host can communicate.

- **Default gateway** - Identifies the router to send a packet to when the destination is not on the same local network subnet.

When a host sends a packet to a device that is on the same IP network, the packet is simply forwarded out of the host interface to the destination device.

When a host sends a packet to a device on a different IP network, then the packet is forwarded to the default gateway, because a host device cannot communicate directly with devices outside of the local network. The default gateway is the destination that routes traffic from the local network to devices on remote networks. It is often used to connect a local network to the Internet.

The default gateway is usually the address of the interface on the router connected to the local network. The router maintains routing table entries of all connected networks as well as entries of remote networks, and determines the best path to reach those destinations.

For example, if PC1 sends a packet to the Web Server located at 176.16.1.99, it would discover that the Web Server is not on the local network and it, therefore, must send the packet to the Media Access Control (MAC) address of its default gateway. The Packet protocol data unit (PDU) in the figure identifies the source and destination IP and MAC addresses.

Note   A router is also usually configured with its own default gateway. This is sometimes known as the Gateway of Last Resort.

Refer to
Online Course
for Illustration

1.1.2.3   Document Network Addressing

When designing a new network or mapping an existing network, document the network. At a minimum, the documentation should identify:

- Device names

- Interfaces used in the design

- IP addresses and subnet masks

- Default gateway addresses

As the figure shows, this information is captured by creating two useful network documents:

- **Topology diagram** - Provides a visual reference that indicates the physical connectivity and logical Layer 3 addressing. Often created using software, such as Microsoft Visio.

■ **An addressing table** - A table that captures device names, interfaces, IPv4 addresses, subnet masks, and default gateway addresses.

Refer to
Online Course
for Illustration

1.1.2.4   Enable IP on a Host

A host can be assigned IP address information either:

■ **Statically** - The host is manually assigned the correct IP address, subnet mask, and default gateway. The DNS server IP address can also be configured.

■ **Dynamically** - IP address information is provided by a server using the Dynamic Host Configuration Protocol (DHCP). The DHCP server provides a valid IP address, subnet mask, and default gateway for end devices. Other information may be provided by the server.

Figure 1 and Figure 2 provide static and dynamic IPv4 address configuration examples.

Statically assigned addresses are commonly used to identify specific network resources, such as network servers and printers. They can also be used in smaller networks with few hosts. However, most host devices acquire their IPv4 address information by accessing a DHCP server. In large enterprises, dedicated DHCP servers providing services to many LANs are implemented. In a smaller branch or small office setting, DHCP services can be provided by a Cisco Catalyst switch or a Cisco ISR.

Refer to
Online Course
for Illustration

1.1.2.5   Device LEDs

Host computers connect to a wired network using a network interface and RJ-45 Ethernet cable. Most network interfaces have one or two LED link indicators next to the interface. Typically, a green LED means a good connection while a blinking green LED indicates network activity.

If the link light is not on, then there may be a problem with either the network cable or the network itself. The switch port where the connection terminates would also have an LED indicator lit. If one or both ends are not lit, try a different network cable.

Note   The actual function of the LEDs varies between computer manufacturers.

Similarly, network infrastructure devices commonly use multiple LED indicators to provide a quick status view. For example, a Cisco Catalyst 2960 switch has several status LEDs to help monitor system activity and performance. These LEDs are generally lit green when the switch is functioning normally and lit amber when there is a malfunction.

Cisco ISRs use various LED indicators to provide status information. A Cisco 1941 router is shown in the figure. The LEDs on the router help the network administrator conduct some basic troubleshooting. Each device has a unique set of LEDs. Consult the device-specific documentation for an accurate description of the LEDs.

Refer to
Online Course
for Illustration

1.1.2.6   Console Access

In a production environment, infrastructure devices are commonly accessed remotely using Secure Shell (SSH) or HyperText Transfer Protocol Secure (HTTPS). Console access is really only required when initially configuring a device, or if remote access fails.

Console access requires:

■ **Console cable** – RJ-45-to-DB-9 console cable

■ **Terminal emulation software** – Tera Term, PuTTY, HyperTerminal

The cable is connected between the serial port of the host and the console port on the device. Most computers and notebooks no longer include built-in serial ports. If the host does not have a serial port, the USB port can be used to establish a console connection. A special USB-to-RS-232 compatible serial port adapter is required when using the USB port.

The Cisco ISR G2 supports a USB serial console connection. To establish connectivity, a USB Type-A to USB Type-B (mini-B USB) is required, as well as an operating system device driver. This device driver is available from http://www.cisco.com. Although these routers have two console ports, only one console port can be active at a time. When a cable is plugged into the USB console port, the RJ-45 port becomes inactive. When the USB cable is removed from the USB port, the RJ-45 port becomes active.

The table in Figure 1 summarizes the console connection requirements. Figure 2 displays the various ports and cables required.

Refer to
Online Course
for Illustration

1.1.2.7   Enable IP on a Switch

Network infrastructure devices require IP addresses to enable remote management. Using the device IP address, the network administrator can remotely connect to the device using Telnet, SSH, HTTP, or HTTPS.

A switch does not have a dedicated interface to which an IP address can be assigned. Instead, the IP address information is configured on a virtual interface called a switched virtual interface (SVI).

For example, in Figure 1, the SVI on the Layer 2 switch S1 is assigned the IP address 192.168.10.2/24 and a default gateway of the router located at 192.168.10.1.

Use the Syntax Checker in Figure 2 to configure the Layer 2 switch S2.

Refer to
Interactive Graphic
in online course.

1.1.2.8   Activity - Document an Addressing Scheme

Refer to **Packet
Tracer Activity**
for this chapter

1.1.2.9   Packet Tracer - Documenting the Network

Background/Scenario

Your job is to document the addressing scheme and connections used in the Central portion of the network. You will need to use a variety of commands to gather the required information.

Refer to
Online Course
for Illustration

1.1.3   Basic Settings on a Router

1.1.3.1   Configure Basic Router Settings

Cisco routers and Cisco switches have many similarities. They support a similar modal operating system, similar command structures, and many of the same commands. In addition, both devices have similar initial configuration steps.

When configuring a Cisco switch or router, the following basic tasks should be performed first:

- **Name the device** - Distinguishes it from other routers.

- **Secure management access** - Secures privileged EXEC, user EXEC, and Telnet access, and encrypts passwords to their highest level.

- **Configure a banner** - Provides legal notification of unauthorized access.

Note   Always save the changes on a router and verify the basic configuration and router operations.

Figures 1 through 4 provide examples of configuring basic settings on router R1:

- In Figure 1, the device is named.

- In Figure 2, management access is secured.

- In Figure 3, a banner is configured.

- In Figure 4, the configuration is saved.

Use the Syntax Checker in Figure 5 to configure router R2.

Refer to
Online Course
for Illustration

1.1.3.2   Configure an IPv4 Router Interface

One distinguishing feature between switches and routers is the type of interfaces supported by each. For example, Layer 2 switches support LANs and, therefore, have multiple FastEthernet or Gigabit Ethernet ports.

Routers support LANs and WANs and can interconnect different types of networks; therefore, they support many types of interfaces. For example, G2 ISRs have one or two integrated Gigabit Ethernet interfaces and High-Speed WAN Interface Card (HWIC) slots to accommodate other types of network interfaces, including serial, DSL, and cable interfaces.

To be available, an interface must be:

- **If using IPv4, configured with an address and a subnet mask** - Use the `ip address` `ip-address subnet-mask` interface configuration command.

- **Activated** - By default, LAN and WAN interfaces are not activated (`shutdown`). To enable an interface, it must be activated using the `no shutdown` command. (This is similar to powering on the interface.) The interface must also be connected to another device (a hub, a switch, or another router) for the physical layer to be active.

Optionally, the interface could also be configured with a short description. It is good practice to configure a description on each interface. The description text is limited to 240 characters. On production networks, a description can be helpful in troubleshooting by providing information about the type of network to which the interface is connected. If the interface connects to an ISP or service carrier, it is helpful to enter the third party connection and contact information.

Depending on the type of interface, additional parameters may be required. For example, in the lab environment, the serial interface connecting to the serial cable end labeled DCE must be configured with the **clock rate** command.

Note Accidentally using the **clock rate** command on a DTE interface generates a %Er-ror: This command applies only to DCE interface message.

Figures 1 through 3 provide examples of configuring the router interfaces of R1.

Use the Syntax Checker in Figure 4 to configure router R2.

Refer to
Online Course
for Illustration

1.1.3.3 Configure an IPv6 Router Interface

Configuring an IPv6 interface is similar to configuring an interface for IPv4. Most IPv6 configuration and verification commands in the Cisco IOS are very similar to their IPv4 counterparts. In many cases, the only difference uses **ipv6** in place of **ip** in commands.

An IPv6 interface must be:

■ **Configured with IPv6 address and subnet mask** - Use the **ipv6 address** *ipv6-address/prefix-length* **[link-local | eui-64]** interface configuration command.

■ **Activated** - The interface must be activated using the **no shutdown** command.

Note An interface can generate its own IPv6 link-local address without having a global unicast address by using the **ipv6 enable** interface configuration command.

Unlike IPv4, IPv6 interfaces will typically have more than one IPv6 address. At a minimum, an IPv6 device must have an IPv6 link-local address but will most likely also have an IPv6 global unicast address. IPv6 also supports the ability for an interface to have multiple IPv6 global unicast addresses from the same subnet. The following commands can be used to statically create a global unicast or link-local IPv6 address:

■ **ipv6 address** *ipv6-address / prefix-length* - Creates a global unicast IPv6 address as specified.

■ **ipv6 address** *ipv6-address / prefix-length* **eui-64** - Configures a global unicast IPv6 address with an interface identifier (ID) in the low-order 64 bits of the IPv6 address using the EUI-64 process.

■ **ipv6 address** *ipv6-address / prefix-length* **link-local** - Configures a static link-local address on the interface that is used instead of the link-local address that is automatically configured when the global unicast IPv6 address is assigned to the interface or enabled using the **ipv6 enable** interface command. Recall, the **ipv6 enable** interface command is used to automatically create an IPv6 link-local address whether or not an IPv6 global unicast address has been assigned.

In the example topology shown in Figure 1, R1 must be configured to support the following IPv6 network addresses:

- 2001:0DB8:ACAD:0001:/64 or 2001:DB8:ACAD:1::/64

- 2001:0DB8:ACAD:0002:/64 or 2001:DB8:ACAD:2::/64

- 2001:0DB8:ACAD:0003:/64 or 2001:DB8:ACAD:3::/64

When the router is configured using the `ipv6 unicast-routing` global configuration command, the router begins sending ICMPv6 Router Advertisement messages out the interface. This enables a PC connected to the interface to automatically configure an IPv6 address and to set a default gateway without needing the services of a DHCPv6 server. Alternatively, a PC connected to the IPv6 network can get its IPv6 address statically assigned, as shown in Figure 2. Notice that the default gateway address configured for PC1 is the IPv6 global unicast address of the R1 GigabitEthernet 0/0 interface.

The router interfaces in the example topology must be configured and enabled as shown in Figures 3 through 5.

Use the Syntax Checker in Figure 6 to configure the IPv6 global unicast addresses on router R2.

Refer to **Online Course** for Illustration

1.1.3.4   Configure an IPv4 Loopback Interface

Another common configuration of Cisco IOS routers is enabling a loopback interface.

The loopback interface is a logical interface internal to the router. It is not assigned to a physical port and can therefore never be connected to any other device. It is considered a software interface that is automatically placed in an UP state, as long as the router is functioning.

The loopback interface is useful in testing and managing a Cisco IOS device because it ensures that at least one interface will always be available. For example, it can be used for testing purposes, such as testing internal routing processes, by emulating networks behind the router.

Additionally, the IPv4 address assigned to the loopback interface can be significant to processes on the router that use an interface IPv4 address for identification purposes, such as the Open Shortest Path First (OSPF) routing process. By enabling a loopback interface, the router will use the always available loopback interface address for identification, rather than an IP address assigned to a physical port that may go down.

Enabling and assigning a loopback address is simple:

```
Router(config)# interface loopback number
Router(config-if)# ip address ip-address subnet-mask
Router(config-if)# exit
```

Multiple loopback interfaces can be enabled on a router. The IPv4 address for each loopback interface must be unique and unused by any other interface.

Refer to **Packet Tracer Activity** for this chapter

1.1.3.5   Packet Tracer - Configuring IPv4 and IPv6 Interfaces

Background/Scenario

Routers R1 and R2 each have two LANs. Your task is to configure the appropriate addressing on each device and verify connectivity between the LANs.

Refer to
Online Course
for Illustration

1.1.4   Verify Connectivity of Directly Connected Networks

1.1.4.1   Verify Interface Settings

There are several `show` commands that can be used to verify the operation and configuration of an interface. The following three commands are especially useful to quickly identify an interface status:

- `show ip interface brief` - Displays a summary for all interfaces including the IPv4 address of the interface and current operational status.

- `show ip route` - Displays the contents of the IPv4 routing table stored in RAM. In Cisco IOS 15, active interfaces should appear in the routing table with two related entries identified by the code 'C' (Connected) or 'L' (Local). In previous IOS versions, only a single entry with the code 'C' will appear.

- `show running-config interface` *interface-id* - Displays the commands configured on the specified interface.

Figure 1 displays the output of the `show ip interface brief` command. The output reveals that the LAN interfaces and the WAN link are all activated and operational as indicated by the Status of "up" and Protocol of "up". A different output would indicate a problem with either the configuration or the cabling.

Note   In Figure 1, the Embedded-Service-Engine0/0 interface is displayed because Cisco ISRs G2 have dual core CPUs on the motherboard. The Embedded-Service-Engine0/0 interface is outside the scope of this course.

Figure 2 displays the output of the `show ip route` command. Notice the three directly connected network entries and the three local host route interface entries. A local host route has an administrative distance of 0. It also has a /32 mask for IPv4, and a /128 mask for IPv6. The local host route is for routes on the router owning the IP address. It is used to allow the router to process packets destined to that IP.

Figure 3 displays the output of the `show running-config interface` command. The output displays the current commands configured on the specified interface.

The following two commands are used to gather more detailed interface information:

- `show interfaces` - Displays interface information and packet flow count for all interfaces on the device.

- `show ip interface` - Displays the IPv4 related information for all interfaces on a router.

Use the Syntax Checker in Figures 4 and 5 to verify the interfaces on R1.

Refer to
Online Course
for Illustration

1.1.4.2   Verify IPv6 Interface Settings

The commands to verify the IPv6 interface configuration are similar to the commands used for IPv4.

The **show ipv6 interface brief** command in Figure 1 displays a summary for each of the interfaces. The [up/up] output on the same line as the interface name indicates the Layer 1/Layer 2 interface state. This is the same as the Status and Protocol columns in the equivalent IPv4 command.

The output displays two configured IPv6 addresses per interface. One address is the IPv6 global unicast address that was manually entered. The other address, which begins with FE80, is the link-local unicast address for the interface. A link-local address is automatically added to an interface whenever a global unicast address is assigned. An IPv6 network interface is required to have a link-local address, but not necessarily a global unicast address.

The **show ipv6 interface gigabitethernet 0/0** command output shown in Figure 2 displays the interface status and all of the IPv6 addresses belonging to the interface. Along with the link local address and global unicast address, the output includes the multicast addresses assigned to the interface, beginning with prefix FF02.

The **show ipv6 route** command shown in Figure 3 can be used to verify that IPv6 networks and specific IPv6 interface addresses have been installed in the IPv6 routing table. The **show ipv6 route** command will only display IPv6 networks, not IPv4 networks.

Within the routing table, a 'c' next to a route indicates that this is a directly connected network. When the router interface is configured with a global unicast address and is in the "up/up" state, the IPv6 prefix and prefix length is added to the IPv6 routing table as a connected route.

The IPv6 global unicast address configured on the interface is also installed in the routing table as a local route. The local route has a /128 prefix. Local routes are used by the routing table to efficiently process packets with the interface address of the router as the destination.

The **ping** command for IPv6 is identical to the command used with IPv4 except that an IPv6 address is used. As shown in Figure 4, the **ping** command is used to verify Layer 3 connectivity between R1 and PC1.

Other useful IPv6 verification commands include:

- **show interface**
- **show ipv6 routers**

1.1.4.3   Filter Show Command Output

Refer to **Online Course** for Illustration

Commands that generate multiple screens of output are, by default, paused after 24 lines. At the end of the paused output, the --More-- text displays. Pressing **Enter** displays the next line and pressing the spacebar displays the next set of lines. Use the **terminal length** *number* command to specify the number of lines to be displayed. A value of 0 (zero) prevents the router from pausing between screens of output.

Another very useful feature that improves the user experience in the command-line interface (CLI) is the filtering of **show** output. Filtering commands can be used to display specific sections of output. To enable the filtering command, enter a pipe (|) character after the **show** command and then enter a filtering parameter and a filtering expression.

The filtering parameters that can be configured after the pipe include:

- **section** - Shows entire section that starts with the filtering expression
- **include** - Includes all output lines that match the filtering expression
- **exclude** - Excludes all output lines that match the filtering expression
- **begin** - Shows all the output lines from a certain point, starting with the line that matches the filtering expression

Note   Output filters can be used in combination with any `show` command.

Figures 1 to 4 provide examples of the various output filters.

Use the Syntax Checker in Figure 5 to filter output.

Refer to
Online Course
for Illustration

1.1.4.4   Command History Feature

The command history feature is useful, because it temporarily stores the list of executed commands to be recalled.

To recall commands in the history buffer, press **Ctrl+P** or the **Up Arrow** key. The command output begins with the most recent command. Repeat the key sequence to recall successively older commands. To return to more recent commands in the history buffer, press **Ctrl+N** or the **Down Arrow** key. Repeat the key sequence to recall successively more recent commands.

By default, command history is enabled and the system captures the last 10 command lines in its history buffer. Use the `show history` privileged EXEC command to display the contents of the buffer.

It is also practical to increase the number of command lines that the history buffer records during the current terminal session only. Use the `terminal history size` user EXEC command to increase or decrease the size of the buffer.

Figure 1 displays a sample of the `terminal history size` and `show history` commands.

Use the Syntax Checker in Figure 2 to practice the two EXEC commands.

Refer to **Packet Tracer Activity** for this chapter

1.1.4.5   Packet Tracer - Configuring and Verifying a Small Network

Background/Scenario

In this activity, you will configure a router with basic settings including IP addressing. You will also configure a switch for remote management and configure the PCs. After you have successfully verified connectivity, you will use `show` commands to gather information about the network.

Refer to **Lab Activity** for this chapter

1.1.4.6   Lab - Configuring Basic Router Settings with IOS CLI

In this lab, you will complete the following objectives:

- Part 1: Set Up the Topology and Initialize Devices
- Part 2: Configure Devices and Verify Connectivity

- Part 3: Display Router Information
- Part 4: Configure IPv6 and Verify Connectivity

Refer to
Lab Activity
for this chapter

1.1.4.7   Lab - Configuring Basic Router Settings with CCP

In this lab, you will complete the following objectives:

- Part 1: Set Up the Topology and Initialize Devices
- Part 2: Configure Devices and Verify Connectivity
- Part 3: Configure Router to Allow CCP Access
- Part 4: (Optional) Install and Setup CCP on PC-A
- Part 5: Configure R1 Settings Using CCP
- Part 6: Use CCP Utilities

Refer to
Online Course
for Illustration

1.2   Routing Decisions

1.2.1   Switching Packets Between Networks

1.2.1.1   Router Switching Function

A primary function of a router is to forward packets toward their destination. This is accomplished by using a switching function, which is the process used by a router to accept a packet on one interface and forward it out of another interface. A key responsibility of the switching function is to encapsulate packets in the appropriate data link frame type for the outgoing data link.

Note   In this context, the term "switching" literally means moving packets from source to destination and should not be confused with the function of a Layer 2 switch.

After the router has determined the exit interface using the path determination function, the router must encapsulate the packet into the data link frame of the outgoing interface.

What does a router do with a packet received from one network and destined for another network? The router performs the following three major steps:

Step 1.   De-encapsulates the Layer 3 packet by removing the Layer 2 frame header and trailer.

Step 2.   Examines the destination IP address of the IP packet to find the best path in the routing table.

Step 3.   If the router finds a path to the destination, it encapsulates the Layer 3 packet into a new Layer 2 frame and forwards the frame out the exit interface.

As shown in the figure, devices have Layer 3 IPv4 addresses and Ethernet interfaces have Layer 2 data link addresses. For example, PC1 is configured with IPv4 address 192.168.1.10

and an example MAC address of 0A-10. As a packet travels from the source device to the final destination device, the Layer 3 IP addresses do not change. However, the Layer 2 data link addresses change at every hop as the packet is de-encapsulated and re-encapsulated in a new frame by each router. It is very likely that the packet is encapsulated in a different type of Layer 2 frame than the one in which it was received. For example, an Ethernet encapsulated frame might be received by the router on a FastEthernet interface, and then processed to be forwarded out of a serial interface as a Point-to-Point Protocol (PPP) encapsulated frame.

Refer to **Online Course** for Illustration

1.2.1.2 Send a Packet

In the animation in the figure, PC1 is sending a packet to PC2. PC1 must determine if the destination IPv4 address is on the same network. PC1 determines its own subnet by doing an **AND** operation on its own IPv4 address and subnet mask. This produces the network address that PC1 belongs to. Next, PC1 does this same **AND** operation using the packet destination IPv4 address and the PC1 subnet mask.

If the destination network address is the same network as PC1, then PC1 does not use the default gateway. Instead, PC1 refers to its ARP cache for the MAC address of the device with that destination IPv4 address. If the MAC address is not in the cache, then PC1 generates an ARP request to acquire the address to complete the packet and send it to the destination. If the destination network address is on a different network, then PC1 forwards the packet to its default gateway.

To determine the MAC address of the default gateway, PC1 checks its ARP table for the IPv4 address of the default gateway and its associated MAC address.

If an ARP entry does not exist in the ARP table for the default gateway, PC1 sends an ARP request. Router R1 sends back an ARP reply. PC1 can then forward the packet to the MAC address of the default gateway, the Fa0/0 interface of router R1.

A similar process is used for IPv6 packets. Instead of the ARP process, IPv6 address resolution uses ICMPv6 Neighbor Solicitation and Neighbor Advertisement messages. IPv6-to-MAC address mapping are kept in a table similar to the ARP cache, called the neighbor cache.

Refer to **Online Course** for Illustration

1.2.1.3 Forward to the Next Hop

The following processes take place when R1 receives the Ethernet frame from PC1:

1. R1 examines the destination MAC address, which matches the MAC address of the receiving interface, FastEthernet 0/0. R1, therefore, copies the frame into its buffer.

2. R1 identifies the Ethernet Type field as 0x800, which means that the Ethernet frame contains an IPv4 packet in the data portion of the frame.

3. R1 de-encapsulates the Ethernet frame.

4. Because the destination IPv4 address of the packet does not match any of the directly connected networks of R1, R1 consults its routing table to route this packet. R1 searches the routing table for a network address that would include the destination IPv4 address of the packet as a host address within that network. In this example, the routing table has a route for the 192.168.4.0/24 network. The destination IPv4 address of the packet is 192.168.4.10, which is a host IPv4 address on that network.

The route that R1 finds to the 192.168.4.0/24 network has a next-hop IPv4 address of 192.168.2.2 and an exit interface of FastEthernet 0/1. This means that the IPv4 packet is encapsulated in a new Ethernet frame with the destination MAC address of the IPv4 address of the next-hop router.

Because the exit interface is on an Ethernet network, R1 must resolve the next-hop IPv4 address with a destination MAC address using ARP:

1. R1 looks up the next-hop IPv4 address of 192.168.2.2 in its ARP cache. If the entry is not in the ARP cache, R1 would send an ARP request out of its FastEthernet 0/1 interface and R2 would send back an ARP reply. R1 would then update its ARP cache with an entry for 192.168.2.2 and the associated MAC address.

2. The IPv4 packet is now encapsulated into a new Ethernet frame and forwarded out the FastEthernet 0/1 interface of R1.

The animation in the figure illustrates how R1 forwards the packet to R2.

Refer to
Online Course
for Illustration

1.2.1.4   Packet Routing

The following processes take place when R2 receives the frame on its Fa0/0 interface:

1. R2 examines the destination MAC address, which matches the MAC address of the receiving interface, FastEthernet 0/0. R2, therefore, copies the frame into its buffer.

2. R2 identifies the Ethernet Type field as 0x800, which means that the Ethernet frame contains an IPv4 packet in the data portion of the frame.

3. R2 de-encapsulates the Ethernet frame.

4. Because the destination IPv4 address of the packet does not match any of the interface addresses of R2, R2 consults its routing table to route this packet. R2 searches the routing table for the destination IPv4 address of the packet using the same process R1 used.

   The routing table of R2 has a route to the 192.168.4.0/24 network, with a next-hop IPv4 address of 192.168.3.2 and an exit interface of Serial 0/0/0. Because the exit interface is not an Ethernet network, R2 does not have to resolve the next-hop IPv4 address with a destination MAC address.

5. The IPv4 packet is now encapsulated into a new data link frame and sent out the Serial 0/0/0 exit interface.

When the interface is a point-to-point (P2P) serial connection, the router encapsulates the IPv4 packet into the proper data link frame format used by the exit interface (HDLC, PPP, etc.). Because there are no MAC addresses on serial interfaces, R2 sets the data link destination address to an equivalent of a broadcast.

The animation in the figure illustrates how R2 forwards the packet to R3.

Refer to
Online Course
for Illustration

1.2.1.5   Reach the Destination

The following processes take place when the frame arrives at R3:

1. R3 copies the data link PPP frame into its buffer.

2. R3 de-encapsulates the data link PPP frame.

3. R3 searches the routing table for the destination IPv4 address of the packet. The routing table has a route to a directly connected network on R3. This means that the packet can be sent directly to the destination device and does not need to be sent to another router.

Because the exit interface is a directly connected Ethernet network, R3 must resolve the destination IPv4 address of the packet with a destination MAC address:

1. R3 searches for the destination IPv4 address of the packet in its Address Resolution Protocol (ARP) cache. If the entry is not in the ARP cache, R3 sends an ARP request out of its FastEthernet 0/0 interface. PC2 sends back an ARP reply with its MAC address. R3 then updates its ARP cache with an entry for 192.168.4.10 and the MAC address that is returned in the ARP reply.

2. The IPv4 packet is encapsulated into a new Ethernet data link frame and sent out the FastEthernet 0/0 interface of R3.

3. When PC2 receives the frame, it examines the destination MAC address, which matches the MAC address of the receiving interface, its Ethernet network interface card (NIC). PC2, therefore, copies the rest of the frame into its buffer.

4. PC2 identifies the Ethernet Type field as 0x800, which means that the Ethernet frame contains an IPv4 packet in the data portion of the frame.

5. PC2 de-encapsulates the Ethernet frame and passes the IPv4 packet to the IPv4 process of its operating system.

The animation in the figure illustrates how R3 forwards the packet to PC2.

Refer to
Interactive Graphic
in online course.

1.2.1.6   Activity - Match Layer 2 and Layer 3 Addressing

Refer to
Online Course
for Illustration

1.2.2   Path Determination

1.2.2.1   Routing Decisions

A primary function of a router is to determine the best path to use to send packets. To determine the best path, the router searches its routing table for a network address that matches the destination IP address of the packet.

The routing table search results in one of three path determinations:

■ **Directly connected network** - If the destination IP address of the packet belongs to a device on a network that is directly connected to one of the interfaces of the router, that packet is forwarded directly to the destination device. This means that the destination IP address of the packet is a host address on the same network as the interface of the router.

■ **Remote network** - If the destination IP address of the packet belongs to a remote network, then the packet is forwarded to another router. Remote networks can only be reached by forwarding packets to another router.

■ **No route determined** - If the destination IP address of the packet does not belong to either a connected or remote network, the router determines if there is a Gateway of Last Resort available. A Gateway of Last Resort is set when a default route is configured on a router. If there is a default route, the packet is forwarded to the Gateway of Last Resort. If the router does not have a default route, then the packet is discarded. If the packet is discarded, the router sends an ICMP unreachable message to the source IP address of the packet.

The logic flowchart in the figure illustrates the router packet forwarding decision process.

Refer to
Online Course
for Illustration

1.2.2.2   Best Path

Determining the best path involves the evaluation of multiple paths to the same destination network and selecting the optimum or shortest path to reach that network. Whenever multiple paths to the same network exist, each path uses a different exit interface on the router to reach that network.

The best path is selected by a routing protocol based on the value or metric it uses to determine the distance to reach a network. A metric is the quantitative value used to measure the distance to a given network. The best path to a network is the path with the lowest metric.

Dynamic routing protocols typically use their own rules and metrics to build and update routing tables. The routing algorithm generates a value, or a metric, for each path through the network. Metrics can be based on either a single characteristic or several characteristics of a path. Some routing protocols can base route selection on multiple metrics, combining them into a single metric.

The following lists some dynamic protocols and the metrics they use:

■ **Routing Information Protocol (RIP)** - Hop count

■ **Open Shortest Path First (OSPF)** - Cisco's cost based on cumulative bandwidth from source to destination

■ **Enhanced Interior Gateway Routing Protocol (EIGRP)** - Bandwidth, delay, load, reliability

The animation in the figure highlights how the path may be different depending on the metric being used.

Refer to
Online Course
for Illustration

1.2.2.3   Load Balancing

What happens if a routing table has two or more paths with identical metrics to the same destination network?

When a router has two or more paths to a destination with equal cost metrics, then the router forwards the packets using both paths equally. This is called equal cost load balancing. The routing table contains the single destination network, but has multiple exit interfaces, one for each equal cost path. The router forwards packets using the multiple exit interfaces listed in the routing table.

If configured correctly, load balancing can increase the effectiveness and performance of the network. Equal cost load balancing can be configured to use both dynamic routing protocols and static routes.

Note   Only EIGRP supports unequal cost load balancing.

The animation in the figure provides an example of equal cost load balancing.

Refer to
Online Course
for Illustration

1.2.2.4 Administrative Distance

It is possible for a router to be configured with multiple routing protocols and static routes. If this occurs, the routing table may have more than one route source for the same destination network. For example, if both RIP and EIGRP are configured on a router, both routing protocols may learn of the same destination network. However, each routing protocol may decide on a different path to reach the destination based on that routing protocol's metrics. RIP chooses a path based on hop count, whereas EIGRP chooses a path based on its composite metric. How does the router know which route to use?

Cisco IOS uses what is known as the administrative distance (AD) to determine the route to install into the IP routing table. The AD represents the "trustworthiness" of the route; the lower the AD, the more trustworthy the route source. For example, a static route has an AD of 1, whereas an EIGRP-discovered route has an AD of 90. Given two separate routes to the same destination, the router chooses the route with the lowest AD. When a router has the choice of a static route and an EIGRP route, the static route takes precedence. Similarly, a directly connected route with an AD of 0 takes precedence over a static route with an AD of 1.

The figure lists various routing protocols and their associated ADs.

Refer to
Interactive Graphic
in online course.

1.2.2.5 Activity - Order the Steps in the Packet Forwarding Process

Refer to
Online Course
for Illustration

1.3 Router Operation

1.3.1 Analyze the Routing Table

1.3.1.1 The Routing Table

The routing table of a router stores information about:

- **Directly connected routes** - These routes come from the active router interfaces. Routers add a directly connected route when an interface is configured with an IP address and is activated.

- **Remote routes** - These are remote networks connected to other routers. Routes to these networks can either be statically configured or dynamically configured using dynamic routing protocols.

Specifically, a routing table is a data file in RAM that is used to store route information about directly connected and remote networks. The routing table contains network or next hop associations. These associations tell a router that a particular destination can be optimally reached by sending the packet to a specific router that represents the next hop on the way to the final destination. The next hop association can also be the outgoing or exit interface to the next destination.

The figure identifies the directly connected networks and remote networks of router R1.

Refer to
Online Course
for Illustration

1.3.1.2   Routing Table Sources

On a Cisco IOS router, the `show ip route` command can be used to display the IPv4 routing table of a router. A router provides additional route information, including how the route was learned, how long the route has been in the table, and which specific interface to use to get to a predefined destination.

Entries in the routing table can be added as:

- **Local Route interfaces** - Added when an interface is configured and active. This entry is only displayed in IOS 15 or newer for IPv4 routes and all IOS releases for IPv6 routes.

- **Directly connected interfaces** - Added to the routing table when an interface is configured and active.

- **Static routes** - Added when a route is manually configured and the exit interface is active.

- **Dynamic routing protocol** - Added when routing protocols that dynamically learn about the network, such as EIGRP or OSPF, are implemented and networks are identified.

The sources of the routing table entries are identified by a code. The code identifies how the route was learned. For instance, common codes include:

- **L** - Identifies the address assigned to a router's interface. This allows the router to efficiently determine when it receives a packet for the interface instead of being forwarded.

- **C** - Identifies a directly connected network.

- **S** - Identifies a static route created to reach a specific network.

- **D** - Identifies a dynamically learned network from another router using EIGRP.

- **O** - Identifies a dynamically learned network from another router using the OSPF routing protocol.

Note   Other codes are beyond the scope of this chapter.

The figure shows the routing table of R1 in a simple network.

Refer to
Online Course
for Illustration

1.3.1.3   Remote Network Routing Entries

As a network administrator, it is imperative to know how to interpret the content of an IPv4 and IPv6 routing table. The figure displays an IPv4 routing table entry on R1 for the route to remote network 10.1.1.0.

The entry identifies the following information:

- **Route source** - Identifies how the route was learned.

- **Destination network** - Identifies the address of the remote network.

- **Administrative distance** - Identifies the trustworthiness of the route source. Lower values indicate preferred route source.

- **Metric** - Identifies the value assigned to reach the remote network. Lower values indicate preferred routes.

- **Next-hop** - Identifies the IPv4 address of the next router to forward the packet to.

- **Route timestamp** - Identifies how much time has passed since the route was learned.

- **Outgoing interface** - Identifies the exit interface to use to forward a packet toward the final destination.

Refer to Interactive Graphic in online course.

1.3.1.4   Activity - Interpret the Content of a Routing Table Entry

Refer to Online Course for Illustration

1.3.2   Directly Connected Routes

1.3.2.1   Directly Connected Interfaces

A newly deployed router, without any configured interfaces, has an empty routing table, as shown in the figure.

Before the interface state is considered up/up and added to the IPv4 routing table, the interface must:

- Be assigned a valid IPv4 or IPv6 address

- Be activated with the `no shutdown` command

- Receive a carrier signal from another device (router, switch, host, etc.)

When the interface is up, the network of that interface is added to the routing table as a directly connected network.

Refer to Online Course for Illustration

1.3.2.2   Directly Connected Route Table Entries

An active, properly configured, directly connected interface actually creates two routing table entries. The figure displays the IPv4 routing table entries on R1 for the directly connected network 192.168.10.0.

The routing table entry for directly connected interfaces is simpler than the entries for remote networks. The entries contain the following information:

- **Route source** - Identifies how the route was learned. Directly connected interfaces have two route source codes. 'C' identifies a directly connected network. 'L' identifies the IPv4 address assigned to the router's interface.

- **Destination network** - The address of the remote network.

- **Outgoing interface** - Identifies the exit interface to use when forwarding packets to the destination network.

Note   Prior to IOS 15, local route routing table entries (L) were not displayed in the IPv4 routing table. Local route (L) entries have always been a part of the IPv6 routing table.

Refer to
Online Course
for Illustration

1.3.2.3   Directly Connected Examples

The examples in Figures 1 to 3 show the steps to configure and activate the interfaces attached to R1. Notice the Layer 1 and 2 informational messages generated as each interface is activated.

As each interface is added, the routing table automatically adds the connected ('c') and local ('L') entries. Figure 4 provides an example of the routing table with the directly connected interfaces of R1 configured and activated.

Use the Syntax Checker in Figure 5 to configure and activate the interfaces connected to R2.

Refer to
Online Course
for Illustration

1.3.2.4   Directly Connected IPv6 Example

The example in Figure 1 shows the configuration steps for the directly connected interfaces of R1 with the indicated IPv6 addresses. Notice the Layer 1 and Layer 2 informational messages generated as each interface is configured and activated.

The `show ipv6 route` command shown in Figure 2 is used to verify that IPv6 networks and specific IPv6 interface addresses have been installed in the IPv6 routing table. Like IPv4, a 'c' next to a route indicates that this is a directly connected network. An 'L' indicates the local route. In an IPv6 network, the local route has a /128 prefix. Local routes are used by the routing table to efficiently process packets with a destination address of the interface of the router.

Notice that there is also a route installed to the FF00::/8 network. This route is required for multicast routing.

Figure 3 displays how the `show ipv6 route` command can be combined with a specific network destination to display the details of how that route was learned by the router.

Figure 4 displays how connectivity to R2 can be verified using the `ping` command.

In Figure 5, notice what happens when the G0/0 LAN interface of R2 is the target of the `ping` command. The pings are unsuccessful. This is because R1 does not have an entry in the routing table to reach the 2001:DB8:ACAD:4::/64 network.

R1 requires additional information to reach a remote network. Remote network route entries can be added to the routing table using either:

- Static routing
- Dynamic routing protocols

Refer to **Packet Tracer Activity** for this chapter

1.3.2.5   Packet Tracer - Investigating Directly Connected Routes
Background

The network in the activity is already configured. You will log in to the routers and use `show` commands to discover and answer the questions below about the directly connected routes.

Refer to
Online Course
for Illustration

1.3.3 Statically Learned Routes

1.3.3.1 Static Routes

After directly connected interfaces are configured and added to the routing table, then static or dynamic routing can be implemented.

Static routes are manually configured. They define an explicit path between two networking devices. Unlike a dynamic routing protocol, static routes are not automatically updated and must be manually reconfigured if the network topology changes. The benefits of using static routes include improved security and resource efficiency. Static routes use less bandwidth than dynamic routing protocols, and no CPU cycles are used to calculate and communicate routes. The main disadvantage to using static routes is the lack of automatic reconfiguration if the network topology changes.

There are two common types of static routes in the routing table:

■ Static route to a specific network

■ Default static route

A static route can be configured to reach a specific remote network. IPv4 static routes are configured using the **ip route** network mask {next-hop-ip | exit-intf} global configuration command. A static route is identified in the routing table with the code 's'.

A default static route is similar to a default gateway on a host. The default static route specifies the exit point to use when the routing table does not contain a path for the destination network.

A default static route is useful when a router has only one exit point to another router, such as when the router connects to a central router or service provider.

To configure an IPv4 default static route, use the **ip route 0.0.0.0 0.0.0.0** {exit-intf | next-hop-ip} global configuration command.

The figure provides a simple scenario of how default and static routes can be applied.

Refer to
Online Course
for Illustration

1.3.3.2 Static Route Examples

Figure 1 shows the configuration of an IPv4 default static route on R1 to the Serial 0/0/0 interface. Notice that the configuration of the route generated an 's*' entry in the routing table. The 's' signifies that the route source is a static route while the asterisk (*) identifies this route as a possible candidate to be the default route. In fact, it has been chosen as the default route as evidenced by the line that reads, "Gateway of Last Resort is 0.0.0.0 to network 0.0.0.0."

Figure 2 shows the configuration of two static routes from R2 to reach the two LANs on R1. The route to 192.168.10.0/24 has been configured using the exit interface while the route to 192.168.11.0/24 has been configured using the next hop IPv4 address. Although both are acceptable, there are some differences in how they operate. For instance, notice how different they look in the routing table. Also notice that because these static routes were to specific networks, the output indicates that the Gateway of Last Resort is not set.

Note   Static and default static routes are discussed in detail in the next chapter.

Use the Syntax Checker in Figure 3 to configure a default static route on router R1 going to R2.

Use the Syntax Checker in Figure 4 to configure static routes on router R2 to reach the R1 LANs.

Refer to
Online Course
for Illustration

1.3.3.3   Static IPv6 Route Examples

Like IPv4, IPv6 supports static and default static routes. They are used and configured like IPv4 static routes.

To configure a default static IPv6 route, use the `ipv6 route ::/0` {`ipv6-address` | `interface-type interface-number`} global configuration command.

Figure 1 shows the configuration of a default static route on R1 to the Serial 0/0/0 interface.

Notice in the output shown in Figure 2 that the default static route configuration generated an 's' entry in the routing table. The 's' signifies that the route source is a static route. Unlike the IPv4 static route, there is no asterisk (*) or Gateway of Last Resort explicitly identified.

Like IPv4, static routes are routes explicitly configured to reach a specific remote network. Static IPv6 routes are configured using the `ipv6 route` `ipv6-prefix/prefix-length`{`ipv6-address`|`interface-type interface-number`} global configuration command.

The example in Figure 3 shows the configuration of two static routes from R2 to reach the two LANs on R1. The route to the 2001:0DB8:ACAD:2::/64 LAN is configured with an exit interface, while the route to the 2001:0DB8:ACAD:1::/64 LAN is configured with the next hop IPv6 address. The next hop IPv6 address can be either an IPv6 global unicast or link-local address.

Figure 4 shows the routing table with the new static routes installed.

Figure 5 confirms remote network connectivity to the 2001:0DB8:ACAD:4::/64 LAN on R2 from R1.

Refer to
Online Course
for Illustration

1.3.4   Dynamic Routing Protocols

1.3.4.1   Dynamic Routing

Dynamic routing protocols are used by routers to share information about the reachability and status of remote networks. Dynamic routing protocols perform several activities, including network discovery and maintaining routing tables.

Network discovery is the ability of a routing protocol to share information about the networks that it knows about with other routers that are also using the same routing protocol. Instead of depending on manually configured static routes to remote networks on every router, a dynamic routing protocol allows the routers to automatically learn about these networks from other routers. These networks, and the best path to each, are added to the routing table of the router, and identified as a network learned by a specific dynamic routing protocol.

During network discovery, routers exchange routes and update their routing tables. Routers have converged after they have finished exchanging and updating their routing tables. Routers then maintain the networks in their routing tables.

The figure provides a simple scenario of how two neighboring routers would initially exchange routing information. In this simplified message, exchange R1 introduces itself and the networks it can reach. R2 responds and provides R1 with its networks.

Refer to **Online Course** for Illustration

1.3.4.2   IPv4 Routing Protocols

A router running a dynamic routing protocol does not only make a best path determination to a network, it also determines a new best path if the initial path becomes unusable (or if the topology changes). For these reasons, dynamic routing protocols have an advantage over static routes. Routers that use dynamic routing protocols automatically share routing information with other routers and compensate for any topology changes without involving the network administrator.

Cisco ISR routers can support a variety of dynamic IPv4 routing protocols including:

- **EIGRP** - Enhanced Interior Gateway Routing Protocol
- **OSPF** - Open Shortest Path First
- **IS-IS** - Intermediate System-to-Intermediate System
- **RIP** - Routing Information Protocol

To determine which routing protocols are supported by the IOS, use the `router ?` command in global configuration mode as shown in the figure.

Note   The focus of this course is on EIGRP and OSPF. RIP will be discussed only for legacy reasons; the other routing protocols supported by the IOS are beyond the scope of the CCNA certification.

Refer to **Online Course** for Illustration

1.3.4.3   IPv4 Dynamic Routing Examples

In this dynamic routing example, assume that R1 and R2 have been configured to support the dynamic routing protocol EIGRP. The routers also advertise directly connected networks. R2 advertises that it is the default gateway to other networks.

The output in the figure displays the routing table of R1 after the routers have exchanged updates and converged. Along with the connected and link local interfaces, there are three 'D' entries in the routing table.

- The entry beginning with 'D*EX' identifies that the source of this entry was EIGRP ('D'). The route is a candidate to be a default route ('*'), and the route is an external route ('*EX') forwarded by EIGRP.
- The other two 'D' entries are routes installed in the routing table based on the update from R2 advertising its LANs.

Refer to **Online Course** for Illustration

1.3.4.4   IPv6 Routing Protocols

As shown in the figure, ISR routers can support dynamic IPv6 routing protocols including:

- RIPng (RIP next generation)
- OSPFv3
- EIGRP for IPv6

Support for dynamic IPv6 routing protocols is dependent on hardware and IOS version. Most of the modifications in the routing protocols are to support the longer IPv6 addresses and different header structures.

To enable IPv6 routers to forward traffic, you must configure the `ipv6 unicast-routing` global configuration command.

Refer to
Online Course
for Illustration

1.3.4.5   IPv6 Dynamic Routing Examples

Routers R1 and R2 have been configured with the dynamic routing protocol EIGRP for IPv6. (This is the IPv6 equivalent of EIGRP for IPv4.)

To view the routing table on R1, enter the `show ipv6 route` command, as shown in the figure. The output in the figure displays the routing table of R1 after the routers have exchanged updates and converged. Along with the connected and local routes, there are two 'D' entries (EIGRP routes) in the routing table.

Refer to
Online Course
for Illustration

Refer to
Lab Activity
for this chapter

1.4   Summary

1.4.1.1   Class Activity - We Really Could Use a Map!

Activity - We Really Could Use a Map!

Scenario

Use the Ashland and Richmond routing tables shown in the file provided with this activity.

With the help of a classmate, draw a network topology using the information from the tables.

To assist you with this activity, follow these guidelines:

- **Start with the Ashland router** - use its routing table to identify ports and IP addresses/networks.

- **Add the Richmond router** - use its routing table to identify ports and IP addresses/networks.

- Add any other intermediary and end devices as specified by the tables.

In addition, record answers from your group to the reflection questions provided with this activity.

Be prepared to share your work with another group and/or the class.

Refer to
Online Course
for Illustration

1.4.1.2   Summary

This chapter introduced the router. The main purpose of a router is to connect multiple networks and forward packets from one network to the next. This means that a router typically has multiple interfaces. Each interface is a member or host on a different IP network.

Cisco IOS uses what is known as the administrative distance (AD) to determine the route to install into the IP routing table. The routing table is a list of networks known by the router. The routing table includes network addresses for its own interfaces, which are the directly connected networks, as well as network addresses for remote networks. A remote network is a network that can only be reached by forwarding the packet to another router.

Remote networks are added to the routing table in one of two ways: either by the network administrator manually configuring static routes or by implementing a dynamic routing protocol. Static routes do not have as much overhead as dynamic routing protocols; however, static routes can require more maintenance if the topology is constantly changing or is unstable.

Dynamic routing protocols automatically adjust to changes without any intervention from the network administrator. Dynamic routing protocols require more CPU processing and also use a certain amount of link capacity for routing updates and messages. In many cases, a routing table will contain both static and dynamic routes.

Routers make their primary forwarding decision at Layer 3, the Network layer. However, router interfaces participate in Layers 1, 2, and 3. Layer 3 IP packets are encapsulated into a Layer 2 data link frame and encoded into bits at Layer 1. Router interfaces participate in Layer 2 processes associated with their encapsulation. For example, an Ethernet interface on a router participates in the ARP process like other hosts on that LAN.

The Cisco IP routing table is not a flat database. The routing table is actually a hierarchical structure that is used to speed up the lookup process when locating routes and forwarding packets.

Components of the IPv6 routing table are very similar to the IPv4 routing table. For instance, it is populated using directly connected interfaces, static routes and dynamically learned routes.

Go to the online course to take the quiz and exam.

Chapter 1 Quiz

This quiz is designed to provide an additional opportunity to practice the skills and knowledge presented in the chapter and to prepare for the chapter exam. You will be allowed multiple attempts and the grade does not appear in the gradebook.

Chapter 1 Exam

The chapter exam assesses your knowledge of the chapter content.

Your Chapter Notes

2.0 Static Routing

2.0.1.1 Introduction

Routing is at the core of every data network, moving information across an internetwork from source to destination. Routers are the devices responsible for the transfer of packets from one network to the next.

Routers learn about remote networks either dynamically, using routing protocols, or manually, or using static routes. In many cases, routers use a combination of both dynamic routing protocols and static routes. This chapter focuses on static routing.

Static routes are very common and do not require the same amount of processing and overhead as dynamic routing protocols.

In this chapter, sample topologies will be used to configure IPv4 and IPv6 static routes and to present troubleshooting techniques. In the process, several important IOS commands and the resulting output will be examined. An introduction to the routing table using both directly connected networks and static routes will be included.

This chapter will also contrast classful routing and the widely implemented classless routing methods. It will cover Classless Inter-Domain Routing (CIDR) and the variable-length subnet mask (VLSM) methods. CIDR and VLSM have helped conserve the IPv4 address space using subnetting and summarization techniques

Refer to
Lab Activity
for this chapter

2.0.1.2 Class Activity - Which Way Should We Go

Activity - Which Way Should We Go?

A huge sporting event is about to take place in your city. To attend the event, you make concise plans to arrive at the sports arena on time to see the entire game.

There are two routes you can take to drive to the event:

- **Highway route** - It is easy to follow and fast driving speeds are allowed.

- **Alternative, direct route** - You found this route using a city map. Depending on conditions, such as the amount of traffic or congestion, this just may be the way to get to the arena on time!

With a partner, discuss these options. Choose a preferred route to arrive at the arena in time to see every second of the huge sporting event.

Compare your optional preferences to network traffic, which route would you choose to deliver data communications for your small- to medium-sized business? Would it be the fastest, easiest route or the alternative, direct route? Justify your choice.

Complete the modeling activity .pdf and be prepared to justify your answers to the class or with another group.

Refer to
Online Course
for Illustration

2.1 Static Routing Implementation

2.1.1 Static Routing

2.1.1.1 Reach Remote Networks

A router can learn about remote networks in one of two ways:

- **Manually** - Remote networks are manually entered into the route table using static routes.

- **Dynamically** - Remote routes are automatically learned using a dynamic routing protocol.

Figure 1 provides a sample scenario of static routing. Figure 2 provides a sample scenario of dynamic routing using EIGRP.

A network administrator can manually configure a static route to reach a specific network. Unlike a dynamic routing protocol, static routes are not automatically updated and must be manually reconfigured any time the network topology changes. A static route does not change until the administrator manually reconfigures it.

Refer to
Online Course
for Illustration

2.1.1.2 Why Use Static Routing?

Static routing provides some advantages over dynamic routing, including:

- Static routes are not advertised over the network, resulting in better security.

- Static routes use less bandwidth than dynamic routing protocols, no CPU cycles are used to calculate and communicate routes.

- The path a static route uses to send data is known.

Static routing has the following disadvantages:

- Initial configuration and maintenance is time-consuming.

- Configuration is error-prone, especially in large networks.

- Administrator intervention is required to maintain changing route information.

- Does not scale well with growing networks; maintenance becomes cumbersome.

- Requires complete knowledge of the whole network for proper implementation.

In the figure, dynamic and static routing features are compared. Notice that the advantages of one method are the disadvantages of the other.

Static routes are useful for smaller networks with only one path to an outside network. They also provide security in a larger network for certain types of traffic or links to other networks that need more control. It is important to understand that static and dynamic routing are not mutually exclusive. Rather, most networks use a combination of dynamic routing protocols and static routes. This may result in the router having multiple paths to a destination network via static routes and dynamically learned routes. However, the administrative distance (AD) of a static route is 1. Therefore, a static route will take precedence over all dynamically learned routes.

Refer to
Online Course
for Illustration

2.1.1.3   When to Use Static Routes

Static routing has three primary uses:

- Providing ease of routing table maintenance in smaller networks that are not expected to grow significantly.

- Routing to and from stub networks. A stub network is a network accessed by a single route, and the router has only one neighbor.

- Using a single default route to represent a path to any network that does not have a more specific match with another route in the routing table. Default routes are used to send traffic to any destination beyond the next upstream router.

The figure shows an example of a stub network connection and a default route connection. Notice in the figure that any network attached to R1 would only have one way to reach other destinations, whether to networks attached to R2, or to destinations beyond R2. This means that network 172.16.3.0 is a stub network and R1 is a stub router. Running a routing protocol between R2 and R1 is a waste of resources.

In this example, a static route can be configured on R2 to reach the R1 LAN. Additionally, because R1 has only one way to send out non-local traffic, a default static route can be configured on R1 to point to R2 as the next hop for all other networks.

Refer to
Interactive Graphic
in online course.

2.1.1.4   Activity - Identify the Advantages and Disadvantages of Static Routing

Refer to
Online Course
for Illustration

2.1.2   Types of Static Routes

2.1.2.1   Static Route Applications

As shown in the figure, static routes are most often used to connect to a specific network or to provide a Gateway of Last Resort for a stub network. They can also be used to:

- Reduce the number of routes advertised by summarizing several contiguous networks as one static route

- Create a backup route in case a primary route link fails

The following types of IPv4 and IPv6 static routes will be discussed:

- Standard static route

- Default static route

- Summary static route

- Floating static route

Refer to
Online Course
for Illustration

2.1.2.2   Standard Static Route

Both IPv4 and IPv6 support the configuration of static routes. Static routes are useful when connecting to a specific remote network.

The figure shows that R2 can be configured with a static route to reach the stub network 172.16.3.0/24.

Note   The example is highlighting a stub network, but in fact, a static route can be used to connect to any network.

Refer to
Online Course
for Illustration

2.1.2.3   Default Static Route

A default static route is a route that matches all packets. A default route identifies the gateway IP address to which the router sends all IP packets that it does not have a learned or static route. A default static route is simply a static route with 0.0.0.0/0 as the destination IPv4 address. Configuring a default static route creates a Gateway of Last Resort.

Note   All routes that identify a specific destination with a larger subnet mask take precedence over the default route.

Default static routes are used:

■ When no other routes in the routing table match the packet destination IP address. In other words, when a more specific match does not exist. A common use is when connecting a company's edge router to the ISP network.

■ When a router has only one other router to which it is connected. This condition is known as a stub router.

Refer to the figure for a sample scenario of implementing default static routing.

Refer to
Online Course
for Illustration

2.1.2.4   Summary Static Route

To reduce the number of routing table entries, multiple static routes can be summarized into a single static route if:

■ The destination networks are contiguous and can be summarized into a single network address.

■ The multiple static routes all use the same exit interface or next-hop IP address.

In the figure, R1 would require four separate static routes to reach the 172.20.0.0/16 to 172.23.0.0/16 networks. Instead, one summary static route can be configured and still provide connectivity to those networks.

Refer to
Online Course
for Illustration

2.1.2.5   Floating Static Route

Another type of static route is a floating static route. Floating static routes are static routes that are used to provide a backup path to a primary static or dynamic route, in the event of a link failure. The floating static route is only used when the primary route is not available.

To accomplish this, the floating static route is configured with a higher administrative distance than the primary route. Recall that the administrative distance represents the trustworthiness of a route. If multiple paths to the destination exist, the router will choose the path with the lowest administrative distance.

For example, assume that an administrator wants to create a floating static route as a backup to an EIGRP-learned route. The floating static route must be configured with a higher administrative distance than EIGRP. EIGRP has an administrative distance of 90. If the floating static route is configured with an administrative distance of 95, the dynamic route learned through EIGRP is preferred to the floating static route. If the EIGRP-learned route is lost, the floating static route is used in its place.

In the figure, the Branch router typically forwards all traffic to the HQ router over the private WAN link. In this example, the routers exchange route information using EIGRP. A floating static route, with an administrative distance of 91 or higher, could be configured to serve as a backup route. If the private WAN link fails and the EIGRP route disappears from the routing table, the router selects the floating static route as the best path to reach the HQ LAN.

Refer to
Interactive Graphic
in online course.

2.1.2.6   Activity - Identify the Type of Static Route

Refer to
Online Course
for Illustration

2.2   Configure Static and Default Routes

2.2.1   Configure IPv4 Static Routes

2.2.1.1   ip route Command

Static routes are configured using the **ip route** global configuration command. The syntax of the command is:

```
Router(config)# ip route network-address subnet-mask { ip-address | interface-type
interface-number [ ip-address ]} [ distance ] [ name name ] [ permanent ] [ tag
tag ]
```

The following parameters are required to configure static routing:

- *network-address* - Destination network address of the remote network to be added to the routing table, often this is referred to as the prefix.

- *subnet-mask* - Subnet mask, or just mask, of the remote network to be added to the routing table. The subnet mask can be modified to summarize a group of networks.

One or both of the following parameters must also be used:

- *ip-address* - The IP address of the connecting router to use to forward the packet to the remote destination network. Commonly referred to as the next hop.

- *exit-intf* - The outgoing interface to use to forward the packet to the next hop.

As shown in the figure, the command syntax commonly used is **ip route** *network-address subnet-mask* {*ip-address* | *exit-intf*}.

The*distance* parameter is used to create a floating static route by setting an administrative distance that is higher than a dynamically learned route.

Note   The remaining parameters are not relevant for this chapter or for CCNA studies.

Refer to
Online Course
for Illustration

2.2.1.2   Next-Hop Options

In this example, Figures 1 to 3 display the routing tables of R1, R2, and R3. Notice that each router has entries only for directly connected networks and their associated local addresses. None of the routers have any knowledge of any networks beyond their directly connected interfaces.

For example, R1 has no knowledge of networks:

- 172.16.1.0/24 - LAN on R2

- 192.168.1.0/24 - Serial network between R2 and R3

- 192.168.2.0/24 - LAN on R3

Figure 4 displays a successful ping from R1 to R2. Figure 5 displays an unsuccessful ping to the R3 LAN. This is because R1 does not have an entry in its routing table for the R3 LAN network.

The next hop can be identified by an IP address, exit interface, or both. How the destination is specified creates one of the three following route types:

- **Next-hop route** - Only the next-hop IP address is specified.

- **Directly connected static route** - Only the router exit interface is specified.

- **Fully specified static route** - The next-hop IP address and exit interface are specified.

Refer to
Online Course
for Illustration

2.2.1.3   Configure a Next-Hop Static Route

In a next-hop static route, only the next-hop IP address is specified. The output interface is derived from the next hop. For example, in Figure 1, three next-hop static routes are configured on R1 using the IP address of the next hop, R2.

Before any packet is forwarded by a router, the routing table process must determine the exit interface to use to forward the packet. This is known as route resolvability. The route resolvability process will vary depending upon the type of forwarding mechanism being used by the router. CEF (Cisco Express Forwarding) is the default behavior on most platforms running IOS 12.0 or later.

Figure 2 details the basic packet forwarding process in the routing table for R1 without the use of CEF. When a packet is destined for the 192.168.2.0/24 network, R1:

1. Looks for a match in the routing table and finds that it has to forward the packets to the next-hop IPv4 address 172.16.2.2, as indicated by the label 1 in the figure. Every route that references only a next-hop IPv4 address and does not reference an exit interface must have the next-hop IPv4 address resolved using another route in the routing table with an exit interface.

2. R1 must now determine how to reach 172.16.2.2; therefore, it searches a second time for a 172.16.2.2 match. In this case, the IPv4 address matches the route for the directly connected network 172.16.2.0/24 with the exit interface Serial 0/0/0, as indicated by the label 2 in the figure. This lookup tells the routing table process that this packet is forwarded out of that interface.

It actually takes two routing table lookup processes to forward any packet to the 192.168.2.0/24 network. When the router performs multiple lookups in the routing table before forwarding a packet, it is performing a process known as a recursive lookup. Because recursive lookups consume router resources, they should be avoided when possible.

A recursive static route is valid (that is, it is a candidate for insertion in the routing table) only when the specified next hop resolves, either directly or indirectly, to a valid exit interface.

Note   CEF provides optimized lookup for efficient packet forwarding by using two main data structures stored in the data plane: a FIB (Forwarding Information Base), which is a copy of the routing table and an adjacency table that includes Layer 2 addressing information. The information combined in both of these tables work together so there is no recursive lookup needed for next-hop IP address lookups. In other words, a static route using a next-hop IP requires only a single lookup when CEF is enabled on the router.

Use the Syntax Checker in Figures 3 and 4 to configure and verify next-hop static routes on R2 and R3.

Refer to
Online Course
for Illustration

2.2.1.4   Configure a Directly Connected Static Route

When configuring a static route, another option is to use the exit interface to specify the next-hop address. In older IOS versions, prior to CEF, this method is used to avoid the recursive lookup problem.

In Figure 1, three directly connected static routes are configured on R1 using the exit interface. The routing table for R1 in Figure 2 shows that when a packet is destined for the 192.168.2.0/24 network, R1 looks for a match in the routing table, and finds that it can forward the packet out of its Serial 0/0/0 interface. No other lookups are required.

Notice how the routing table looks different for the route configured with an exit interface than the route configured with a recursive entry.

Configuring a directly connected static route with an exit interface allows the routing table to resolve the exit interface in a single search, instead of two searches. Although the routing table entry indicates "directly connected", the administrative distance of the static route is still 1. Only a directly connected interface can have an administrative distance of 0.

Note   For point-to-point interfaces, you can use static routes that point to the exit interface or to the next-hop address. For multipoint/broadcast interfaces, it is more suitable to use static routes that point to a next-hop address.

Use the Syntax Checker in Figures 3 and 4 to configure and verify directly connected static routes on R2 and R3.

Although static routes that use only an exit interface on point-to-point networks are common, the use of the default CEF forwarding mechanism makes this practice unnecessary.

Refer to
Online Course
for Illustration

2.2.1.5   Configure a Fully Specified Static Route

Fully Specified Static Route

In a fully specified static route, both the output interface and the next-hop IP address are specified. This is another type of static route that is used in older IOSs, prior to CEF. This form of static route is used when the output interface is a multi-access interface and it is necessary to explicitly identify the next hop. The next hop must be directly connected to the specified exit interface.

Suppose that the network link between R1 and R2 is an Ethernet link and that the GigabitEthernet 0/1 interface of R1 is connected to that network, as shown in Figure 1. CEF is not enabled. To eliminate the recursive lookup, a directly connected static route can be implementing using the following command:

```
R1(config)# ip route 192.168.2.0 255.255.255.0 GigabitEthernet 0/1
```

However, this may cause unexpected or inconsistent results. The difference between an Ethernet multi-access network and a point-to-point serial network is that a point-to-point network has only one other device on that network, the router at the other end of the link. With Ethernet networks, there may be many different devices sharing the same multi-access network, including hosts and even multiple routers. By only designating the Ethernet exit interface in the static route, the router will not have sufficient information to determine which device is the next-hop device.

R1 knows that the packet needs to be encapsulated in an Ethernet frame and sent out the GigabitEthernet 0/1 interface. However, R1 does not know the next-hop IPv4 address and therefore it cannot determine the destination MAC address for the Ethernet frame.

Depending upon the topology and the configurations on other routers, this static route may or may not work. It is recommended that when the exit interface is an Ethernet network, that a fully specified static route is used including both the exit interface and the next-hop address.

As shown in Figure 2, when forwarding packets to R2, the exit interface is GigabitEthernet 0/1 and the next-hop IPv4 address is 172.16.2.2.

Note   With the use of CEF, a fully specified static route is no longer necessary. A static route using a next-hop address should be used.

Use the Syntax Checker in Figure 3 and 4 to configure and verify fully specified static routes on R2 and R3.

Refer to
Online Course
for Illustration

2.2.1.6   Verify a Static Route

Along with **ping** and **traceroute**, useful commands to verify static routes include:

- **show ip route**

- **show ip route static**

- **show ip route** *network*

Figure 1 displays sample output of the `show ip route static` command. In the example, the output is filtered using the pipe and `begin` parameter. The output reflects the use of static routes using the next-hop address.

Figure 2 displays sample output of the `show ip route 192.168.2.1` command.

Figure 3 verifies the `ip route` configuration in the running configuration.

Use the Syntax Checker in Figure 4 to verify the routing settings of R2.

Use the Syntax Checker in Figure 5 to verify the routing settings of R3.

Refer to
Online Course
for Illustration

2.2.2   Configure IPv4 Default Routes

2.2.2.1   Default Static Route

A default route is a static route that matches all packets. Rather than storing all routes to all networks in the routing table, a router can store a single default route to represent any network that is not in the routing table.

Routers commonly use default routes that are either configured locally or learned from another router, using a dynamic routing protocol. A default route is used when no other routes in the routing table match the destination IP address of the packet. In other words, if a more specific match does not exist, then the default route is used as the Gateway of Last Resort.

Default static routes are commonly used when connecting:

- An edge router to a service provider network

- A stub router (a router with only one upstream neighbor router)

As shown in the figure, the command syntax for a default static route is similar to any other static route, except that the network address is `0.0.0.0` and the subnet mask is `0.0.0.0`. The basic command syntax of a default static route is:

- `ip route 0.0.0.0 0.0.0.0` { *ip-address* | *exit-intf* }

Note   An IPv4 default static route is commonly referred to as a quad-zero route.

Refer to
Online Course
for Illustration

2.2.2.2   Configure a Default Static Route

R1 can be configured with three static routes to reach all of the remote networks in the example topology. However, R1 is a stub router because it is only connected to R2. Therefore, it would be more efficient to configure a default static route.

The example in the figure configures a default static route on R1. With the configuration shown in the example, any packets not matching more specific route entries are forwarded to 172.16.2.2.

Refer to
Online Course
for Illustration

2.2.2.3   Verify a Default Static Route

In the figure, the `show ip route static` command output displays the contents of the routing table. Note the asterisk (*) next to the route with code 's'. As displayed in the

Codes table in the figure, the asterisk indicates that this static route is a candidate default route, which is why it is selected as the Gateway of Last Resort.

The key to this configuration is the /0 mask. Recall that the subnet mask in a routing table determines how many bits must match between the destination IP address of the packet and the route in the routing table. A binary 1 indicates that the bits must match. A binary 0 indicates that the bits do not have to match. A /0 mask in this route entry indicates that none of the bits are required to match. The default static route matches all packets for which a more specific match does not exist.

Refer to **Packet Tracer Activity** for this chapter

2.2.2.4   Packet Tracer - Configuring IPv4 Static and Default Routes

Background/Scenario

In this activity, you will configure static and default routes. A static route is a route that is entered manually by the network administrator to create a route that is reliable and safe. There are four different static routes that are used in this activity: a recursive static route, a directly connected static route, a fully specified static route, and a default route.

Refer to **Lab Activity** for this chapter

2.2.2.5   Lab - Configuring IPv4 Static and Default Routes

In this lab, you will complete the following objectives:

■ Part 1: Set Up the Topology and Initialize Devices

■ Part 2: Configure Basic Device Settings and Verify Connectivity

■ Part 3: Configure Static Routes

■ Part 4: Configure and Verify a Default Route

Refer to **Online Course** for Illustration

2.2.3   Configure IPv6 Static Routes

2.2.3.1   The ipv6 route Command

Static routes for IPv6 are configured using the **ipv6 route** global configuration command. Figure 1 shows the simplified version of the command syntax:

```
Router(config)# ipv6 route ipv6-prefix/prefix-length { ipv6-address | exit-intf }
```

Most of parameters are identical to the IPv4 version of the command. IPv6 static routes can also be implemented as:

■ Standard IPv6 static route

■ Default IPv6 static route

■ Summary IPv6 static route

■ Floating IPv6 static route

As with IPv4, these routes can be configured as recursive, directly connected, or fully specified.

The **ipv6 unicast-routing** global configuration command must be configured to enable the router to forward IPv6 packets. Figure 2 displays the enabling of IPv6 unicast routing.

Use the Syntax Checker in Figures 3 and 4 to enable IPv6 unicast routing on R2 and R3.

Refer to
Online Course
for Illustration

2.2.3.2 Next-Hop Options

In this example, Figures 1 to 3 display the routing tables of R1, R2, and R3. Each router has entries only for directly connected networks and their associated local addresses. None of the routers have any knowledge of any networks beyond their directly connected interfaces.

For example, R1 has no knowledge of networks:

- 2001:DB8:ACAD:2::/64 - LAN on R2
- 2001:DB8:ACAD:5::/64 - Serial network between R2 and R3
- 2001:DB8:ACAD:3::/64 - LAN on R3

Figure 4 displays a successful ping from R1 to R2. Figure 5 displays an unsuccessful ping to the R3 LAN. This is because R1 does not have an entry in its routing table for that network.

The next hop can be identified by an IPv6 address, exit interface, or both. How the destination is specified creates one of three route types:

- **Next-hop static IPv6 route** - Only the next-hop IPv6 address is specified.
- **Directly connected static IPv6 route** - Only the router exit interface is specified.
- **Fully specified static IPv6 route** - The next-hop IPv6 address and exit interface are specified.

Refer to
Online Course
for Illustration

2.2.3.3 Configure a Next-Hop Static IPv6 Route

In a next-hop static route, only the next-hop IPv6 address is specified. The output interface is derived from the next hop. For instance, in Figure 1, three next-hop static routes are configured on R1.

As with IPv4, before any packet is forwarded by the router, the routing table process must resolve the route to determine the exit interface to use to forward the packet. The route resolvability process will vary depending upon the type of forwarding mechanism being used by the router. CEF (Cisco Express Forwarding) is the default behavior on most platforms running IOS 12.0 or later.

Figure 2 details the basic packet forwarding route resolvability process in the routing table for R1 without the use of CEF. When a packet is destined for the 2001:DB8:ACAD:3::/64 network, R1:

1. Looks for a match in the routing table and finds that it has to forward the packets to the next-hop IPv6 address 2001:DB8:ACAD:4::2. Every route that references only a next-hop IPv6 address and does not reference an exit interface must have the next-hop IPv6 address resolved using another route in the routing table with an exit interface.

2. R1 must now determine how to reach 2001:DB8:ACAD:4::2; therefore, it searches a second time looking for a match. In this case, the IPv6 address matches the route for the directly connected network 2001:DB8:ACAD:4::/64 with the exit interface Serial 0/0/0. This lookup tells the routing table process that this packet is forwarded out of that interface.

Therefore, it actually takes two routing table lookup processes to forward any packet to the 2001:DB8:ACAD:3::/64 network. When the router has to perform multiple lookups in the routing table before forwarding a packet, it is performing a process known as a recursive lookup.

A recursive static IPv6 route is valid (that is, it is a candidate for insertion in the routing table) only when the specified next hop resolves, either directly or indirectly, to a valid exit interface.

Use the Syntax Checker in Figure 3 and Figure 4 to configure next-hop static IPv6 routes.

Refer to
Online Course
for Illustration

2.2.3.4   Configure a Directly Connected Static IPv6 Route

When configuring a static route on point-to-point networks, an alternative to using the next-hop IPv6 address is to specify the exit interface. This is an alternative used in older IOSs or whenever CEF is disabled, to avoid the recursive lookup problem.

For instance, in Figure 1, three directly connected static routes are configured on R1 using the exit interface.

The IPv6 routing table for R1 in Figure 2 shows that when a packet is destined for the 2001:DB8:ACAD:3::/64 network, R1 looks for a match in the routing table and finds that it can forward the packet out of its Serial 0/0/0 interface. No other lookups are required.

Notice how the routing table looks different for the route configured with an exit interface than the route configured with a recursive entry.

Configuring a directly connected static route with an exit interface allows the routing table to resolve the exit interface in a single search instead of two searches. Recall that with the use of the CEF forwarding mechanism, static routes with an exit interface are considered unnecessary. A single lookup is performed using a combination of the FIB and adjacency table stored in the data plane.

Use the Syntax Checker in Figure 3 and Figure 4 to configure directly connected static IPv6 routes.

Refer to
Online Course
for Illustration

2.2.3.5   Configure a Fully Specified Static IPv6 Route

In a fully specified static route, both the output interface and the next-hop IPv6 address are specified. Similar to fully specified static routes used with IPv4, this would be used if CEF were not enabled on the router and the exit interface was on a multi-access network. With CEF, a static route using only a next-hop IPv6 address would be the preferred method even when the exit interface is a multi-access network.

Unlike IPv4, there is a situation in IPv6 when a fully specified static route must be used. If the IPv6 static route uses an IPv6 link-local address as the next-hop address, a fully specified static route including the exit interface must be used. Figure 1 shows an example of a fully qualified IPv6 static route using an IPv6 link-local address as the next-hop address.

The reason a fully specified static route must be used is because IPv6 link-local addresses are not contained in the IPv6 routing table. Link-local addresses are only unique on a given link or network. The next-hop link-local address may be a valid address on multiple networks connected to the router. Therefore, it is necessary that the exit interface be included.

In Figure 1, a fully specified static route is configured using R2's link-local address as the next-hop address. Notice that IOS requires that an exit interface be specified.

Figure 2 shows the IPv6 routing table entry for this route. Notice that both the next-hop link-local address and the exit interface are included.

Use the Syntax Checker in Figure 3 to configure fully specified static IPv6 routes on R2 to reach R1's LAN using a link-local address.

Refer to
Online Course
for Illustration

2.2.3.6   Verify IPv6 Static Routes

Along with `ping` and `traceroute`, useful commands to verify static routes include:

- `show ipv6 route`

- `show ipv6 route static`

- `show ipv6 route` *network*

Figure 1 displays sample output of the `show ipv6 route static` command. The output reflects the use of static routes using next-hop global unicast addresses.

Figure 2 displays sample output from the `show ip route 2001:DB8:ACAD:3::` command.

Refer to
Online Course
for Illustration

Figure 3 verifies the `ipv6 route` configuration in the running configuration.

2.2.4   Configure IPv6 Default Routes

2.2.4.1   Default Static IPv6 Route

A default route is a static route that matches all packets. Instead of routers storing routes for all of the networks in the Internet, they can store a single default route to represent any network that is not in the routing table.

Routers commonly use default routes that are either configured locally or learned from another router, using a dynamic routing protocol. They are used when no other routes match the packet's destination IP address in the routing table. In other words, if a more specific match does not exist, then use the default route as the Gateway of Last Resort.

Default static routes are commonly used when connecting:

- A company's edge router to a service provider network.

- A router with only an upstream neighbor router. The router has no other neighbors and is, therefore, referred to as a stub router.

As shown in the figure, the command syntax for a default static route is similar to any other static route, except that the ipv6-prefix/prefix-length is `::/0`, which matches all routes.

The basic command syntax of a default static route is:

- `ipv6 route ::/0 {` *ipv6-address* `|` *exit-intf* `}`

Refer to
Online Course
for Illustration

2.2.4.2   Configure a Default Static IPv6 Route

R1 can be configured with three static routes to reach all of the remote networks in our topology. However, R1 is a stub router because it is only connected to R2. Therefore, it would be more efficient to configure a default static IPv6 route.

The example in the figure displays a configuration for a default static IPv6 route on R1.

Refer to
Online Course
for Illustration

2.2.4.3   Verify a Default Static Route

In Figure 1, the `show ipv6 route static` command output displays the contents of the routing table.

Unlike IPv4, IPv6 does not explicitly state that the default IPv6 is the Gateway of Last Resort.

The key to this configuration is the `::/0` mask. Recall that the ipv6 prefix-length in a routing table determines how many bits must match between the destination IP address of the packet and the route in the routing table. The `::/0` mask indicates that none of the bits are required to match. As long as a more specific match does not exist, the default static IPv6 route matches all packets.

Figure 2 displays a successful ping to the R3 LAN interface.

Refer to **Packet Tracer Activity** for this chapter

2.2.4.4   Packet Tracer - Configuring IPv6 Static and Default Routes

In this activity, you will configure IPv6 static and default routes. A static route is a route that is entered manually by the network administrator to create a route that is reliable and safe. There are four different static routes used in this activity: a recursive static route; a directly connected static route; a fully specified static route; and a default route.

Refer to **Lab Activity** for this chapter

2.2.4.5   Lab - Configuring IPv6 Static and Default Routes

In this lab, you will complete the following objectives:

- Part 1: Build the Network and Configure Basic Device Settings
- Part 2: Configure IPv6 Static and Default Routes

Refer to
Online Course
for Illustration

2.3   Review of CIDR and VLSM

2.3.1   Classful Addressing

2.3.1.1   Classful Network Addressing

Released in 1981, RFC 790 and RFC 791 describe how IPv4 network addresses were initially allocated based on a classification system. In the original specification of IPv4, the authors established the classes to provide three different sizes of networks for large, medium, and small organizations. As a result, class A, B, and C addresses were defined with a specific format for the high order bits. High order bits are the far left bits in a 32-bit address.

As shown in the figure:

- **Class A addresses begin with 0** - Intended for large organizations; includes all addresses from 0.0.0.0 (**0**0000000) to 127.255.255.255 (**0**1111111). The 0.0.0.0 address is reserved for default routing and the 127.0.0.0 address is reserved for loopback testing.

- **Class B addresses begin with 10** - Intended for medium-to-large organizations; includes all addresses from 128.0.0.0 (**10**000000) to 191.255.255.255 (**10**111111).

- **Class C addresses begin with 110** - Intended for small-to-medium organizations; includes all addresses from 192.0.0.0 (**110**00000) to 223.255.255.255 (**110**11111).

The remaining addresses were reserved for multicasting and future uses.

- **Class D Multicast addresses begin with 1110** - Multicast addresses are used to identify a group of hosts that are part of a multicast group. This helps reduce the amount of packet processing that is done by hosts, particularly on broadcast media (i.e., Ethernet LANs). Routing protocols, such as RIPv2, EIGRP, and OSPF use designated multicast addresses (RIP = 224.0.0.9, EIGRP = 224.0.0.10, OSPF 224.0.0.5, and 224.0.0.6).

- **Class E Reserved IP addresses begin with 1111** - These addresses were reserved for experimental and future use.

Links:

"Internet Protocol," http://www.ietf.org/rfc/rfc791.txt

"Internet Multicast Addresses," http://www.iana.org/assignments/multicast-addresses

2.3.1.2 Classful Subnet Masks

Refer to **Online Course** for Illustration

As specified in RFC 790, each network class has a default subnet mask associated with it.

As shown in Figure 1, class A networks used the first octet to identify the network portion of the address. This is translated to a 255.0.0.0 classful subnet mask. Because only 7 bits were left in the first octet (remember, the first bit is always 0), this made 2 to the 7th power, or 128 networks. The actual number is 126 networks, because there are two reserved class A addresses (i.e., 0.0.0.0/8 and 127.0.0.0/8). With 24 bits in the host portion, each class A address had the potential for over 16 million individual host addresses.

As shown in Figure 2, class B networks used the first two octets to identify the network portion of the network address. With the first two bits already established as 1 and 0, 14 bits remained in the first two octets for assigning networks, which resulted in 16,384 class B network addresses. Because each class B network address contained 16 bits in the host portion, it controlled 65,534 addresses. (Recall that two addresses were reserved for the network and broadcast addresses.)

As shown in Figure 3, class C networks used the first three octets to identify the network portion of the network address. With the first three bits established as 1 and 1 and 0, 21 bits remained for assigning networks for over 2 million class C networks. But, each class C network only had 8 bits in the host portion, or 254 possible host addresses.

An advantage of assigning specific default subnet masks to each class is that it made routing update messages smaller. Classful routing protocols do not include the subnet mask information in their updates. The receiving router applies the default mask based on the value of the first octet which identifies the class.

Refer to
Online Course
for Illustration

2.3.1.3 Classful Routing Protocol Example

Using classful IP addresses meant that the subnet mask of a network address could be determined by the value of the first octet, or more accurately, the first three bits of the address. Routing protocols, such as RIPv1, only need to propagate the network address of known routes and do not need to include the subnet mask in the routing update. This is due to the router receiving the routing update determining the subnet mask simply by examining the value of the first octet in the network address, or by applying its ingress interface mask for subnetted routes. The subnet mask was directly related to the network address.

In Figure 1, R1 sends an update to R2. In the example, R1 knows that subnet 172.16.1.0 belongs to the same major classful network as the outgoing interface. Therefore, it sends a RIP update to R2 containing subnet 172.16.1.0. When R2 receives the update, it applies the receiving interface subnet mask (/24) to the update and adds 172.16.1.0 to the routing table.

In Figure 2, R2 sends an update to R3. When sending updates to R3, R2 summarizes subnets 172.16.1.0/24, 172.16.2.0/24, and 172.16.3.0/24 into the major classful network 172.16.0.0. Because R3 does not have any subnets that belong to 172.16.0.0, it applies the classful mask for a class B network, which is /16.

Refer to
Online Course
for Illustration

2.3.1.4 Classful Addressing Waste

The classful addressing specified in RFCs 790 and 791 resulted in a tremendous waste of address space. In the early days of the Internet, organizations were assigned an entire classful network address from the A, B, or C class.

As illustrated in the figure:

- Class A had 50% of the total address space. However, only 126 organizations could be assigned a class A network address. Ridiculously, each of these organizations could provide addresses for up to 16 million hosts. Very large organizations were allocated entire class A address blocks. Some companies and governmental organizations still have class A addresses. For example, General Electric owns 3.0.0.0/8, Apple Computer owns 17.0.0.0/8, and the U.S. Postal Service owns 56.0.0.0/8.

- Class B had 25% of the total address space. Up to 16,384 organizations could be assigned a class B network address and each of these networks could support up to 65,534 hosts. Only the largest organizations and governments could ever hope to use all 65,000 addresses. Like class A networks, many IP addresses in the class B address space were wasted.

- Class C had 12.5 % of the total address space. Many more organizations were able to get class C networks, but were limited in the total number of hosts that they could connect. In fact, in many cases, class C addresses were often too small for most mid-size organizations.

- Classes D and E are used for multicasting and reserved addresses.

The overall result was that the classful addressing was a very wasteful addressing scheme. A better network addressing solution had to be developed. For this reason, Classless Inter-Domain Routing (CIDR) was introduced in 1993.

Refer to
Online Course
for Illustration

2.3.2   CIDR

2.3.2.1   Classless Inter-Domain Routing

Just as the Internet was growing at an exponential rate in the early 1990s, so were the size of the routing tables that were maintained by Internet routers under classful IP addressing. For this reason, the IETF introduced CIDR in RFC 1517 in 1993.

CIDR replaced the classful network assignments and address classes (A, B, and C) became obsolete. Using CIDR, the network address is no longer determined by the value of the first octet. Instead, the network portion of the address is determined by the subnet mask, also known as the network prefix, or prefix length (i.e., /8, /19, etc.).

ISPs are no longer limited to a /8, /16, or /24 subnet mask. They can now more efficiently allocate address space using any prefix length, starting with /8 and larger (i.e., /8, /9, /10, etc.). The figure shows how blocks of IP addresses can be assigned to a network based on the requirements of the customer, ranging from a few hosts to hundreds or thousands of hosts.

CIDR also reduces the size of routing tables and manages the IPv4 address space more efficiently using:

- **Route summarization** - Also known as prefix aggregation, routes are summarized into a single route to help reduce the size of routing tables. For instance, one summary static route can replace several specific static route statements.

- **Supernetting** - Occurs when the route summarization mask is a smaller value than the default traditional classful mask.

Note   A supernet is always a route summary, but a route summary is not always a supernet.

Refer to
Online Course
for Illustration

2.3.2.2   CIDR and Route Summarization

In the figure, notice that ISP1 has four customers, and that each customer has a variable amount of IP address space. The address space of the four customers can be summarized into one advertisement to ISP2. The 192.168.0.0/20 summarized or aggregated route includes all the networks belonging to Customers A, B, C, and D. This type of route is known as a supernet route. A supernet summarizes multiple network addresses with a mask that is smaller than the classful mask.

Determining the summary route and subnet mask for a group of networks can be done in the following three steps:

Step 1.   List the networks in binary format.

Step 2.   Count the number of far left matching bits. This identifies the prefix length or subnet mask for the summarized route.

Step 3.   Copy the matching bits and then add zero bits to the rest of the address to determine the summarized network address.

The summarized network address and subnet mask can now be used as the summary route for this group of networks.

Summary routes can be configured by both static routes and classless routing protocols.

Refer to
Online Course
for Illustration

2.3.2.3   Static Routing CIDR Example

Creating smaller routing tables makes the routing table lookup process more efficient, because there are fewer routes to search. If one static route can be used instead of multiple static routes, the size of the routing table is reduced. In many cases, a single static route can be used to represent dozens, hundreds, or even thousands of routes.

Summary CIDR routes can be configured using static routes. This helps to reduce the size of routing tables.

In Figure 1, R1 has been configured to reach the identified networks in the topology. Although acceptable, it would be more efficient to configure a summary static route.

Figure 2 provides a solution using CIDR summarization. The six static route entries could be reduced to 172.16.0.0/13 entry. The example removes the six static route entries and replaces them with a summary static route.

Refer to
Online Course
for Illustration

2.3.2.4   Classless Routing Protocol Example

Classful routing protocols cannot send supernet routes. This is because the receiving router automatically applies the default classful subnet mask to the network address in the routing update. If the topology in the figure contained a classful routing protocol, then R3 would only install 172.16.0.0/16 in the routing table.

Propagating VLSM and supernet routes requires a classless routing protocol such as RIPv2, OSPF, or EIGRP. Classless routing protocols advertise network addresses with their associated subnet masks. With a classless routing protocol, R2 can summarize networks 172.16.0.0/16, 172.17.0.0/16, 172.18.0.0/16, and 172.19.0.0/16, and advertise a supernet summary static route 172.16.0.0/14 to R3. R3 then installs the supernet route 172.16.0.0/14 in its routing table.

Note   When a supernet route is in a routing table, for example, as a static route, a classful routing protocol does not include that route in its updates.

Refer to
Online Course
for Illustration

2.3.3   VLSM

2.3.3.1   Fixed-Length Subnet Masking

With fixed-length subnet masking (FLSM), the same number of addresses is allocated for each subnet. If all the subnets have the same requirements for the number of hosts, these fixed size address blocks would be sufficient. However, most often that is not the case.

Note   FLSM is also referred to as traditional subnetting.

The topology shown in Figure 1 requires that network address 192.168.20.0/24 be subnetted into seven subnets: one subnet for each of the four LANs (Building A to D), and one for each of the three WAN connections between routers.

Figure 2 highlights how traditional subnetting can borrow 3 bits from the host portion in the last octet to meet the subnet requirement of seven subnets. For example, under the Host portion, the Subnet portion highlights how borrowing 3 bits creates 8 subnets while the Host portion highlights 5 host bits providing 30 usable hosts IP addresses per subnet. This scheme creates the needed subnets and meets the host requirement of the largest LAN.

Although this traditional subnetting meets the needs of the largest LAN and divides the address space into an adequate number of subnets, it results in significant waste of unused addresses.

For example, only two addresses are needed in each subnet for the three WAN links. Because each subnet has 30 usable addresses, there are 28 unused addresses in each of these subnets. As shown in Figure 3, this results in 84 unused addresses (28 x 3). Further, this limits future growth by reducing the total number of subnets available. This inefficient use of addresses is characteristic of traditional subnetting of classful networks.

Applying a traditional subnetting scheme to this scenario is not very efficient and is wasteful. In fact, this example is a good model for showing how subnetting a subnet can be used to maximize address utilization. Subnetting a subnet, or using variable-length subnet mask (VLSM), was designed to avoid wasting addresses.

2.3.3.2   Variable-Length Subnet Masking

Refer to **Online Course** for Illustration

In traditional subnetting the same subnet mask is applied for all the subnets. This means that each subnet has the same number of available host addresses.

As illustrated in Figure 1, traditional subnetting creates subnets of equal size. Each subnet in a traditional scheme uses the same subnet mask.

With VLSM the subnet mask length varies depending on how many bits have been borrowed for a particular subnet, thus the "variable" part of variable-length subnet mask. As shown in Figure 2, VLSM allows a network space to be divided into unequal parts.

VLSM subnetting is similar to traditional subnetting in that bits are borrowed to create subnets. The formulas to calculate the number of hosts per subnet and the number of subnets created still apply. The difference is that subnetting is not a single pass activity. With VLSM, the network is first subnetted, and then the subnets are subnetted again. This process can be repeated multiple times to create subnets of various sizes.

2.3.3.3   VLSM in Action

Refer to **Online Course** for Illustration

VLSM allows the use of different masks for each subnet. After a network address is subnetted, those subnets can be further subnetted. VLSM is simply subnetting a subnet. VLSM can be thought of as sub-subnetting.

The figure shows the network 10.0.0.0/8 that has been subnetted using the subnet mask of /16, which makes 256 subnets. That is 10.0.0.0/16, 10.1.0.0/16, 10.2.0.0/16, ..., 10.255.0.0/16. Four of these /16 subnets are displayed in the figure. Any of these /16 subnets can be subnetted further.

Click the Play button in the figure to view the animation. In the animation:

■ The 10.1.0.0/16 subnet is subnetted again with the /24 mask.

■ The 10.2.0.0/16 subnet is subnetted again with the /24 mask.

- The 10.3.0.0/16 subnet is subnetted again with the /28 mask

- The 10.4.0.0/16 subnet is subnetted again with the /20 mask.

Individual host addresses are assigned from the addresses of "sub-subnets". For example, the figure shows the 10.1.0.0/16 subnet divided into /24 subnets. The 10.1.4.10 address would now be a member of the more specific subnet 10.1.4.0/24.

Refer to
Online Course
for Illustration

2.3.3.4   Subnetting Subnets

Another way to view the VLSM subnets is to list each subnet and its sub-subnets.

In Figure 1, the 10.0.0.0/8 network is the starting address space and is subnetted with a /16 mask. Borrowing 8 bits (going from /8 to /16) creates 256 subnets that range from 10.0.0.0/16 to 10.255.0.0/16.

In Figure 2, the 10.1.0.0/16 subnet is further subnetted by borrowing 8 more bits. This creates 256 subnets with a /24 mask. This mask allows 254 host addresses per subnet. The subnets ranging from 10.1.0.0/24 to 10.1.255.0/24 are subnets of the subnet 10.1.0.0/16.

In Figure 3, the 10.2.0.0/16 subnet is also further subnetted with a /24 mask allowing 254 host addresses per subnet. The subnets ranging from 10.2.0.0/24 to 10.2.255.0/24 are subnets of the subnet 10.2.0.0/16.

In Figure 4, the 10.3.0.0/16 subnet is further subnetted with a /28 mask, thus creating 4,096 subnets and allowing 14 host addresses per subnet. The subnets ranging from 10.3.0.0/28 to 10.3.255.240/28 are subnets of the subnet 10.3.0.0/16.

In Figure 5, the 10.4.0.0/16 subnet is further subnetted with a /20 mask, thus creating 16 subnets and allowing 4,094 host addresses per subnet. The subnets ranging from 10.4.0.0/20 to 10.4.240.0/20 are subnets of the subnet 10.4.0.0/16. These /20 subnets are big enough to subnet even further, allowing more networks.

Refer to
Online Course
for Illustration

2.3.3.5   VLSM Example

Careful consideration must be given to the design of a network addressing scheme. For example, the sample topology in Figure 1 requires seven subnets.

Using traditional subnetting, the first seven address blocks are allocated for LANs and WANs, as shown in Figure 2. This scheme results in 8 subnets with 30 usable addresses each (/27). While this scheme works for the LAN segments, there are many wasted addresses in the WAN segments.

If an addressing scheme is designed for a new network, the address blocks can be assigned in a way that minimizes waste and keeps unused blocks of addresses contiguous. It can be more difficult to do this when adding to an existing network.

As shown in Figure 3, to use the address space more efficiently, /30 subnets are created for WAN links. To keep the unused blocks of addresses together, the last /27 subnet is further subnetted to create the /30 subnets. The first 3 subnets were assigned to WAN links creating subnets 192.168.20.224/30, 192.168.20.228/30, and 192.168.20.232/30. Designing the addressing scheme in this way leaves three unused /27 subnets and five unused /30 subnets.

Figures 4 to 7 display sample configurations on all four routers to implement the VLSM addressing scheme.

Refer to **Packet Tracer Activity** for this chapter

2.3.3.6   Packet Tracer - Designing and Implementing a VLSM Addressing Scheme

Background/Scenario

In this activity, you are given a network address to develop a VLSM addressing scheme for the network shown in the included topology.

Refer to **Lab Activity** for this chapter

2.3.3.7   Lab - Designing and Implementing Addressing with VLSM

In this lab, you will complete the following objectives:

- Part 1: Examine the Network Requirements
- Part 2: Design the VLSM Address Scheme
- Part 3: Cable and Configure the IPv4 Network

Refer to **Online Course** for Illustration

2.4   Configure Summary and Floating Static Routes

2.4.1   Configure IPv4 Summary Routes

2.4.1.1   Route Summarization

Route summarization, also known as route aggregation, is the process of advertising a contiguous set of addresses as a single address with a less-specific, shorter subnet mask. CIDR is a form of route summarization and is synonymous with the term supernetting.

CIDR ignores the limitation of classful boundaries, and allows summarization with masks that are smaller than that of the default classful mask. This type of summarization helps reduce the number of entries in routing updates and lowers the number of entries in local routing tables. It also helps reduce bandwidth utilization for routing updates and results in faster routing table lookups.

In the figure, R1 requires a summary static route to reach networks in the range of 172.20.0.0/16 to 172.23.0.0/16.

Refer to **Online Course** for Illustration

2.4.1.2   Calculate a Summary Route

Summarizing networks into a single address and mask can be done in three steps:

Step 1.   List the networks in binary format. Figure 1 lists networks 172.20.0.0/16 to 172.23.0.0/16 in binary format.

Step 2.   Count the number of far-left matching bits to determine the mask for the summary route. Figure 2 highlights the 14 far left matching bits. This is the prefix, or subnet mask, for the summarized route: /14 or 255.252.0.0.

Step 3.   Copy the matching bits and then add zero bits to determine the summarized network address. Figure 3 shows that the matching bits with zeros at the end results in the network address 172.20.0.0. The four networks - 172.20.0.0/16,

172.21.0.0/16, 172.22.0.0/16, and 172.23.0.0/16 - can be summarized into the single network address and prefix 172.20.0.0/14.

Figure 4 displays R1 configured with a summary static route to reach networks 172.20.0.0/16 to 172.23.0.0/16.

Refer to
Online Course
for Illustration

2.4.1.3   Summary Static Route Example

Multiple static routes can be summarized into a single static route if:

- The destination networks are contiguous and can be summarized into a single network address.

- The multiple static routes all use the same exit interface or next-hop IP address.

Consider the example in Figure 1. All routers have connectivity using static routes.

Figure 2 displays the static routing table entries for R3. Notice that it has three static routes that can be summarized because they share the same two first octets.

Figure 3 displays the steps to summarize those three networks:

Step 1.   Write out the networks to summarize in binary.

Step 2.   To find the subnet mask for summarization, start with the far left bit, work to the right, finding all the bits that match consecutively until a column of bits that do not match is found, identifying the summary boundary.

Step 3.   Count the number of far left matching bits; in our example, it is 22. This number identifies the subnet mask for the summarized route as /22 or 255.255.252.0.

Step 4.   To find the network address for summarization, copy the matching 22 bits and add all 0 bits to the end to make 32 bits.

After the summary route is identified, replace the existing routes with the one summary route.

Figure 4 displays how the three existing routes are removed and then the new summary static route is configured.

Figure 5 confirms that the summary static route in is the routing table of R3.

Refer to
Interactive Graphic
in online course.

2.4.1.4   Activity - Determine the Summary Network Address and Prefix

Refer to **Packet
Tracer Activity**
for this chapter

2.4.1.5   Packet Tracer - Configuring IPv4 Route Summarization - Scenario 1

In this activity, you will calculate and configure summary routes. Router summarization, also known as route aggregation, is the process of advertising a contiguous set of addresses as a single address.

Refer to **Packet Tracer Activity** for this chapter

2.4.1.6   Packet Tracer - Configuring IPv4 Route Summarization - Scenario 2

In this activity, you will calculate and configure summary routes. Router summarization, also known as route aggregation, is the process of advertising a contiguous set of addresses as a single address. After calculating summary routes for each LAN, you must summarize a route which includes all networks in the topology in order for the ISP to reach each LAN.

Refer to **Online Course** for Illustration

2.4.2   Configure IPv6 Summary Routes

2.4.2.1   Summarize IPv6 Network Addresses

Aside from the fact that IPv6 addresses are 128 bits long and written in hexadecimal, summarizing IPv6 addresses is actually similar to the summarization of IPv4 addresses. It just requires a few extra steps due to the abbreviated IPv6 addresses and hex conversion.

Multiple static IPv6 routes can be summarized into a single static IPv6 route if:

■ The destination networks are contiguous and can be summarized into a single network address.

■ The multiple static routes all use the same exit interface or next-hop IPv6 address.

Refer to the network in the Figure 1. R1 currently has four static IPv6 routes to reach networks 2001:DB8:ACAD:1::/64 to 2001:DB8:ACAD:4::/64.

Figure 2 displays the IPv6 static routes installed in the IPv6 routing table.

Refer to **Online Course** for Illustration

2.4.2.2   Calculate IPv6 Network Addresses

Summarizing IPv6 networks into a single IPv6 prefix and prefix-length can be done in seven steps as shown in Figures 1 to 7:

Step 1.   List the network addresses (prefixes) and identify the part where the addresses differ.

Step 2.   Expand the IPv6 if it is abbreviated.

Step 3.   Convert the differing section from hex to binary.

Step 4.   Count the number of far left matching bits to determine the prefix-length for the summary route.

Step 5.   Copy the matching bits and then add zero bits to determine the summarized network address (prefix).

Step 6.   Convert the binary section back to hex.

Step 7.   Append the prefix of the summary route (result of Step 4).

Refer to **Online Course** for Illustration

2.4.2.3   Configure an IPv6 Summary Address

After the summary route is identified, replace the existing routes with the single summary route.

Figure 1 displays how the four existing routes are removed and then the new summary static IPv6 route is configured.

Figure 2 confirms that the summary static route is in the routing table of R1.

Refer to **Packet Tracer Activity** for this chapter

2.4.2.4   Packet Tracer - Configuring IPv6 Route Summarization

In this activity, you will calculate, configure, and verify a summary route for all the networks R1 can access through R2. R1 is configured with a loopback interface. Instead of adding a LAN or another network to R1, we can use a loopback interface to simplify testing when verifying routing.

Refer to **Lab Activity** for this chapter

2.4.2.5   Lab - Calculating Summary Routes with IPv4 and IPv6

In this lab, you will complete the following objectives:

- Part 1: Calculate IPv4 Summary Routes

- Part 2: Calculate IPv6 Summary Routes

Refer to **Online Course** for Illustration

2.4.3   Configure Floating Static Routes

2.4.3.1   Floating Static Routes

Floating static routes are static routes that have an administrative distance greater than the administrative distance of another static route or dynamic routes. They are very useful when providing a backup to a primary link, as shown in the figure.

By default, static routes have an administrative distance of 1, making them preferable to routes learned from dynamic routing protocols. For example, the administrative distances of some common dynamic routing protocols are:

- EIGRP = 90

- IGRP = 100

- OSPF = 110

- IS-IS = 115

- RIP = 120

The administrative distance of a static route can be increased to make the route less desirable than that of another static route or a route learned through a dynamic routing protocol. In this way, the static route "floats" and is not used when the route with the better administrative distance is active. However, if the preferred route is lost, the floating static route can take over, and traffic can be sent through this alternate route.

A floating static route can be used to provide a backup route to multiple interfaces or networks on a router. It is also encapsulation independent, meaning it can be used to forward packets out any interface, regardless of encapsulation type.

An important consideration of a floating static route is that it is affected by convergence time. A route that is continuously dropping and re-establishing a connection can cause the backup interface to be activated unnecessarily.

Refer to
Online Course
for Illustration

2.4.3.2 Configure a Floating Static Route

IPv4 static routes are configured using the `ip route` global configuration command and specifying an administrative distance. If no administrative distance is configured, the default value (1) is used.

Refer to the topology in Figure 1. In this scenario, the preferred route from R1 is to R2. The connection to R3 should be used for backup only.

R1 is configured with a default static route pointing to R2. Because no administrative distance is configured, the default value (1) is used for this static route. R1 is also configured with a floating static default pointing to R3 with an administrative distance of 5. This value is greater than the default value of 1 and, therefore, this route floats and is not present in the routing table, unless the preferred route fails.

Figure 2 verifies that the default route to R2 is installed in the routing table. Note that the backup route to R3 is not present in the routing table.

Use the Syntax Checker in Figure 3 to configure R3 similarly to R1.

Refer to
Online Course
for Illustration

2.4.3.3 Test the Floating Static Route

Because the default static route on R1 to R2 has an administrative distance of 1, traffic from R1 to R3 should go through R2. The output in Figure 1 confirms that traffic between R1 and R3 flows through R2.

What would happen if R2 failed? To simulate this failure both serial interfaces of R2 are shut down, as shown in Figure 2.

Notice in Figure 3 that R1 automatically generates messages indicating that the serial interface to R2 is down. A look at the routing table verifies that the default route is now pointing to R3 using the floating static default route configured for next-hop 10.10.10.2.

The output in Figure 4 confirms that traffic now flows directly between R1 and R3.

Note Configuring IPv6 floating static routes is outside of the scope of this chapter.

Refer to **Packet
Tracer Activity**
for this chapter

2.4.3.4 Packet Tracer - Configuring a Floating Static Route

In this activity, you will configure a floating static route. A floating static route is used as a backup route. It has a manually configured administrative distance greater than that of the primary route and therefore would not be in the routing table until the primary route fails. You will test failover to the backup route, and then restore connectivity to the primary route.

Refer to
Online Course
for Illustration

2.5   Troubleshoot Static and Default Route Issues

2.5.1   Packet Processing with Static Routes

2.5.1.1   Static Routes and Packet Forwarding

The following example describes the packet forwarding process with static routes.

In the figure, click the Play button to see the animation, where PC1 is sending a packet to PC3:

1. The packet arrives on the GigabitEthernet 0/0 interface of R1.

2. R1 does not have a specific route to the destination network, 192.168.2.0/24; therefore, R1 uses the default static route.

3. R1 encapsulates the packet in a new frame. Because the link to R2 is a point-to-point link, R1 adds an "all 1s" address for the Layer 2 destination address.

4. The frame is forwarded out of the Serial 0/0/0 interface. The packet arrives on the Serial 0/0/0 interface on R2.

5. R2 de-encapsulates the frame and looks for a route to the destination. R2 has a static route to 192.168.2.0/24 out of the Serial 0/0/1 interface.

6. R2 encapsulates the packet in a new frame. Because the link to R3 is a point-to-point link, R2 adds an "all 1s" address for the Layer 2 destination address.

7. The frame is forwarded out of the Serial 0/0/1 interface. The packet arrives on the Serial 0/0/1 interface on R3.

8. R3 de-encapsulates the frame and looks for a route to the destination. R3 has a connected route to 192.168.2.0/24 out of the GigabitEthernet 0/0 interface.

9. R3 looks up the ARP table entry for 192.168.2.10 to find the Layer 2 Media Access Control (MAC) address for PC3. If no entry exists, R3 sends an Address Resolution Protocol (ARP) request out of the GigabitEthernet 0/0 interface, and PC3 responds with an ARP reply, which includes the PC3 MAC address.

10. R3 encapsulates the packet in a new frame with the MAC address of the GigabitEthernet 0/0 interface as the source Layer 2 address and the MAC address of PC3 as the destination MAC address.

11. The frame is forwarded out of GigabitEthernet 0/0 interface. The packet arrives on the network interface card (NIC) interface of PC3.

Refer to
Online Course
for Illustration

2.5.2   Troubleshoot IPv4 Static and Default Route Configuration

2.5.2.1   Troubleshoot a Missing Route

Networks are subject to forces that can cause their status to change quite often:

- An interface fails.

- A service provider drops a connection.

■ Links become oversaturated.

■ An administrator enters a wrong configuration.

When there is a change in the network, connectivity may be lost. Network administrators are responsible for pinpointing and solving the problem. To find and solve these issues, a network administrator must be familiar with tools to help isolate routing problems quickly.

Common IOS troubleshooting commands include:

■ `ping`

■ `traceroute`

■ `show ip route`

■ `show ip interface brief`

■ `show cdp neighbors detail`

Figure 1 displays the result of an extended ping from the source interface of R1 to the LAN interface of R3. An extended ping is when the source interface or source IP address is specified.

Figure 2 displays the result of a traceroute from R1 to the R3 LAN.

Figure 3 displays the routing table of R1.

Figure 4 provides a quick status of all interfaces on the router.

Figure 5 provides a list of directly connected Cisco devices. This command validates Layer 2 (and therefore Layer 1) connectivity. For example, if a neighbor device is listed in the command output, but it cannot be pinged, then Layer 3 addressing should be investigated.

<table>
<tr><td>Refer to
Online Course
for Illustration</td></tr>
</table>

2.5.2.2 Solve a Connectivity Problem

Finding a missing (or misconfigured) route is a relatively straightforward process, if the right tools are used in a methodical manner.

For instance, in this example, the user at PC1 reports that he cannot access resources on the R3 LAN. This can be confirmed by pinging the LAN interface of R3 using the LAN interface of R1 as the source (see Figure 1). The results show that there is no connectivity between these LANs.

A traceroute in Figure 2 reveals that R2 is not responding as expected. For some reason, R2 forwards the traceroute back to R1. R1 returns it to R2. This loop would continue until the time to live (TTL) value decrements to zero, in which case, the router would then send an Internet Control Message Protocol (ICMP) destination unreachable message to R1.

The next step is to investigate the routing table of R2, because it is the router displaying a strange forwarding pattern. The routing table in Figure 3 reveals that the 192.168.2.0/24 network is configured incorrectly. A static route to the 192.168.2.0/24 network has been configured using the next-hop address 172.16.2.1. Using the configured next-hop address, packets destined for the 192.168.2.0/24 network are sent back to R1. It is clear from the topology that the 192.168.2.0/24 network is connected to R3, not R1. Therefore, the static route to the 192.168.2.0/24 network on R2 must use next-hop 192.168.1.1, not 172.16.2.1.

Figure 4 shows output from the running configuration that reveals the incorrect `ip route` statement. The incorrect route is removed and the correct route is then entered.

Figure 5 verifies that R1 can now reach the LAN interface of R3. As a last step in confirmation, the user on PC1 should also test connectivity to the 192.168.2.0/24 LAN.

Refer to **Packet Tracer Activity** for this chapter

2.5.2.3   Packet Tracer - Solving the Missing Route

In this activity, PC1 reports that they cannot access resources at Server. Locate the problem, decide on an appropriate solution and resolve the issue.

Refer to **Packet Tracer Activity** for this chapter

2.5.2.4   Packet Tracer - Troubleshooting VLSM and Route Summarization

In this activity, the network is already addressed using VLSM and configured with static routes. But there is a problem. Locate the issue or issues, determine the best solution, implement the solution, and verify connectivity.

Refer to **Lab Activity** for this chapter

2.5.2.5   Lab - Troubleshooting Static Routes

In this lab, you will complete the following objectives:

- Part 1: Build the Network and Configure Basic Device Settings
- Part 2: Troubleshoot Static Routes in an IPv4 Network
- Part 3: Troubleshoot Static Routes in an IPv6 Network

Refer to **Online Course** for Illustration

2.6   Summary

Refer to **Lab Activity** for this chapter

2.6.1.1   Class Activity - Make It Static

Activity - Make It Static!

As the use of IPv6 addressing becomes more prevalent, it is important for network administrators to be able to direct network traffic between routers.

To prove that you are able to direct IPv6 traffic correctly and review the IPv6 default static route curriculum concepts, use the topology as shown in the .pdf file provided, specifically for this activity.

Work with a partner to write an IPv6 statement for each of the three scenarios. Try to write the route statements without the assistance of completed labs, Packet Tracer files, etc.

Scenario 1

IPv6 default static route from R2 directing all data through your S0/0/0 interface to the next hop address on R1.

Scenario 2

IPv6 default static route from R3 directing all data through your S0/0/1 interface to the next hop address on R2.

Scenario 3

IPv6 default static route from R2 directing all data through your S0/0/1 interface to the next hop address on R3.

When complete, get together with another group and compare your written answers. Discuss any differences found in your comparisons.

Refer to **Packet Tracer Activity** for this chapter

2.6.1.2   Packet Tracer Skills Integration Challenge

The network administrator asked you to implement IPv4 and IPv6 static and default routing in the test environment shown in the topology. Configure each static and default route as directly connected.

Refer to **Online Course** for Illustration

2.6.1.3   Summary

In this chapter, you learned how IPv4 and IPv6 static routes can be used to reach remote networks. Remote networks are networks that can only be reached by forwarding the packet to another router. Static routes are easily configured. However, in large networks, this manual operation can become quite cumbersome. Static routes are still used, even when a dynamic routing protocol is implemented.

Static routes can be configured with a next-hop IP address, which is commonly the IP address of the next-hop router. When a next-hop IP address is used, the routing table process must resolve this address to an exit interface. On point-to-point serial links, it is usually more efficient to configure the static route with an exit interface. On multi-access networks, such as Ethernet, both a next-hop IP address and an exit interface can be configured on the static route.

Static routes have a default administrative distance of 1. This administrative distance also applies to static routes configured with a next-hop address, as well as an exit interface.

A static route is only entered in the routing table if the next-hop IP address can be resolved through an exit interface. Whether the static route is configured with a next-hop IP address or exit interface, if the exit interface that is used to forward that packet is not in the routing table, the static route is not included in the routing table.

Using CIDR, several static routes can be configured as a single summary route. This means fewer entries in the routing table and results in a faster routing table lookup process. CIDR also manages the IPv4 address space more efficiently.

VLSM subnetting is similar to traditional subnetting in that bits are borrowed to create subnets. With VLSM, the network is first subnetted, and then the subnets are subnetted again. This process can be repeated multiple times to create subnets of various sizes

The ultimate summary route is a default route, configured with a 0.0.0.0 network address and a 0.0.0.0 subnet mask for IPv4, and the prefix/prefix-length ::/0 for IPv6. If there is not a more specific match in the routing table, the routing table uses the default route to forward the packet to another router.

A floating static route can be configured to back up a main link by manipulating its administrative value.

Go to the online course to take the quiz and exam.

Chapter 2 Quiz

This quiz is designed to provide an additional opportunity to practice the skills and knowledge presented in the chapter and to prepare for the chapter exam. You will be allowed multiple attempts and the grade does not appear in the gradebook.

Chapter 2 Exam

The chapter exam assesses your knowledge of the chapter content.

Your Chapter Notes

Routing Dynamically

3.0 Routing Dynamically

3.0.1.1 Introduction

The data networks that we use in our everyday lives to learn, play, and work range from small, local networks to large, global internetworks. At home, a user may have a router and two or more computers. At work, an organization may have multiple routers and switches servicing the data communication needs of hundreds or even thousands of PCs.

Routers forward packets by using information in the routing table. Routes to remote networks can be learned by the router in two ways: static routes and dynamic routes.

In a large network with numerous networks and subnets, configuring and maintaining static routes between these networks requires a great deal of administrative and operational overhead. This operational overhead is especially cumbersome when changes to the network occur, such as a down link or implementing a new subnet. Implementing dynamic routing protocols can ease the burden of configuration and maintenance tasks and give the network scalability.

This chapter introduces dynamic routing protocols. It explores the benefits of using dynamic routing protocols, how different routing protocols are classified, and the metrics routing protocols use to determine the best path for network traffic. Other topics covered in this chapter include the characteristics of dynamic routing protocols and how the various routing protocols differ. Network professionals must understand the different routing protocols available in order to make informed decisions about when to use static or dynamic routing. They also need to know which dynamic routing protocol is most appropriate in a particular network environment.

Refer to Lab Activity for this chapter

3.0.1.2 Class Activity How Much Does This Cost?

Activity - How Much Does This Cost?

This modeling activity illustrates the network concept of routing cost.

You will be a member of a team of five students who travel routes to complete the activity scenarios. One digital camera or bring your own device (BYOD) with camera, a stopwatch, and the student file for this activity will be required per group. One person will function as the photographer and event recorder, as selected by each group. The remaining four team members will actively participate in the scenarios below.

A school or university classroom, hallway, outdoor track area, school parking lot, or any other location can serve as the venue for these activities.

Activity 1

The tallest person in the group establishes a start and finish line by marking 15 steps from start to finish, indicating the distance of the team route. Each student will take 15 steps from the start line toward the finish line and then stop on the 15th step—no further steps are allowed.

Note   Not all of the students may reach the same distance from the start line due to their height and stride differences. The photographer will take a group picture of the entire team's final location after taking the 15 steps required.

Activity 2

A new start and finish line will be established; however, this time, a longer distance for the route will be established than the distance specified in Activity 1. No maximum steps are to be used as a basis for creating this particular route. One at a time, students will "walk the new route from beginning to end twice".

Each team member will count the steps taken to complete the route. The recorder will time each student and at the end of each team member's route, record the time that it took to complete the full route and how many steps were taken, as recounted by each team member and recorded on the team's student file.

After both activities have been completed, teams will use the digital picture taken for Activity 1 and their recorded data from Activity 2 file to answer the reflection questions.

Group answers can be discussed as a class, time permitting.

Refer to
Online Course
for Illustration

3.1   Dynamic Routing Protocols

3.1.1   Dynamic Routing Protocol Operation

3.1.1.1   The Evolution of Dynamic Routing Protocols

Dynamic routing protocols have been used in networks since the late 1980s. One of the first routing protocols was Routing Information Protocol (RIP). RIP version 1 (RIPv1) was released in 1988, but some of the basic algorithms within the protocol were used on the Advanced Research Projects Agency Network (ARPANET) as early as 1969.

As networks evolved and became more complex, new routing protocols emerged. The RIP routing protocol was updated to accommodate growth in the network environment, into RIPv2. However, the newer version of RIP still does not scale to the larger network implementations of today. To address the needs of larger networks, two advanced routing protocols were developed: Open Shortest Path First (OSPF) and Intermediate System-to-Intermediate System (IS-IS). Cisco developed the Interior Gateway Routing Protocol (IGRP) and Enhanced IGRP (EIGRP), which also scales well in larger network implementations.

Additionally, there was the need to connect different internetworks and provide routing between them. The Border Gateway Protocol (BGP) is now used between Internet service providers (ISPs). BGP is also used between ISPs and their larger private clients to exchange routing information.

Figure 1 displays the timeline of when the various protocols were introduced.

Figure 2 classifies the protocols.

With the advent of numerous consumer devices using IP, the IPv4 addressing space is nearly exhausted; thus, IPv6 has emerged. To support the communication based on IPv6, newer versions of the IP routing protocols have been developed, see the IPv6 row in the figure.

RIP is the simplest of dynamic routing protocols and is used in this section to provide a basic level of routing protocol understanding.

Refer to
Online Course
for Illustration

3.1.1.2   Purpose of Dynamic Routing Protocols

Routing protocols are used to facilitate the exchange of routing information between routers. A routing protocol is a set of processes, algorithms, and messages that are used to exchange routing information and populate the routing table with the routing protocol's choice of best paths. The purpose of dynamic routing protocols includes:

■ Discovery of remote networks

■ Maintaining up-to-date routing information

■ Choosing the best path to destination networks

■ Ability to find a new best path if the current path is no longer available

The main components of dynamic routing protocols include:

■ **Data structures** - Routing protocols typically use tables or databases for its operations. This information is kept in RAM.

■ **Routing protocol messages** - Routing protocols use various types of messages to discover neighboring routers, exchange routing information, and other tasks to learn and maintain accurate information about the network.

■ **Algorithm** - An algorithm is a finite list of steps used to accomplish a task. Routing protocols use algorithms for facilitating routing information and for best path determination.

The figure highlights the data structures, routing protocol messages, and routing algorithm used by EIGRP.

Refer to
Online Course
for Illustration

3.1.1.3   The Role of Dynamic Routing Protocols

Routing protocols allow routers to dynamically share information about remote networks and automatically add this information to their own routing tables; see the animation in the figure.

Routing protocols determine the best path, or route, to each network. That route is then added to the routing table. A primary benefit of dynamic routing protocols is that routers exchange routing information when there is a topology change. This exchange allows routers to automatically learn about new networks and also to find alternate paths when there is a link failure to a current network.

Compared to static routing, dynamic routing protocols require less administrative overhead. However, the expense of using dynamic routing protocols is dedicating part of a router's resources for protocol operation, including CPU time and network link bandwidth. Despite the benefits of dynamic routing, static routing still has its place. There are times when static routing is more appropriate and other times when dynamic routing is the better choice. Networks with moderate levels of complexity may have both static and dynamic routing configured.

Refer to
Interactive Graphic
in online course.

3.1.1.4   Activity - Identify Components of a Routing Protocol

Refer to
Online Course
for Illustration

3.1.2   Dynamic versus Static Routing

3.1.2.1   Using Static Routing

Before identifying the benefits of dynamic routing protocols, consider the reasons why network professionals use static routing. Dynamic routing certainly has several advantages over static routing; however, static routing is still used in networks today. In fact, networks typically use a combination of both static and dynamic routing.

Static routing has several primary uses, including:

- Providing ease of routing table maintenance in smaller networks that are not expected to grow significantly.

- Routing to and from a stub network, which is a network with only one default route out and no knowledge of any remote networks.

- Accessing a single default route (which is used to represent a path to any network that does not have a more specific match with another route in the routing table).

The figure provides a sample scenario of static routing.

Refer to
Online Course
for Illustration

3.1.2.2   Static Routing Scorecard

The table in the figure highlights the advantages and disadvantages of static routing. Static routing is easy to implement in a small network. Static routes stay the same, which makes them fairly easy to troubleshoot. Static routes do not send update messages and, therefore, require very little overhead.

The disadvantages of static routing include:

- They are not easy to implement in a large network.

- Managing the static configurations can become time consuming.

- If a link fails, a static route cannot reroute traffic.

Refer to
Online Course
for Illustration

3.1.2.3   Using Dynamic Routing Protocols

Dynamic routing protocols help the network administrator manage the time-consuming and exacting process of configuring and maintaining static routes.

Imagine maintaining the static routing configurations for the seven routers in Figure 1.

What if the company grew and now had four regions and 28 routers to manage, as shown in Figure 2? What happens when a link goes down? How do you ensure that redundant paths are available?

Dynamic routing is the best choice for large networks like the one shown.

Refer to
Online Course
for Illustration

3.1.2.4   Dynamic Routing Scorecard

The table in the figure highlights the advantages and disadvantages of dynamic routing. Dynamic routing protocols work well in any type of network consisting of several routers. They are scalable and automatically determine better routes if there is a change in the topology. Although there is more to the configuration of dynamic routing protocols, they are simpler to configure in a large network.

There are disadvantages to dynamic routing. Dynamic routing requires knowledge of additional commands. It is also less secure than static routing because the interfaces identified by the routing protocol send routing updates out. Routes taken may differ between packets. The routing algorithm uses additional CPU, RAM, and link bandwidth.

Notice how dynamic routing addresses the disadvantages of static routing.

Refer to
Interactive Graphic
in online course.

3.1.2.5   Activity - Compare Static and Dynamic Routing

Refer to
Online Course
for Illustration

3.1.3   Routing Protocol Operating Fundamentals

3.1.3.1   Dynamic Routing Protocol Operation

All routing protocols are designed to learn about remote networks and to quickly adapt whenever there is a change in the topology. The method that a routing protocol uses to accomplish this depends upon the algorithm it uses and the operational characteristics of that protocol.

In general, the operations of a dynamic routing protocol can be described as follows:

1. The router sends and receives routing messages on its interfaces.

2. The router shares routing messages and routing information with other routers that are using the same routing protocol.

3. Routers exchange routing information to learn about remote networks.

4. When a router detects a topology change the routing protocol can advertise this change to other routers.

Click Play in the figure to view an animation of dynamic routing protocols in operation.

Refer to
Online Course
for Illustration

3.1.3.2   Cold Start

All routing protocols follow the same patterns of operation. To help illustrate this, consider the following scenario in which all three routers are running RIPv2.

When a router powers up, it knows nothing about the network topology. It does not even know that there are devices on the other end of its links. The only information that a router has is from its own saved configuration file stored in NVRAM. After a router boots successfully, it applies the saved configuration. If the IP addressing is configured correctly, then the router initially discovers its own directly connected networks.

Click Play in the figure to view an animation of the initial discovery of connected networks for each router.

Notice how the routers proceed through the boot up process and then discovers any directly connected networks and subnet masks. This information is added to their routing tables as follows:

- R1 adds the 10.1.0.0 network available through interface FastEthernet 0/0 and 10.2.0.0 is available through interface Serial 0/0/0.

- R2 adds the 10.2.0.0 network available through interface Serial 0/0/0 and 10.3.0.0 is available through interface Serial 0/0/1.

- R3 adds the 10.3.0.0 network available through interface Serial 0/0/1 and 10.4.0.0 is available through interface FastEthernet 0/0.

With this initial information, the routers then proceed to find additional route sources for their routing tables.

Refer to
Online Course
for Illustration

3.1.3.3   Network Discovery

After initial boot up and discovery, the routing table is updated with all directly connected networks and the interfaces those networks reside on.

If a routing protocol is configured, the next step is for the router to begin exchanging routing updates to learn about any remote routes.

The router sends an update packet out all interfaces that are enabled on the router. The update contains the information in the routing table, which currently are all directly connected networks.

At the same time, the router also receives and processes similar updates from other connected routers. Upon receiving an update, the router checks it for new network information. Any networks that are not currently listed in the routing table are added.

Refer to the figure for a topology setup between three routers, R1, R2, and R3. Based on this topology, below is a listing of the different updates that R1, R2, and R3 send and receive during initial convergence.

R1:

- Sends an update about network 10.1.0.0 out the Serial0/0/0 interface

- Sends an update about network 10.2.0.0 out the FastEthernet0/0 interface

- Receives update from R2 about network 10.3.0.0 and increments the hop count by 1

- Stores network 10.3.0.0 in the routing table with a metric of 1

R2:

- Sends an update about network 10.3.0.0 out the Serial 0/0/0 interface

- Sends an update about network 10.2.0.0 out the Serial 0/0/1 interface

- Receives an update from R1 about network 10.1.0.0 and increments the hop count by 1

- Stores network 10.1.0.0 in the routing table with a metric of 1

- Receives an update from R3 about network 10.4.0.0 and increments the hop count by 1

- Stores network 10.4.0.0 in the routing table with a metric of 1

R3:

- Sends an update about network 10.4.0.0 out the Serial 0/0/1 interface

- Sends an update about network 10.3.0.0 out the FastEthernet0/0

- Receives an update from R2 about network 10.2.0.0 and increments the hop count by 1

- Stores network 10.2.0.0 in the routing table with a metric of 1

Click Play in the figure to view an animation of R1, R2, and R3 starting the initial exchange.

After this first round of update exchanges, each router knows about the connected networks of their directly connected neighbors. However, did you notice that R1 does not yet know about 10.4.0.0 and that R3 does not yet know about 10.1.0.0? Full knowledge and a converged network do not take place until there is another exchange of routing information.

Refer to
Online Course
for Illustration

3.1.3.4 Exchanging the Routing Information

At this point the routers have knowledge about their own directly connected networks and about the connected networks of their immediate neighbors. Continuing the journey toward convergence, the routers exchange the next round of periodic updates. Each router again checks the updates for new information.

Refer to the figure for a topology setup between three routers, R1, R2, and R3. After initial discovery is complete, each router continues the convergence process by sending and receiving the following updates.

R1:

- Sends an update about network 10.1.0.0 out the Serial 0/0/0 interface

- Sends an update about networks 10.2.0.0 and 10.3.0.0 out the FastEthernet0/0 interface

- Receives an update from R2 about network 10.4.0.0 and increments the hop count by 1

- Stores network 10.4.0.0 in the routing table with a metric of 2

- Same update from R2 contains information about network 10.3.0.0 with a metric of 1. There is no change; therefore, the routing information remains the same

R2:

- Sends an update about networks 10.3.0.0 and 10.4.0.0 out of Serial 0/0/0 interface

- Sends an update about networks 10.1.0.0 and 10.2.0.0 out of Serial 0/0/1 interface

- Receives an update from R1 about network 10.1.0.0. There is no change; therefore, the routing information remains the same

- Receives an update from R3 about network 10.4.0.0. There is no change; therefore, the routing information remains the same

R3:

- Sends an update about network 10.4.0.0 out the Serial 0/0/1 interface

- Sends an update about networks 10.2.0.0 and 10.3.0.0 out the FastEthernet0/0 interface

- Receives an update from R2 about network 10.1.0.0 and increments the hop count by 1

- Stores network 10.1.0.0 in the routing table with a metric of 2

- Same update from R2 contains information about network 10.2.0.0 with a metric of 1. There is no change; therefore, the routing information remains the same

Click Play in the figure to view an animation of R1, R2, and R3 sending the latest routing table to their neighbors.

Distance vector routing protocols typically implement a routing loop prevention technique known as split horizon. Split horizon prevents information from being sent out the same interface from which it was received. For example, R2 does not send an update containing the network 10.1.0.0 out of Serial 0/0/0, because R2 learned about network 10.1.0.0 through Serial 0/0/0.

After routers within a network have converged, the router can then use the information within the route table to determine the best path to reach a destination. Different routing protocols have different ways of calculating the best path.

Refer to **Online Course** for Illustration

3.1.3.5 Achieving Convergence

The network has converged when all routers have complete and accurate information about the entire network, as shown in Figure 1. Convergence time is the time it takes routers to share information, calculate best paths, and update their routing tables. A network is not completely operable until the network has converged; therefore, most networks require short convergence times.

Convergence is both collaborative and independent. The routers share information with each other, but must independently calculate the impacts of the topology change on their own routes. Because they develop an agreement with the new topology independently, they are said to converge on this consensus.

Convergence properties include the speed of propagation of routing information and the calculation of optimal paths. The speed of propagation refers to the amount of time it takes for routers within the network to forward routing information.

As shown in Figure 2, routing protocols can be rated based on the speed to convergence; the faster the convergence, the better the routing protocol. Generally, older protocols, such as RIP, are slow to converge, whereas modern protocols, such as EIGRP and OSPF, converge more quickly.

Refer to **Packet Tracer Activity** for this chapter

3.1.3.6 Packet Tracer - Investigating Convergence

This activity will help you identify important information in routing tables and witness the process of network convergence.

Refer to **Online Course** for Illustration

3.1.4 Types of Routing Protocols

3.1.4.1 Classifying Routing Protocols

Routing protocols can be classified into different groups according to their characteristics. Specifically, routing protocols can be classified by their:

- **Purpose** - Interior Gateway Protocol (IGP) or Exterior Gateway Protocol (EGP)

- **Operation** - Distance vector, link-state protocol, or path-vector protocol

- **Behavior** - Classful (legacy) or classless protocol

For example, IPv4 routing protocols are classified as follows:

- **RIPv1 (legacy)** - IGP, distance vector, classful protocol

- **IGRP (legacy)** - IGP, distance vector, classful protocol developed by Cisco (deprecated from 12.2 IOS and later)

- **RIPv2** - IGP, distance vector, classless protocol

- **EIGRP** - IGP, distance vector, classless protocol developed by Cisco

- **OSPF** - IGP, link-state, classless protocol

- **IS-IS** - IGP, link-state, classless protocol

- **BGP** - EGP, path-vector, classless protocol

The classful routing protocols, RIPv1 and IGRP, are legacy protocols and are only used in older networks. These routing protocols have evolved into the classless routing protocols, RIPv2 and EIGRP, respectively. Link-state routing protocols are classless by nature.

Figure 1 displays a hierarchical view of dynamic routing protocol classification.

Figures 2 to 5 highlight the purpose, operation, and behavior of the various routing protocols.

Refer to **Online Course** for Illustration

3.1.4.2 IGP and EGP Routing Protocols

An autonomous system (AS) is a collection of routers under a common administration such as a company or an organization. An AS is also known as a routing domain. Typical examples of an AS are a company's internal network and an ISP's network.

The Internet is based on the AS concept; therefore, two types of routing protocols are required:

- **Interior Gateway Protocols (IGP)** - Used for routing within an AS. It is also referred to as intra-AS routing. Companies, organizations, and even service providers use an IGP on their internal networks. IGPs include RIP, EIGRP, OSPF, and IS-IS.

- **Exterior Gateway Protocols (EGP)** - Used for routing between AS. It is also referred to as inter-AS routing. Service providers and large companies may interconnect using an EGP. The Border Gateway Protocol (BGP) is the only currently-viable EGP and is the official routing protocol used by the Internet.

Note   Because BGP is the only EGP available, the term EGP is rarely used; instead, most engineers simply refer to BGP.

The example in the figure provides simple scenarios highlighting the deployment of IGPs, BGP, and static routing:

- **ISP-1** - This is an AS and it uses IS-IS as the IGP. It interconnects with other autonomous systems and service providers using BGP to explicitly control how traffic is routed.

- **ISP-2** - This is an AS and it uses OSPF as the IGP. It interconnects with other autonomous systems and service providers using BGP to explicitly control how traffic is routed.

- **AS-1** - This is a large organization and it uses EIGRP as the IGP. Because it is multihomed (i.e., connects to two different service providers), it uses BGP to explicitly control how traffic enters and leaves the AS.

- **AS-2** - This is a medium-sized organization and it uses OSPF as the IGP. It is also multihomed; therefore, it uses BGP to explicitly control how traffic enters and leaves the AS.

- **AS-3** - This is a small organization with older routers within the AS; it uses RIP as the IGP. BGP is not required because it is single-homed (i.e., connects to one service provider). Instead, static routing is implemented between the AS and the service provider.

Note   BGP is beyond the scope of this course and is not discussed in detail.

Refer to
Online Course
for Illustration

3.1.4.3   Distance Vector Routing Protocols

Distance vector means that routes are advertised by providing two characteristics:

- **Distance** - Identifies how far it is to the destination network and is based on a metric such as the hop count, cost, bandwidth, delay, and more.

- **Vector** - Specifies the direction of the next-hop router or exit interface to reach the destination.

For example, in the figure, R1 knows that the distance to reach network 172.16.3.0/24 is one hop and that the direction is out of the interface S0/0/0 toward R2.

A router using a distance vector routing protocol does not have the knowledge of the entire path to a destination network. Distance vector protocols use routers as sign posts along the path to the final destination. The only information a router knows about a remote network is the distance or metric to reach that network and which path or interface to use to get there. Distance vector routing protocols do not have an actual map of the network topology.

There are four distance vector IPv4 IGPs:

- **RIPv1** - First generation legacy protocol

- **RIPv2** - Simple distance vector routing protocol

■ **IGRP** - First generation Cisco proprietary protocol (obsolete and replaced by EIGRP)

■ **EIGRP** - Advanced version of distance vector routing

Refer to
Online Course
for Illustration

3.1.4.4 Link-State Routing Protocols

In contrast to distance vector routing protocol operation, a router configured with a link-state routing protocol can create a complete view or topology of the network by gathering information from all of the other routers.

To continue our analogy of sign posts, using a link-state routing protocol is like having a complete map of the network topology. The sign posts along the way from source to destination are not necessary, because all link-state routers are using an identical map of the network. A link-state router uses the link-state information to create a topology map and to select the best path to all destination networks in the topology.

RIP-enabled routers send periodic updates of their routing information to their neighbors. Link-state routing protocols do not use periodic updates. After the network has converged, a link-state update is only sent when there is a change in the topology. For example, the link-state update in the animation is not sent until the 172.16.3.0 network goes down.

Click Play in the figure to view link-state operations.

Link-state protocols work best in situations where:

■ The network design is hierarchical, usually occurring in large networks

■ Fast convergence of the network is crucial

■ The administrators have good knowledge of the implemented link-state routing protocol

There are two link-state IPv4 IGPs:

■ **OSPF** - Popular standards based routing protocol

■ **IS-IS** - Popular in provider networks

Refer to
Online Course
for Illustration

3.1.4.5 Classful Routing Protocols

The biggest distinction between classful and classless routing protocols is that classful routing protocols do not send subnet mask information in their routing updates. Classless routing protocols include subnet mask information in the routing updates.

The two original IPv4 routing protocols developed were RIPv1 and IGRP. They were created when network addresses were allocated based on classes (i.e., class A, B, or C). At that time, a routing protocol did not need to include the subnet mask in the routing update, because the network mask could be determined based on the first octet of the network address.

Note Only RIPv1 and IGRP are classful. All other IPv4 and IPv6 routing protocols are classless. Classful addressing has never been a part of IPv6.

The fact that RIPv1 and IGRP do not include subnet mask information in their updates means that they cannot provide variable-length subnet masks (VLSMs) and classless inter-domain routing (CIDR).

Classful routing protocols also create problems in discontiguous networks. A discontiguous network is when subnets from the same classful major network address are separated by a different classful network address.

To illustrate the shortcoming of classful routing, refer to the topology in the Figure 1. Notice that the LANs of R1 (172.16.1.0/24) and R3 (172.16.2.0/24) are both subnets of the same class B network (172.16.0.0/16). They are separated by different classful network addresses (192.168.1.0/30 and 192.168.2.0/30).

When R1 forwards an update to R2, RIPv1 does not include the subnet mask information with the update; it only forwards the class B network address 172.16.0.0.

R2 receives and processes the update. It then creates and adds an entry for the class B 172.16.0.0/16 network in the routing table, as shown in Figure 2.

Figure 3 shows that when R3 forwards an update to R2, it also does not include the subnet mask information and therefore only forwards the classful network address 172.16.0.0.

In Figure 4, R2 receives and processes the update and adds another entry for the classful network address 172.16.0.0/16 to its routing table. When there are two entries with identical metrics in the routing table, the router shares the load of the traffic equally among the two links. This is known as load balancing.

As shown in Figure 5, this has a negative effect on a discontiguous network. Notice the erratic behavior of the `ping` and `traceroute` commands.

3.1.4.6   Classless Routing Protocols

Refer to **Online Course** for Illustration

Modern networks no longer use classful IP addressing and the subnet mask cannot be determined by the value of the first octet. The classless IPv4 routing protocols (RIPv2, EIGRP, OSPF, and IS-IS) all include the subnet mask information with the network address in routing updates. Classless routing protocols support VLSM and CIDR.

IPv6 routing protocols are classless. The distinction whether a routing protocol is classful or classless typically only applies to IPv4 routing protocols. All IPv6 routing protocols are considered classless because they include the prefix-length with the IPv6 address.

Figures 1 through 5 illustrate how classless routing solves the issues created with classful routing:

- **Figure 1** - In this discontiguous network design, the classless protocol RIPv2 has been implemented on all three routers. When R1 forwards an update to R2, RIPv2 includes the subnet mask information with the update 172.16.1.0/24.

- **Figure 2** - R2 receives, processes, and adds two entries in the routing table. The first line displays the classful network address 172.16.0.0 with the /24 subnet mask of the update. This is known as the parent route. The second entry displays the VLSM network address 172.16.1.0 with the exit and next-hop address. This is referred to as the child route. Parent routes never include an exit interface or next-hop IP address.

- **Figure 3** - When R3 forwards an update to R2, RIPv2 includes the subnet mask information with the update 172.16.2.0/24.

■ **Figure 4** - R2 receives, processes, and adds another child route entry 172.16.2.0/24 under the parent route entry 172.16.0.0.

■ **Figure 5** - R2 is now aware of the subnetted networks.

Refer to
Online Course
for Illustration

3.1.4.7 Routing Protocol Characteristics

Routing protocols can be compared based on the following characteristics:

■ **Speed of Convergence** - Speed of convergence defines how quickly the routers in the network topology share routing information and reach a state of consistent knowledge. The faster the convergence, the more preferable the protocol. Routing loops can occur when inconsistent routing tables are not updated due to slow convergence in a changing network.

■ **Scalability** - Scalability defines how large a network can become, based on the routing protocol that is deployed. The larger the network is, the more scalable the routing protocol needs to be.

■ **Classful or Classless (Use of VLSM)** - Classful routing protocols do not include the subnet mask and cannot support VLSM. Classless routing protocols include the subnet mask in the updates. Classless routing protocols support VLSM and better route summarization.

■ **Resource Usage** - Resource usage includes the requirements of a routing protocol such as memory space (RAM), CPU utilization, and link bandwidth utilization. Higher resource requirements necessitate more powerful hardware to support the routing protocol operation, in addition to the packet forwarding processes.

■ **Implementation and Maintenance** - Implementation and maintenance describes the level of knowledge that is required for a network administrator to implement and maintain the network based on the routing protocol deployed.

The table in the figure summarizes the characteristics of each routing protocol.

Refer to
Online Course
for Illustration

3.1.4.8 Routing Protocol Metrics

There are cases when a routing protocol learns of more than one route to the same destination. To select the best path, the routing protocol must be able to evaluate and differentiate between the available paths. This is accomplished through the use of routing metrics.

A metric is a measurable value that is assigned by the routing protocol to different routes based on the usefulness of that route. In situations where there are multiple paths to the same remote network, the routing metrics are used to determine the overall "cost" of a path from source to destination. Routing protocols determine the best path based on the route with the lowest cost.

Different routing protocols use different metrics. The metric used by one routing protocol is not comparable to the metric used by another routing protocol. Two different routing protocols might choose different paths to the same destination.

The animation in the figure shows that RIP would choose the path with the least amount of hops; whereas, OSPF would choose the path with the highest bandwidth.

Refer to **Interactive Graphic** in online course.

3.1.4.9   Activity - Classify Dynamic Routing Protocols

Refer to **Interactive Graphic** in online course.

3.1.4.10   Activity - Compare Routing Protocols

Refer to **Interactive Graphic** in online course.

3.1.4.11   Activity - Match the Metric to the Protocol

Refer to **Online Course** for Illustration

3.2   Distance Vector Dynamic Routing

3.2.1   Distance Vector Routing Protocol Operation

3.2.1.1   Distance Vector Technologies

Distance vector routing protocols share updates between neighbors. Neighbors are routers that share a link and are configured to use the same routing protocol. The router is only aware of the network addresses of its own interfaces and the remote network addresses it can reach through its neighbors. Routers using distance vector routing are not aware of the network topology.

Some distance vector routing protocols send periodic updates. For example, RIP sends a periodic update to all of its neighbors every 30 seconds. RIP does this even if the topology has not changed; it continues to send updates. RIPv1 reaches all of its neighbors by sending updates to the all-hosts IPv4 address of 255.255.255.255, a broadcast.

The broadcasting of periodic updates is inefficient because the updates consume bandwidth and consume network device CPU resources. Every network device has to process a broadcast message. RIPv2 and EIGRP, instead, use multicast addresses so that only neighbors that need updates will receive them. EIGRP can also send a unicast message to only the affected neighbor. Additionally, EIGRP only sends an update when needed, instead of periodically.

As shown in the figure, the two modern IPv4 distance vector routing protocols are RIPv2 and EIGRP. RIPv1 and IGRP are listed only for historical accuracy.

Refer to **Online Course** for Illustration

3.2.1.2   Distance Vector Algorithm

At the core of the distance vector protocol is the routing algorithm. The algorithm is used to calculate the best paths and then send that information to the neighbors.

The algorithm used for the routing protocols defines the following processes:

■ Mechanism for sending and receiving routing information

■ Mechanism for calculating the best paths and installing routes in the routing table

■ Mechanism for detecting and reacting to topology changes

In the animation in the figure, R1 and R2 are configured with the RIP routing protocol. The algorithm sends and receives updates. Both R1 and R2 then glean new information from the update. In this case, each router learns about a new network. The algorithm on each router makes its calculations independently and updates the routing table with the new information. When the LAN on R2 goes down, the algorithm constructs a triggered update and sends it to R1. R1 then removes the network from the routing table.

Different routing protocols use different algorithms to install routes in the routing table, send updates to neighbors, and make path determination decisions. For example:

- RIP uses the Bellman-Ford algorithm as its routing algorithm. It is based on two algorithms developed in 1958 and 1956 by Richard Bellman and Lester Ford, Jr.

- IGRP and EIGRP use the Diffusing Update Algorithm (DUAL) routing algorithm developed by Dr. J.J. Garcia-Luna-Aceves at SRI International.

Refer to
Interactive Graphic
in online course.

3.2.1.3   Activity - Identify Distance Vector Terminology

Refer to
Online Course
for Illustration

3.2.2   Types of Distance Vector Routing Protocols

3.2.2.1   Routing Information Protocol

The Routing Information Protocol (RIP) was a first generation routing protocol for IPv4 originally specified in RFC 1058. It is easy to configure, making it a good choice for small networks.

RIPv1 has the following key characteristics:

- Routing updates are broadcasted (255.255.255.255) every 30 seconds.

- The hop count is used as the metric for path selection.

- A hop count greater than 15 hops is deemed infinite (too far). That 15th hop router would not propagate the routing update to the next router.

In 1993, RIPv1 evolved to a classless routing protocol known as RIP version 2 (RIPv2). RIPv2 introduced the following improvements:

- **Classless routing protocol** - It supports VLSM and CIDR, because it includes the subnet mask in the routing updates.

- **Increased efficiency** - It forwards updates to multicast address 224.0.0.9, instead of the broadcast address 255.255.255.255.

- **Reduced routing entries** - It supports manual route summarization on any interface.

- **Secure** - It supports an authentication mechanism to secure routing table updates between neighbors.

The table in the figure summarizes the differences between RIPv1 and RIPv2.

RIP updates are encapsulated into a UDP segment, with both source and destination port numbers set to UDP port 520.

In 1997, the IPv6 enabled version of RIP was released. RIPng is based on RIPv2. It still has a 15 hop limitation and the administrative distance is 120.

Refer to
Online Course
for Illustration

3.2.2.2   Enhanced Interior-Gateway Routing Protocol

The Interior Gateway Routing Protocol (IGRP) was the first proprietary IPv4 routing protocol developed by Cisco in 1984. It used the following design characteristics:

■ Bandwidth, delay, load, and reliability are used to create a composite metric.

■ Routing updates are broadcast every 90 seconds, by default.

In 1992, IGRP was replaced by Enhanced IGRP (EIGRP). Like RIPv2, EIGRP also introduced support for VLSM and CIDR. EIGRP increases efficiency, reduces routing updates, and supports secure message exchange.

The table in the figure summarizes the differences between IGRP and EIGRP.

EIGRP also introduced:

■ **Bounded triggered updates** - It does not send periodic updates. Only routing table changes are propagated, whenever a change occurs. This reduces the amount of load the routing protocol places on the network. Bounded triggered updates means that EIGRP only sends to the neighbors that need it. It uses less bandwidth, especially in large networks with many routes.

■ **Hello keepalive mechanism** - A small Hello message is periodically exchanged to maintain adjacencies with neighboring routers. This means a very low usage of network resources during normal operation, instead of the periodic updates.

■ **Maintains a topology table** - Maintains all the routes received from neighbors (not only the best paths) in a topology table. DUAL can insert backup routes into the EIGRP topology table.

■ **Rapid convergence** - In most cases, it is the fastest IGP to converge because it maintains alternate routes, enabling almost instantaneous convergence. If a primary route fails, the router can use the alternate route identified. The switchover to the alternate route is immediate and does not involve interaction with other routers.

■ **Multiple network layer protocol support** - EIGRP uses Protocol Dependent Modules (PDM), which means that it is the only protocol to include support for protocols other than IPv4 and IPv6, such as legacy IPX and AppleTalk.

Refer to
Interactive Graphic
in online course.

3.2.2.3   Activity - Compare RIP and EIGRP

Refer to **Packet
Tracer Activity**
for this chapter

3.2.2.4   Packet Tracer - Comparing RIP and EIGRP Path Selection

PCA and **PCB** need to communicate. The path that the data takes between these end devices can travel through **R1**, **R2**, and **R3**, or it can travel through **R4** and **R5**. The process by which routers select the best path depends on the routing protocol. We will examine the behavior of two distance vector routing protocols, Enhanced Interior Gateway Routing Protocol (EIGRP) and Routing Information Protocol version 2 (RIPv2).

Refer to
Online Course
for Illustration

3.3   RIP and RIPng Routing

3.3.1   Configuring the RIP Protocol

3.3.1.1   Router RIP Configuration Mode

Although RIP is rarely used in modern networks, it is useful as a foundation for under-standing basic network routing. For this reason, this section provides a brief overview of how to configure basic RIP settings and to verify RIPv2.

Refer to the reference topology in Figure 1 and the addressing table in Figure 2. In this sce-nario, all routers have been configured with basic management features and all interfaces identified in the reference topology are configured and enabled. There are no static routes configured and no routing protocols enabled; therefore, remote network access is currently impossible. RIPv2 is used as the dynamic routing protocol. To enable RIP, use the `router rip` command, as shown in Figure 3. This command does not directly start the RIP pro-cess. Instead, it provides access to the router configuration mode where the RIP routing settings are configured.

To disable and eliminate RIP, use the `no router rip` global configuration command. This command stops the RIP process and erases all existing RIP configurations.

Figure 4 displays the various RIP commands that can be configured. The highlighted key-words are covered in this section.

Refer to
Online Course
for Illustration

3.3.1.2   Advertising Networks

By entering the RIP router configuration mode, the router is instructed to run RIP. But the router still needs to know which local interfaces it should use for communication with other routers, as well as which locally connected networks it should advertise to those routers.

To enable RIP routing for a network, use the `network` *network-address* router configura-tion mode command. Enter the classful network address for each directly connected net-work. This command:

- Enables RIP on all interfaces that belong to a specific network. Associated interfaces now both send and receive RIP updates.

- Advertises the specified network in RIP routing updates sent to other routers every 30 seconds.

Note   If a subnet address is entered, the IOS automatically converts it to the classful net-work address. Remember RIPv1 is a classful routing protocol for IPv4. For example, enter-ing the `network 192.168.1.32` command would automatically be converted to `network 192.168.1.0` in the running configuration file. The IOS does not give an error message, but instead corrects the input and enters the classful network address.

In Figure 1, the `network` command is used to advertise the R1 directly connected net-works.

Use the Syntax Checker in Figure 2 to configure a similar configuration on R2 and R3.

Refer to
Online Course
for Illustration

3.3.1.3   Examining Default RIP Settings

The `show ip protocols` command displays the IPv4 routing protocol settings currently configured on the router. This output displayed in Figure 1 confirms most RIP parameters including:

1. RIP routing is configured and running on router R1.

2. The values of various timers; for example, the next routing update, is sent by R1 in 16 seconds.

3. The version of RIP configured is currently RIPv1.

4. R1 is currently summarizing at the classful network boundary.

5. The classful networks are advertised by R1. These are the networks that R1 include in its RIP updates.

6. The RIP neighbors are listed including their next-hop IP address, the associated AD that R2 uses for updates sent by this neighbor and when the last update was received from this neighbor.

Note   This command is also very useful when verifying the operations of other routing protocols (i.e., EIGRP and OSPF).

The `show ip route` command displays the RIP routes installed in the routing table. In Figure 2, R1 now knows about the highlighted networks.

Use the Syntax Checker in Figure 3 to verify the R2 and R3 RIP settings and routes.

Refer to
Online Course
for Illustration

3.3.1.4   Enabling RIPv2

By default, when a RIP process is configured on a Cisco router, it is running RIPv1, as shown in Figure 1. However, even though the router only sends RIPv1 messages, it can interpret both RIPv1 and RIPv2 messages. A RIPv1 router ignores the RIPv2 fields in the route entry.

Use the `version 2` router configuration mode command to enable RIPv2, as shown in Figure 2. Notice how the `show ip protocols` command verifies that R2 is now configured to send and receive version 2 messages only. The RIP process now includes the subnet mask in all updates, making RIPv2 a classless routing protocol.

Note   Configuring `version 1` enables RIPv1 only, while configuring `no version` returns the router to the default setting of sending version 1 updates but listening for version 1 or version 2 updates.

Figure 3 verifies that there are no RIP routes still in the routing table. This is because R1 is now only listening for RIPv2 updates. R2 and R3 are still sending RIPv1 updates. Therefore, the `version 2` command must be configured on all routers in the routing domain.

Use the Syntax Checker in Figure 4 to enable RIPv2 on R2 and R3.

Refer to
Online Course
for Illustration

3.3.1.5 Disabling Auto Summarization

As shown in Figure 1, RIPv2 automatically summarizes networks at major network boundaries by default, just like RIPv1.

To modify the default RIPv2 behavior of automatic summarization, use the `no auto-summary` router configuration mode command as shown in Figure 2. This command has no effect when using RIPv1. When automatic summarization has been disabled, RIPv2 no longer summarizes networks to their classful address at boundary routers. RIPv2 now includes all subnets and their appropriate masks in its routing updates. The `show ip protocols` now states that `automatic network summarization is not in effect`.

Note RIPv2 must be enabled before automatic summarization is disabled.

Use the Syntax Checker in Figure 3 to disable automatic summarization on R2 and R3.

Refer to
Online Course
for Illustration

3.3.1.6 Configuring Passive Interfaces

By default, RIP updates are forwarded out all RIP enabled interfaces. However, RIP updates really only need to be sent out interfaces connecting to other RIP enabled routers.

For instance, refer to the topology in Figure 1. RIP sends updates out of its G0/0 interface even though no RIP device exists on that LAN. R1 has no way of knowing this and, as a result, sends an update every 30 seconds. Sending out unneeded updates on a LAN impacts the network in three ways:

- **Wasted Bandwidth** - Bandwidth is used to transport unnecessary updates. Because RIP updates are either broadcasted or multicasted; therefore, switches also forward the updates out all ports.

- **Wasted Resources** - All devices on the LAN must process the update up to the transport layers, at which point the devices will discard the update.

- **Security Risk** - Advertising updates on a broadcast network is a security risk. RIP updates can be intercepted with packet sniffing software. Routing updates can be modified and sent back to the router, corrupting the routing table with false metrics that misdirect traffic.

Use the `passive-interface` router configuration command to prevent the transmission of routing updates through a router interface, but still allow that network to be advertised to other routers. The command stops routing updates out the specified interface. However, the network that the specified interface belongs to is still advertised in routing updates that are sent out other interfaces.

There is no need for R1, R2, and R3 to forward RIP updates out of their LAN interfaces. The configuration in Figure 2 identifies the R1 G0/0 interface as passive. The `show ip protocols` command is then used to verify that the Gigabit Ethernet interface was passive. Notice that the G0/0 interface is no longer listed as sending or receiving version 2 updates, but instead is now listed under the Passive Interface(s) section. Also notice that the network 192.168.1.0 is still listed under Routing for Networks, which means that this network is still included as a route entry in RIP updates that are sent to R2.

Note All routing protocols support the `passive-interface` command.

Use the Syntax Checker in Figure 3 to configure the LAN interface as a passive interface on R2 and R3.

As an alternative, all interfaces can be made passive using the `passive-interface default` command. Interfaces that should not be passive can be re-enabled using the `no passive-interface` command.

Refer to
Online Course
for Illustration

3.3.1.7   Propagating a Default Route

Refer to Figure 1. In this scenario, R1 is single-homed to a service provider. Therefore, all that is required for R1 to reach the Internet is a default static route going out of the Serial 0/0/1 interface.

Similar default static routes could be configured on R2 and R3, but it is much more scalable to enter it one time on the edge router R1 and then have R1 propagate it to all other routers using RIP. To provide Internet connectivity to all other networks in the RIP routing domain, the default static route needs to be advertised to all other routers that use the dynamic routing protocol.

To propagate a default route, the edge router must be configured with:

- A default static route using the `ip route 0.0.0.0 0.0.0.0` *exit-intf next-hop-ip* command.

- The `default-information originate` router configuration command. This instructs R1 router to originate default information, by propagating the static default route in RIP updates.

The example in Figure 2 configures a fully specified default static route to the service provider and then the route is propagated by RIP. Notice that R1 now has a Gateway of Last Resort and default route installed in its routing table.

Use the Syntax Checker in Figure 3 to verify that the default route has been propagated to R2 and R3.

Refer to **Packet
Tracer Activity**
for this chapter

3.3.1.8   Packet Tracer - Configuring RIPv2

Although RIP is rarely used in modern networks, it is useful as a foundation for understanding basic network routing. In this activity, you will configure a default route, RIP version 2 with appropriate network statements and passive interfaces, and verify full connectivity.

Refer to
Online Course
for Illustration

3.3.2   Configuring the RIPng Protocol

3.3.2.1   Advertising IPv6 Networks

As with its IPv4 counterpart, RIPng is rarely used in modern networks. It is also useful as a foundation for understanding basic network routing. For this reason, this section provides a brief overview of how to configure basic RIPng.

Refer to the reference topology in the figure. In this scenario, all routers have been configured with basic management features and all interfaces identified in the reference topology are configured and enabled. There are no static routes configured and no routing protocols enabled; therefore, remote network access is currently impossible.

To enable an IPv6 router to forward IPv6 packets, the `ipv6 unicast-routing` must be configured.

Unlike RIPv2, RIPng is enabled on an interface and not in router configuration mode. In fact, there is no `network` *network-address* command available in RIPng. Instead, use the `ipv6 rip` *domain-name* `enable` interface configuration command.

In Figure 1, IPv6 unicast routing is enabled and the Gigabit Ethernet 0/0 and Serial 0/0/0 interfaces are enabled for RIPng using the domain name RIP-AS.

Use the Syntax Checker in Figure 2 to configure a similar configuration on R2 and R3.

The process to propagate a default route in RIPng is identical to RIPv2 except that an IPv6 default static route must be specified. For example, assume that R1 had an Internet connection from a Serial 0/0/1 interface to IP address 2001:DB8:FEED:1::1/64. To propagate a default route, R3 would have to be configured with:

- A default static route using the `ipv6 route 0::/0 2001:DB8:FEED:1::1` global configuration command.

- The `ipv6 rip` *domain-name* `default-information originate` interface configuration mode command. This instructs R3 to be the source of the default route information and propagate the default static route in RIPng updates sent out of the configured interface.

<table>
<tr><td>Refer to
Online Course
for Illustration</td></tr>
</table>

3.3.2.2 Examining the RIPng Configuration

In Figure 1, the `show ipv6 protocols` command does not provide the same amount of information as its IPv4 counterpart. However, it does confirm the following parameters:

1. That RIPng routing is configured and running on router R1.

2. The interfaces configured with RIPng.

The `show ipv6 route` command displays the routes installed in the routing table as shown in Figure 2. The output confirms that R1 now knows about the highlighted RIPng networks.

Notice that the R2 LAN is advertised as two hops away. This is because there is a difference in the way RIPv2 and RIPng calculate the hop counts. With RIPv2 (and RIPv1), the metric to the R2 LAN would be one hop. This is because the metric (hop count) that is displayed in the IPv4 routing table is the number of hops required to reach the remote network (counting the next-hop router as the first hop). In RIPng, the sending router already considers itself to be one hop away; therefore, R2 advertises its LAN with a metric of 1. When R1 receives the update, it adds another hop count of 1 to the metric. Therefore, R1 considers the R2 LAN to be two hops away. Similarly it considers the R3 LAN to be three hops away.

Appending the `rip` keyword to the command as shown in Figure 3 only lists RIPng networks.

Use the Syntax Checker in Figure 4 to verify the R2 and R3.

Refer to **Packet Tracer Activity** for this chapter

3.3.2.3   Packet Tracer - Configuring RIPng

RIPng (RIP Next Generation) is a distance vector routing protocol for routing IPv6 addresses. RIPng is based on RIPv2 and has the same administrative distance and 15 hop limitation. This activity will help you become more familiar with RIPng.

Refer to **Lab Activity** for this chapter

3.3.2.4   Lab - Configuring RIPv2

In this lab you will complete the following objectives:

- Part 1: Build the Network and Configure Basic Device Settings

- Part 2: Configure and Verify RIPv2 Routing

- Part 3: Configure IPv6 on Devices

- Part 4: Configure and Verify RIPng Routing

Refer to **Online Course** for Illustration

3.4   Link-State Dynamic Routing

3.4.1   Link-State Routing Protocol Operation

3.4.1.1   Shortest Path First Protocols

Link-state routing protocols are also known as shortest path first protocols and are built around Edsger Dijkstra's shortest path first (SPF) algorithm. The SPF algorithm is discussed in more detail in a later section.

The IPv4 link-state routing protocols are shown in the figure:

- Open Shortest Path First (OSPF)

- Intermediate System-to-Intermediate System (IS-IS)

Link-state routing protocols have the reputation of being much more complex than their distance vector counterparts. However, the basic functionality and configuration of link-state routing protocols is equally straight-forward.

Just like RIP and EIGRP, basic OSPF operations can be configured using the:

- `router ospf` *process-id* global configuration command

- `network` command to advertise networks

Refer to **Online Course** for Illustration

3.4.1.2   Dijkstra's Algorithm

All link-state routing protocols apply Dijkstra's algorithm to calculate the best path route. The algorithm is commonly referred to as the shortest path first (SPF) algorithm. This algorithm uses accumulated costs along each path, from source to destination, to determine the total cost of a route.

In the figure, each path is labeled with an arbitrary value for cost. The cost of the shortest path for R2 to send packets to the LAN attached to R3 is 27. Each router determines its own cost to each destination in the topology. In other words, each router calculates the SPF algorithm and determines the cost from its own perspective.

Note   The focus of this section is on cost, which is determined by the SPF tree. For this reason, the graphics throughout this section show the connections of the SPF tree, not the topology. All links are represented with a solid black line.

Refer to
Online Course
for Illustration

3.4.1.3   SPF Example

The table in Figure 1 displays the shortest path and the accumulated cost to reach the identified destination networks from the perspective of R1.

The shortest path is not necessarily the path with the least number of hops. For example, look at the path to the R5 LAN. It might be assumed that R1 would send directly to R4 instead of to R3. However, the cost to reach R4 directly (22) is higher than the cost to reach R4 through R3 (17).

Observe the shortest path for each router to reach each of the LANs, as shown in Figures 2 to 5.

Refer to
Online Course
for Illustration

3.4.2   Link-State Updates

3.4.2.1   Link-State Routing Process

So exactly how does a link-state routing protocol work? With link-state routing protocols, a link is an interface on a router. Information about the state of those links is known as link-states.

Examine the topology in the figure. All routers in the topology will complete the following generic link-state routing process to reach a state of convergence:

1.   Each router learns about its own links and its own directly connected networks. This is done by detecting that an interface is in the up state.

2.   Each router is responsible for meeting its neighbors on directly connected networks. Link state routers do this by exchanging Hello packets with other link-state routers on directly connected networks.

3.   Each router builds a Link-State Packet (LSP) containing the state of each directly connected link. This is done by recording all the pertinent information about each neighbor, including neighbor ID, link type, and bandwidth.

4.   Each router floods the LSP to all neighbors. Those neighbors store all LSPs received in a database. They then flood the LSPs to their neighbors until all routers in the area have received the LSPs. Each router stores a copy of each LSP received from its neighbors in a local database.

5.   Each router uses the database to construct a complete map of the topology and computes the best path to each destination network. Like having a road map, the router now has a complete map of all destinations in the topology and the routes to reach them. The SPF algorithm is used to construct the map of the topology and to determine the best path to each network.

Note This process is the same for both OSPF for IPv4 and OSPF for IPv6. The examples in this section refer to OSPF for IPv4.

Refer to
Online Course
for Illustration

3.4.2.2 Link and Link-State

The first step in the link-state routing process is that each router learns about its own links, its own directly connected networks. When a router interface is configured with an IP address and subnet mask, the interface becomes part of that network.

Refer to the topology in Figure 1. For purposes of this discussion, assume that R1 was previously configured and had full connectivity to all neighbors. However, R1 lost power briefly and had to restart.

During boot up R1 loads the saved startup configuration file. As the previously configured interfaces become active, R1 learns about its own directly connected networks. Regardless of the routing protocols used, these directly connected networks are now entries in the routing table.

As with distance vector protocols and static routes, the interface must be properly configured with an IPv4 address and subnet mask, and the link must be in the up state before the link-state routing protocol can learn about a link. Also, like distance vector protocols, the interface must be included in one of the `network` router configuration statements before it can participate in the link-state routing process.

Figure 1 shows R1 linked to four directly connected networks:

- FastEthernet 0/0 - 10.1.0.0/16
- Serial 0/0/0 - 10.2.0.0/16
- Serial 0/0/1 - 10.3.0.0/16
- Serial 0/1/0 - 10.4.0.0/16

As shown in Figures 2 to 5, the link-state information includes:

- The interface's IPv4 address and subnet mask
- The type of network, such as Ethernet (broadcast) or Serial point-to-point link
- The cost of that link
- Any neighbor routers on that link

Note Cisco's implementation of OSPF specifies the OSPF routing metric as the cost of the link based on the bandwidth of the outgoing interface. For the purposes of this chapter, we are using arbitrary cost values to simplify the demonstration.

Refer to
Online Course
for Illustration

3.4.2.3 Say Hello

The second step in the link-state routing process is that each router is responsible for meeting its neighbors on directly connected networks.

Routers with link-state routing protocols use a Hello protocol to discover any neighbors on its links. A neighbor is any other router that is enabled with the same link-state routing protocol.

Click Play in the figure to view an animation on the link-state neighbor discovery process with Hello packets.

In the animation, R1 sends Hello packets out its links (interfaces) to discover if there are any neighbors. R2, R3, and R4 reply to the Hello packet with their own Hello packets because these routers are configured with the same link-state routing protocol. There are no neighbors out the FastEthernet 0/0 interface. Because R1 does not receive a Hello on this interface, it does not continue with the link-state routing process steps for the FastEthernet 0/0 link.

When two link-state routers learn that they are neighbors, they form an adjacency. These small Hello packets continue to be exchanged between two adjacent neighbors and serves as a keepalive function to monitor the state of the neighbor. If a router stops receiving Hello packets from a neighbor, that neighbor is considered unreachable and the adjacency is broken.

Refer to
Online Course
for Illustration

3.4.2.4 Building the Link-State Packet

The third step in the link-state routing process is that each router builds a link-state packet (LSP) containing the state of each directly connected link.

After a router has established its adjacencies, it can build its LSPs that contain the link-state information about its links. A simplified version of the LSP from R1 displayed in the figure would contain the following:

1. R1; Ethernet network 10.1.0.0/16; Cost 2

2. R1 -> R2; Serial point-to-point network; 10.2.0.0/16; Cost 20

3. R1 -> R3; Serial point-to-point network; 10.3.0.0/16; Cost 5

4. R1 -> R4; Serial point-to-point network; 10.4.0.0/16; Cost 20

Refer to
Online Course
for Illustration

3.4.2.5 Flooding the LSP

The fourth step in the link-state routing process is that each router floods the LSP to all neighbors, who then store all LSPs received in a database.

Each router floods its link-state information to all other link-state routers in the routing area. Whenever a router receives an LSP from a neighboring router, it immediately sends that LSP out all other interfaces except the interface that received the LSP. This process creates a flooding effect of LSPs from all routers throughout the routing area.

Click Play in the figure to view an animation on LSP flooding.

In the animation, notice how the LSPs are flooded almost immediately after being received without any intermediate calculations. Link-state routing protocols calculate the SPF algorithm after the flooding is complete. As a result, link-state routing protocols reach convergence very quickly.

Remember that LSPs do not need to be sent periodically. An LSP only needs to be sent:

- During initial startup of the routing protocol process on that router (e.g., router restart)

- Whenever there is a change in the topology (e.g., a link going down or coming up, a neighbor adjacency being established or broken)

In addition to the link-state information, other information is included in the LSP, such as sequence numbers and aging information, to help manage the flooding process. This information is used by each router to determine if it has already received the LSP from another router or if the LSP has newer information than what is already contained in the link-state database. This process allows a router to keep only the most current information in its link-state database.

Refer to **Online Course** for Illustration

3.4.2.6   Building the Link-State Database

The final step in the link-state routing process is that each router uses the database to construct a complete map of the topology and computes the best path to each destination network.

Eventually, all routers receive an LSP from every other link-state router in the routing area. These LSPs are stored in the link-state database.

The example in the figure displays the link-state database content of R1.

As a result of the flooding process, R1 has learned the link-state information for each router in its routing area. Notice that R1 also includes its own link-state information in the link-state database.

With a complete link-state database, R1 can now use the database and the shortest path first (SPF) algorithm to calculate the preferred path or shortest path to each network resulting in the SPF tree.

Refer to **Online Course** for Illustration

3.4.2.7   Building the SPF Tree

Each router in the routing area uses the link-state database and SPF algorithm to construct the SPF tree.

For example, using the link-state information from all other routers, R1 can now begin to construct an SPF tree of the network. To begin, the SPF algorithm interprets each router's LSP to identify networks and associated costs.

In Figure 1, R1 identifies its directly connected networks and costs.

In Figures 2 through 5, R1 keeps adding any unknown network and associated costs to the SPF tree. Notice that R1 ignores any networks it has already identified.

The SPF algorithm then calculates the shortest paths to reach each individual network resulting in the SPF tree as shown in Figure 6. R1 now has a complete topology view of the link-state area.

Each router constructs its own SPF tree independently from all other routers. To ensure proper routing, the link-state databases used to construct those trees must be identical on all routers.

Refer to
Online Course
for Illustration

3.4.2.8   Adding OSPF Routes to the Routing Table

Using the shortest path information determined by the SPF algorithm, these paths can now be added to the routing table. The figure shows the routes that have now been added to R1's IPv4 routing table.

The routing table also includes all directly connected networks and routes from any other sources, such as static routes. Packets are now forwarded according to these entries in the routing table.

Refer to
Interactive Graphic
in online course.

3.4.2.9   Activity - Building the Link-State Database and SPF Tree

Refer to
Online Course
for Illustration

3.4.3   Why Use Link-State Routing Protocols

3.4.3.1   Why Use Link-State Protocols?

As shown in the figure, there are several advantages of link-state routing protocols compared to distance vector routing protocols.

- **Builds a Topological Map** - Link-state routing protocols create a topological map, or SPF tree of the network topology. Because link-state routing protocols exchange link-states, the SPF algorithm can build an SPF tree of the network. Using the SPF tree, each router can independently determine the shortest path to every network.

- **Fast Convergence** - When receiving an LSP, link-state routing protocols immediately flood the LSP out all interfaces except for the interface from which the LSP was received. In contrast, RIP needs to process each routing update and update its routing table before flooding them out other interfaces.

- **Event-driven Updates** - After the initial flooding of LSPs, link-state routing protocols only send out an LSP when there is a change in the topology. The LSP contains only the information regarding the affected link. Unlike some distance vector routing protocols, link-state routing protocols do not send periodic updates.

- **Hierarchical Design** - Link-state routing protocols use the concept of areas. Multiple areas create a hierarchical design to networks, allowing for better route aggregation (summarization) and the isolation of routing issues within an area.

Link-state protocols also have a few disadvantages compared to distance vector routing protocols:

- **Memory Requirements** - Link-state protocols require additional memory to create and maintain the link-state database and SPF tree.

- **Processing Requirements** - Link-state protocols can also require more CPU processing than distance vector routing protocols. The SPF algorithm requires more CPU time than distance vector algorithms such as Bellman-Ford, because link-state protocols build a complete map of the topology.

- **Bandwidth Requirements** - The flooding of link-state packets can adversely affect the available bandwidth on a network. This should only occur during initial startup of routers, but can also be an issue on unstable networks.

Refer to
Online Course
for Illustration

3.4.3.2   Disadvantages of Link-State Protocols

Modern link-state routing protocols are designed to minimize the effects on memory, CPU, and bandwidth. The use and configuration of multiple areas can reduce the size of the link-state databases. Multiple areas can also limit the amount of link-state information flooding in a routing domain and send LSPs only to those routers that need them. When there is a change in the topology, only those routers in the affected area receive the LSP and run the SPF algorithm. This can help isolate an unstable link to a specific area in the routing domain.

For example, in the figure, there are three separate routing domains: area 1, area 0, and area 51. If a network in area 51 goes down, the LSP with the information about this downed link is only flooded to other routers in that area. Only those routers in area 51 need to update their link-state databases, rerun the SPF algorithm, create a new SPF tree, and update their routing tables. Routers in other areas learn that this route is down, but this is done with a type of LSP that does not cause them to rerun their SPF algorithm. Routers in other areas can update their routing tables directly.

Refer to
Online Course
for Illustration

3.4.3.3   Protocols that Use Link-State

There are only two link-state routing protocols, OSPF and IS-IS.

Open Shortest Path First (OSPF) is the most popular implementation. It was designed by the Internet Engineering Task Force (IETF) OSPF Working Group. The development of OSPF began in 1987 and there are two current versions in use:

- **OSPFv2** - OSPF for IPv4 networks (RFC 1247 and RFC 2328)
- **OSPFv3** - OSPF for IPv6 networks (RFC 2740)

Note   With the OSPFv3 Address Families feature, OSPFv3 includes support for both IPv4 and IPv6.

IS-IS was designed by International Organization for Standardization (ISO) and is described in ISO 10589. The first incarnation of this routing protocol was developed at Digital Equipment Corporation (DEC) and is known as DECnet Phase V. Radia Perlman was the chief designer of the IS-IS routing protocol.

IS-IS was originally designed for the OSI protocol suite and not the TCP/IP protocol suite. Later, Integrated IS-IS, or Dual IS-IS, included support for IP networks. Although IS-IS has been known as the routing protocol used mainly by ISPs and carriers, more enterprise networks are beginning to use IS-IS.

OSPF and IS-IS share many similarities and also have many differences. There are many pro-OSPF and pro-IS-IS factions who discuss and debate the advantages of one routing protocol over the other. Both routing protocols provide the necessary routing functionality.

Refer to
Online Course
for Illustration

3.5 The Routing Table

3.5.1 Parts of an IPv4 Route Entry

3.5.1.1 Routing Table Entries

The topology displayed in Figure 1 is used as the reference topology for this section. Notice that in the topology:

- R1 is the edge router that connects to the Internet. Therefore, it is propagating a default static route to R2 and R3.

- R1, R2, and R3 contain discontiguous networks separated by another classful network.

- R3 is also introducing a 192.168.0.0/16 supernet route.

Figure 2 displays the IPv4 routing table of R1 with directly connected, static, and dynamic routes.

Note The routing table hierarchy in Cisco IOS was originally implemented with the classful routing scheme. Although the routing table incorporates both classful and classless addressing, the overall structure is still built around this classful scheme.

Refer to
Online Course
for Illustration

3.5.1.2 Directly Connected Entries

As highlighted in Figure 1, the routing table of R1 contains three directly connected networks. Notice that two routing table entries are automatically created when an active router interface is configured with an IP address and subnet mask.

Figure 2 displays one of the routing table entries on R1 for the directly connected network 172.16.1.0. These entries were automatically added to the routing table when the GigabitEthernet 0/0 interface was configured and activated. The entries contain the following information:

- **Route source** - Identifies how the route was learned. Directly connected interfaces have two route source codes. C identifies a directly connected network. Directly connected networks are automatically created whenever an interface is configured with an IP address and activated. L identifies that this is a local route. Local routes are automatically created whenever an interface is configured with an IP address and activated.

- **Destination network** - The address of the remote network and how that network is connected.

- **Outgoing interface** - Identifies the exit interface to use when forwarding packets to the destination network.

Note Local routing table entries did not appear in routing tables prior to IOS release 15.

A router typically has multiple interfaces configured. The routing table stores information about both directly connected and remote routes. As with directly connected networks, the route source identifies how the route was learned. For instance, common codes for remote networks include:

- **S** - Identifies that the route was manually created by an administrator to reach a specific network. This is known as a static route.

- **D** - Identifies that the route was learned dynamically from another router using the EIGRP routing protocol.

- **O** - Identifies that the route was learned dynamically from another router using the OSPF routing protocol.

- **R** - Identifies that the route was learned dynamically from another router using the RIP routing protocol.

Refer to
Online Course
for Illustration

3.5.1.3   Remote Network Entries

The figure displays an IPv4 routing table entry on R1 for the route to remote network 172.16.4.0 on R3. The entry identifies the following information:

- **Route source** - Identifies how the route was learned.

- **Destination network** - Identifies the address of the remote network.

- **Administrative distance** - Identifies the trustworthiness of the route source.

- **Metric** - Identifies the value assigned to reach the remote network. Lower values indicate preferred routes.

- **Next hop** - Identifies the IPv4 address of the next router to forward the packet to.

- **Route timestamp** - Identifies from when the route was last heard.

- **Outgoing interface** - Identifies the exit interface to use to forward a packet toward the final destination.

Refer to
Interactive Graphic
in online course.

3.5.1.4   Activity - Identify Parts of an IPv4 Routing Table Entry

Refer to
Online Course
for Illustration

3.5.2   Dynamically Learned IPv4 Routes

3.5.2.1   Routing Table Terms

A dynamically built routing table provides a great deal of information, as shown in the figure. Therefore, it is crucial to understand the output generated by the routing table. Special terms are applied when discussing the contents of a routing table.

The Cisco IP routing table is not a flat database. The routing table is actually a hierarchical structure that is used to speed up the lookup process when locating routes and forwarding packets. Within this structure, the hierarchy includes several levels.

Routes are discussed in terms of:

- Ultimate route
- Level 1 route
- Level 1 parent route
- Level 2 child routes

Refer to
Online Course
for Illustration

3.5.2.2 Ultimate Route

An ultimate route is a routing table entry that contains either a next-hop IPv4 address or an exit interface. Directly connected, dynamically learned, and local routes are ultimate routes.

In the figure, the highlighted areas are examples of ultimate routes. Notice that all of these routes specify either a next-hop IPv4 address or an exit interface.

Refer to
Online Course
for Illustration

3.5.2.3 Level 1 Route

A level 1 route is a route with a subnet mask equal to or less than the classful mask of the network address. Therefore, a level 1 route can be a:

- **Network route** - A network route that has a subnet mask equal to that of the classful mask.

- **Supernet route** - A supernet route is a network address with a mask less than the classful mask, for example, a summary address.

- **Default route** - A default route is a static route with the address 0.0.0.0/0.

The source of the level 1 route can be a directly connected network, static route, or a dynamic routing protocol.

Figure 1 highlights how level 1 routes are also ultimate routes.

Figure 2 highlights level 1 routes.

Refer to
Online Course
for Illustration

3.5.2.4 Level 1 Parent Route

As illustrated in Figure 1, a level 1 parent route is a level 1 network route that is subnetted. A parent route can never be an ultimate route.

Figure 2 highlights the level 1 parent routes in the routing table of R1. In the routing table, it basically provides a heading for the specific subnets it contains. Each entry displays the classful network address, the number of subnets and the number of different subnet masks that the classful address has been subdivided into.

Refer to
Online Course
for Illustration

3.5.2.5 Level 2 Child Route

A level 2 child route is a route that is a subnet of a classful network address. As illustrated in Figure 1, a level 1 parent route is a level 1 network route that is subnetted. A level 1 parent routes contain level 2 child routes, as shown in Figure 2.

Like a level 1 route, the source of a level 2 route can be a directly connected network, a static route, or a dynamically learned route. Level 2 child routes are also ultimate routes.

Note The routing table hierarchy in Cisco IOS has a classful routing scheme. A level 1 parent route is the classful network address of the subnet route. This is the case even if a classless routing protocol is the source of the subnet route.

Figure 3 highlights the child routes in the routing table of R1.

Refer to
Interactive Graphic
in online course.

3.5.2.6   Activity - Identify Parent and Child IPv4 Routes

Refer to
Online Course
for Illustration

3.5.3   The IPv4 Route Lookup Process

3.5.3.1   Route Lookup Process

When a packet arrives on a router interface, the router examines the IPv4 header, identifies the destination IPv4 address, and proceeds through the router lookup process.

In Figure 1, the router examines level 1 network routes for the best match with the destination address of the IPv4 packet.

1. If the best match is a level 1 ultimate route, then this route is used to forward the packet.

2. If the best match is a level 1 parent route, proceed to the next step.

   In Figure 2, the router examines child routes (the subnet routes) of the parent route for a best match.

3. If there is a match with a level 2 child route, that subnet is used to forward the packet.

4. If there is not a match with any of the level 2 child routes, proceed to the next step.

   In Figure 3, the router continues searching level 1 supernet routes in the routing table for a match, including the default route, if there is one.

5. If there is now a lesser match with a level 1 supernet or default routes, the router uses that route to forward the packet.

6. If there is not a match with any route in the routing table, the router drops the packet.

Note A route referencing only a next-hop IP address and not an exit interface must be resolved to a route with an exit interface. A recursive lookup is performed on the next-hop IP address until the route is resolved to an exit interface.

Refer to
Online Course
for Illustration

3.5.3.2   Best Route = Longest Match

What is meant by the router must find the best match in the routing table? Best match is equal to the longest match.

For there to be a match between the destination IPv4 address of a packet and a route in the routing table, a minimum number of far left bits must match between the IPv4 address of the packet and the route in the routing table. The subnet mask of the route in the routing table is used to determine the minimum number of far left bits that must match. Remember that an IPv4 packet only contains the IPv4 address and not the subnet mask.

The best match is the route in the routing table that has the most number of far left matching bits with the destination IPv4 address of the packet. The route with the greatest number of equivalent far left bits, or the longest match, is always the preferred route.

In the figure, a packet is destined for 172.16.0.10. The router has three possible routes that match this packet: 172.16.0.0/12, 172.16.0.0/18, and 172.16.0.0/26. Of the three routes, 172.16.0.0/26 has the longest match and is therefore chosen to forward the packet. Remember, for any of these routes to be considered a match there must be at least the number of matching bits indicated by the subnet mask of the route.

Refer to
Interactive Graphic
in online course.

3.5.3.3 Activity - Determine the Longest Match Route

Refer to
Online Course
for Illustration

3.5.4 Analyze an IPv6 Routing Table

3.5.4.1 IPv6 Routing Table Entries

Components of the IPv6 routing table are very similar to the IPv4 routing table. For instance, it is populated using directly connected interfaces, static routes, and dynamically learned routes.

Because IPv6 is classless by design, all routes are effectively level 1 ultimate routes. There is no level 1 parent of level 2 child routes.

The topology displayed in the figure is used as the reference topology for this section. Notice that in the topology:

- R1, R2, and R3 are configured in a full mesh topology. All routers have redundant paths to various networks.

- R2 is the edge router and connects to the ISP; however, a default static route is not being advertised.

- EIGRP for IPv6 has been configured on all three routers.

Refer to
Online Course
for Illustration

3.5.4.2 Directly Connected Entries

The routing table of R1 is displayed in Figure 1 using the **show ipv6 route** command. Although, the command output is displayed slightly differently than in the IPv4 version, it still contains the relevant route information.

Figure 2 highlights the connected network and local routing table entries of the directly connected interfaces. The three entries were added when the interfaces were configured and activated.

As shown in Figure 3, directly connected route entries display the following information:

- **Route source** - Identifies how the route was learned. Directly connected interfaces have two route source codes (C identifies a directly connected network while L identifies that this is a local route.)

- **Directly connected network** - The IPv6 address of the directly connected network.

■ **Administrative distance** - Identifies the trustworthiness of the route source. IPv6 uses the same distances as IPv4. A value of 0 indicates the best, most trustworthy source.

■ **Metric** - Identifies the value assigned to reach the remote network. Lower values indicate preferred routes.

■ **Outgoing interface** - Identifies the exit interface to use when forwarding packets to the destination network.

Note   The serial links have reference bandwidths configured to observe how EIGRP metrics select the best route. The reference bandwidth is not a realistic representation of modern networks. It is used only to provide a visual sense of link speed.

Refer to
Online Course
for Illustration

3.5.4.3   Remote IPv6 Network Entries

Figure 1 highlights the routing table entries for the three remote networks (i.e., R2 LAN, R3 LAN, and the link between R2 and R3). The three entries were added by the EIGRP.

Figure 2 displays a routing table entry on R1 for the route to remote network 2001:DB8:CAFE:3::/64 on R3. The entry identifies the following information:

■ **Route source** - Identifies how the route was learned. Common codes include O (OSPF), D (EIGRP), R (RIP), and S (Static route).

■ **Destination network** - Identifies the address of the remote IPv6 network.

■ **Administrative distance** - Identifies how trustworthiness of the route source. IPv6 uses the same distances as IPv4.

■ **Metric** - Identifies the value assigned to reach the remote network. Lower values indicate preferred routes.

■ **Next hop** - Identifies the IPv6 address of the next router to forward the packet to.

■ **Outgoing interface** - Identifies the exit interface to use to forward a packet toward the final destination.

When an IPv6 packet arrives on a router interface, the router examines the IPv6 header and identifies the destination IPv6 address. The router then proceeds through the following router lookup process.

The router examines level 1 network routes for the best match with the destination address of the IPv6 packet. Just like IPv4, the longest match is the best match. For example, if there are multiple matches in the routing table, the router chooses the route with the longest match. A match is made by matching the far left bits of the packet's destination IPv6 address with the IPv6 prefix and prefix-length in the IPv6 routing table.

Refer to
Interactive Graphic
in online course.

3.5.4.4   Activity - Identify Parts of an IPv6 Routing Table Entry

Refer to
Online Course
for Illustration

Refer to
Lab Activity
for this chapter

3.6   Summary

3.6.1.1   Class Activity IPv6 - Details, Details...

IPv6 – Details, Details...

After studying the concepts presented in this chapter concerning IPv6, you should be able to read a routing table easily and interpret the IPv6 routing information listed within it.

With a partner, use the IPv6 routing table diagram and the .pdf provided with this activity.

Record your answers to the Reflection questions.

Then compare your answers with, at least, one other group from the class.

Refer to
Online Course
for Illustration

3.6.1.2   Summary

Dynamic routing protocols are used by routers to facilitate the exchange of routing information between routers. The purpose of dynamic routing protocols includes: discovery of remote networks, maintaining up-to-date routing information, choosing the best path to destination networks, and ability to find a new best path if the current path is no longer available. While dynamic routing protocols require less administrative overhead than static routing, they do require dedicating part of a router's resources for protocol operation, including CPU time and network link bandwidth.

Networks typically use a combination of both static and dynamic routing. Dynamic routing is the best choice for large networks and static routing is better for stub networks.

Routing protocols are responsible for discovering remote networks, as well as maintaining accurate network information. When there is a change in the topology routing protocols propagate that information throughout the routing domain. The process of bringing all routing tables to a state of consistency, where all of the routers in the same routing domain or area have complete and accurate information about the network, is called convergence. Some routing protocols converge faster than others.

Routing protocols can be classified as either classful or classless, distance-vector or link-state, and an interior gateway protocol or an exterior gateway protocol.

Distance vector protocols use routers as "sign posts" along the path to the final destination. The only information a router knows about a remote network is the distance or metric to reach that network and which path or interface to use to get there. Distance vector routing protocols do not have an actual map of the network topology.

A router configured with a link-state routing protocol can create a complete view or topology of the network by gathering information from all of the other routers.

Metrics are used by routing protocols to determine the best path or shortest path to reach a destination network. Different routing protocols may use different metrics. Typically, a lower metric means a better path. Metrics can be determined by hops, bandwidth, delay, reliability, and load.

Routers sometimes learn about multiple routes to the same network from both static routes and dynamic routing protocols. When a router learns about a destination network from more than one routing source, Cisco routers use the administrative distance value to determine which source to use. Each dynamic routing protocol has a unique administrative value, along with static routes and directly connected networks. The lower the administrative value, the more preferred the route source. A directly connected network is always the preferred source, followed by static routes and then various dynamic routing protocols.

The `show ip protocols` command displays the IPv4 routing protocol settings currently configured on the router. For IPv6, use `show ipv6 protocols`.

With link-state routing protocols such as OSPF, a link is an interface on a router. Information about the state of those links is known as link-states. All link-state routing protocols apply Dijkstra's algorithm to calculate the best path route. The algorithm is commonly referred to as the shortest path first (SPF) algorithm. This algorithm uses accumulated costs along each path, from source to destination, to determine the total cost of a route.

Go to the online course to take the quiz and exam.

Chapter 3 Quiz

This quiz is designed to provide an additional opportunity to practice the skills and knowledge presented in the chapter and to prepare for the chapter exam. You will be allowed multiple attempts and the grade does not appear in the gradebook.

Chapter 3 Exam

The chapter exam assesses your knowledge of the chapter content.

Your Chapter Notes

EIGRP

4.0 EIGRP

4.0.1.1 Introduction

Enhanced Interior Gateway Routing Protocol (EIGRP) is an advanced distance vector routing protocol developed by Cisco Systems. As the name suggests, EIGRP is an enhancement of another Cisco routing protocol IGRP (Interior Gateway Routing Protocol). IGRP is an older classful, distance vector routing protocol, now obsolete since IOS 12.3.

EIGRP is a distance vector routing protocol that includes features found in link-state routing protocols. EIGRP is suited for many different topologies and media. In a well-designed network, EIGRP can scale to include multiple topologies and can provide extremely quick convergence times with minimal network traffic.

This chapter introduces EIGRP and provides basic configuration commands to enable it on a Cisco IOS router. It also explores the operation of the routing protocol and provides more detail on how EIGRP determines best path.

Refer to
Lab Activity
for this chapter

4.0.1.2 Class Activity - Classless EIGRP

Activity - Classless EIGRP

Scenario

EIGRP was introduced as a distance vector routing protocol in 1992. It was originally designed to work as a proprietary protocol on Cisco devices only. In 2013, EIGRP became a multi-vendor routing protocol, meaning that it can be used by other device vendors in addition to Cisco devices.

Complete the reflection questions which accompany the PDF file for this activity. Save your work and be prepared to share your answers with the class.

Refer to
Online Course
for Illustration

4.1 Characteristics of EIGRP

4.1.1 Basic Features of EIGRP

4.1.1.1 Features of EIGRP

EIGRP was initially released in 1992 as a proprietary protocol available only on Cisco devices. In 2013, Cisco released a basic functionality of EIGRP as an open standard to the IETF as an informational RFC. This means that other networking vendors can now implement EIGRP on their equipment to interoperate with both Cisco and non-Cisco routers running EIGRP.

However, advanced features of EIGRP, such as EIGRP stub, needed for the Dynamic Multipoint Virtual Private Network (DMVPN) deployment, will not be released to the IETF. As an informational RFC, Cisco will continue to maintain control of EIGRP.

EIGRP includes features of both link-state and distance vector routing protocols. However, EIGRP is still based on the key distance vector routing protocol principle, in which information about the rest of the network is learned from directly connected neighbors.

EIGRP is an advanced distance vector routing protocol that includes features not found in other distance vector routing protocols like RIP and IGRP.

Diffusing Update Algorithm

As the computational engine that drives EIGRP, the Diffusing Update Algorithm (DUAL) resides at the center of the routing protocol. DUAL guarantees loop-free and backup paths throughout the routing domain. Using DUAL, EIGRP stores all available backup routes for destinations so that it can quickly adapt to alternate routes when necessary.

Establishing Neighbor Adjacencies

EIGRP establishes relationships with directly connected routers that are also enabled for EIGRP. Neighbor adjacencies are used to track the status of these neighbors.

Reliable Transport Protocol

The Reliable Transport Protocol (RTP) is unique to EIGRP and provides delivery of EIGRP packets to neighbors. RTP and the tracking of neighbor adjacencies set the stage for DUAL.

Partial and Bounded Updates

EIGRP uses the terms, partial and bounded, when referring to its updates. Unlike RIP, EIGRP does not send periodic updates and route entries do not age out. The term partial means that the update only includes information about the route changes, such as a new link or a link becoming unavailable. The term bounded refers to the propagation of partial updates that are sent only to those routers that the changes affect. This minimizes the bandwidth that is required to send EIGRP updates.

Equal and Unequal Cost Load Balancing

EIGRP supports equal cost load balancing and unequal cost load balancing, which allows administrators to better distribute traffic flow in their networks.

Note   The term hybrid routing protocol is used in some older documentation to define EIGRP. However, this term is misleading because EIGRP is not a hybrid between distance vector and link-state routing protocols. EIGRP is solely a distance vector routing protocol; therefore, Cisco no longer uses this term to refer to it.

Refer to Online Course for Illustration

4.1.1.2   Protocol Dependent Modules

EIGRP has the capability for routing several different protocols including IPv4 and IPv6 using protocol-dependent modules (PDMs). Although now obsolete, EIGRP also used PDMs to route Novell's IPX and Apple Computer's AppleTalk network layer protocols.

The PDMs are responsible for network layer protocol-specific tasks. An example is the EIGRP module, which is responsible for sending and receiving EIGRP packets that are encapsulated in IPv4. The EIGRP module is also responsible for parsing EIGRP packets and informing DUAL of the new information that is received. EIGRP asks DUAL to make routing decisions, but the results are stored in the IPv4 routing table. Also, EIGRP PDMs are responsible for redistributing routes that are learned by other routing protocols.

PDMs are responsible for the specific routing tasks for each network layer protocol, including:

- Maintaining the neighbor and topology tables of EIGRP routers that belong to that protocol suite

- Building and translating protocol-specific packets for DUAL

- Interfacing DUAL to the protocol-specific routing table

- Computing the metric and passing this information to DUAL

- Implement filtering and access lists

- Perform redistribution functions to and from other routing protocols

When a router discovers a new neighbor, it records the neighbor's address and interface as an entry in the neighbor table. One neighbor table exists for each protocol-dependent module, such as IPv4. EIGRP also maintains a topology table. The topology table contains all destinations that are advertised by neighboring routers. There is also a separate topology table for each PDM.

Refer to
Online Course
for Illustration

4.1.1.3   Reliable Transport Protocol

EIGRP uses Reliable Transport Protocol (RTP) for the delivery and reception of EIGRP packets. EIGRP was designed as a network layer independent routing protocol; because of this design EIGRP cannot use the services of UDP or TCP. This allows EIGRP to be used for protocols other than those from the TCP/IP protocol suite, such as IPX and AppleTalk. The figure conceptually shows how RTP operates.

Although "reliable" is part of its name, RTP includes both reliable delivery and unreliable delivery of EIGRP packets, similar to TCP and UDP, respectively. Reliable RTP requires an acknowledgment to be returned by the receiver to the sender. An unreliable RTP packet does not require an acknowledgment. For example, an EIGRP update packet is sent reliably over RTP and requires an acknowledgment. An EIGRP Hello packet is also sent over RTP, but unreliably. This means that EIGRP Hello packets do not require an acknowledgment.

RTP can send EIGRP packets as unicast or multicast.

- Multicast EIGRP packets for IPv4 use the reserved IPv4 multicast address 224.0.0.10.

- Multicast EIGRP packets for IPv6 are sent to the reserved IPv6 multicast address FF02::A.

Refer to
Online Course
for Illustration

4.1.1.4   Authentication

Like other routing protocols, EIGRP can be configured for authentication. RIPv2, EIGRP, OSPF, IS-IS, and BGP can each be configured to authenticate their routing information.

It is a good practice to authenticate transmitted routing information. Doing so ensures that routers only accept routing information from other routers that have been configured with the same password or authentication information.

Note   Authentication does not encrypt the EIGRP routing updates.

Refer to
Online Course
for Illustration

4.1.2   Types of EIGRP Packets

4.1.2.1   EIGRP Packet Types

EIGRP uses five different packet types, some in pairs. EIGRP packets are sent using either RTP reliable or unreliable delivery and can be sent as a unicast, multicast, or sometimes both. EIGRP packet types are also called EIGRP packet formats or EIGRP messages.

As shown in Figure 1, the five EIGRP packet types include:

Hello packets - Used for neighbor discovery and to maintain neighbor adjacencies.

■ Sent with unreliable delivery

■ Multicast (on most network types)

Update packets - Propagates routing information to EIGRP neighbors.

■ Sent with reliable delivery

■ Unicast or multicast

Acknowledgment packets - Used to acknowledge the receipt of an EIGRP message that was sent using reliable delivery.

■ Sent with unreliable delivery

■ Unicast

Query packets - Used to query routes from neighbors.

■ Sent with reliable delivery

■ Unicast or multicast

Reply packets - Sent in response to an EIGRP query.

■ Sent with unreliable delivery

■ Unicast

Figure 2 shows that EIGRP messages are typically encapsulated in IPv4 or IPv6 packets. EIGRP for IPv4 messages use IPv4 as the network layer protocol. The IPv4 protocol field uses 88 to indicate the data portion of the packet is an EIGRP for IPv4 message. EIGRP for IPv6 messages are encapsulated in IPv6 packets using the next header field of 88. Similar, to the protocol field for IPv4, the IPv6 next header field indicates the type of data carried in the IPv6 packet.

Refer to
Online Course
for Illustration

4.1.2.2   EIGRP Hello Packets

EIGRP uses small Hello packets to discover other EIGRP-enabled routers on directly connected links. Hello packets are used by routers to form EIGRP neighbor adjacencies, also known as neighbor adjacencies.

EIGRP Hello packets are sent as IPv4 or IPv6 multicasts, and use RTP unreliable delivery. This means that the receiver does not reply with an acknowledgment packet.

- The reserved EIGRP multicast address for IPv4 is 224.0.0.10.

- The reserved EIGRP multicast address for IPv6 is FF02::A.

EIGRP routers discover neighbors and establish adjacencies with neighbor routers using the Hello packet. On most networks, EIGRP Hello packets are sent multicast every five seconds. However, on multipoint, nonbroadcast multiple access (NBMA) networks, such as X.25, Frame Relay, and Asynchronous Transfer Mode (ATM) interfaces with access links of T1 (1.544 Mb/s) or slower, Hello packets are sent unicast every 60 seconds.

EIGRP also uses Hello packets to maintain established adjacencies. An EIGRP router assumes that as long as it receives Hello packets from a neighbor, the neighbor and its routes remain viable.

EIGRP uses a Hold timer to determine the maximum time the router should wait to receive the next Hello before declaring that neighbor as unreachable. By default, the hold time is three times the Hello interval, or 15 seconds on most networks and 180 seconds on low-speed NBMA networks. If the hold time expires, EIGRP declares the route as down and DUAL searches for a new path by sending out queries.

Refer to
Online Course
for Illustration

4.1.2.3   EIGRP Update and Acknowledgment Packets

EIGRP Update Packets

EIGRP sends Update packets to propagate routing information. Update packets are sent only when necessary. EIGRP updates contain only the routing information needed and are sent only to those routers that require it.

Unlike RIP, EIGRP (another distance vector routing protocol) does not send periodic updates and route entries do not age out. Instead, EIGRP sends incremental updates only when the state of a destination changes. This may include when a new network becomes available, an existing network becomes unavailable, or a change occurs in the routing metric for an existing network.

EIGRP uses the terms, partial and bounded, when referring to its updates. The term partial means that the update only includes information about the route changes. The term bounded refers to the propagation of partial updates that are sent only to those routers that the changes affect.

By sending only the routing information that is needed, only to those routers that need it, EIGRP minimizes the bandwidth that is required to send EIGRP updates.

EIGRP update packets use reliable delivery, which means the sending router requires an acknowledgment. Update packets are sent as a multicast when required by multiple routers, or as a unicast when required by only a single router. In the figure, because the links are point-to-point, the updates are sent as unicasts.

EIGRP Acknowledgment Packets

EIGRP sends Acknowledgment (ACK) packets when reliable delivery is used. An EIGRP acknowledgment is an EIGRP Hello packet without any data. RTP uses reliable delivery for EIGRP update, query, and reply packets. EIGRP acknowledgment packets are always sent as an unreliable unicast. Unreliable delivery makes sense; otherwise, there would be an endless loop of acknowledgments.

In the figure, R2 has lost connectivity to the LAN attached to its Gigabit Ethernet interface. R2 immediately sends an update to R1 and R3 noting the downed route. R1 and R3 respond with an acknowledgment to let R2 know that they have received the update.

Note   Some documentation refers to the Hello and acknowledgment as a single type of EIGRP packet.

Refer to
Online Course
for Illustration

4.1.2.4   EIGRP Query and Reply Packets

EIGRP Query Packets

DUAL uses query and reply packets when searching for networks and other tasks. Queries and replies use reliable delivery. Queries can use multicast or unicast, whereas replies are always sent as unicast.

In the figure, R2 has lost connectivity to the LAN and it sends out queries to all EIGRP neighbors searching for any possible routes to the LAN. Because queries use reliable delivery, the receiving router must return an EIGRP acknowledgment. The acknowledgment informs the sender of the query that it has received the query message. To keep this example simple, acknowledgments were omitted in the graphic.

EIGRP Reply Packets

All neighbors must send a reply, regardless of whether or not they have a route to the downed network. Because replies also use reliable delivery, routers such as R2, must send an acknowledgment.

It may not be obvious why R2 would send out a query for a network it knows is down. Actually, only R2's interface that is attached to the network is down. Another router could be attached to the same LAN and have an alternate path to this same network. Therefore, R2 queries for such a router before completely removing the network from its topology table.

Refer to
Interactive Graphic
in online course.

4.1.2.5   Activity - Identify the EIGRP Packet Type

Refer to
Interactive Graphic
in online course.

4.1.2.6   Video Demonstration - Observing EIGRP Protocol Communications

Refer to
Online Course
for Illustration

4.1.3   EIGRP Messages

4.1.3.1   Encapsulating EIGRP Messages

The data portion of an EIGRP message is encapsulated in a packet. This data field is called type, length, value (TLV). The types of TLVs relevant to this course are EIGRP parameters, IP internal routes, and IP external routes.

The EIGRP packet header is included with every EIGRP packet, regardless of its type. The EIGRP packet header and TLV are then encapsulated in an IPv4 packet. In the IPv4 packet header, the protocol field is set to 88 to indicate EIGRP, and the IPv4 destination address is set to the multicast 224.0.0.10. If the EIGRP packet is encapsulated in an Ethernet frame, the destination MAC address is also a multicast address, 01-00-5E-00-00-0A.

Figures 1 to 4 show the Data Link Ethernet Frame. EIGRP for IPv4 is encapsulated in an IPv4 packet. EIGRP for IPv6 would use a similar type of encapsulation. EIGRP for IPv6 is encapsulated using an IPv6 header. The IPv6 destination address would be the multicast address FF02::A and the next header field would be set to 88.

Refer to
Online Course
for Illustration

4.1.3.2 EIGRP Packet Header and TLV

Every EIGRP message includes the header, as shown in Figure 1. Important fields include the Opcode field and the Autonomous System Number field. Opcode specifies the EIGRP packet type as follows:

- Update

- Query

- Reply

- Hello

The autonomous system number specifies the EIGRP routing process. Unlike RIP, multiple instances of EIGRP can run on a network; the autonomous system number is used to track each running EIGRP process.

Figure 2 shows the EIGRP parameter's TLV. The EIGRP parameter's message includes the weights that EIGRP uses for its composite metric. By default, only bandwidth and delay are weighted. Both are weighted equally; therefore, the K1 field for bandwidth and the K3 field for delay are both set to one (1). The other K values are set to zero (0).

The Hold Time is the amount of time the EIGRP neighbor receiving this message should wait before considering the advertising router to be down.

Figure 3 shows the IP Internal Routes TLV. The IP internal message is used to advertise EIGRP routes within an autonomous system. Important fields include the metric fields (delay and bandwidth), the subnet mask field (prefix length), and the destination field.

Delay is calculated as the sum of delays from source to destination in units of 10 microseconds. Bandwidth is the lowest configured bandwidth of any interface along the route.

The subnet mask is specified as the prefix length or the number of network bits in the subnet mask. For example, the prefix length for the subnet mask 255.255.255.0 is 24, because 24 is the number of network bits.

The Destination field stores the address of the destination network. Although only 24 bits are shown in this figure, this field varies based on the value of the network portion of the 32-bit network address. For example, the network portion of 10.1.0.0/16 is 10.1; therefore, the Destination field stores the first 16 bits. Because the minimum length of this field is 24 bits, the remainder of the field is padded with zeros. If a network address is longer than 24 bits (192.168.1.32/27, for example), then the Destination field is extended for another 32 bits (for a total of 56 bits) and the unused bits are padded with zeros.

Figure 4 shows the IP External Routes TLV. The IP external message is used when external routes are imported into the EIGRP routing process. In this chapter, we will import or redistribute a default static route into EIGRP. Notice that the bottom half of the IP External Routes TLV includes all the fields used by the IP Internal TLV.

Note   The maximum transmission unit (MTU) is not a metric used by EIGRP. The MTU is included in the routing updates, but it is not used to determine the routing metric.

Refer to **Online Course** for Illustration

4.2   Configuring EIGRP for IPv4

4.2.1   Configuring EIGRP with IPv4

4.2.1.1   EIGRP Network Topology

Figure 1 displays the topology that is used in this course to configure EIGRP for IPv4. The types of serial interfaces and their associated bandwidths may not necessarily reflect the more common types of connections found in today's networks. The bandwidths of the serial links used in this topology were chosen to help explain the calculation of the routing protocol metrics and the process of best path selection.

The routers in the topology have a starting configuration, including addresses on the interfaces. There is currently no static routing or dynamic routing configured on any of the routers.

Figures 2, 3, and 4 display the interface configurations for the three EIGRP routers in the topology. Only routers R1, R2, and R3 are part of the EIGRP routing domain. The ISP router is used as the routing domain's gateway to the Internet.

Refer to **Online Course** for Illustration

4.2.1.2   Autonomous System Numbers

EIGRP uses the `router eigrp` *autonomous-system* command to enable the EIGRP process. The autonomous system number referred to in the EIGRP configuration is not associated with the Internet Assigned Numbers Authority (IANA) globally assigned autonomous system numbers used by external routing protocols.

So what is the difference between the IANA globally assigned autonomous system number and the EIGRP autonomous system number?

An IANA globally assigned autonomous system is a collection of networks under the administrative control of a single entity that presents a common routing policy to the Internet. In the figure, companies A, B, C, and D are all under the administrative control of ISP1. ISP1 presents a common routing policy for all of these companies when advertising routes to ISP2.

The guidelines for the creation, selection, and registration of an autonomous system are described in RFC 1930. Global autonomous system numbers are assigned by IANA, the same authority that assigns IP address space. The local regional Internet registry (RIR) is responsible for assigning an autonomous system number to an entity from its block of assigned autonomous system numbers. Prior to 2007, autonomous system numbers were

16-bit numbers ranging from 0 to 65,535. Today, 32-bit autonomous system numbers are assigned increasing the number of available autonomous system numbers to over 4 billion.

Usually Internet Service Providers (ISPs), Internet backbone providers, and large institutions connecting to other entities require an autonomous system number. These ISPs and large institutions use the exterior gateway routing protocol, Border Gateway Protocol (BGP), to propagate routing information. BGP is the only routing protocol that uses an actual autonomous system number in its configuration.

The vast majority of companies and institutions with IP networks do not need an autonomous system number, because they are controlled by a larger entity, such as an ISP. These companies use interior gateway protocols, such as RIP, EIGRP, OSPF, and IS-IS to route packets within their own networks. They are one of many independent and separate networks within the autonomous system of the ISP. The ISP is responsible for the routing of packets within its autonomous system and between other autonomous systems.

The autonomous system number used for EIGRP configuration is only significant to the EIGRP routing domain. It functions as a process ID to help routers keep track of multiple, running instances of EIGRP. This is required because it is possible to have more than one instance of EIGRP running on a network. Each instance of EIGRP can be configured to support and exchange routing updates for different networks.

Refer to
Online Course
for Illustration

4.2.1.3 The Router EIGRP Command

The Cisco IOS includes the processes to enable and configure several different types of dynamic routing protocols. The `router` global configuration mode command is used to begin the configuration of any dynamic routing protocol. The topology shown in Figure 1 is used to demonstrate this command.

As shown in Figure 2, when followed by a question mark (?), the `router` global configuration mode command lists of all the available routing protocols supported by this specific IOS release running on the router.

The following global configuration mode command is used to enter the router configuration mode for EIGRP and begin the configuration of the EIGRP process:

```
Router(config)# router eigrp autonomous-system
```

The *autonomous-system* argument can be assigned to any 16-bit value between the number 1 and 65,535. All routers within the EIGRP routing domain must use the same autonomous system number.

Figure 3 shows the configuration of the EIGRP process on routers R1, R2, and R3. Notice that the prompt changes from a global configuration mode prompt to router configuration mode.

In this example, 1 identifies this particular EIGRP process running on this router. To establish neighbor adjacencies, EIGRP requires all routers in the same routing domain to be configured with the same autonomous system number. In Figure 3, that same EIGRP is enabled on all three routers using the same autonomous system number of 1.

Note Both EIGRP and OSPF can support multiple instances of each routing protocol, although this type of multiple routing protocol implementation is not usually needed or recommended.

The `router eigrp` *autonomous-system* command does not start the EIGRP process itself. The router does not start sending updates. Rather, this command only provides access to configure the EIGRP settings.

To completely remove the EIGRP routing process from a device, use the `no router eigrp` *autonomous-system* global configuration mode command, which stops the EIGRP process and removes all existing EIGRP router configurations.

Refer to
Online Course
for Illustration

4.2.1.4   EIGRP Router ID

Determining the Router ID

The EIGRP router ID is used to uniquely identify each router in the EIGRP routing domain. The router ID is used in both EIGRP and OSPF routing protocols, although the role of the router ID is more significant in OSPF.

In EIGRP IPv4 implementations, the use of the router ID is not that apparent. EIGRP for IPv4 uses the 32-bit router ID to identify the originating router for redistribution of external routes. The need for a router ID becomes more evident in the discussion of EIGRP for IPv6. While the router ID is necessary for redistribution, the details of EIGRP redistribution are beyond the scope of this curriculum. For purposes of this curriculum, it is only necessary to understand what the router ID is and how it is derived.

Cisco routers derive the router ID based on three criteria, in the following precedence:

1. Use the IPv4 address configured with the `eigrp router-id` router configuration mode command.

2. If the router ID is not configured, the router chooses the highest IPv4 address of any of its loopback interfaces.

3. If no loopback interfaces are configured, the router chooses the highest active IPv4 address of any of its physical interfaces.

If the network administrator does not explicitly configure a router ID using the `eigrp router-id` command, EIGRP generates its own router ID using either a loopback or physical IPv4 address. A loopback address is a virtual interface and is automatically in the up state when configured. The interface does not need to be enabled for EIGRP, meaning that it does not need to be included in one of the EIGRP network commands. However, the interface must be in the up/up state.

Using the criteria described above, the figure shows the default EIGRP router IDs that are determined by the routers' highest active IPv4 address.

Note   The `eigrp router-id` command is used to configure the router ID for EIGRP. Some versions of IOS will accept the command `router-id`, without first specifying `eigrp`. The running-config, however, will display `eigrp router-id` regardless of which command is used.

Refer to
Online Course
for Illustration

4.2.1.5   Configuring the EIGRP Router ID

The **eigrp router-id** command is used to configure the EIGRP router ID and takes precedence over any loopback or physical interface IPv4 addresses. The command syntax is:

```
Router(config)# router eigrp autonomous-system
Router(config-router)# eigrp router-id ipv4-address
```

Note   The IPv4 address used to indicate the router ID is actually any 32-bit number displayed in dotted-decimal notation.

The router ID can be configured with any IPv4 address with two exceptions: 0.0.0.0 and 255.255.255.255. The router ID should be a unique 32-bit number in the EIGRP routing domain; otherwise, routing inconsistencies can occur.

Figure 1 shows the configuration of the EIGRP router ID for routers R1 and R2 using the **router eigrp** *autonomous-system* command.

Loopback Address Used as the Router ID

Another option to specify the EIGRP router ID is to use an IPv4 loopback address. The advantage of using a loopback interface, instead of the IPv4 address of a physical interface, is that unlike physical interfaces, it cannot fail. There are no actual cables or adjacent devices on which the loopback interface depends for being in the up state. Therefore, using a loopback address for the router ID can provide a more consistent router ID than using an interface address.

If the **eigrp router-id** command is not used and loopback interfaces are configured, EIGRP chooses the highest IPv4 address of any of its loopback interfaces. The following commands are used to enable and configure a loopback interface:

```
Router(config)# interface loopback number
Router(config-if)# ip address ipv4-address subnet-mask
```

Note   The EIGRP router ID is not changed, unless the EIGRP process is removed with the **no router eigrp** command or if the router ID is manually configured with the **eigrp router-id** command.

Verifying the EIGRP Process

Figure 2 shows the **show ip protocols** output for R1, including its router ID. The **show ip protocols** command displays the parameters and current state of any active routing protocol processes, including both EIGRP and OSPF. The **show ip protocols** command displays different types of output specific to each routing protocol.

Use the Syntax Checker in Figure 3 to configure and verify the router ID for R3.

Refer to
Online Course
for Illustration

4.2.1.6   The Network Command

EIGRP router configuration mode allows for the configuration of the EIGRP routing protocol. Figure 1 shows that R1, R2, and R3 all have networks that should be included within a single EIGRP routing domain. To enable EIGRP routing on an interface, use the **network** router configuration mode command and enter the classful network address for each directly connected network.

The **network** command has the same function as in all IGP routing protocols. The **network** command in EIGRP:

- Enables any interface on this router that matches the network address in the **network** router configuration mode command to send and receive EIGRP updates.

- The network of the interfaces is included in EIGRP routing updates.

```
Router(config-router)# network ipv4-network-address
```

The *ipv4-network-address* argument is the classful IPv4 network address for this interface. Figure 2 shows the network commands configured for R1. In the figure, a single classful **network** statement, **network 172.16.0.0**, is used on R1 to include both interfaces in subnets 172.16.1.0/24 and 172.16.3.0/30. Notice that only the classful network address is used.

Figure 3 shows the **network** command used to enable EIGRP on R2's interfaces for subnets 172.16.1.0/24 and 172.16.2.0/24. When EIGRP is configured on R2's S0/0/0 interface, DUAL sends a notification message to the console stating that a neighbor adjacency with another EIGRP router on that interface has been established. This new adjacency happens automatically because both R1 and R2 use the same **eigrp 1** autonomous system number, and both routers now send updates on their interfaces in the 172.16.0.0 network.

By default, the **eigrp log-neighbor-changes** router configuration mode command is enabled. This command is used to:

- Display any changes in EIGRP neighbor adjacencies.

- Help verify neighbor adjacencies during configuration of EIGRP.

- Advise the network administrator when any EIGRP adjacencies have been removed.

Refer to **Online Course** for Illustration

4.2.1.7   The Network Command and Wildcard Mask

By default, when using the **network** command and an IPv4 network address, such as 172.16.0.0, all interfaces on the router that belong to that classful network address are enabled for EIGRP. However, there may be times when the network administrator does not want to include all interfaces within a network when enabling EIGRP. For example, in Figure 1, assume that an administrator wants to enable EIGRP on R2, but only for the subnet 192.168.10.8 255.255.255.252, on the S0/0/1 interface.

To configure EIGRP to advertise specific subnets only, use the *wildcard-mask* option with the network command:

```
Router(config-router)# network network-address [ wildcard-mask ]
```

Think of a wildcard mask as the inverse of a subnet mask. The inverse of subnet mask 255.255.255.252 is 0.0.0.3. To calculate the inverse of the subnet mask, subtract the subnet mask from 255.255.255.255 as follows:

```
  255.255.255.255
- 255.255.255.252  Subtract the subnet mask
  ---------------
    0.  0.  0.  3  Wildcard mask
```

Figure 2 continues the EIGRP network configuration of R2. The `network 192.168.10.8 0.0.0.3` command specifically enables EIGRP on the S0/0/1 interface, a member of the 192.168.10.8 255.255.255.252 subnet.

Some IOS versions also let you enter the subnet mask instead of a wildcard mask. Figure 3 shows an example of configuring the same S0/0/1 interface on R2, but this time using a subnet mask in the `network` command. However, if the subnet mask is used, the IOS converts the command to the *wildcard-mask* format within the configuration. This is verified in the `show running-config` output in Figure 3.

Use the Syntax Checker in Figure 4 to configure the EIGRP `network` commands for router R3.

**Refer to
Online Course
for Illustration**

4.2.1.8   Passive Interface

As soon as a new interface is enabled within the EIGRP network, EIGRP attempts to form a neighbor adjacency with any neighboring routers to send and receive EIGRP updates.

At times it may be necessary, or advantageous, to include a directly connected network in the EIGRP routing update, but not allow any neighbor adjacencies off of that interface to form. The `passive-interface` command can be used to prevent the neighbor adjacencies. There are two primary reasons for enabling the `passive-interface` command:

■ To suppress unnecessary update traffic, such as when an interface is a LAN interface, with no other routers connected

■ To increase security controls, such as preventing unknown rogue routing devices from receiving EIGRP updates

Figure 1 shows R1, R2, and R3 do not have neighbors on their GigabitEthernet 0/0 interfaces.

The `passive-interface` router configuration mode command disables the transmission and receipt of EIGRP Hello packets on these interfaces.

```
Router(config)# router eigrp as-number
Router(config-router)# passive-interface interface-type interface-number
```

Figure 2 shows the `passive-interface` command configured to suppress Hello packets on the LANs for R1 and R3. R2 is configured using the Syntax Checker.

Without a neighbor adjacency, EIGRP cannot exchange routes with a neighbor. Therefore, the `passive-interface` command prevents the exchange of routes on the interface. Although EIGRP does not send or receive routing updates on an interface configured with the `passive-interface` command, it still includes the address of the interface in routing updates sent out of other non-passive interfaces.

Note   To configure all interfaces as passive, use the `passive-interface default` command. To disable the interface as passive, use the `no passive-interface` command.

An example of using the passive interface to increase security controls is when a network must connect to a third-party organization, for which the local administrator has no control, such as when connecting to an ISP network. In this case, the local network administrator would need to advertise the interface link through their own network, but would not want the third-party organization to receive or send routing updates to the local routing device, as this is a security risk.

Verifying the Passive Interface

To verify whether any interface on a router is configured as passive, use the `show ip protocols` privileged EXEC mode command, as shown in Figure 3. Notice that although R3's GigabitEthernet 0/0 interface is a passive interface, EIGRP still includes the interface's network address of 192.168.1.0 network in its routing updates.

Use the Syntax Checker in Figure 4 to configure R2 to suppress EIGRP Hello packets on its GigabitEthernet 0/0 interface.

Refer to
Online Course
for Illustration

4.2.2   Verifying EIGRP with IPv4

4.2.2.1   Verifying EIGRP: Examining Neighbors

Before EIGRP can send or receive any updates, routers must establish adjacencies with their neighbors. EIGRP routers establish adjacencies with neighbor routers by exchanging EIGRP Hello packets.

Use the `show ip eigrp neighbors` command to view the neighbor table and verify that EIGRP has established an adjacency with its neighbors. For each router, you should be able to see the IPv4 address of the adjacent router and the interface that this router uses to reach that EIGRP neighbor. Using this topology, each router has two neighbors listed in the neighbor table.

The `show ip eigrp neighbors` command output includes:

- **H column** - Lists the neighbors in the order that they were learned.
- **Address** - IPv4 address of the neighbor.
- **Interface** - Local interface on which this Hello packet was received.
- **Hold** - Current hold time. When a Hello packet is received, this value is reset to the maximum hold time for that interface, and then counts down to zero. If zero is reached, the neighbor is considered down.
- **Uptime** - Amount of time since this neighbor was added to the neighbor table.
- Smooth Round Trip Timer (SRTT) and Retransmission Timeout (RTO) - Used by RTP to manage reliable EIGRP packets.
- **Queue Count** - Should always be zero. If more than zero, then EIGRP packets wait to be sent.
- **Sequence Number** - Used to track updates, queries, and reply packets.

The `show ip eigrp neighbors` command is very useful for verifying and troubleshooting EIGRP. If a neighbor is not listed after adjacencies have been established with a router's neighbors, check the local interface to ensure it is activated with the `show ip interface brief` command. If the interface is active, try pinging the IPv4 address of the neighbor.

If the ping fails, it means that the neighbor interface is down and must be activated. If the ping is successful and EIGRP still does not see the router as a neighbor, examine the following configurations:

■ Are both routers configured with the same EIGRP autonomous system number?

■ Is the directly connected network included in the EIGRP `network` statements?

Refer to
Online Course
for Illustration

4.2.2.2   Verifying EIGRP: show ip protocols Command

The `show ip protocols` command displays the parameters and other information about the current state of any active IPv4 routing protocol processes configured on the router. The `show ip protocols` command displays different types of output specific to each routing protocol.

The output in Figure 1 indicates several EIGRP parameters, including:

1. EIGRP is an active dynamic routing protocol on R1 configured with the autonomous system number 1.

2. The EIGRP router ID of R1 is 1.1.1.1.

3. The EIGRP administrative distances on R1 are internal AD of 90 and external of 170 (default values).

4. By default, EIGRP does not automatically summarize networks. Subnets are included in the routing updates.

5. The EIGRP neighbor adjacencies R1 has with other routers used to receive EIGRP routing updates.

Note   Prior to IOS 15, automatic summarization was enabled, by default, for EIGRP.

The output from the `show ip protocols` command is useful in debugging routing operations. Information in the Routing Information Sources field can help identify a router suspected of delivering bad routing information. The Routing Information Sources field lists all the EIGRP routing sources the Cisco IOS software uses to build its IPv4 routing table. For each source, note the following:

■ IPv4 address

■ Administrative distance

■ Time the last update was received from this source

As shown in Figure 2, EIGRP has a default AD of 90 for internal routes and 170 for routes imported from an external source, such as default routes. When compared to other IGPs, EIGRP is the most preferred by the Cisco IOS, because it has the lowest administrative distance. EIGRP has a third AD value of 5, for summary routes.

Refer to
Online Course
for Illustration

4.2.2.3   Verifying EIGRP: Examine the IPv4 routing table

Another way to verify that EIGRP and other functions of the router are configured properly is to examine the IPv4 routing tables with the `show ip route` command. As with any dynamic routing protocol, the network administrator must verify the information in the routing table to ensure that it is populated as expected, based on configurations entered. For this reason, it is important to have a good understanding of the routing protocol configuration commands, as well as the routing protocol operations and the processes used by the routing protocol to build the IP routing table.

Note   The outputs used throughout this course are from Cisco IOS 15. Prior to IOS 15, EIGRP automatic summarization was enabled by default. The state of automatic summarization can make a difference in the information displayed in the IPv4 routing table. If a previous version of the IOS is used, automatic summarization can be disabled using the **no auto-summary** router configuration mode command:

```
Router(config-router)# no auto-summary
```

Figure 1 shows the topology for R1, R2, and R3.

In Figure 2, the IPv4 routing table is examined using the **show ip route** command. EIGRP routes are denoted in the routing table with a **D**. The letter D was used to represent EIGRP because the protocol is based upon the DUAL algorithm.

The **show ip route** command verifies that routes received by EIGRP neighbors are installed in the IPv4 routing table. The **show ip route** command displays the entire routing table, including remote networks learned dynamically, directly connected and static routes. For this reason, it is normally the first command used to check for convergence. After routing is correctly configured on all routers, the **show ip route** command reflects that each router has a full routing table, with a route to each network in the topology.

Notice that R1 has installed routes to three IPv4 remote networks in its IPv4 routing table:

- 172.16.2.0/24 network via router R2 using its Serial0/0/0 interface
- 192.168.1.0/24 network via router R3 using its Serial0/0/1 interface
- 192.168.10.8/30 network via both R2 using its Serial0/0/0 interface and via R3 using its Serial0/0/1 interface

R1 has two paths to the 192.168.10.8/30 network, because its cost or metric to reach that network is the same or equal using both routers. These are known as equal cost routes. R1 uses both paths to reach this network, which is known as load balancing. The EIGRP metric is discussed later in this chapter.

Figure 3 displays the routing table for R2. Notice similar results are displayed including an equal cost route for the 192.168.10.4/30 network.

Figure 4 displays the routing table for R3. Similar to the results for R1 and R2, remote networks are learned using EIGRP, including an equal cost route for the 172.16.3.0/30 network.

Refer to **Packet Tracer Activity** for this chapter

4.2.2.4   Packet Tracer - Configuring Basic EIGRP with IPv4

In this activity, you will implement basic EIGRP configurations including **network** commands, passive interfaces, and disabling automatic summarization. You will then verify your EIGRP configuration using a variety of **show** commands and testing end-to-end connectivity.

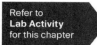

4.2.2.5   Lab - Configuring Basic EIGRP with IPv4

In this lab, you will complete the following objectives:

- Part 1: Build the Network and Verify Connectivity

- Part 2: Configure EIGRP Routing

- Part 3: Verify EIGRP Routing

- Part 4: Configure Bandwidth and Passive Interfaces

Refer to
Online Course
for Illustration

4.3   Operation of EIGRP

4.3.1   EIGRP Initial Route Discovery

4.3.1.1   EIGRP Neighbor Adjacency

The goal of any dynamic routing protocol is to learn about remote networks from other routers and to reach convergence in the routing domain. Before any EIGRP update packets can be exchanged between routers, EIGRP must first discover its neighbors. EIGRP neighbors are other routers running EIGRP on directly connected networks.

EIGRP uses Hello packets to establish and maintain neighbor adjacencies. For two EIGRP routers to become neighbors, several parameters between the two routers must match. For example, two EIGRP routers must use the same EIGRP metric parameters and both must be configured using the same autonomous system number.

Each EIGRP router maintains a neighbor table, which contains a list of routers on shared links that have an EIGRP adjacency with this router. The neighbor table is used to track the status of these EIGRP neighbors.

The figure shows two EIGRP routers exchanging initial EIGRP Hello packets. When an EIGRP enabled router receives a Hello packet on an interface, it adds that router to its neighbor table.

1. A new router (R1) comes up on the link and sends an EIGRP Hello packet through all of its EIGRP-configured interfaces.

2. Router R2 receives the Hello packet on an EIGRP-enabled interface. R2 replies with an EIGRP update packet that contains all the routes it has in its routing table, except those learned through that interface (split horizon). However, the neighbor adjacency is not established until R2 also sends an EIGRP Hello packet to R1.

3. After both routers have exchanged Hellos, the neighbor adjacency is established. R1 and R2 update their EIGRP neighbor tables adding the adjacent router as a neighbor.

Refer to
Online Course
for Illustration

4.3.1.2   EIGRP Topology Table

EIGRP updates contain networks that are reachable from the router sending the update. As EIGRP updates are exchanged between neighbors, the receiving router adds these entries to its EIGRP topology table.

Each EIGRP router maintains a topology table for each routed protocol configured, such as IPv4 and IPv6. The topology table includes route entries for every destination that the router learns from its directly connected EIGRP neighbors.

The figure shows the continuation of the initial route discovery process from the previous page. It now shows the update of the topology table.

When a router receives an EIGRP routing update, it adds the routing information to its EIGRP topology table and replies with an EIGRP acknowledgment.

1. R1 receives the EIGRP update from neighbor R2 and includes information about the routes that the neighbor is advertising, including the metric to each destination. R1 adds all update entries to its topology table. The topology table includes all destinations advertised by neighboring (adjacent) routers and the cost (metric) to reach each network.

2. EIGRP update packets use reliable delivery; therefore, R1 replies with an EIGRP acknowledgment packet informing R2 that it has received the update.

3. R1 sends an EIGRP update to R2 advertising the routes that it is aware of, except those learned from R2 (split horizon).

4. R2 receives the EIGRP update from neighbor R1 and adds this information to its own topology table.

5. R2 responds to the R1's EIGRP update packet with an EIGRP acknowledgment.

Refer to
Online Course
for Illustration

4.3.1.3   EIGRP Convergence

The figure illustrates the final steps of the initial route discovery process.

1. After receiving the EIGRP update packets from R2, using the information in the topology table, R1 updates its IP routing table with the best path to each destination, including the metric and the next-hop router.

2. Similar to R1, R2 updates its IP routing table with the best path routes to each network.

At this point, EIGRP on both routers is considered to be in the converged state.

Refer to
Interactive Graphic
in online course.

4.3.1.4   Activity - Identify the Steps in Establishing EIGRP Neighbor Adjacencies

Refer to
Online Course
for Illustration

4.3.2   Metrics

4.3.2.1   EIGRP Composite Metric

By default, EIGRP uses the following values in its composite metric to calculate the preferred path to a network:

■ **Bandwidth** - The slowest bandwidth among all of the outgoing interfaces, along the path from source to destination.

■ **Delay** - The cumulative (sum) of all interface delay along the path (in tens of microseconds).

The following values can be used, but are not recommended, because they typically result in frequent recalculation of the topology table:

■ **Reliability** - Represents the worst reliability between the source and destination, which is based on keepalives.

■ **Load** - Represents the worst load on a link between the source and destination, which is computed based on the packet rate and the configured bandwidth of the interface.

Note Although the MTU is included in the routing table updates, it is not a routing metric used by EIGRP.

The Composite Metric

Figure 1 shows the composite metric formula used by EIGRP. The formula consists of values K1 to K5, known as EIGRP metric weights. K1 and K3 represent bandwidth and delay, respectively. K2 represents load, and K4 and K5 represent reliability. By default, K1 and K3 are set to 1, and K2, K4, and K5 are set to 0. The result is that only the bandwidth and delay values are used in the computation of the default composite metric. EIGRP for IPv4 and EIGRP for IPv6 use the same formula for the composite metric.

The metric calculation method (k values) and the EIGRP autonomous system number must match between EIGRP neighbors. If they do not match, the routers do not form an adjacency.

The default k values can be changed with the **metric weights** router configuration mode command:

```
Router(config-router)# metric weights tos k1 k2 k3 k4 k5
```

Note Modifying the **metric weights** value is generally not recommended and beyond the scope of this course. However, its relevance is important in establishing neighbor adjacencies. If one router has modified the metric weights and another router has not, an adjacency does not form.

Verifying the k Values

The **show ip protocols** command is used to verify the k values. The command output for R1 is shown in Figure 2. Notice that the k values on R1 are set to the default.

Refer to
Online Course
for Illustration

4.3.2.2 Examining Interface Values

Examining the Metric Values

The **show interface** command displays interface information, including the parameters used to compute the EIGRP metric. The figure shows the **show interface** command for the Serial 0/0/0 interface on R1.

■ **BW** - Bandwidth of the interface (in kilobits per second).

■ **DLY** - Delay of the interface (in microseconds).

- **Reliability** - Reliability of the interface as a fraction of 255 (255/255 is 100% reliability), calculated as an exponential average over five minutes. By default, EIGRP does not include its value in computing its metric.

- **Txload, Rxload** - Transmit and receive load on the interface as a fraction of 255 (255/255 is completely saturated), calculated as an exponential average over five minutes. By default, EIGRP does not include its value in computing its metric.

Note   Throughout this course, bandwidth is referenced as kb/s. However, router output displays bandwidth using the Kbit/sec abbreviation. Router output also displays delay as usec. In this course, delay is referenced as microseconds.

4.3.2.3 Bandwidth Metric

Refer to **Online Course** for Illustration

The bandwidth metric is a static value used by some routing protocols, such as EIGRP and OSPF, to calculate their routing metric. The bandwidth is displayed in kilobits per second (kb/s). Most serial interfaces use the default bandwidth value of 1544 kb/s or 1,544,000 b/s (1.544 Mb/s). This is the bandwidth of a T1 connection. However, some serial interfaces use a different default bandwidth value. Figure 1 shows the topology used throughout this section. The types of serial interfaces and their associated bandwidths may not necessarily reflect the more common types of connections found in networks today.

Always verify bandwidth with the `show interfaces` command.

The default value of the bandwidth may or may not reflect the actual physical bandwidth of the interface. If actual bandwidth of the link differs from the default bandwidth value, the bandwidth value should be modified.

Configuring the Bandwidth Parameter

On most serial links, the bandwidth metric defaults to 1544 kb/s. Because both EIGRP and OSPF use bandwidth in default metric calculations, a correct value for bandwidth is very important to the accuracy of routing information.

Use the following interface configuration mode command to modify the bandwidth metric:

```
Router(config-if)# bandwidth kilobits-bandwidth-value
```

Use the `no bandwidth` command to restore the default value.

In Figure 2, the link between R1 and R2 has a bandwidth of 64 kb/s, and the link between R2 and R3 has a bandwidth of 1,024 kb/s. The figure shows the configurations used on all three routers to modify the bandwidth on the appropriate serial interfaces.

Verifying the Bandwidth Parameter

Use the `show interfaces` command to verify the new bandwidth parameters, as shown in Figure 3. It is important to modify the bandwidth metric on both sides of the link to ensure proper routing in both directions.

Modifying the bandwidth value does not change the actual bandwidth of the link. The `bandwidth` command only modifies the bandwidth metric used by routing protocols, such as EIGRP and OSPF.

4.3.2.4   Delay Metric

Delay is the measure of the time it takes for a packet to traverse a route. The delay (DLY) metric is a static value based on the type of link to which the interface is connected and is expressed in microseconds. Delay is not measured dynamically. In other words, the router does not actually track how long packets take to reach the destination. The delay value, much like the bandwidth value, is a default value that can be changed by the network administrator.

When used to determine the EIGRP metric, delay is the cumulative (sum) of all interface delays along the path (measured in tens of microseconds).

The table in Figure 1 shows the default delay values for various interfaces. Notice that the default value is 20,000 microseconds for serial interfaces and 10 microseconds for GigabitEthernet interfaces.

Use the `show interface` command to verify the delay value on an interface, as shown in Figure 2. Although an interface with various bandwidths can have the same delay value, by default, Cisco recommends not modifying the delay parameter, unless the network administrator has a specific reason to do so.

4.3.2.5   Calculating the EIGRP Metric

Although EIGRP automatically calculates the routing table metric used to choose the best path, it is important that the network administrator understands how these metrics were determined.

The figure shows the composite metric used by EIGRP. Using the default values for K1 and K3, the calculation can be simplified to the slowest bandwidth (or minimum bandwidth), plus the sum of all of the delays.

In other words, by examining the bandwidth and delay values for all of the outgoing interfaces of the route, we can determine the EIGRP metric as follows:

Step 1.   Determine the link with the slowest bandwidth. Use that value to calculate bandwidth (10,000,000/bandwidth).

Step 2.   Determine the delay value for each outgoing interface on the way to the destination. Add the delay values and divide by 10 (sum of delay/10).

Step 3.   Add the computed values for bandwidth and delay, and multiply the sum by 256 to obtain the EIGRP metric.

The routing table output for R2 shows that the route to 192.168.1.0/24 has an EIGRP metric of 3,012,096.

4.3.2.6   Calculating the EIGRP Metric

Figure 1 displays the three router topology. This example illustrates how EIGRP determines the metric displayed in R2's routing table for the 192.168.1.0/24 network.

Bandwidth

EIGRP uses the slowest bandwidth in its metric calculation. The slowest bandwidth can be determined by examining each interface between R2 and the destination network 192.168.1.0. The Serial 0/0/1 interface on R2 has a bandwidth of 1,024 kb/s. The

GigabitEthernet 0/0 interface on R3 has a bandwidth of 1,000,000 kb/s. Therefore, the slowest bandwidth is 1,024 kb/s and is used in the calculation of the metric.

EIGRP divides a reference bandwidth value of 10,000,000 by the interface bandwidth value in kb/s. This results in higher bandwidth values receiving a lower metric and lower bandwidth values receiving a higher metric. 10,000,000 is divided by 1,024. If the result is not a whole number, then the value is rounded down. In this case, 10,000,000 divided by 1,024 equals 9,765.625. The .625 is dropped to yield 9,765 for the bandwidth portion of the composite metric, as shown in Figure 2.

Delay

The same outgoing interfaces are used to determine the delay value, as shown in Figure 3.

EIGRP uses the sum of all delays to the destination. The Serial 0/0/1 interface on R2 has a delay of 20,000 microseconds. The Gigabit 0/0 interface on R3 has a delay of 10 microseconds. The sum of these delays is divided by 10. In the example, (20,000+10)/10 results in a value of 2,001 for the delay portion of the composite metric.

Calculate Metric

Use the calculated values for bandwidth and delay in the metric formula. This results in a metric of 3,012,096, as shown in Figure 4. This value matches the value shown in the routing table for R2.

Refer to
Interactive Graphic
in online course.

4.3.2.7 Activity - Calculate the EIGRP Metric

Refer to
Online Course
for Illustration

4.3.3 DUAL and the Topology Table

4.3.3.1 DUAL Concepts

EIGRP uses the Diffusing Update Algorithm (DUAL) to provide the best loop-free path and loop-free backup paths.

DUAL uses several terms, which are discussed in more detail throughout this section:

- Successor

- Feasible Distance (FD)

- Feasible Successor (FS)

- Reported Distance (RD) or Advertised Distance (AD)

- Feasible Condition or Feasibility Condition (FC)

These terms and concepts are at the center of the loop avoidance mechanism of DUAL.

Refer to
Online Course
for Illustration

4.3.3.2 Introduction to DUAL

EIGRP uses convergence algorithm DUAL. Convergence is critical to a network to avoid routing loops.

Routing loops, even temporary ones, can be detrimental to network performance. Distance vector routing protocols, such as RIP, prevent routing loops with hold-down timers and split horizon. Although EIGRP uses both of these techniques, it uses them somewhat differently; the primary way that EIGRP prevents routing loops is with the DUAL algorithm.

Click Play in the figure to view the basic operation of DUAL.

The DUAL algorithm is used to obtain loop-freedom at every instance throughout a route computation. This allows all routers involved in a topology change to synchronize at the same time. Routers that are not affected by the topology changes are not involved in the recomputation. This method provides EIGRP with faster convergence times than other distance vector routing protocols.

The decision process for all route computations is done by the DUAL Finite State Machine (FSM). An FSM is a workflow model, similar to a flow chart that is composed of the following:

- A finite number of stages (states)

- Transitions between those stages

- Operations

The DUAL FSM tracks all routes, uses EIGRP metrics to select efficient, loop-free paths, and identify the routes with the least-cost path to be inserted into the routing table.

Recomputation of the DUAL algorithm can be processor-intensive. EIGRP avoids recomputation whenever possible by maintaining a list of backup routes that DUAL has already determined to be loop-free. If the primary route in the routing table fails, the best backup route is immediately added to the routing table.

Refer to
Online Course
for Illustration

4.3.3.3   Successor and Feasible Distance

Figure 1 shows the topology for this topic. A successor is a neighboring router that is used for packet forwarding and is the least-cost route to the destination network. The IP address of a successor is shown in a routing table entry right after the word via.

FD is the lowest calculated metric to reach the destination network. FD is the metric listed in the routing table entry as the second number inside the brackets. As with other routing protocols, this is also known as the metric for the route.

Examining the routing table for R2 in Figure 2, notice that EIGRP's best path for the 192.168.1.0/24 network is through router R3, and that the feasible distance is 3,012,096. This is the metric that was calculated in the previous topic.

Refer to
Online Course
for Illustration

4.3.3.4   Feasible Successors, Feasibility Condition, and Reported Distance

DUAL can converge quickly after a change in the topology because it can use backup paths to other networks without recomputing DUAL. These backup paths are known as Feasible Successors (FSs).

An FS is a neighbor that has a loop-free backup path to the same network as the successor, and it satisfies the Feasibility Condition (FC). R2's successor for the 192.168.1.0/24 network is R3, providing the best path or lowest metric to the destination network. Notice in Figure 1, that R1 provides an alternative path, but is it an FS? Before R1 can be an FS for R2, R1 must first meet the FC.

The FC is met when a neighbor's Reported Distance (RD) to a network is less than the local router's feasible distance to the same destination network. If the reported distance is less, it represents a loop-free path. The reported distance is simply an EIGRP neighbor's feasible distance to the same destination network. The reported distance is the metric that a router reports to a neighbor about its own cost to that network.

In Figure 2, R1's feasible distance to 192.168.1.0/24 is 2,170,112.

- R1 reports to R2 that its FD to 192.168.1.0/24 is 2,170,112.

- From R2's perspective, 2,170,112 is R1's RD.

R2 uses this information to determine if R1 meets the FC and, therefore, can be an FS.

As shown in Figure 3, because the RD of R1 (2,170,112) is less than R2's own FD (3,012,096), R1 meets the FC.

R1 is now an FS for R2 to the 192.168.1.0/24 network.

If there is a failure in R2's path to 192.168.1.0/24 via R3 (successor), then R2 immediately installs the path via R1 (FS) in its routing table. R1 becomes the new successor for R2's path to this network, as shown in Figure 4.

Refer to
Online Course
for Illustration

4.3.3.5   Topology Table: show ip eigrp topology Command

Figure 1 shows the topology.

The EIGRP topology table contains all of the routes that are known to each EIGRP neighbor. As an EIGRP router learns routes from its neighbors, those routes are installed in its EIGRP topology table.

As shown in Figure 2, use the `show ip eigrp topology` command to view the topology table. The topology table lists all successors and FSs that DUAL has calculated to destination networks. Only the successor is installed into the IP routing table.

Refer to
Online Course
for Illustration

4.3.3.6   Topology Table: show ip eigrp topology Command (Cont.)

As shown in Figure 1, the first line in the topology table displays:

- **P** - Route in the passive state. When DUAL is not performing its diffusing computations to determine a path for a network, the route is in a stable mode, known as the passive state. If DUAL recalculates or searches for a new path, the route is in an active state and displays an A. All routes in the topology table should be in the passive state for a stable routing domain.

- **192.168.1.0/24** - Destination network that is also found in the routing table.

- **1 successors** - Displays the number of successors for this network. If there are multiple equal cost paths to this network, there are multiple successors.

- **FD is 3012096** - FD, the EIGRP metric to reach the destination network. This is the metric displayed in the IP routing table.

As shown in Figure 2, the first subentry in the output shows the successor:

- **via 192.168.10.10** - Next-hop address of the successor, R3. This address is shown in the routing table.

- **3012096** - FD to 192.168.1.0/24. It is the metric shown in the IP routing table.

- **2816** - RD of the successor and is R3's cost to reach this network.

■ **Serial 0/0/1** - Outbound interface used to reach this network, also shown in the routing table.

As shown in Figure 3, the second subentry shows the FS, R1 (if there is not a second entry, then there are no FSs):

■ **via 172.16.3.1** - Next-hop address of the FS, R1.

■ **41024256** - R2's new FD to 192.168.1.0/24, if R1 became the new successor and would be the new metric displayed in the IP routing table.

■ **2170112** - RD of the FS, or R1's metric to reach this network. RD must be less than the current FD of 3,012,096 to meet the FC.

■ **Serial 0/0/0** - This is the outbound interface used to reach FS, if this router becomes the successor.

Refer to
Online Course
for Illustration

4.3.3.7   Topology Table: No Feasible Successor

To see how DUAL uses successors and FSs, examine the router table of R1, assuming the network is converged, as shown in Figure 1.

Figure 2 displays a partial output from the `show ip route` command on R1. The route to 192.168.1.0/24 shows that the successor is R3 via 192.168.10.6 with an FD of 2,170,112.

The IP routing table only includes the best path, the successor. To see if there are any FSs, we must examine the EIGRP topology table. The topology table in Figure 3 only shows the successor 192.168.10.6, which is R3. There are no FSs. By looking at the actual physical topology or network diagram, it is obvious that there is a backup route to 192.168.1.0/24 through R2. R2 is not an FS because it does not meet the FC. Although, looking at the topology, it is obvious that R2 is a backup route, EIGRP does not have a map of the network topology. EIGRP is a distance vector routing protocol and only knows about remote network information through its neighbors.

DUAL does not store the route through R2 in the topology table. All links can be displayed using the `show ip eigrp topology all-links` command. This command displays links whether they satisfy the FC or not.

As shown in Figure 4, the `show ip eigrp topology all-links` command shows all possible paths to a network, including successors, FSs, and even those routes that are not FSs. R1's FD to 192.168.1.0/24 is 2,170,112 via the successor R3. For R2 to be considered a FS, it must meet the FC. R2's RD to R1 to reach 192.168.1.0/24 must be less the R1's current FD. Per the figure, R2's RD is 3,012,096, which is higher than R1's current FD of 2,170,112.

Even though R2 looks like a viable backup path to 192.168.1.0/24, R1 has no idea that the path is not a potential loop back through itself. EIGRP is a distance vector routing protocol, without the ability to see a complete, loop-free topological map of the network. DUAL's method of guaranteeing that a neighbor has a loop-free path is that the neighbor's metric must satisfy the FC. By ensuring that the RD of the neighbor is less than its own FD, the router can assume that this neighboring router is not part of its own advertised route; thus, always avoiding the potential for a loop.

R2 can be used as a successor if R3 fails; however, there is a longer delay before adding it to the routing table. Before R2 can be used as a successor, DUAL must do further processing.

Refer to
Interactive Graphic
in online course.

4.3.3.8   Activity - Determine the Feasible Successor

Refer to
Online Course
for Illustration

4.3.4   DUAL and Convergence

4.3.4.1   DUAL Finite State Machine (FSM)

The centerpiece of EIGRP is DUAL and its EIGRP route-calculation engine. The actual name of this technology is DUAL Finite State Machine (FSM). This FSM contains all of the logic used to calculate and compare routes in an EIGRP network. The figure shows a simplified version of the DUAL FSM.

An FSM is an abstract machine, not a mechanical device with moving parts. FSMs define a set of possible states that something can go through, what events cause those states, and what events result from those states. Designers use FSMs to describe how a device, computer program, or routing algorithm reacts to a set of input events.

FSMs are beyond the scope of this course; however, the concept is used to examine some of the output from EIGRP's FSM using the `debug eigrp fsm` command. Use this command to examine what DUAL does when a route is removed from the routing table.

Refer to
Online Course
for Illustration

4.3.4.2   DUAL: Feasible Successor

R2 is currently using R3 as the successor to 192.168.1.0/24. In addition, R2 currently lists R1 as an FS, as shown in Figure 1.

The `show ip eigrp topology` output for R2 in Figure 2 verifies that R3 is the successor and R1 is the FS for the 192.168.1.0/24 network. To understand how DUAL can use a FS when the path using the successor is no longer available, a link failure is simulated between R2 and R3.

Before simulating the failure, DUAL debugging must be enabled using the `debug eigrp fsm` command on R2, as shown in Figure 3. A link failure is simulated using the `shutdown` command on the Serial 0/0/1 interface on R2.

The `debug` output displays the activity generated by DUAL when a link goes down. R2 must inform all EIGRP neighbors of the lost link, as well as update its own routing and topology tables. This example only shows selected `debug` output. In particular, notice that the DUAL FSM searches for and finds an FS for the route in the EIGRP topology table.

The FS R1 now becomes the successor and is installed in the routing table as the new best path to 192.168.1.0/24, as shown in Figure 4. With an FS, this change in the routing table happens almost immediately.

As shown in Figure 5, the topology table for R2 now shows R1 as the successor and there are no new FSs. If the link between R2 and R3 is made active again, then R3 returns as the successor and R1 once again becomes the FS.

Refer to
Online Course
for Illustration

4.3.4.3   DUAL: No Feasible Successor

Occasionally, the path to the successor fails and there are not any FSs. In this instance, DUAL does not have a guaranteed loop-free backup path to the network, so the path is not in the topology table as an FS. If there are not any FSs in the topology table, DUAL puts the network into the active state. DUAL actively queries its neighbors for a new successor.

R1 is currently using R3 as the successor to 192.168.1.0/24, as shown in Figure 1. However, R1 does not have R2 listed as an FS, because R2 does not satisfy the FC. To understand how DUAL searches for a new successor when there is no FS, a link failure is simulated between R1 and R3.

Before the link failure is simulated, DUAL debugging is enabled with the **debug eigrp fsm** command on R1, as shown in Figure 2. A link failure is simulated using the **shutdown** command on the Serial 0/0/1 interface on R1.

When the successor is no longer available and there is no feasible successor, DUAL puts the route into an active state. DUAL sends EIGRP queries asking other routers for a path to the network. Other routers return EIGRP replies, letting the sender of the EIGRP query know whether or not they have a path to the requested network. If none of the EIGRP replies have a path to this network, the sender of the query does not have a route to this network.

The selected debug output in Figure 2 shows the 192.168.1.0/24 network put into the active state and EIGRP queries sent to other neighbors. R2 replies with a path to this network, which becomes the new successor and is installed into the routing table.

If the sender of the EIGRP queries receives EIGRP replies that include a path to the requested network, the preferred path is added as the new successor and added to the routing table. This process takes longer than if DUAL had an FS in its topology table and was able to quickly add the new route to the routing table. On Figure 3, notice that R1 has a new route to the 192.168.1.0/24 network. The new EIGRP successor is router R2.

Figure 4 shows that the topology table for R1 now has R2 as the successor with no new FSs. If the link between R1 and R3 is made active again, R3 returns as the successor. However, R2 is still not the FS, because it does not meet the FC.

Refer to **Packet
Tracer Activity**
for this chapter

4.3.4.4   Packet Tracer - Investigating DUAL FSM

In this activity, you will modify the EIGRP metric formula to cause a change in the topology. This allows you to see how EIGRP reacts when a neighbor goes down due to unforeseen circumstances. You will then use the **debug** command to view topology changes and how the DUAL Finite State Machine determines successor and feasible successor paths to re-converge the network.

Refer to
Online Course
for Illustration

4.4   Configuring EIGRP for IPv6

4.4.1   EIGRP for IPv4 vs. IPv6

4.4.1.1   EIGRP for IPv6

Similar to its IPv4 counterpart, EIGRP for IPv6 exchanges routing information to populate the IPv6 routing table with remote prefixes. EIGRP for IPv6 was made available in Cisco IOS, Release 12.4(6)T.

Note   In IPv6, the network address is referred to as the prefix and the subnet mask is called the prefix length.

EIGRP for IPv4 runs over the IPv4 network layer, communicating with other EIGRP IPv4 peers, and advertising only IPv4 routes. EIGRP for IPv6 has the same functionality as EIGRP for IPv4, but uses IPv6 as the network layer transport, communicating with EIGRP for IPv6 peers and advertising IPv6 routes.

EIGRP for IPv6 also uses DUAL as the computation engine to guarantee loop-free paths and backup paths throughout the routing domain.

As with all IPv6 routing protocols, EIGRP for IPv6 has separate processes from its IPv4 counterpart. The processes and operations are basically the same as in the IPv4 routing protocol; however, they run independently. EIGRP for IPv4 and EIGRP for IPv6 each have separate EIGRP neighbor tables, EIGRP topology tables, and IP routing tables, as shown in the figure. EIGRP for IPv6 is a separate protocol-dependent module (PDM).

The EIGRP for IPv6 configuration and verification commands are very similar those used in EIGRP for IPv4. These commands are described later in this section.

Refer to
Online Course
for Illustration

4.4.1.2   Comparing EIGRP for IPv4 and IPv6

The following is a comparison of the main features of EIGRP for IPv4 and EIGRP for IPv6:

- **Advertised routes** - EIGRP for IPv4 advertises IPv4 networks; whereas, EIGRP for IPv6 advertises IPv6 prefixes.

- **Distance vector** - Both EIGRP for IPv4 and IPv6 are advanced distance vector routing protocols. Both protocols use the same administrative distances.

- **Convergence technology** - EIGRP for IPv4 and IPv6 both use the DUAL algorithm. Both protocols use the same DUAL techniques and processes, including successor, FS, FD, and RD.

- **Metric** - Both EIGRP for IPv4 and IPv6 use bandwidth, delay, reliability, and load for their composite metric. Both routing protocols use the same composite metric and use only bandwidth and delay, by default.

- **Transport protocol** - The Reliable Transport Protocol (RTP) is responsible for guaranteed delivery of EIGRP packets to all neighbors for both protocols, EIGRP for IPv4 and IPv6.

- **Update messages** - Both EIGRP for IPv4 and IPv6 send incremental updates when the state of a destination changes. The terms, partial and bounded, are used when referring to updates for both protocols.

- **Neighbor discovery mechanism** - EIGRP for IPv4 and EIGRP for IPv6 use a simple Hello mechanism to learn about neighboring routers and form adjacencies.

- **Source and destination addresses** - EIGRP for IPv4 sends messages to the multicast address 224.0.0.10. These messages use the source IPv4 address of the outbound interface. EIGRP for IPv6 sends its messages to the multicast address FF02::A. EIGRP for IPv6 messages are sourced using the IPv6 link-local address of the exit interface.

- **Authentication** - EIGRP for IPv4 can use either plaintext authentication or Message Digest 5 (MD5) authentication. EIGRP for IPv6 uses MD5.

- **Router ID** - Both EIGRP for IPv4 and EIGRP for IPv6 use a 32-bit number for the EIGRP router ID. The 32-bit router ID is represented in dotted-decimal notation and is commonly referred to as an IPv4 address. If the EIGRP for IPv6 router has not been configured with an IPv4 address, the `eigrp router-id` command must be used to configure a 32-bit router ID. The process for determining the router ID is the same for both EIGRP for IPv4 and IPv6.

4.4.1.3 IPv6 Link-local Addresses

Refer to **Online Course** for Illustration

Routers running a dynamic routing protocol, such as EIGRP exchange messages between neighbors on the same subnet or link. Routers only need to send and receive routing protocol messages with their directly connected neighbors. These messages are always sent from the source IP address of the router that is doing the forwarding.

IPv6 link-local addresses are ideal for this purpose. An IPv6 link-local address enables a device to communicate with other IPv6-enabled devices on the same link and only on that link (subnet). Packets with a source or destination link-local address cannot be routed beyond the link from where the packet originated.

EIGRP for IPv6 messages are sent using:

- **Source IPv6 address** - This is the IPv6 link-local address of the exit interface.

- **Destination IPv6 address** - When the packet needs to be sent to a multicast address, it is sent to the IPv6 multicast address FF02::A, the all-EIGRP-routers with link-local scope. If the packet can be sent as a unicast address, it is sent to the link-local address of the neighboring router.

Note   IPv6 link-local addresses are in the FE80::/10 range. The /10 indicates that the first 10 bits are 1111 1110 10xx xxxx, which results in the first hextet having a range of 1111 1110 1000 0000 (FE80) to 1111 1110 1011 1111 (FEBF).

Refer to
Interactive Graphic
in online course.

4.4.1.4 Activity - Compare EIGRPv4 and EIGRPv6

Refer to
Online Course
for Illustration

4.4.2 Configuring EIGRP for IPv6

4.4.2.1 EIGRP for IPv6 Network Topology

Figure 1 shows the network topology that is used for configuring EIGRP for IPv6. If the network is running dual-stack, using both IPv4 and IPv6 on all devices, EIGRP for both IPv4 and IPv6 can be configured on all the routers. However, in this section, the focus is solely on EIGRP for IPv6.

Only the IPv6 global unicast addresses have been configured on each router.

Figures 2, 3, and 4 display the starting interface configurations on each router. Notice the interface bandwidth values from the previous EIGRP for IPv4 configuration. Because EIGRP for IPv4 and IPv6 use the same metrics, modifying the bandwidth parameters influences both routing protocols.

Refer to
Online Course
for Illustration

4.4.2.2 Configuring IPv6 Link-local Addresses

Link-local addresses are automatically created when an IPv6 global unicast address is assigned to the interface. Global unicast addresses are not required on an interface; however, IPv6 link-local addresses are.

Unless configured manually, Cisco routers create the link-local address using FE80::/10 prefix and the EUI-64 process, as shown in Figure 1. EUI-64 involves using the 48-bit Ethernet MAC address, inserting FFFE in the middle and flipping the seventh bit. For serial interfaces, Cisco uses the MAC address of an Ethernet interface. A router with several serial interfaces can assign the same link-local address to each IPv6 interface, because link-local addresses only need to be local on the link.

Link-local addresses created using the EUI-64 format, or in some cases random interface IDs, make it difficult to recognize and remember those addresses. Because IPv6 routing protocols use IPv6 link-local addresses for unicast addressing and next hop address information in the routing table, it is common practice to make it an easily recognizable address. Configuring the link-local address manually provides the ability to create an address that is recognizable and easier to remember.

Link-local addresses can be configured manually using the same interface configuration mode command used to create IPv6 global unicast addresses, but with different parameters:

```
Router(config-if)# ipv6 address link-local-address link-local
```

A link-local address has a prefix within the range FE80 to FEBF. When an address begins with this hextet (16-bit segment), the **link-local** keyword must follow the address.

Figure 2 shows the configuration of a link-local address using the **ipv6 address** interface configuration mode command. The link-local address FE80::1 is used to make it easily recognizable as belonging to router R1. The same IPv6 link-local address is configured on all of R1's interfaces. FE80::1 can be configured on each link because it only has to be unique on that link.

Similar to R1, in Figure 3, router R2 is configured with FE80::2 as the IPv6 link-local address on all of its interfaces.

Use the Syntax Checker on Figure 4 to configure FE80::3 as the link-local address on all of R3's interfaces.

As shown in Figure 5, the `show ipv6 interface brief` command is used to verify the IPv6 link-local and global unicast addresses on all interfaces.

Refer to **Online Course** for Illustration

4.4.2.3 Configuring the EIGRP for IPv6 Routing Process

The `ipv6 unicast-routing` global configuration mode command enables IPv6 routing on the router. This command is required before any IPv6 routing protocol can be configured. This command is not required to configure IPv6 addresses on the interfaces, but is necessary for the router to be enabled as an IPv6 router.

EIGRP for IPv6

The following global configuration mode command is used to enter router configuration mode for EIGRP for IPv6:

```
Router(config)# ipv6 router eigrp autonomous-system
```

Similar to EIGRP for IPv4, the `autonomous-system` value must be the same on all routers in the routing domain. In Figure 1, the EIGRP for IPv6 routing process could not be configured until IPv6 routing was enabled with the `ipv6 unicast-routing` global configuration mode command.

Router ID

As shown in Figure 2, the `eigrp router-id` command is used to configure the router ID. EIGRP for IPv6 uses a 32 bit value for the router ID. To obtain that value, EIGRP for IPv6 uses the same process as EIGRP for IPv4. The `eigrp router-id` command takes precedence over any loopback or physical interface IPv4 addresses. If an EIGRP for IPv6 router does not have any active interfaces with an IPv4 address, then the `eigrp router-id` command is required.

The router ID should be a unique 32-bit number in the EIGRP for IP routing domain; otherwise, routing inconsistencies can occur.

Note The `eigrp router-id` command is used to configure the router ID for EIGRP. Some versions of IOS will accept the command `router-id`, without first specifying `eigrp`. The running-config, however, will display `eigrp router-id` regardless of which command is used.

No Shutdown Command

By default, the EIGRP for IPv6 process is in a shutdown state. The `no shutdown` command is required to activate the EIGRP for IPv6 process, as shown in Figure 3. This command is not required for EIGRP for IPv4. Although, EIGRP for IPv6 is enabled, neighbor adjacencies and routing updates cannot be sent and received until EIGRP is activated on the appropriate interfaces.

Both the `no shutdown` command and a router ID are required for the router to form neighbor adjacencies.

Figure 4 shows the complete EIGRP for IPv6 configuration for router R2.

Use the Syntax Checker in Figure 5 to configure the EIGRP for IPv6 process on router R3.

Refer to
Online Course
for Illustration

4.4.2.4   ipv6 eigrp Interface Command

EIGRP for IPv6 uses a different method to enable an interface for EIGRP. Instead of using the `network` router configuration mode command in to specify matching interface addresses, EIGRP for IPv6 is configured directly on the interface.

Use the following interface configuration mode command to enable EIGRP for IPv6 on an interface:

```
Router(config-if)# ipv6 eigrp autonomous-system
```

The *autonomous-system* value must be the same as the autonomous system number used to enable the EIGRP routing process. Similar to the `network` command used in EIGRP for IPv4, the `ipv6 eigrp interface` command:

- Enables the interface to form adjacencies and send or receive EIGRP for IPv6 updates

- Includes the prefix (network) of this interface in EIGRP for IPv6 routing updates

Figure 1 shows the configuration to enable EIGRP for IPv6 on routers R1 and R2 interfaces. Notice the message following the serial 0/0/0 interface in R2:

```
%DUAL-5-NBRCHANGE: EIGRP-IPv6 2: Neighbor FE80::1 (Serial0/0/0) is up: new adja-
cency
```

This message indicates that R2 has now formed an EIGRP-IPv6 adjacency with the neighbor at link-local address FE80::1. Because static link-local addresses were configured on all three routers, it is easy to determine that this adjacency is with router R1 (FE80::1).

Use the Syntax Checker in Figure 2 to enable EIGRP for IPv6 on R3's interfaces.

Passive Interface with EIGRP for IPv6

The same `passive-interface` command used for IPv4 is used to configure an interface as passive with EIGRP for IPv6. As shown in Figure 3, the `show ipv6 protocols` command is used to verify the configuration.

Refer to
Online Course
for Illustration

4.4.3   Verifying EIGRP for IPv6

4.4.3.1   Verifying EIGRP for IPv6: Examining Neighbors

Similar to EIGRP for IPv4, before any EIGRP for IPv6 updates can be sent or received, routers must establish adjacencies with their neighbors, as shown in Figure 1.

Use the `show ipv6 eigrp neighbors` command to view the neighbors' table and verify that EIGRP for IPv6 has established an adjacency with its neighbors. The output shown in Figure 2 displays the IPv6 link-local address of the adjacent neighbor and the interface that this router uses to reach that EIGRP neighbor. Using meaningful link-local addresses makes it easy to recognize the neighbors R2 at FE80::2 and R3 at FE80::3.

The output from the `show ipv6 eigrp neighbor` command includes:

- **H column** - Lists the neighbors in the order they were learned.

- **Address** - IPv6 link-local address of the neighbor.

- **Interface** - Local interface on which this Hello packet was received.

- **Hold** - Current hold time. When a Hello packet is received, this value is reset to the maximum hold time for that interface and then counts down to zero. If zero is reached, the neighbor is considered down.

- **Uptime** - Amount of time since this neighbor was added to the neighbor table.

- **SRTT** and **RTO** - Used by RTP to manage reliable EIGRP packets.

- **Queue Count** - Should always be zero. If it is more than zero, then EIGRP packets are waiting to be sent.

- **Sequence Number** - Used to track updates, queries, and reply packets.

The `show ipv6 eigrp neighbors` command is useful for verifying and troubleshooting EIGRP for IPv6. If an expected neighbor is not listed, ensure that both ends of the link are up/up using the `show ipv6 interface brief` command. The same requirements exist for establishing neighbor adjacencies with EIGRP for IPv6 as it does for IPv4. If both sides of the link have active interfaces, check to see:

- Are both routers configured with the same EIGRP autonomous system number?

- Is the interface enabled for EIGRP for IPv6 with the correct autonomous system number?

Refer to **Online Course** for Illustration

4.4.3.2   Verifying EIGRP for IPv6: show ip protocols Command

The `show ipv6 protocols` command displays the parameters and other information about the state of any active IPv6 routing protocol processes currently configured on the router. The `show ipv6 protocols` command displays different types of output specific to each IPv6 routing protocol.

The output in the figure indicates several EIGRP for IPv6 parameters previously discussed, including:

1. EIGRP for IPv6 is an active dynamic routing protocol on R1 configured with the autonomous system number 2.

2. These are the *k* values used to calculate the EIGRP composite metric. K1 and K3 are 1, by default, and K2, K4, and K5 are 0, by default.

3. The EIGRP for IPv6 router ID of R1 is 1.0.0.0.

4. Same as EIGRP for IPv4, EIGRP for IPv6 administrative distances have internal AD of 90 and external of 170 (default values).

5. The interfaces enabled for EIGRP for IPv6.

The output from the `show ipv6 protocols` command is useful in debugging routing operations. The Interfaces section shows which interfaces EIGRP for IPv6 have been enabled. This is useful in verifying that EIGRP is enabled on all of the appropriate interfaces with the correct autonomous system number.

Refer to
Online Course
for Illustration

4.4.3.3   Verifying EIGRP for IPv6: Examine the IPv6 Routing Table

As with any routing protocol, the goal is to populate the IP routing table with routes to remote networks and the best paths to reaching those networks. As with IPv4, it is important to examine the IPv6 routing table and determine whether it is populated with the correct routes.

The IPv6 routing table is examined using the **show ipv6 route** command. EIGRP for IPv6 routes are denoted in the routing table with a D, similar to its counterpart for IPv4.

Figure 1 shows that R1 has installed three EIGRP routes to remote IPv6 networks in its IPv6 routing table:

- 2001:DB8:CAFE:2::/64 via R3 (FE80::3) using its Serial 0/0/1 interface
- 2001:DB8:CAFE:3::/64 via R3 (FE80::3) using its Serial 0/0/1 interface
- 2001:DB8:CAFE:A002::/64 via R3 (FE80::3) using its Serial 0/0/1 interface

All three routes are using router R3 as the next-hop router (successor). Notice that the routing table uses the link-local address as the next-hop address. Because each router has had all its interfaces configured with a unique and distinguishable link-local address, it is easy to recognize that the next-hop router via FE80::3 is router R3.

Figure 2 displays the IPv6 routing table for R2.

Figure 3 displays the routing table for R3. Notice that R3 has two equal cost paths to the 2001:DB8:CAFE:A001::/64. One path is via R1 at FE80::1 and the other path is via R2 at FE80::2.

Refer to **Packet Tracer Activity** for this chapter

4.4.3.4   Packet Tracer - Configuring Basic EIGRP with IPv6

In this activity, you will configure the network with EIGRP routing for IPv6. You will also assign router IDs, configure passive interfaces, verify the network is fully converged, and display routing information using **show** commands.

- EIGRP for IPv6 has the same overall operation and features as EIGRP for IPv4. There are a few major differences between them:
- EIGRP for IPv6 is configured directly on the router interfaces.
- With EIGRP for IPv6, a router-ID is required on each router or the routing process does not start.
- The EIGRP for IPv6 routing process uses a shutdown feature.

Refer to **Lab Activity** for this chapter

4.4.3.5   Lab - Configuring Basic EIGRP for IPv6

In this lab, you will complete the following objectives:

- Part 1: Build the Network and Verify Connectivity
- Part 2: Configure EIGRP for IPv6 Routing
- Part 3: Verify EIGRP for IPv6 Routing
- Part 4: Configure and Verify Passive Interfaces

Refer to
Online Course
for Illustration

Refer to
Lab Activity
for this chapter

4.5   Summary

4.5.1.1   Class Activity - Portfolio RIP and EIGRP

Activity - Portfolio RIP and EIGRP

Scenario

You are preparing a portfolio file for comparison of RIP and EIGRP routing protocols.

Think of a network with three interconnected routers with each router providing a LAN for PCs, printers, and other end devices. The graphic on this page depicts one example of a topology like this.

In this modeling activity scenario, you will be creating, addressing and configuring a topology, using verification commands, and comparing/contrasting RIP and EIGRP routing protocol outputs.

Complete the PDF reflection questions accompanying this activity. Save your work and be prepared to share your answers with the class. Also save a copy of your work for later use within this course or for portfolio reference.

Refer to
Online Course
for Illustration

4.5.1.2   Summary

EIGRP (Enhanced Interior Gateway Routing Protocol) is a classless, distance vector routing protocol. EIGRP is an enhancement of another Cisco routing protocol IGRP (Interior Gateway Routing Protocol) which is now obsolete. EIGRP was initially released in 1992 as a Cisco proprietary protocol available only on Cisco devices. In 2013, Cisco released a basic functionality of EIGRP as an open standard, to the IETF.

EIGRP uses the source code of "D" for DUAL in the routing table. EIGRP has a default administrative distance of 90 for internal routes and 170 for routes imported from an external source, such as default routes.

EIGRP is an advanced distance vector routing protocol that includes features not found in other distance vector routing protocols like RIP. These features include: Diffusing Update Algorithm (DUAL), establishing neighbor adjacencies, Reliable Transport Protocol (RTP), partial and bounded updates, and equal and unequal cost load balancing.

EIGRP uses PDMs (Protocol Dependent Modules) giving it the capability to support different Layer 3 protocols including IPv4 and IPv6. EIGRP uses RTP (Reliable Transport Protocol) as the transport layer protocol for the delivery of EIGRP packets. EIGRP uses reliable delivery for EIGRP updates, queries and replies; and uses unreliable delivery for EIGRP Hellos and acknowledgments. Reliable RTP means an EIGRP acknowledgment must be returned.

Before any EIGRP updates are sent, a router must first discover their neighbors. This is done with EIGRP Hello packets. The Hello and hold-down values do not need to match for two routers to become neighbors. The `show ip eigrp neighbors` command is used to view the neighbor table and verify that EIGRP has established an adjacency with its neighbors.

EIGRP does not send periodic updates like RIP. EIGRP sends partial or bounded updates, which includes only the route changes and only to those routers that are affected by the change. EIGRP composite metric uses bandwidth, delay, reliability, and load to determine the best path. By default only bandwidth and delay are used.

At the center of EIGRP is DUAL (Diffusing Update Algorithm). The DUAL finite state machine is used to determine best path and potential backup paths to every destination network. The successor is a neighboring router that is used to forward the packet using the least-cost route to the destination network. Feasible distance (FD) is the lowest calculated metric to reach the destination network through the successor. A feasible successor (FS) is a neighbor who has a loop-free backup path to the same network as the successor, and also meets the feasibility condition. The feasibility condition (FC) is met when a neighbor's reported distance (RD) to a network is less than the local router's feasible distance to the same destination network. The reported distance is simply an EIGRP neighbor's feasible distance to the destination network.

EIGRP is configured with the `router eigrp` *autonomous-system* command. The autonomous-system value is actually a process-id and must be the same on all routers in the EIGRP routing domain. The `network` command is similar to that used with RIP. The network is the classful network address of the directly connected interfaces on the router. A wildcard mask is an optional parameter that can be used to include only specific interfaces.

Go to the online course to take the quiz and exam.

Chapter 4 Quiz

This quiz is designed to provide an additional opportunity to practice the skills and knowledge presented in the chapter and to prepare for the chapter exam. You will be allowed multiple attempts and the grade does not appear in the gradebook.

Chapter 4 Exam

The chapter exam assesses your knowledge of the chapter content.

Your Chapter Notes

EIGRP Advanced Configurations and Troubleshooting

5.0 EIGRP Advanced Configurations and Troubleshooting

5.0.1.1 Introduction

EIGRP is a versatile routing protocol that can be fine-tuned in many ways. Two of the most important tuning capabilities are the ability to summarize routes and the ability to implement load balancing. Other tuning capabilities include being able to propagate a default, fine-tune timers, and implement authentication between EIGRP neighbors to increase security.

This chapter discusses these additional tuning features and the configuration mode commands to implement these features for both IPv4 and IPv6.

Refer to **Lab Activity** for this chapter

5.0.1.2 Class Activity - EIGRP - Back to the Future

Activity - EIGRP – Back to the Future

Scenario

This chapter teaches you how to maintain your EIGRP networks and to influence them to do what you want them to do. EIGRP concepts from this chapter include:

- Autosummarization
- Load balancing
- Default routes
- Hold down timers
- Authentication

With a partner, write 10 EIGRP review questions based on the previous chapter's curriculum content. Three of the questions must focus on the bulleted items above. Ideally, Multiple Choice, True/False, or Fill in the Blank question types will be designed. As you design your questions, ensure that you record the curriculum section and page numbers of the supporting content in case you need to refer back for answer verification.

Save your work and then meet with another group, or the entire class, and quiz them using the questions you developed.

Refer to
Online Course
for Illustration

5.1   Advanced EIGRP Configurations

5.1.1   Autosummarization

5.1.1.1   Network Topology

To configure tuning features of EIGRP, it is necessary to start with a basic implementation of EIGRP.

Figure 1 shows the network topology used for this chapter.

Figures 2, 3, and 4 show the IPv4 interface configurations and the EIGRP implementations on R1, R2, and R3, respectively.

The types of serial interfaces and their associated bandwidths may not necessarily reflect the more common types of connections found in networks today. The bandwidths of the serial links used in this topology help explain the calculation of the routing protocol metrics and the process of best path selection.

Notice that the `bandwidth` commands on the serial interfaces were used to modify the default bandwidth of 1,544 Kb/s.

In this chapter, the ISP router is used as the routing domain's gateway to the Internet. All three routers are running Cisco IOS, Release 15.2.

Refer to
Online Course
for Illustration

5.1.1.2   EIGRP Autosummarization

One of the most common tuning methods of EIGRP is enabling and disabling automatic route summarization. Route summarization allows a router to group networks together and advertises them as one large group using a single, summarized route. The ability to summarize routes is necessary due to the rapid growth of networks.

A border router is a router that sits at the edge of a network. This router must be able to advertise all of the known networks within its route table to a connecting network router or ISP router. This convergence can potentially result in very large route tables. Imagine if a single router had 10 different networks and had to advertise all 10 route entries to a connecting router. What if that connecting router also had 10 networks, and had to advertise all 20 routes to an ISP router? If every enterprise router followed this pattern, the routing table of the ISP router would be huge.

Summarization decreases the number of entries in routing updates and lowers the number of entries in local routing tables. It also reduces bandwidth utilization for routing updates and results in faster routing table lookups.

To limit the number of routing advertisements and the size of routing tables, routing protocols such as EIGRP, use autosummarization at classful boundaries. This means that EIGRP recognizes subnets as a single Class A, B, or C network, and creates only one entry in the routing table for the summary route. As a result, all traffic destined for the subnets travels across that one path.

The figure shows an example of how autosummarization works. Routers R1 and R2 are both configured using EIGRP for IPv4 with autosummarization. R1 has three subnets in its routing table: 172.16.1.0/24, 172.16.2.0/24, and 172.16.3.0/24. In the classful network addressing architecture, these subnets are all considered part of a larger class B network,

172.16.0.0/16. Because EIGRP on router R1 is configured for autosummarization, when it sends its routing update to R2, it summarizes the three /24 subnets as a single network of 172.16.0.0/16, which reduces the number of routing updates sent and the number of entries in R2's IPv4 routing table.

All traffic destined for the three subnets travels across the one path. R2 does not maintain routes to individual subnets and no subnet information is learned. In an enterprise network, the path chosen to reach the summary route may not be the best choice for the traffic that is trying to reach each individual subnet. The only way that all routers can find the best routes for each individual subnet is for neighbors to send subnet information. In this situation, autosummarization should be disabled. When autosummarization is disabled, updates include subnet information.

Refer to
Online Course
for Illustration

5.1.1.3 Configuring EIGRP Autosummarization

EIGRP for IPv4 autosummarization is disabled by default beginning with Cisco IOS Release 15.0(1)M and 12.2(33). Prior to this, autosummarization was enabled by default. This meant that EIGRP performed auto-summarization each time the EIGRP topology crossed a border between two different major class networks.

In Figure 1, the output from the **show ip protocols** command on R1 indicates that EIGRP autosummarization is disabled. This router is running IOS 15.2; therefore, EIGRP autosummarization is disabled by default. Figure 2 shows the current routing table for R3. Notice that the IPv4 routing table for R3 contains all of the networks and subnets within the EIGRP routing domain.

To enable autosummarization for EIGRP, use the **auto-summary** command in router configuration mode, as shown in Figure 3:

```
R1(config)# router eigrp as-number
R1(config-router)# auto-summary
```

The **no** form of this command is used to disable autosummarization .

Use the Syntax Checker in Figure 4 to enable autosummarization for R3.

Refer to
Online Course
for Illustration

5.1.1.4 Verifying Auto-Summary: show ip protocols

In Figure 1, notice the EIGRP routing domain has three classful networks:

■ 172.16.0.0/16 class B network consisting of 172.16.1.0/24, 172.16.2.0/24, and 172.16.3.0/30 subnets

■ 192.168.10.0/24 class C network consisting of the 192.168.10.4/30 and 192.168.10.8/30 subnets

■ 192.168.1.0/24 class C network, which is not subnetted

The output from R1's **show ip protocols** command in Figure 2 shows that autosummarization is now enabled. The output also indicates the networks that are summarized and on which interfaces. Notice that R1 summarizes two networks in its EIGRP routing updates:

■ 192.168.10.0/24 sent out the GigabitEthernet 0/0 and Serial 0/0/0 interfaces

■ 172.16.0.0/16 sent out the Serial 0/0/1 interface

R1 has the subnets 192.168.10.4/30 and 192.168.10.8/30 in its IPv4 routing table.

As indicated in Figure 3, R1 summarizes the 192.168.10.4/30 and 192.168.10.8/30 subnet. It forwards the summarized address of 192.168.10.0/24 to its neighbors on its Serial 0/0/0 and GigabitEthernet 0/0 interfaces. Because R1 does not have any EIGRP neighbors on its GigabitEthernet 0/0 interface, the summarized routing update is only received by R2.

As indicated in Figure 4, R1 also has the 172.16.1.0/24, 172.16.2.0/24, and 172.16.3.0/30 subnets in its IPv4 routing table. R3 selects R1 as the successor to 172.16.0.0/16 because it has a lower feasible distance. The R3 S0/0/0 interface connecting to R1 uses a default bandwidth of 1,544 kb/s. The R3 link to R2 has a higher feasible distance because the R3 S0/0/1 interface has been configured with a lower bandwidth of 1,024 kb/s.

Notice that the 172.16.0.0/16 summarized update is not sent out R1's GigabitEthernet 0/0 and Serial 0/0/0 interfaces. This is because these two interfaces are members of the same 172.16.0.0/16 class B network. The 172.16.1.0/24 non-summarized routing update is sent by R1 to R2. Summarized updates are only sent out interfaces on different major classful networks.

5.1.1.5 Verifying Auto-Summary: Topology Table

Refer to
Online Course
for Illustration

In Figure 1, routers R1 and R2 will send R3 a summarized EIGRP routing update of 172.16.0.0/16. Routing tables for R1 and R2 contain subnets of the 172.16.0.0/16 network; therefore, both routers send the summary advertisement across a different major network to R3.

Figure 2 shows the output from the `show ip eigrp topology all-links` command used to view R3's complete EIGRP topology table. This verifies that R3 has received the 172.16.0.0/16 summary route from both R1 at 192.168.10.5 and R2 at 192.168.10.9. The first entry via 192.168.10.5 is the successor and the second entry via 192.168.10.9 is the feasible successor. R1 is the successor because its 1,544 kb/s link with R3 gives R3 a better EIGRP cost to 172.16.0.0/16 than R2, which is using a slower 1,024 kb/s link.

The `all-links` option shows all received updates, whether the route qualifies as a feasible successor (FS) or not. In this instance, R2 does qualify as an FS. R2 is considered an FS because its reported distance (RD) of 2,816 is less than the feasible distance (FD) of 2,170,112 via R1.

5.1.1.6 Verifying Auto-Summary: Routing Table

Refer to
Online Course
for Illustration

Examine the routing table to verify that the summarized route was received.

Figure 1 shows R3's routing table prior to autosummarization, and then with autosummarization enabled using the `auto-summary` command. Notice that with autosummarization enabled, R3's routing table now only contains the single class B network address 172.16.0.0/16. The successor or next-hop router is R1 via 192.168.10.5.

Note Autosummarization is only an option with EIGRP for IPv4. Classful addressing does not exist in IPv6; therefore, there is no need for autosummarization with EIGRP for IPv6.

When enabling autosummarization, it is also necessary to understand the Null interface. Figure 2 shows the routing table for R1. Notice the two entries highlighted are using an exit interface of Null0. EIGRP has automatically included a summary route to Null0 for two classful networks 192.168.10.0/24 and 172.16.0.0/16.

The Null0 interface is a virtual IOS interface that is a route to nowhere, commonly known as "the bit bucket." Packets that match a route with a Null0 exit interface are discarded.

EIGRP for IPv4 automatically includes a Null0 summary route whenever the following conditions exist:

- There is at least one subnet that was learned via EIGRP.
- There are two or more **network** EIGRP router configuration mode commands.
- Autosummarization is enabled.

The purpose of the Null0 summary route is to prevent routing loops for destinations that are included in the summary, but do not actually exist in the routing table.

Refer to
Online Course
for Illustration

5.1.1.7   Summary Route

The figure illustrates a scenario where a routing loop could occur:

1. R1 has a default route, 0.0.0.0/0 via the ISP router.

2. R1 sends a routing update to R2 containing the default route.

3. R2 installs the default route from R1 in its IPv4 routing table.

4. R2's routing table contains the 172.16.1.0/24, 172.16.2.0/24, and 172.16.3.0/24 subnets in its routing table.

5. R2 sends a summarized update to R1 for the 172.16.0.0/16 network.

6. R1 installs the summarized route for 172.16.0.0/16 via R2.

7. R1 receives a packet for 172.16.4.10. Because R1 has a route for 172.16.0.0/16 via R2, it forwards the packet to R2.

8. R2 receives the packet with the destination address 172.16.4.10 from R1. The packet does not match any specific route so using the default route in its routing table R2 forwards the packet back to R1.

9. The packet for 172.16.4.10 is looped between R1 and R2 until the TTL expires and the packet is dropped.

Refer to
Online Course
for Illustration

5.1.1.8   Summary Route (Cont.)

EIGRP uses the Null0 interface to prevent these types of routing loops. The figure illustrates a scenario where a Null0 route prevents the routing loop illustrated in the previous example:

1. R1 has a default route, 0.0.0.0/0 via the ISP router.

2. R1 sends a routing update to R2 containing the default route.

3. R2 installs the default route from R1 in its IPv4 routing table.

4. R2's routing table contains the 172.16.1.0/24, 172.16.2.0/24, and 172.16.3.0/24 subnets in its routing table.

5. R2 installs the 172.16.0.0/16 summary route to Null0 in its routing table.

6. R2 sends a summarized update to R1 for the 172.16.0.0/16 network.

7. R1 installs the summarized route for 172.16.0.0/16 via R2.

8. R1 receives a packet for 172.16.4.10. Because R1 has a route for 172.16.0.0/16 via R2, it forwards the packet to R2.

9. R2 receives the packet with the destination address 172.16.4.10 from R1. The packet does not match any specific subnet of 172.16.0.0 but does match the 172.16.0.0/16 summary route to Null0. Using the Null0 route, the packet is discarded.

A summary route on R2 for 172.16.0.0/16 to the Null0 interface, discards any packets that begin with 172.16.x.x, but do not have a longer match with any of the subnets: 172.16.1.0/24, 172.16.2.0/24, or 172.16.3.0/24.

Even if R2 has a default route of 0.0.0.0/0 in its routing table, the Null0 route is a longer match.

Note The Null0 summary route is removed when autosummary is disabled using the **no auto-summary** router configuration mode command.

Refer to **Interactive Graphic** in online course.

5.1.1.9   Activity - Determine the Classful Summarization

Refer to **Interactive Graphic** in online course.

5.1.1.10   Activity - Determine the Exit Interface for a Given Packet

Refer to **Online Course** for Illustration

5.1.2   Manual Summarization

5.1.2.1   Manual Summary Routes

EIGRP can be configured to summarize routes, whether or not autosummarization (**auto-summary**) is enabled. Because EIGRP is a classless routing protocol and includes the subnet mask in the routing updates, manual summarization can include supernet routes. Remember, a supernet is an aggregation of multiple major classful network addresses.

In Figure 1, two more networks are added to router R3 using loopback interfaces: 192.168.2.0/24 and 192.168.3.0/24. Although the loopback interfaces are virtual interfaces, they are used to represent physical networks for this example.

Figure 2 shows the commands on R3 to configure the two loopback interfaces and the configuration to enable both interfaces for EIGRP.

To verify that R3 sent EIGRP update packets to R1 and R2, the routing tables are examined on both routers.

In Figure 3, only the pertinent routes are shown. R1 and R2 routing tables show these additional networks in their routing tables: 192.168.2.0/24 and 192.168.3.0/24. Instead of sending three separate networks, R3 can summarize the 192.168.1.0/24, 192.168.2.0/24, and 192.168.3.0/24 networks as a single route.

Refer to
Online Course
for Illustration

5.1.2.2   Configuring EIGRP Manual Summary Routes

Determining the Summary EIGRP Route

Figure 1 shows the two manual summary routes that are configured on R3. These summary routes are sent out of the Serial 0/0/0 and Serial 0/0/1 interfaces to R3's EIGRP neighbors.

To determine the summary of these three networks, the same method is used to determine summary static routes, as shown in Figure 2:

Step 1.   Write out the networks to be summarized in binary.

Step 2.   To find the subnet mask for summarization, start with the far left bit.

Step 3.   Working from left to right, find all the bits that match consecutively.

Step 4.   When there is a column of bits that do not match, stop. This is the summary boundary.

Step 5.   Count the number of far left matching bits, which in this example is 22. This number is used to determine the subnet mask for the summarized route: /22 or 255.255.252.0.

Step 6.   To find the network address for summarization, copy the matching 22 bits and add all 0 bits to the end to make 32 bits.

The result is the summary network address and mask for 192.168.0.0/22.

Configure EIGRP Manual Summarization

To establish EIGRP manual summarization on a specific EIGRP interface, use the following interface configuration mode command:

```
Router(config-if)# ip summary-address eigrp as-number network-address subnet-mask
```

Figure 2 shows the configuration to propagate a manual summary route on R3's Serial 0/0/0 interface. Because R3 has two EIGRP neighbors, the EIGRP manual summarization must be configured on both Serial 0/0/0 and Serial 0/0/1.

Use the Syntax Checker in Figure 3 to configure the same manual summary route on R3's Serial 0/0/1 interface.

Refer to
Online Course
for Illustration

5.1.2.3   Verifying Manual Summary Routes

The figure illustrates that, after the summary route is configured, the routing tables of R1 and R2 no longer include the individual 192.168.1.0/24, 192.168.2.0/24, and 192.168.3.0/24 networks. Instead, they show a single summary route of 192.168.0.0/22. Summary routes reduce the number of total routes in routing tables, which makes the routing table lookup process more efficient. Summary routes also require less bandwidth utilization for the routing updates, because a single route can be sent instead of multiple individual routes.

Refer to
Online Course
for Illustration

5.1.2.4   EIGRP for IPv6: Manual Summary Routes

While autosummarization is not available for EIGRP IPv6 networks, it is possible to enable manual summarization for EIGRP IPv6.

Figure 1 shows an EIGRP IPv6 topology with four loopback addresses configured on R3. These virtual addresses are used to represent physical networks in R3's IPv6 routing table. These networks can be manually summarized in EIGRP for IPv6.

Figure 2 shows the configuration of the IPv6 loopback addresses on R3. Only four loopback addresses are shown in the topology and configured on R3; however, for this example it is assumed that all 2001:DB8:ACAD::/48 subnets can be reachable via R3.

To configure EIGRP for IPv6 manual summarization on a specific EIGRP interface, use the following interface configuration mode command:

```
Router(config-if)# ipv6 summary-address eigrp as-number prefix/prefix-length
```

Figure 3 shows the configuration to propagate an EIGRP for IPv6 manual summary route to R1 and R2 for the 2001:DB8:ACAD::/48 prefix. Similar to EIGRP for IPv4, R3 includes a summary route to null0 as a loop prevention mechanism.

The reception of the manual summary route can be verified by examining the routing table of the other routers in the routing domain. Figure 4 shows the 2001:DB8:ACAD::/48 route in the IPv6 routing table of R1.

Refer to **Packet Tracer Activity** for this chapter

5.1.2.5   Packet Tracer - Configuring EIGRP Manual Summary Routes for IPv4 and IPv6

In this activity, you will calculate and configure summary routes for the IPv4 and IPv6 networks. EIGRP is already configured; however, you are required to configure IPv4 and IPv6 summary routes on the specified interfaces. EIGRP will replace the current routes with a more specific summary route thereby reducing the size of the routing tables.

Refer to **Online Course** for Illustration

5.1.3   Default Route Propagation

5.1.3.1   Propagating a Default Static Route

Propagating a Default Static Route

Using a static route to 0.0.0.0/0 as a default route is not routing protocol-dependent. The "quad zero" static default route can be used with any currently supported routing protocols. The static default route is usually configured on the router that has a connection to a network outside the EIGRP routing domain; for example, to an ISP.

In Figure 1, R2 is the gateway router connecting the EIGRP routing domain with the Internet. When the static default route is configured, it is necessary to propagate that route throughout the EIGRP domain, as shown in Figure 2.

One method of propagating a static default route within the EIGRP routing domain is by using the `redistribute static` command. The `redistribute static` command tells EIGRP to include static routes in its EIGRP updates to other routers. Figure 3 shows the configuration of the static default route and the `redistribute static` command on router R2.

Figure 4 verifies that the default route has been received by router R2 and installed in its IPv4 routing table.

In Figure 5, the `show ip protocols` command verifies that R2 is redistributing static routes within the EIGRP routing domain.

Refer to
Online Course
for Illustration

5.1.3.2   Verifying the Propagated Default Route

The figure displays a portion of the IPv4 routing tables for R1 and R3.

In the routing tables for R1 and R3, notice the routing source and administrative distance for the new default route learned using EIGRP. The entry for the EIGRP learned default route is identified by the following:

- **D** - This route was learned from an EIGRP routing update.

- ***** - The route is a candidate for a default route.

- **EX** - The route is an external EIGRP route, in this case a static route outside of the EIGRP routing domain.

- **170** - This is the administrative distance of an external EIGRP route.

Notice that R1 selects R3 as the successor to the default route because it has a lower feasible distance. Default routes provide a default path to outside the routing domain and, like summary routes, minimize the number of entries in the routing table.

Refer to
Online Course
for Illustration

5.1.3.3   EIGRP for IPv6: Default Route

Recall that EIGRP maintains separate tables for IPv4 and IPv6; therefore, an IPv6 default route must be propagated separately, as shown in Figure 1. Similar to EIGRP for IPv4, a default static route is configured on the gateway router (R2), as shown in Figure 2:

```
R2(config)# ipv6 route ::/0 serial 0/1/0
```

The ::/0 prefix and prefix-length is equivalent to the 0.0.0.0 0.0.0.0 address and subnet mask used in IPv4. Both are all-zero addresses with a /0 prefix-length.

The IPv6 default static route is redistributed into the EIGRP for IPv6 domain using the same **redistribute static** command used in EIGRP for IPv4.

Note   Some IOSs may require that the **redistribute static** command include the EIGRP metric parameters before the static route can be redistributed.

Verifying Propagation of Default Route

The propagation of the IPv6 static default route can be verified by examining R1's IPv6 routing table using the **show ipv6 route** command, as shown in Figure 3. Notice that the successor or next-hop address is not R2, but R3. This is because R3 provides a better path to R2, at a lower cost metric than R1.

Refer to **Packet
Tracer Activity**
for this chapter

5.1.3.4   Packet Tracer - Propagating a Default Route in EIGRP for IPv4 and IPv6

In this activity, you will configure and propagate a default route in EIGRP for IPv4 and IPv6 networks. EIGRP is already configured. However, you are required to configure an IPv4 and an IPv6 default route. Then, you will configure the EIGRP routing process to propagate the default route to downstream EIGRP neighbors. Finally, you will verify the default routes by pinging hosts outside the EIGRP routing domain.

Refer to
Online Course
for Illustration

5.1.4   Fine-tuning EIGRP Interfaces

5.1.4.1   EIGRP Bandwidth Utilization

EIGRP Bandwidth for IPv4

By default, EIGRP uses only up to 50 percent of an interface's bandwidth for EIGRP information. This prevents the EIGRP process from over-utilizing a link and not allowing enough bandwidth for the routing of normal traffic.

Use the **ip bandwidth-percent eigrp** command to configure the percentage of bandwidth that can be used by EIGRP on an interface.

```
Router(config-if)# ip bandwidth-percent eigrp as-number percent
```

In Figure 1, R1 and R2 share a very slow 64 kb/s link. The configuration to limit how much bandwidth EIGRP uses is shown, along with the **bandwidth** command. The **ip bandwidth-percent eigrp** command uses the amount of configured bandwidth (or the default bandwidth) when calculating the percent that EIGRP can use. In this example, EIGRP is limited to no more than 50 percent of the link's bandwidth, as shown in Figure 2. Therefore, EIGRP never uses more the 32 kb/s of the link' bandwidth for EIGRP packet traffic.

To restore the default value, use the **no** form of this command.

Use the Syntax Checker in Figure 3 to limit the bandwidth used by EIGRP between R2 and R3, to 75 percent of the link's bandwidth.

EIGRP Bandwidth for IPv6

To configure the percentage of bandwidth that can be used by EIGRP for IPv6 on an interface, use the **ipv6 bandwidth-percent eigrp** command in interface configuration mode. To restore the default value, use the **no** form of this command.

```
Router(config-if)# ipv6 bandwidth-percent eigrp as-number percent
```

Figure 4 shows the configuration of the interfaces between R1 and R2 to limit the bandwidth used by EIGRP for IPv6.

Refer to
Online Course
for Illustration

5.1.4.2   Hello and Hold Timers

Hello Intervals and Hold times with EIGRP for IPv4

EIGRP uses a lightweight Hello protocol to establish and monitor the connection status its neighbor. The Hold time tells the router the maximum time that the router should wait to receive the next Hello before declaring that neighbor as unreachable.

Hello intervals and Hold times are configurable on a per-interface basis and do not have to match with other EIGRP routers to establish or maintain adjacencies. The command to configure a different Hello interval is:

```
Router(config-if)# ip hello-interval eigrp as-number seconds
```

If the Hello interval is changed, ensure that the Hold time value is equal to, or greater than, the Hello interval. Otherwise, neighbor adjacency goes down after the Hold time expires and before the next Hello interval. Use the following command to configure a different Hold time:

```
Router(config-if)# ip hold-time eigrp as-number seconds
```

The *seconds* value for both Hello and Hold time intervals can range from 1 to 65,535.

Figure 1 shows the configuration of R1 to use a 60-second Hello interval and 180-second Hold time. The **no** form can be used on both of these commands to restore the default values.

The Hello interval time and Hold time do not need to match for two routers to form an EIGRP adjacency.

Use the Syntax Checker in Figure 2 to configure the adjacent interface on R2 with the same values as R1.

Hello Intervals and Hold times with EIGRP for IPv6

EIGRP for IPv6 uses the same Hello interval and Hold times as EIGRP for IPv4. The interface configuration mode commands are similar to those for IPv4:

```
Router(config-if)# ipv6 hello-interval eigrp as-number seconds
Router(config-if)# ipv6 hold-time eigrp as-number seconds
```

Figure 3 shows the Hello interval and Hold times configurations for R1 and R2 with EIGRP for IPv6.

5.1.4.3 Load Balancing IPv4

Refer to
Online Course
for Illustration

Equal-cost load balancing is the ability of a router to distribute outbound traffic using all interfaces that have the same metric from the destination address. Load balancing uses network segments and bandwidth more efficiently. For IP, Cisco IOS Software applies load balancing using up to four equal-cost paths by default.

Figure 1 shows the EIGRP for IPv4 network topology. In this topology, R3 has two EIGRP equal-cost routes for the network between R1 and R2, 172.16.3.0/30. One route is via R1 at 192.168.10.4/30 and the other route is via R2 at 192.168.10.8/30.

The **show ip protocols** command can be used to verify the number of equal-cost paths currently configured on the router. The output in Figure 2 shows that R3 is using the default of four equal-cost paths.

The routing table maintains both routes. Figure 3 shows that R3 has two EIGRP equal-cost routes for the 172.16.3.0/30 network. One route is via R1 at 192.168.10.5 and the other route is via R2 at 192.168.10.9. Looking at the topology in Figure 1, it may seem as if the path via R1 is the better route because there is a 1544 kb/s link between R3 and R1, whereas the link to R2 is only a 1024 kb/s link. However, EIGRP only uses the slowest bandwidth in its composite metric which is the 64 Kb/s link between R1 and R2. Both paths have the same 64 Kb/s link as the slowest bandwidth, this results in both paths being equal.

When a packet is process-switched, load balancing over equal-cost paths occurs on a per-packet basis. When packets are fast-switched, load balancing over equal-cost paths occurs on a per-destination basis. Cisco Express Forwarding (CEF) can perform both per packet and per-destination load balancing.

Cisco IOS, by default, allows load balancing using up to four equal-cost paths; however, this can be modified. Using the **maximum-paths** router configuration mode command, up to 32 equal-cost routes can be kept in the routing table.

```
Router(config-router)# maximum-paths value
```

The *value* argument refers to the number of paths that should be maintained for load balancing. If the value is set to **1**, load balancing is disabled.

Refer to
Online Course
for Illustration

5.1.4.4   Load Balancing IPv6

Figure 1 shows the EIGRP for IPv6 network topology. The serial links in the topology have the same bandwidth that is used in the EIGRP for IPv4 topology.

Similar to the previous scenario for IPv4, R3 has two EIGRP equal-cost routes for the network between R1 and R2, 2001:DB8:CAFE:A001::/64. One route is via R1 at FE80::1 and the other route is via R2 at FE80::2.

Figure 2 shows that the EIGRP metrics are the same in the IPv6 routing table and in the IPv4 routing table for the 2001:DB8:CAFE:A001::/64 and 172.16.3.0/30 networks. This is because the EIGRP composite metric is the same for both EIGRP for IPv6 and for IPv4.

Note   EIGRP for IPv4 and IPv6 can also balance traffic across multiple routes that have different metrics. This type of balancing is called unequal-cost load balancing.

Refer to
Interactive Graphic
in online course.

5.1.4.5   Activity - Determine the EIGRP Fine Tuning Commands

Refer to
Online Course
for Illustration

5.1.5   Secure EIGRP

5.1.5.1   Routing Protocol Authentication Overview

Routing Protocol Authentication

Network administrators must be aware that routers are at risk from attack just as much as end-user devices. Anyone with a packet sniffer, such as Wireshark, can read information propagating between routers. In general, routing systems can be attacked through the disruption of peer devices or the falsification of routing information.

Disruption of peers is the less critical of the two attacks because routing protocols heal themselves, making the disruption last only slightly longer than the attack itself.

The falsification of routing information is a more subtle class of attack that targets the information carried within the routing protocol. The consequences of falsifying routing information are as follows:

- Redirect traffic to create routing loops

- Redirect traffic to monitor on an insecure line

- Redirect traffic to discard it

A method to protect routing information on the network is to authenticate routing protocol packets using the Message Digest 5 (MD5) algorithm. MD5 allows the routers to compare signatures that should all be the same, confirming that it is from a credible source.

The three components of such a system include:

- Encryption algorithm, which is generally public knowledge

- Key used in the encryption algorithm, which is a secret shared by the routers authenticating their packets

- Contents of the packet itself

In the figure, click the Play button to view an animation of how each router authenticates the routing information. Generally, the originator of the routing information produces a signature using the key and routing data it is about to send as inputs to the encryption algorithm. The router receiving the routing data can then repeat the process using the same key and the same routing data it has received. If the signature the receiver computes is the same as the signature, the sender computes the update is authenticated and considered reliable.

Routing protocols such as RIPv2, EIGRP, OSPF, IS-IS, and BGP all support various forms of MD5 authentication.

Refer to
Online Course
for Illustration

5.1.5.2 Configuring EIGRP with MD5 Authentication

EIGRP message authentication ensures that routers only accept routing messages from other routers that know the same pre-shared key. Without authentication configured, if an unauthorized person introduces another router with different or conflicting route information on the network, the routing tables on the legitimate routers can become corrupt and a DoS attack may ensue. Thus, when authentication is added to the EIGRP messages sent between routers, it prevents someone from purposely, or accidentally, adding another router to the network and causing a problem.

EIGRP supports routing protocol authentication using MD5. The configuration of EIGRP message authentication consists of two steps: the creation of a key chain and key, and the configuration of EIGRP authentication to use that keychain and key.

Step 1.   Create a Key Chain and KeyRouting authentication requires a key on a keychain to function. Before authentication can be enabled, create a keychain and at least one key.

a.   In global configuration mode, create the key chain. Although multiple keys can be configured, this section focuses on the use of a single key.

```
Router(config)# key chain name-of-chain
```

b.   Specify the key ID. The key ID is the number used to identify an authentication key within a key chain. The range of keys is from 0 to 2,147,483,647. It is recommended that the key number be the same on all routers in the configuration.

```
Router(config-keychain)# key key-id
```

c.   Specify the key string for the key. The key string is similar to a password. Routers exchanging authentication keys must be configured using the same key string.

```
Router(config-keychain-key )# key-string key-string-text
```

Step 2.   Configure EIGRP Authentication Using Key Chain and KeyConfigure EIGRP to perform message authentication with the previously defined key. Complete this configuration on all interfaces enabled for EIGRP.

a.   a. In global configuration mode, specify the interface on which to configure EIGRP message authentication.

```
Router(config)# interface type number
```

b. b. Enable EIGRP message authentication. The **md5** keyword indicates that the MD5 hash is to be used for authentication.

```
Router(config-if)# ip authentication mode eigrp as-number md5
```

c. c. Specify the keychain that should be used for authentication. The *name-of-chain* argument specifies the key chain that was created in Step 1.

```
Router(config-if)# ip authentication key-chain eigrp as-number name-of-chain
```

Each key has its own key ID, which is stored locally. The combination of the key ID and the interface associated with the message uniquely identifies the authentication algorithm and MD5 authentication key in use. The key chain and the routing update are processed using the MD5 algorithm to produce a unique signature.

Refer to
Online Course
for Illustration

5.1.5.3   EIGRP Authentication Example

To authenticate routing updates, all EIGRP-enabled interfaces must be configured to support authentication. Figure 1 shows the IPv4 topology and which interfaces are configured with authentication.

Figure 2 shows the configuration for router R1 using the **EIGRP_KEY** key chain and the **cisco123** key string. After R1 is configured, the other routers receive authenticated routing updates. Adjacencies are lost until the neighbors are configured with routing protocol authentication.

Figure 3 shows a similar configuration for router R2. Notice that the same key string, **cisco123**, is used to authenticate information with R1 and ultimately R3.

Use the Syntax Checker in Figure 4 to configure EIGRP authentication for R3.

Configuring EIGRP for IPv6 Authentication

The algorithms and the configuration to authenticate EIGRP for IPv6 messages are the same as EIGRP for IPv4. The only difference is the interface configuration mode commands use **ipv6**, instead of **ip**.

```
Router(config-if)# ipv6 authentication mode eigrp as-number md5
Router(config-if)# ipv6 authentication key-chain eigrp as-number name-of-chain
```

Figure 5 shows the commands to configure EIGRP for IPv6 authentication on router R1 using the **EIGRP_IPV6_KEY** key chain and the **cisco123** key string. Similar configurations would be entered on R2 and R3.

Refer to
Online Course
for Illustration

5.1.5.4   Verify Authentication

After EIGRP message authentication is configured on one router, any adjacent neighbors that have not yet been configured for authentication are no longer EIGRP neighbors. For example, when R1's Serial 0/0/0 interface was configured for MD5 authentication, but R2 had not yet been configured, the following IOS message appeared on R1:

```
%DUAL-5-NBRCHANGE: EIGRP-IPv4 1: Neighbor 172.16.3.2 (Serial0/0/0) is down: authentication mode changed
```

When the adjacent Serial 0/0/0 interface on R2 is configured, the adjacency is re-established and the following IOS message is displayed on R1:

```
%DUAL-5-NBRCHANGE: EIGRP-IPv4 1: Neighbor 172.16.3.2 (Serial0/0/0) is up: new ad-
jacency
```

Similar messages are also displayed on R2.

Adjacencies are only formed when both connecting devices have authentication configured, as shown in Figure 1. To verify that the correct EIGRP adjacencies were formed after being configured for authentication, use the **show ip eigrp neighbors** command on each router. Figure 2 shows that all three routers have re-established neighbor adjacencies after being configured for EIGRP authentication.

To verify the neighbor adjacencies EIGRP for IPv6, use the **show ipv6 eigrp neighbors** command.

Refer to
Lab Activity
for this chapter

5.1.5.5   Lab - Configuring Advanced EIGRP for IPv4 Features
In this lab, you will complete the following objectives:

- Part 1: Build the Network and Configure Basic Device Settings

- Part 2: Configure EIGRP and Verify Connectivity

- Part 3: Configure Summarization for EIGRP

- Part 4: Propagate a Default Route

- Part 5: Fine-Tune EIGRP

- Part 6: Configure EIGRP Authentication

Refer to
Online Course
for Illustration

5.2   Troubleshoot EIGRP

5.2.1   Components of Troubleshooting EIGRP

5.2.1.1   Basic EIGRP Troubleshooting Commands

EIGRP is commonly used in large enterprise networks. Troubleshooting problems related to the exchange of routing information is an essential skill for a network administrator. This is particularly true for administrators who are involved in the implementation and maintenance of large, routed enterprise networks that use EIGRP as the IGP. There are several commands that are useful when troubleshooting an EIGRP network.

The **show ip eigrp neighbors** command verifies that the router recognizes its neighbors. The output in Figure 1 indicates two successful EIGRP neighbor adjacencies on R1.

In Figure 2, the **show ip route** command verifies that the router learned the route to a remote network through EIGRP. The output shows that R1 has learned about four remote networks through EIGRP.

Figure 3 shows the output from the **show ip protocols** command. This command verifies that the EIGRP displays the currently configured values for various properties of any enabled routing protocols.

EIGRP for IPv6

Similar commands and troubleshooting criteria also apply to EIGRP for IPv6.

The following are the equivalent commands used with EIGRP for IPv6:

- Router# **show ipv6 eigrp neighbors**

- Router# **show ipv6 route**

- Router# **show ipv6 protocols**

Refer to
Online Course
for Illustration

5.2.1.2   Components

The figure shows a flowchart for diagnosing EIGRP connectivity issues.

After configuring EIGRP, the first step is to test connectivity to the remote network. If the ping fails, confirm the EIGRP neighbor adjacencies. Neighbor adjacency might not be formed for a number of reasons, including the following:

- The interface between the devices is down.

- The two routers have mismatching EIGRP autonomous system numbers (process IDs).

- Proper interfaces are not enabled for the EIGRP process.

- An interface is configured as passive.

Aside from these issues, there are a number of other, more advanced issues that can cause neighbor adjacencies to not be formed. Two examples are misconfigured EIGRP authentication or mismatched K values, which EIGRP uses to calculate its metric.

If the EIGRP neighbor adjacency is formed between the two routers, but there is still a connection issue, there may be a routing problem. Some issues that may cause a connectivity problem for EIGRP include:

- Proper networks are not being advertised on remote routers.

- An incorrectly-configured passive interface, or an ACL, is blocking advertisements of remote networks.

- Autosummarization is causing inconsistent routing in a discontiguous network.

If all of the required routes are in the routing table, but the path that traffic takes is not correct, verify the interface bandwidth values.

Refer to
Interactive Graphic
in online course.

5.2.1.3   Activity - Identify the Troubleshooting Command

Refer to
Online Course
for Illustration

5.2.2   Troubleshoot EIGRP Neighbor Issues

5.2.2.1   Layer 3 Connectivity

A prerequisite for a neighbor adjacency to form between two directly connected routers is Layer 3 connectivity. By examining the output of the **show ip interface brief** command, a network administrator can verify that the status and protocol of connecting interfaces are up. A ping from one router to another, directly connected router, should confirm IPv4 connectivity between the devices. The figure displays the `show ip interface brief` command output for R1. R1 shows connectivity to R2, and pings are successful.

If the ping is unsuccessful, check the cabling and verify that the interfaces on connected devices are on a common subnet. A log message that states that EIGRP neighbors are `not on common subnet` indicates that there is an incorrect IPv4 address on one of the two EIGRP neighbor interfaces.

EIGRP for IPv6

Similar commands and troubleshooting criteria also apply to EIGRP for IPv6.

The equivalent command used with EIGRP for IPv6 is `show ipv6 interface brief`.

Refer to
Online Course
for Illustration

5.2.2.2 EIGRP Parameters

When troubleshooting an EIGRP network, one of the first things to verify is that all routers that are participating in the EIGRP network are configured with the same autonomous system number. The **router eigrp** *as-number* command starts the EIGRP process and is followed by a number that is the autonomous system number. The value of the `as-number` argument must be the same in all routers that are in the EIGRP routing domain.

Figure 1 shows that all routers should be participating in autonomous system number 1. In Figure 2, the `show ip protocols` command verifies that R1, R2, and R3 all use the same autonomous system number.

EIGRP for IPv6

Similar commands and troubleshooting criteria also apply to EIGRP for IPv6.

The following are the equivalent commands used with EIGRP for IPv6:

- Router(config)# **ipv6 router eigrp** *as-number*

- Router# **show ipv6 protocols**

Note   At the top of the output, "IP Routing is NSF aware" refers to Nonstop Forwarding (NSF). This capability allows the EIGRP peers of a failing router to retain the routing information that it has advertised, and to continue using this information until the failed router resumes normal operation and is able to exchange routing information. For more information refer to: http://www.cisco.com/en/US/docs/ios-xml/ios/iproute_eigrp/configuration/15-mt/eigrp-nsf-awa.html

Refer to
Online Course
for Illustration

5.2.2.3 EIGRP Interfaces

In addition to verifying the autonomous system number, it is necessary to verify that all interfaces are participating in the EIGRP network. The `network` command that is configured under the EIGRP routing process indicates which router interfaces participates in EIGRP. This command is applied to the classful network address of the interface or to a subnet when the wildcard mask is included.

In Figure 1, the `show ip eigrp interfaces` command displays which interfaces are enabled for EIGRP on R1. If connected interfaces are not enabled for EIGRP, then neighbors do not form an adjacency.

In Figure 2, the "Routing for Networks" section of the `show ip protocols` command indicates which networks have been configured; any interfaces in those networks participate in EIGRP.

If the network is not present in this section, use `show running-config` to ensure that the proper `network` command was configured.

In Figure 3, the output from the `show running-config` command confirms that any interfaces with these addresses, or a subnet of these addresses, are enabled for EIGRP.

EIGRP for IPv6

Similar commands and troubleshooting criteria also apply to EIGRP for IPv6.

The following are the equivalent commands used with EIGRP for IPv6:

- Router# `show ipv6 protocols`

- Router# `show ipv6 eigrp interfaces`

Refer to **Interactive Graphic** in online course.

5.2.2.4 Activity - Troubleshoot EIGRP Neighbor Issues

Refer to **Online Course** for Illustration

5.2.3 Troubleshoot EIGRP Routing Table Issues

5.2.3.1 Passive Interface

One reason that route tables may not reflect the correct routes is due to the `passive-interface` command. With EIGRP running on a network, the `passive-interface` command stops both outgoing and incoming routing updates. For this reason, routers do not become neighbors.

To verify whether any interface on a router is configured as passive, use the `show ip protocols` command in privileged EXEC mode. Figure 1 shows that R2's GigabitEthernet 0/0 interface is configured as a passive interface, because there are no neighbors on that link.

In addition to being configured on interfaces that have no neighbors, a passive interface can be enabled on interfaces for security purposes. In Figure 2, notice that the shading for the EIGRP routing domain is different from previous topologies. The 209.165.200.224/27 network is now included in the R2's EIGRP updates. However, for security reasons, the network administrator does not want R2 to form an EIGRP neighbor adjacency with the ISP router.

Figure 3 shows the addition of the 209.165.200.224/27 `network` command on R2. R2 now advertises this network to the other routers in the EIGRP routing domain.

The `passive-interface` router configuration mode command is configured on Serial 0/1/0 to prevent R2's EIGRP updates from being sent to the ISP router. The `show ip eigrp neighbors` command on R2 verifies that R2 has not established a neighbor adjacency with ISP.

Figure 4 shows that R1 has an EIGRP route to the 209.165.200.224/27 network in its IPv4 routing table (R3 will also have an EIGRP route to that network in its IPv4 routing table). However, R2 does not have a neighbor adjacency with the ISP router.

EIGRP for IPv6

Similar commands and troubleshooting criteria also apply to EIGRP for IPv6.

The following are the equivalent commands used with EIGRP for IPv6:

- Router# **show ipv6 protocols**
- Router(config-rtr)# **passive-interface** *type number*

Refer to **Online Course** for Illustration

5.2.3.2   Missing Network Statement

Figure 1 shows that R1's GigabitEthernet 0/1 interface has now been configured with the 10.10.10.1/24 address and is active.

R1 and R3 still have their neighbor adjacency, but a ping test from the R3 router to a R1's G0/1 interface of 10.10.10.1 is unsuccessful. Figure 2 shows a failed connectivity test from R3 to the destination network of 10.10.10.0/24.

In Figure 3, using the **show ip protocols** on the R1 router shows that the network 10.10.10.0/24 is not advertised to EIGRP neighbors.

As shown in Figure 4, R1's EIGRP process is configured to include the advertisement of the 10.10.10.0/24 network.

Figure 5 shows that there is now a route in R3's routing table for the 10.10.10.0/24 network and reachability is verified by pinging R1's GigabitEthernet 0/1 interface.

EIGRP for IPv6

Similar commands and troubleshooting criteria also apply to EIGRP for IPv6.

The following are the equivalent commands used with EIGRP for IPv6:

- Router# **show ipv6 protocols**
- Router# **show ipv6 route**
- Router(config-rtr)# **network** *ipv6-prefix/prefix-length*

Note   Another form of missing route may result from the router filtering inbound or outbound routing updates. ACLs provide filtering for different protocols, and these ACLs may affect the exchange of the routing protocol messages that cause routes to be absent from the routing table. The **show ip protocols** command shows whether there are any ACLs that are applied to EIGRP.

Refer to **Online Course** for Illustration

5.2.3.3   Autosummarization

Another issue that may create problems for the network administrator is EIGRP autosummarization.

Figure 1 shows a different network topology than what has been used throughout this chapter. There is no connection between R1 and R3. R1's LAN has the network address 10.10.10.0/24, while R3's LAN is 10.20.20.0/24. The serial connections between both routers and R2 have the same bandwidth of 1024 kb/s.

R1 and R3 have their LAN and serial interfaces enabled for EIGRP, as shown in Figure 2. Both routers perform EIGRP autosummarization .

EIGRP for IPv4 can be configured to automatically summarize routes at classful boundaries. If there are discontiguous networks, autosummarization causes inconsistent routing.

In Figure 3, R2's routing table shows that it does not receive individual routes for the 10.10.10.0/24 and 10.20.20.0/24 subnets. Both R1 and R3 automatically summarized those subnets to the 10.0.0.0/8 classful boundary when sending EIGRP update packets to R2. The result is that R2 has two equal-cost routes to 10.0.0.0/8 in the routing table, which can result in inaccurate routing and packet loss. Depending upon whether per-packet, per-destination, or CEF load balancing is being used, packets may or may not be forwarded out the proper interface.

In Figure 4, the `show ip protocols` command verifies that autosummarization is performed on both R1 and R3. Notice that both routers summarize the 10.0.0.0/8 network using the same metric.

The `auto-summary` command is disabled by default on Cisco IOS Software versions of 15 and newer versions of 12.2(33). By default, older software has autosummarization enabled. To disable autosummarization, enter the `no auto-summary` command in `router EIGRP` configuration mode.

To correct this problem, R1 and R3 have autosummarization disabled:

```
R1(config)# router eigrp 1
R1(config-router)# no auto-summary
R3(config)# router eigrp 1
R3(config-router)# no auto-summary
```

After autosummarization has been disabled on R1 and R3, R2's routing table now indicates that it receives the individual 10.10.10.0/24 and 10.20.20.0/24 subnets from R1 and R3, respectively, as shown in Figure 5. Accurate routing and connectivity to both subnets is now restored.

EIGRP for IPv6

Classful networks do not exist in IPv6; therefore EIGRP for IPv6 does not support autosummarization. All summarization must be accomplished using EIGRP manual summary routes.

Refer to Interactive Graphic in online course.

5.2.3.4   Activity - Troubleshoot EIGRP Routing Table Issues

Refer to Packet Tracer Activity for this chapter

5.2.3.5   Packet Tracer - Troubleshooting EIGRP for IPv4

In this activity, you will troubleshoot EIGRP neighbor issues. Use show commands to identify errors in the network configuration. Then, you will document the errors you discover and implement an appropriate solution. Finally, you will verify full end-to-end connectivity is restored.

Refer to Lab Activity for this chapter

5.2.3.6   Lab - Troubleshooting Basic EIGRP for IPv4 and IPv6

In this lab, you will complete the following objectives:

■ Part 1: Build the Network and Load Device Configurations

■ Part 2: Troubleshoot Layer 3 Connectivity

- Part 3: Troubleshoot EIGRP for IPv4
- Part 4: Troubleshoot EIGRP for IPv6

Refer to
Lab Activity
for this chapter

5.2.3.7 Lab - Troubleshooting Advanced EIGRP
In this lab, you will complete the following objectives:

- Part 1: Build the Network and Load Device Configurations
- Part 2: Troubleshoot EIGRP

Refer to
Online Course
for Illustration

Refer to
Lab Activity
for this chapter

5.3 Summary

5.3.1.1 Class Activity - Tweaking EIGRP
Scenario

The purpose of this activity is to review EIGRP routing protocol fine-tuning concepts.

You will work with a partner to design one EIGRP topology. This topology is the basis for two parts of the activity. The first uses default settings for all configurations and the second incorporates, at least, three of the following fine-tuning EIGRP options:

- Manual summary route
- Default routes
- Default routes propagation
- Hello interval timer settings

Refer to the labs, Packet Tracer activities, and interactive activities to help you as you progress through this modeling activity.

Directions are listed on the PDF file for this activity. Share your completed work with another group. You may want to save a copy of this activity to a portfolio.

Refer to **Packet Tracer Activity** for this chapter

5.3.1.2 Packet Tracer - Skills Integration Challenge
In this activity, you are tasked with implementing EIGRP for IPv4 and IPv6 on two separate networks. Your task includes enabling EIGRP, assigning router-IDs, changing the Hello timers, configuring EIGRP summary routes, and limiting EIGRP advertisements.

Refer to
Online Course
for Illustration

5.3.1.3 Summary
EIGRP is one of the routing protocols commonly used in large enterprise networks. Modifying EIGRP features and troubleshooting problems is one of the most essential skills for a network engineer involved in the implementation and maintenance of large routed enterprise networks that use EIGRP.

Summarization decreases the number of entries in routing updates and lowers the number of entries in local routing tables. It also reduces bandwidth utilization for routing updates and results in faster routing table lookups. EIGRP for IPv4 autosummarization is disabled by default beginning with Cisco IOS Release 15.0(1)M and 12.2(33). Prior to this, autosummarization was enabled by default. To enable autosummarization for EIGRP use the **auto-summary** command in router configuration mode. Use the **show ip protocols** command to verify the status of autosummarization. Examine the routing table to verify that autosummarization is working.

EIGRP automatically includes summary routes to Null0 to prevent routing loops that are included in the summary but do not actually exist in the routing table. The Null0 interface is a virtual IOS interface that is a route to nowhere, commonly known as "the bit bucket." Packets that match a route with a Null0 exit interface are discarded.

To establish EIGRP manual summarization on a specific EIGRP interface, use the following interface configuration mode command:

```
Router(config-if)# ip summary-address eigrp as-number network-address subnet-mask
```

To configure EIGRP for IPv6 manual summarization on a specific EIGRP interface, use the following interface configuration mode command:

```
Router(config-if)# ipv6 summary-address eigrp as-number prefix/prefix-length
```

One method of propagating a default route within the EIGRP routing domain is to use the **redistribute static** command. This command tells EIGRP to include this static route in its EIGRP updates to other routers. The **show ip protocols** command verifies that static routes within the EIGRP routing domain are being redistributed.

Use the **ip bandwidth-percent eigrp** as-number percent interface configuration mode command to configure the percentage of bandwidth that can be used by EIGRP on an interface.

To configure the percentage of bandwidth that can be used by EIGRP for IPv6 on an interface, use the **ipv6 bandwidth-percent eigrp** command in interface configuration mode. To restore the default value, use the **no** form of this command.

Hello intervals and Hold times are configurable on a per-interface basis in EIGRP and do not have to match with other EIGRP routers to establish or maintain adjacencies.

For IP in EIGRP, Cisco IOS software applies load balancing using up to four equal-cost paths by default. With the **maximum-paths** router configuration mode command, up to 32 equal-cost routes can be kept in the routing table.

EIGRP supports routing protocol authentication using MD5. The algorithms and the configuration to authenticate EIGRP for IPv4 messages are the same as EIGRP for IPv6. The only difference is that the interface configuration mode commands use **ip**, instead of **ipv6**.

```
Router(config-if)# ipv6 authentication mode eigrp as-number md5
Router(config-if)# ipv6 authentication key-chain eigrp as-number name-of-chain
```

To verify that the correct EIGRP adjacencies were formed after being configured for authentication, use the **show ip eigrp neighbors** command on each router.

The **show ip route** command verifies that the router learned EIGRP routes. The **show ip protocols** command is used to verify that EIGRP displays the currently configured values.

Go to the online course to take the quiz and exam.

Chapter 5 Quiz

This quiz is designed to provide an additional opportunity to practice the skills and knowledge presented in the chapter and to prepare for the chapter exam. You will be allowed multiple attempts and the grade does not appear in the gradebook.

Chapter 5 Exam

The chapter exam assesses your knowledge of the chapter content.

Your Chapter Notes

Single-Area OSPF

6.0 Single-Area OSPF

6.0.1.1 Introduction

Open Shortest Path First (OSPF) is a link-state routing protocol that was developed as a replacement for the distance vector routing protocol, RIP. RIP was an acceptable routing protocol in the early days of networking and the Internet. However, RIP's reliance on hop count as the only metric for determining best route quickly became problematic. Using hop count does not scale well in larger networks with multiple paths of varying speeds. OSPF has significant advantages over RIP in that it offers faster convergence and scales to much larger network implementations.

OSPF is a classless routing protocol that uses the concept of areas for scalability. This chapter covers basic, single-area OSPF implementations and configurations.

Refer to **Lab Activity** for this chapter

6.0.1.2 Class Activity - Can Submarines Swim?

Activity - Can Submarines Swim?

Scenario

Edsger Wybe Dijkstra was a famous computer programmer and theoretical physicist. One of his most famous quotes was: "The question of whether computers can think is like the question of whether submarines can swim." Dijkstra's work has been applied, among other things, to routing protocols. He created the Shortest Path First (SPF) algorithm for network routing.

Now, open the PDF provided with this activity and answer the reflection questions. Save your work.

Get together with two of your classmates to compare your answers.

After completing this activity, do you have an idea as to how the OSPF protocol may work?

Refer to **Online Course** for Illustration

6.1 Characteristics of OSPF

6.1.1 Open Shortest Path First

6.1.1.1 Evolution of OSPF

As shown in Figure 1, OSPF version 2 (OSPFv2) is available for IPv4 while OSPF version 3 (OSPFv3) is available for IPv6.

Click the dates in Figure 2 to see historical events related to OSPF.

The initial development of OSPF began in 1987 by the Internet Engineering Task Force (IETF) OSPF Working Group. At that time, the Internet was largely an academic and research network funded by the U.S. government.

In 1989, the specification for OSPFv1 was published in RFC 1131. Two implementations were written. One implementation was developed to run on routers and the other to run on UNIX workstations. The latter implementation became a widespread UNIX process known as GATED. OSPFv1 was an experimental routing protocol and was never deployed.

In 1991, OSPFv2 was introduced in RFC 1247 by John Moy. OSPFv2 offered significant technical improvements over OSPFv1. It is classless by design; therefore, it supports VLSM and CIDR.

At the same time the OSPF was introduced, ISO was working on a link-state routing protocol of their own, Intermediate System-to-Intermediate System (IS-IS). IETF chose OSPF as their recommended Interior Gateway Protocol (IGP).

In 1998, the OSPFv2 specification was updated in RFC 2328, which remains the current RFC for OSPF.

In 1999, OSPFv3 for IPv6 was published in RFC 2740. OSPF for IPv6, created by John Moy, Rob Coltun, and Dennis Ferguson, is not only a new protocol implementation for IPv6, but also a major rewrite of the operation of the protocol.

In 2008, OSPFv3 was updated in RFC 5340 as OSPF for IPv6.

Note   In this chapter, unless explicitly identified as OSPFv2 or OSPFv3, the term OSPF is used to indicate concepts that are shared by both.

Refer to **Online Course** for Illustration

6.1.1.2   Features of OSPF

OSPF features, as shown in Figure 1, include:

- **Classless** - It is classless by design; therefore, it supports VLSM and CIDR.

- **Efficient** - Routing changes trigger routing updates (no periodic updates). It uses the SPF algorithm to choose the best path.

- **Fast convergence** - It quickly propagates network changes.

- **Scalable** - It works well in small and large network sizes. Routers can be grouped into areas to support a hierarchical system.

- **Secure** - It supports Message Digest 5 (MD5) authentication. When enabled, OSPF routers only accept encrypted routing updates from peers with the same pre-shared password.

Administrative distance (AD) is the trustworthiness (or preference) of the route source. OSPF has a default administrative distance of 110. As shown in Figure 2, OSPF is preferred over IS-IS and RIP.

Refer to **Online Course** for Illustration

6.1.1.3   Components of OSPF

All routing protocols share similar components. They all use routing protocol messages to exchange route information. The messages help build data structures, which are then processed using a routing algorithm.

The three main components of the OSPF routing protocol include:

Data Structures

OSPF creates and maintains three databases: (see Figure 1).

- **Adjacency database** - Creates the neighbor table
- **Link-state database (LSDB)** - Creates the topology table
- **Forwarding database** - Creates the routing table

These tables contain a list of neighboring routers to exchange routing information with and are kept and maintained in RAM.

Routing Protocol Messages

OSPF exchanges messages to convey routing information using five types of packets. These packets, as shown in Figure 2, are:

- Hello packet
- Database description packet
- Link-state request packet
- Link-state update packet
- Link-state acknowledgment packet

These packets are used to discover neighboring routers and also to exchange routing information to maintain accurate information about the network.

Algorithm

The CPU processes the neighbor and topology tables using Dijkstra's SPF algorithm. The SPF algorithm is based on the cumulative cost to reach a destination.

The SPF algorithm creates an SPF tree by placing each router at the root of the tree and calculating the shortest path to each node. The SPF tree is then used to calculate the best routes. OSPF places the best routes into the forwarding database, which is used to make the routing table.

Refer to
Online Course
for Illustration

6.1.1.4   Link-State Operation

To maintain routing information, OSPF routers complete the following generic link-state routing process to reach a state of convergence:

1. Establish Neighbor Adjacencies (Figure 1) - OSPF-enabled routers must recognize each other on the network before they can share information. An OSPF-enabled router sends Hello packets out all OSPF-enabled interfaces to determine if neighbors are present on those links. If a neighbor is present, the OSPF-enabled router attempts to establish a neighbor adjacency with that neighbor.

2. Exchange Link-State Advertisements (Figure 2) - After adjacencies are established, routers then exchange link-state advertisements (LSAs). LSAs contain the state and cost of each directly connected link. Routers flood their LSAs to adjacent neighbors. Adjacent neighbors receiving the LSA immediately flood the LSA to other directly connected neighbors, until all routers in the area have all LSAs.

3. Build the Topology Table (Figure 3) - After LSAs are received, OSPF-enabled routers build the topology table (LSDB) based on the received LSAs. This database eventually holds all the information about the topology of the network.

4. Execute the SPF Algorithm (Figures 4 and 5) - Routers then execute the SPF algorithm. The gears in the figure are used to indicate the execution of the SPF algorithm. The SPF algorithm creates the SPF tree.

The content of the R1 SPF tree is displayed in Figure 6.

From the SPF tree, the best paths are inserted into the routing table. Routing decisions are made based on the entries in the routing table.

<table>
<tr><td>Refer to
Online Course
for Illustration</td></tr>
</table>

6.1.1.5   Single-Area and Multiarea OSPF

To make OSPF more efficient and scalable, OSPF supports hierarchical routing using areas. An OSPF area is a group of routers that share the same link-state information in their LSDBs.

OSPF can be implemented in one of two ways:

- **Single-Area OSPF** - In Figure 1, all routers are in one area called the backbone area (area 0).

- **Multiarea OSPF** - In Figure 2, OSPF is implemented using multiple areas, in a hierarchal fashion. All areas must connect to the backbone area (area 0). Routers interconnecting the areas are referred to as Area Border Routers (ABR).

With multiarea OSPF, OSPF can divide one large autonomous system (AS) into smaller areas, to support hierarchical routing. With hierarchical routing, routing still occurs between the areas (interarea routing), while many of the processor intensive routing operations, such as recalculating the database, are kept within an area.

For instance, any time a router receives new information about a topology change within the area (including the addition, deletion, or modification of a link) the router must rerun the SPF algorithm, create a new SPF tree, and update the routing table. The SPF algorithm is CPU-intensive and the time it takes for calculation depends on the size of the area.

Note   Topology changes are distributed to routers in other areas in a distance vector format. In other words, these routers only update their routing tables and do not need to rerun the SPF algorithm.

Too many routers in one area would make the LSDBs very large and increase the load on the CPU. Therefore, arranging routers into areas effectively partitions a potentially large database into smaller and more manageable databases.

The hierarchical-topology possibilities of multiarea OSPF have these advantages:

- **Smaller routing tables** - Fewer routing table entries because network addresses can be summarized between areas. Route summarization is not enabled by default.

- **Reduced link-state update overhead** - Minimizes processing and memory requirements.

- **Reduced frequency of SPF calculations** - Localizes the impact of a topology change within an area. For instance, it minimizes routing update impact because LSA flooding stops at the area boundary.

Figure 3 illustrates these advantages.

For example, R2 is an ABR for area 51. As an ABR, it would summarize the area 51 routes into area 0. When one of the summarized links fails, LSAs are exchanged within area 51 only. Routers in area 51 must rerun the SPF algorithm to identify the best routes. However, the routers in area 0 and area 1 do not receive any updates; therefore, they do not execute the SPF algorithm.

The focus of this chapter is on single-Area OSPF.

Refer to **Interactive Graphic** in online course.

6.1.1.6   Activity - Identify OSPF Features and Terminology

Refer to **Online Course** for Illustration

6.1.2   OSPF Messages

6.1.2.1   Encapsulating OSPF Messages

OSPF messages transmitted over an Ethernet link contain the following information:

- **Data Link Ethernet Frame Header** - Identifies the destination multicast MAC addresses 01-00-5E-00-00-05 or 01-00-5E-00-00-06. (Figure 1)

- **IP Packet Header** - Identifies the IPv4 protocol field 89 which indicates that this is an OSPF packet. It also identifies one of two OSPF multicast addresses, 224.0.0.5 or 224.0.0.6. (Figure 2)

- **OSPF Packet Header** - Identifies the OSPF packet type, the router ID and the area ID. (Figure 3)

- **OSPF Packet Type Specific Data** - Contains the OSPF packet type information. The content differs depending on the packet type. In this case, it is an IPv4 Header. (Figure 4)

Refer to **Online Course** for Illustration

6.1.2.2   Types of OSPF Packets

OSPF uses link-state packets (LSPs) to establish and maintain neighbor adjacencies and exchange routing updates.

The figure shows the five different types of LSPs used by OSPF. Each packet serves a specific purpose in the OSPF routing process:

- **Type 1: Hello packet** - Used to establish and maintain adjacency with other OSPF routers.

- **Type 2: Database Description (DBD) packet** - Contains an abbreviated list of the sending router's LSDB and is used by receiving routers to check against the local LSDB. The LSDB must be identical on all link-state routers within an area to construct an accurate SPF tree.

- **Type 3: Link-State Request (LSR) packet** - Receiving routers can then request more information about any entry in the DBD by sending an LSR.

■ **Type 4: Link-State Update (LSU) packet** - Used to reply to LSRs and to announce new information. LSUs contain seven different types of LSAs.

■ **Type 5: Link-State Acknowledgment (LSAck) packet** - When an LSU is received, the router sends an LSAck to confirm receipt of the LSU. The LSAck data field is empty.

Refer to
Online Course
for Illustration

6.1.2.3 Hello Packet

Hello Packet

The OSPF Type 1 packet is the Hello packet. Hello packets are used to:

■ Discover OSPF neighbors and establish neighbor adjacencies.

■ Advertise parameters on which two routers must agree to become neighbors.

■ Elect the Designated Router (DR) and Backup Designated Router (BDR) on multi-access networks like Ethernet and Frame Relay. Point-to-point links do not require DR or BDR.

The figure displays the fields contained in the Type 1 Hello packet. Important fields shown in the figure include:

■ **Type** - Identifies the type of packet. A one (1) indicates a Hello packet. A value 2 identifies a DBD packet, 3 an LSR packet, 4 an LSU packet, and 5 an LSAck packet.

■ **Router ID** - A 32-bit value expressed in dotted decimal notation (an IPv4 address) used to uniquely identifying the originating router.

■ **Area ID** - Area from which the packet originated.

■ **Network Mask** - Subnet mask associated with the sending interface.

■ **Hello Interval** - Specifies the frequency, in seconds, at which a router sends Hello packets. The default Hello interval on multiaccess networks is 10 seconds. This timer must be the same on neighboring routers; otherwise, an adjacency is not established.

■ **Router Priority** - Used in a DR/BDR election. The default priority for all OSPF routers is 1, but can be manually altered from 0 to 255. The higher the value, the more likely the router becomes the DR on the link.

■ **Dead Interval** - Is the time in seconds that a router waits to hear from a neighbor before declaring the neighboring router out of service. By default, the router Dead Interval is four times the Hello interval. This timer must be the same on neighboring routers; otherwise, an adjacency is not established.

■ **Designated Router (DR)** - Router ID of the DR.

■ **Backup Designated Router (BDR)** - Router ID of the BDR.

■ **List of Neighbors** - List that identifies the router IDs of all adjacent routers.

Click each of the highlighted fields in the figure for more information.

Refer to
Online Course
for Illustration

6.1.2.4   Hello Packet Intervals

As shown in the figure, OSPF Hello packets are transmitted to multicast address 224.0.0.5 in IPv4 and FF02::5 in IPv6 (all OSPF routers) every:

- 10 seconds (default on multiaccess and point-to-point networks)

- 30 seconds (default on nonbroadcast multiaccess [NBMA] networks; for example, Frame Relay)

The Dead interval is the period that the router waits to receive a Hello packet before declaring the neighbor down. If the Dead interval expires before the routers receive a Hello packet, OSPF removes that neighbor from its LSDB. The router floods the LSDB with information about the down neighbor out all OSPF-enabled interfaces.

Cisco uses a default of 4 times the Hello interval:

- 40 seconds (default on multiaccess and point-to-point networks)

- 120 seconds (default on NBMA networks; for example, Frame Relay)

Refer to
Online Course
for Illustration

6.1.2.5   Link-State Updates

Routers initially exchange Type 2 DBD packets, which is an abbreviated list of the sending router's LSDB and is used by receiving routers to check against the local LSDB.

A Type 3 LSR packet is used by the receiving routers to request more information about an entry in the DBD.

The Type 4 LSU packet is used to reply to an LSR packet.

LSUs are also used to forward OSPF routing updates, such as link changes. Specifically, an LSU packet can contain 11 different types of OSPFv2 LSAs, as shown in the figure. OSPFv3 renamed several of these LSAs and also contains two additional LSAs.

Note   The difference between the LSU and LSA terms can sometimes be confusing because these terms are often used interchangeably. However, an LSU contains one or more LSAs.

Refer to
Interactive Graphic
in online course.

6.1.2.6   Activity - Identify the OSPF Packet Types

Refer to
Online Course
for Illustration

6.1.3   OSPF Operation

6.1.3.1   OSPF Operational States

When an OSPF router is initially connected to a network, it attempts to:

- Create adjacencies with neighbors

- Exchange routing information

- Calculate the best routes

- Reach convergence

OSPF progresses through several states while attempting to reach convergence:

- Down state

- Init state

- Two-Way state

- ExStart state

- Exchange state

- Loading state

- Full state

Click the blue boxes in the figure for more information.

6.1.3.2   Establish Neighbor Adjacencies

Refer to
Online Course
for Illustration

When OSPF is enabled on an interface, the router must determine if there is another OSPF neighbor on the link. To accomplish this, the router forwards a Hello packet that contains its router ID out all OSPF-enabled interfaces. The OSPF router ID is used by the OSPF process to uniquely identify each router in the OSPF area. A router ID is an IP address assigned to identify a specific router among OSPF peers.

When a neighboring OSPF-enabled router receives a Hello packet with a router ID that is not within its neighbor list, the receiving router attempts to establish an adjacency with the initiating router.

Refer to R1 in Figure 1. When OSPF is enabled, the enabled Gigabit Ethernet 0/0 interface transitions from the Down state to the Init state. R1 starts sending Hello packets out all OSPF-enabled interfaces to discover OSPF neighbors to develop adjacencies with.

In Figure 2, R2 receives the Hello packet from R1 and adds the R1 router ID to its neighbor list. R2 then sends a Hello packet to R1. The packet contains the R2 Router ID and the R1 Router ID in its list of neighbors on the same interface.

In Figure 3, R1 receives the Hello and adds the R2 Router ID in its list of OSPF neighbors. It also notices its own Router ID in the Hello packet's list of neighbors. When a router receives a Hello packet with its Router ID listed in the list of neighbors, the router transitions from the Init state to the Two-Way state.

The action performed in Two-Way state depends on the type of inter-connection between the adjacent routers:

- If the two adjacent neighbors are interconnected over a point-to-point link, then they immediately transition from the Two-Way state to the database synchronization phase.

- If the routers are interconnected over a common Ethernet network, then a designated router DR and a BDR must be elected.

Because R1 and R2 are interconnected over an Ethernet network, a DR and BDR election takes place. As shown in Figure 4, R2 becomes the DR and R1 is the BDR. This process only occurs on multi-access networks such as Ethernet LANs.

Hello packets are continually exchanged to maintain router information.

Refer to
Online Course
for Illustration

6.1.3.3   OSPF DR and BDR

Why is a DR and BDR election necessary?

Multiaccess networks can create two challenges for OSPF regarding the flooding of LSAs:

- **Creation of multiple adjacencies** - Ethernet networks could potentially interconnect many OSPF routers over a common link. Creating adjacencies with every router is unnecessary and undesirable. It would lead to an excessive number of LSAs exchanged between routers on the same network.

- **Extensive flooding of LSAs** - Link-state routers flood their LSAs any time OSPF is initialized, or when there is a change in the topology. This flooding can become excessive.

To understand the problem with multiple adjacencies, we must study a formula:

For any number of routers (designated as n) on a multiaccess network, there are n $(n - 1)$ / 2 adjacencies.

Figure 1 shows a simple topology of five routers, all of which are attached to the same multiaccess Ethernet network. Without some type of mechanism to reduce the number of adjacencies, collectively these routers would form 10 adjacencies:

$5 (5 - 1) / 2 = 10$

This may not seem like much, but as routers are added to the network, the number of adjacencies increases dramatically, as shown in Figure 2.

To understand the problem of extensive flooding of LSAs, play the animation in Figure 3. In the animation, R2 sends out an LSA. This event triggers every other router to also send out an LSA. Not shown in the animation are the required acknowledgments sent for every LSA received. If every router in a multiaccess network had to flood and acknowledge all received LSAs to all other routers on that same multiaccess network, the network traffic would become quite chaotic.

The solution to managing the number of adjacencies and the flooding of LSAs on a multiaccess network is the DR. On multiaccess networks, OSPF elects a DR to be the collection and distribution point for LSAs sent and received. A BDR is also elected in case the DR fails. All other routers become DROTHERs. A DROTHER is a router that is neither the DR nor the BDR.

Play the animation in Figure 4 to see the role of DR.

Refer to
Online Course
for Illustration

6.1.3.4   Synchronizing OSPF Databases

After the Two-Way state, routers transition to database synchronization states. While the Hello packet was used to establish neighbor adjacencies, the other four types of OSPF packets are used during the process of exchanging and synchronizing LSDBs.

In the ExStart state, a master and slave relationship is created between each router and its adjacent DR and BDR. The router with the higher router ID acts as the master for the Exchange state. In Figure 1, R2 becomes the master.

In the Exchange state, the master and slave routers exchange one or more DBD packets. A DBD packet includes information about the LSA entry header that appears in the router's LSDB. The entries can be about a link or about a network. Each LSA entry header includes information about the link-state type, the address of the advertising router, the link's cost, and the sequence number. The router uses the sequence number to determine the newness of the received link-state information.

In Figure 2, R2 sends a DBD packet to R1. When R1 receives the DBD, it performs the following actions:

1. It acknowledges the receipt of the DBD using the LSAck packet.

2. R1 then sends DBD packets to R2.

3. R2 acknowledges R1.

R1 compares the information received with the information it has in its own LSDB. If the DBD packet has a more current link-state entry, the router transitions to the Loading state.

For example, in Figure 3, R1 sends an LSR regarding network 172.16.6.0 to R2. R2 responds with the complete information about 172.16.6.0 in an LSU packet. Again, when R1 receives an LSU, it sends an LSAck. R1 then adds the new link-state entries into its LSDB.

After all LSRs have been satisfied for a given router, the adjacent routers are considered synchronized and in a full state.

As long as the neighboring routers continue receiving Hello packets, the network in the transmitted LSAs remain in the topology database. After the topological databases are synchronized, updates (LSUs) are sent only to neighbors when:

■ A change is perceived (incremental updates)

■ Every 30 minutes

Refer to Interactive Graphic in online course.

6.1.3.5   Activity - Identify the OSPF States for Establishing Adjacency

Refer to Interactive Graphic in online course.

6.1.3.6   Video Demonstration - Observing OSPF Protocol Communications

Refer to Online Course for Illustration

6.2   Configuring Single-Area OSPFv2

6.2.1   OSPF Router ID

6.2.1.1   OSPF Network Topology

Introduced in 1991, OSPFv2 is a link-state routing protocol for IPv4. OSPF was designed as an alternative to another IPv4 routing protocol, RIP.

The figure shows the topology used for configuring OSPFv2 in this section. The types of serial interfaces and their associated bandwidths may not necessarily reflect the more common types of connections found in networks today. The bandwidths of the serial links used in this topology were chosen to help explain the calculation of the routing protocol metrics and the process of best path selection.

The routers in the topology have a starting configuration, including interface addresses. There is currently no static routing or dynamic routing configured on any of the routers. All interfaces on routers R1, R2, and R3 (except the loopback on R2) are within the OSPF backbone area. The ISP router is used as the routing domain's gateway to the Internet.

Note In this topology the loopback interface is used to simulate the WAN link to the Internet.

Refer to
Online Course
for Illustration

6.2.1.2   Router OSPF Configuration Mode

Figure 1 is the reference topology for this topic. OSPFv2 is enabled using the `router ospf` *process-id* global configuration mode command. The *process-id* value represents a number between 1 and 65,535 and is selected by the network administrator. The *process-id* value is locally significant, which means that it does not have to be the same value on the other OSPF routers to establish adjacencies with those neighbors.

Figure 2 provides an example of entering router OSPF configuration mode on R1.

Note The list of commands has been altered to display only the commands that are used in this chapter. For a complete list of commands, use the Syntax Checkers in Figure 3.

Use the Syntax Checker in Figure 3 to enter OSPF router configuration mode on R2 and list the commands available at the prompt.

Refer to
Online Course
for Illustration

6.2.1.3   Router IDs

Every router requires a router ID to participate in an OSPF domain. The router ID can be defined by an administrator or automatically assigned by the router. The router ID is used by the OSPF-enabled router to:

- **Uniquely identify the router** - The router ID is used by other routers to uniquely identify each router within the OSPF domain and all packets that originate from them.

- **Participate in the election of the DR** - In a multiaccess LAN environment, the election of the DR occurs during initial establishment of the OSPF network. When OSPF links become active, the routing device configured with the highest priority is elected the DR. Assuming there is no priority configured, or there is a tie, then the router with the highest router ID is elected the DR. The routing device with the second highest router ID is elected the BDR.

But how does the router determine the router ID? As illustrated in the figure, Cisco routers derive the router ID based on one of three criteria, in the following preferential order:

- The router ID is explicitly configured using the OSPF `router-id` *rid* router configuration mode command. The *rid* value is any 32-bit value expressed as an IPv4 address. This is the recommended method to assign a router ID.

- If the router ID is not explicitly configured, the router chooses the highest IPv4 address of any of configured loopback interfaces. This is the next best alternative to assigning a router ID.

■ If no loopback interfaces are configured, then the router chooses the highest active IPv4 address of any of its physical interfaces. This is the least recommended method because it makes it more difficult for administrators to distinguish between specific routers.

If the router uses the highest IPv4 address for the router ID, the interface does not need to be OSPF-enabled. This means that the interface address does not need to be included in one of the OSPF **network** commands for the router to use that IP address as the router ID. The only requirement is that the interface is active and in the up state.

Note   The router ID looks like an IP address, but it is not routable and, therefore, is not included in the routing table, unless the OSPF routing process chooses an interface (physical or loopback) that is appropriately defined by a **network** command.

Refer to
Online Course
for Illustration

6.2.1.4   Configuring an OSPF Router ID

Use the **router-id** *rid* router configuration mode command to manually assign a 32-bit value expressed as an IPv4 address to a router. An OSPF router identifies itself to other routers using this router ID.

As shown in Figure 1, R1 is configured with a router ID of 1.1.1.1, R2 with 2.2.2.2, and R3 with 3.3.3.3.

In Figure 2, the router ID 1.1.1.1 is assigned to R1. Use the **show ip protocols** command to verify the router ID.

Note   R1 had never been configured with an OSPF router ID. If it had, then the router ID would have to be modified.

If the router ID is the same on two neighboring routers, the router displays an error message similar to the one below:

```
%OSPF-4-DUP_RTRID1: Detected router with duplicate router ID.
```

To correct this problem, configure all routers so that they have unique OSPF router IDs.

Use the Syntax Checker in Figure 3 to assign the router ID to R2 and R3.

Refer to
Online Course
for Illustration

6.2.1.5   Modifying a Router ID

Sometimes a router ID needs to be changed, for example, when a network administrator establishes a new router ID scheme for the network. However, after a router selects a router ID, an active OSPF router does not allow the router ID to be changed until the router is reloaded or the OSPF process cleared.

In Figure 1, notice that the current router ID is 192.168.10.5. The router ID should be 1.1.1.1.

In Figure 2, the router ID 1.1.1.1 is being assigned to R1. Notice how an informational message appears stating that the OSPF process must be cleared or that the router must be reloaded. The reason is because R1 already has adjacencies with other neighbors using the router ID 192.168.10.5. Those adjacencies must be renegotiated using the new router IP 1.1.1.1.

Clearing the OSPF process is the preferred method to reset the router ID.

In Figure 3, the OSPF routing process is cleared using the `clear ip ospf process` privileged EXEC mode command. This forces OSPF on R1 to transition to the Down and Init states. Notice the adjacency change messages from full to down and then from loading to full. The `show ip protocols` command verifies that the router ID has changed.

Use the Syntax Checker in Figure 4 to modify the router ID for R1.

Refer to
Online Course
for Illustration

6.2.1.6   Using a Loopback Interface as the Router ID

A router ID can also be assigned using a loopback interface.

The IPv4 address of the loopback interface should be configured using a 32-bit subnet mask (255.255.255.255). This effectively creates a host route. A 32-bit host route does not get advertised as a route to other OSPF routers.

The example in the figure displays how to configure a loopback interface with a host route on R1. R1 uses the host route as its router ID, assuming there is no router ID explicitly configured or previously learned.

Note   Some older versions of the IOS do not recognize the `router-id` command; therefore, the best way to set the router ID on those routers is by using a loopback interface.

Refer to
Online Course
for Illustration

6.2.2   Configure Single-Area OSPFv2

6.2.2.1   Enabling OSPF on Interfaces

The `network` command determines which interfaces participate in the routing process for an OSPF area. Any interfaces on a router that match the network address in the `network` command are enabled to send and receive OSPF packets. As a result, the network (or subnet) address for the interface is included in OSPF routing updates.

The basic command syntax is `network` *network-address wildcard-mask* `area` *area-id*.

The `area` *area-id* syntax refers to the OSPF area. When configuring single-area OSPF, the `network` command must be configured with the same *area-id* value on all routers. Although any area ID can be used, it is good practice to use an area ID of 0 with single-area OSPF. This convention makes it easier if the network is later altered to support multi-area OSPF.

The figure displays the reference topology.

Refer to
Online Course
for Illustration

6.2.2.2   Wildcard Mask

OSPFv2 uses the argument combination of *network-address wildcard-mask* to enable OSPF on interfaces. OSPF is classless by design; therefore, the wildcard mask is always required. When identifying interfaces that are participating in a routing process, the wildcard mask is typically the inverse of the subnet mask configured on that interface.

A wildcard mask is a string of 32 binary digits used by the router to determine which bits of the address to examine for a match. In a subnet mask, binary 1 is equal to a match and binary 0 is not a match. In a wildcard mask, the reverse is true:

- **Wildcard mask bit 0** - Matches the corresponding bit value in the address.

- **Wildcard mask bit 1** - Ignores the corresponding bit value in the address.

The easiest method for calculating a wildcard mask is to subtract the network subnet mask from 255.255.255.255.

The example in Figure 1 calculates the wildcard mask from the network address of 192.168.10.0/24. To do so, the subnet mask 255.255.255.0 is subtracted from 255.255.255.255, providing a result of 0.0.0.255. Therefore, 192.168.10.0/24 is 192.168.10.0 with a wildcard mask of 0.0.0.255.

The example in Figure 2 calculates the wildcard mask from the network address of 192.168.10.64/26. Again, the subnet mask 255.255.255.192 is subtracted from 255.255.255.255 providing a result of 0.0.0.63. Therefore, 192.168.10.0/26 is 192.168.10.0 with a wildcard mask of 0.0.0.63.

Refer to
Online Course
for Illustration

6.2.2.3   The network Command

There are several ways to identify the interfaces that will participate in the OSPFv2 routing process.

Figure 1 displays the required commands to determine which interfaces on R1 participate in the OSPFv2 routing process for an area. Notice the use of wildcard masks to identify the respective interfaces based on their network addresses. Because this is a single-area OSPF network, all area IDs are set to 0.

As an alternative, OSPFv2 can be enabled using the `network` *intf-ip-address* `0.0.0.0` *area* *area-id* router configuration mode command.

Figure 2 provides an example of specifying the interface IPv4 address with a quad 0 wildcard mask. Entering `network` `172.16.3.1` `0.0.0.0` `area` `0` on R1 tells the router to enable interface Serial0/0/0 for the routing process. As a result, the OSPFv2 process will advertise the network that is on this interface (172.16.3.0/30).

The advantage of specifying the interface is that the wildcard mask calculation is not necessary. OSPFv2 uses the interface address and subnet mask to determine the network to advertise.

Some IOS versions allow the subnet mask to be entered instead of the wildcard mask. The IOS then converts the subnet mask to the wildcard mask format.

Use the Syntax Checker in Figure 3 to advertise the networks connected to R2.

Note   While completing the Syntax Checker, observe the informational messages describing the adjacency between R1 (1.1.1.1) and R2 (2.2.2.2). The IPv4 addressing scheme used for the router ID makes it easy to identify the neighbor.

Refer to
Online Course
for Illustration

6.2.2.4   Passive Interface

By default, OSPF messages are forwarded out all OSPF-enabled interfaces. However, these messages really only need to be sent out interfaces connecting to other OSPF-enabled routers.

Refer to the topology in the figure. OSPF messages are forwarded out of all three routers G0/0 interface even though no OSPF neighbor exists on that LAN. Sending out unneeded messages on a LAN affects the network in three ways:

- **Inefficient Use of Bandwidth** - Available bandwidth is consumed transporting unnecessary messages. Messages are multicasted; therefore, switches are also forwarding the messages out all ports.

- **Inefficient Use of Resources** - All devices on the LAN must process the message and eventually discard the message.

- **Increased Security Risk** - Advertising updates on a broadcast network is a security risk. OSPF messages can be intercepted with packet sniffing software. Routing updates can be modified and sent back to the router, corrupting the routing table with false metrics that misdirect traffic.

Refer to
Online Course
for Illustration

6.2.2.5   Configuring Passive Interfaces

Use the `passive-interface` router configuration mode command to prevent the transmission of routing messages through a router interface, but still allow that network to be advertised to other routers, as shown in Figure 1. Specifically, the command stops routing messages from being sent out the specified interface. However, the network that the specified interface belongs to is still advertised in routing messages that are sent out other interfaces.

For instance, there is no need for R1, R2, and R3 to forward OSPF messages out of their LAN interfaces. The configuration identifies the R1 G0/0 interface as passive.

It is important to know that a neighbor adjacency cannot be formed over a passive interface. This is because link-state packets cannot be sent or acknowledged.

The `show ip protocols` command is then used to verify that the Gigabit Ethernet interface was passive, as shown in Figure 2. Notice that the G0/0 interface is now listed under the Passive Interface(s) section. The network 172.16.1.0 is still listed under Routing for Networks, which means that this network is still included as a route entry in OSPF updates that are sent to R2 and R3.

Note   OSPFv2 and OSPFv3 both support the `passive-interface` command.

Use the Syntax Checker in Figure 3 to configure the LAN interface as a passive interface on R2.

As an alternative, all interfaces can be made passive using the `passive-interface default` command. Interfaces that should not be passive can be re-enabled using the `no passive-interface` command.

Continue using the Syntax Checker in Figure 3 and configure the LAN interface as a passive interface on R3.

Note   While completing the Syntax Checker, notice the OSPF informational state messages as the interfaces are all rendered passive and then the two serial interfaces are made non-passive.

Refer to
Interactive Graphic
in online course.

6.2.2.6   Activity - Calculate the Subnet and Wildcard Masks

Refer to **Packet
Tracer Activity**
for this chapter

6.2.2.7   Packet Tracer - Configuring OSPFv2 in a Single-area

In this activity, the IP addressing is already configured. You are responsible for configuring the three router topology with basic single-area OSPFv2, and then verifying connectivity between end devices.

Refer to
Online Course
for Illustration

6.2.3   OSPF Cost

6.2.3.1   OSPF Metric = Cost

Recall that a routing protocol uses a metric to determine the best path of a packet across a network. A metric gives indication of the overhead that is required to send packets across a certain interface. OSPF uses cost as a metric. A lower cost indicates a better path than a higher cost.

The cost of an interface is inversely proportional to the bandwidth of the interface. Therefore, a higher bandwidth indicates a lower cost. More overhead and time delays equal a higher cost. Therefore, a 10-Mb/s Ethernet line has a higher cost than a 100-Mb/s Ethernet line.

The formula used to calculate the OSPF cost is:

- **Cost** = *reference bandwidth / interface bandwidth*

The default reference bandwidth is 10^8 (100,000,000); therefore, the formula is:

- **Cost** = *100,000,000 bps / interface bandwidth in bps*

Refer to the table in the figure for a breakdown of the cost calculation. Notice that FastEthernet, Gigabit Ethernet, and 10 GigE interfaces share the same cost, because the OSPF cost value must be an integer. Consequently, because the default reference bandwidth is set to 100 Mb/s, all links that are faster than Fast Ethernet also have a cost of 1.

Refer to
Online Course
for Illustration

6.2.3.2   OSPF Accumulates Costs

The cost of an OSPF route is the accumulated value from one router to the destination network.

For example, in Figure 1, the cost to reach the R2 LAN 172.16.2.0/24 from R1 should be as follows:

- Serial link from R1 to R2 cost = 64

- Gigabit Ethernet link on R2 cost = 1

- Total cost to reach 172.16.2.0/24 = 65

The routing table of R1 in Figure 2 confirms that the metric to reach the R2 LAN is a cost of 65.

Refer to
Online Course
for Illustration

6.2.3.3 Adjusting the Reference Bandwidth

OSPF uses a reference bandwidth of 100 Mb/s for any links that are equal to or faster than a fast Ethernet connection. Therefore, the cost assigned to a fast Ethernet interface with an interface bandwidth of 100 Mb/s would equal 1.

`Cost = 100,000,000 bps / 100,000,000 = 1`

While this calculation works for fast Ethernet interfaces, it is problematic for links that are faster than 100 Mb/s; because the OSPF metric only uses integers as its final cost of a link. If something less than an integer is calculated, OSPF rounds up to the nearest integer. For this reason, from the OSPF perspective, an interface with an interface bandwidth of 100 Mb/s (a cost of 1) has the same cost as an interface with a bandwidth of 100 Gb/s (a cost of 1).

To assist OSPF in making the correct path determination, the reference bandwidth must be changed to a higher value to accommodate networks with links faster than 100 Mb/s.

Adjusting the Reference Bandwidth

Changing the reference bandwidth does not actually affect the bandwidth capacity on the link; rather, it simply affects the calculation used to determine the metric. To adjust the reference bandwidth, use the `auto-cost reference-bandwidth Mb/s` router configuration command. This command must be configured on every router in the OSPF domain. Notice that the value is expressed in Mb/s; therefore, to adjust the costs for:

- Gigabit Ethernet - `auto-cost reference-bandwidth 1000`

- 10 Gigabit Ethernet - `auto-cost reference-bandwidth 10000`

To return to the default reference bandwidth, use the `auto-cost reference-bandwidth 100` command.

The table in Figure 1 displays the OSPF cost if the reference bandwidth is set to Gigabit Ethernet. Although the metric values increase, OSPF makes better choices because it can now distinguish between FastEthernet and Gigabit Ethernet links.

Figure 2 displays the OSPF cost if the reference bandwidth is adjusted to accommodate 10 Gigabit Ethernet links. The reference bandwidth should be adjusted anytime there are links faster than FastEthernet (100 Mb/s).

Note The costs represent whole numbers that have been rounded down.

In Figure 3, all routers have been configured to accommodate the Gigabit Ethernet link with the `auto-cost reference-bandwidth 1000 router` configuration command. The new accumulated cost to reach the R2 LAN 172.16.2.0/24 from R1:

- Serial link from R1 to R2 cost = 647

- Gigabit Ethernet link on R2 cost = 1

- Total cost to reach 172.16.2.0/24 = **648**

Use the `show ip ospf interface s0/0/0` command to verify the current OSPF cost assigned to the R1 serial 0/0/0 interface, as shown in Figure 4. Notice how it displays a cost of 647.

The routing table of R1 in Figure 5 confirms that the metric to reach the R2 LAN is a cost of 648.

Refer to
Online Course
for Illustration

6.2.3.4 Default Interface Bandwidths

All interfaces have default bandwidth values assigned to them. As with reference bandwidth, interface bandwidth values do not actually affect the speed or capacity of the link. Instead, they are used by OSPF to compute the routing metric. Therefore, it is important that the bandwidth value reflect the actual speed of the link so that the routing table has accurate best path information.

Although the bandwidth values of Ethernet interfaces usually match the link speed, some other interfaces may not. For instance, the actual speed of serial interfaces is often different than the default bandwidth. On Cisco routers, the default bandwidth on most serial interfaces is set to 1.544 Mb/s.

Note   Older serial interfaces may default to 128 kb/s.

Refer to the example in Figure 1. Notice that the link between:

- R1 and R2 should be set to 1,544 kb/s (default value)
- R2 and R3 should be set to 1,024 kb/s
- R1 and R3 should be set to 64 kb/s

Use the `show interfaces` command to view the interface bandwidth setting. Figure 2 displays the serial interface 0/0/0 settings for R1. The bandwidth setting is accurate and therefore the serial interface does not have to be adjusted.

Figure 3 displays the serial interface 0/0/1 settings for R1. It also confirms that the interface is using the default interface bandwidth 1,544 kb/s. According to the reference topology, this should be set to 64 kb/s. Therefore, the R1 serial 0/0/1 interface must be adjusted.

Figure 4 displays the resulting cost metric of 647, which is based on the reference bandwidth set to 1,000,000,000 bps and the default interface bandwidth of 1,544 kb/s (1,000,000,000 / 1,544,000).

Refer to
Online Course
for Illustration

6.2.3.5 Adjusting the Interface Bandwidths

Adjusting the Interface Bandwidth

To adjust the interface bandwidth use the `bandwidth` *kilobits* interface configuration command. Use the `no bandwidth` command to restore the default value.

The example in Figure 1 adjusts the R1 Serial 0/0/1 interface bandwidth to 64 kb/s. A quick verification confirms that the interface bandwidth setting is now 64 kb/s.

The bandwidth must be adjusted at each end of the serial links, therefore:

- R2 requires its S0/0/1 interface to be adjusted to 1,024 kb/s.

- R3 requires its serial 0/0/0 to be adjusted to 64 kb/s and its serial 0/0/1 to be adjusted to 1,024 kb/s.

Use the Syntax Checker in Figure 2 to adjust the serial interface of R2 and R3.

Note   A common misconception for students who are new to networking and the Cisco IOS is to assume that the **bandwidth** command changes the physical bandwidth of the link. The command only modifies the bandwidth metric used by EIGRP and OSPF. The command does not modify the actual bandwidth on the link.

Refer to
Online Course
for Illustration

6.2.3.6   Manually Setting the OSPF Cost

As an alternative to setting the default interface bandwidth, the cost can be manually configured on an interface using the **ip ospf cost** *value* interface configuration command.

An advantage of configuring a cost over setting the interface bandwidth is that the router does not have to calculate the metric when the cost is manually configured. In contrast, when the interface bandwidth is configured, the router must calculate the OSPF cost based on the bandwidth. The **ip ospf cost** command is useful in multi-vendor environments where non-Cisco routers may use a metric other than bandwidth to calculate the OSPF costs.

Both the **bandwidth** interface command and the **ip ospf cost** interface command achieve the same result, which is to provide an accurate value for use by OSPF in determining the best route.

For instance, in the example in Figure 1, the interface bandwidth of serial 0/0/1 is reset to the default value and the OSPF cost is manually set to 15,625. Although the interface bandwidth is reset to the default value, the OSPF cost is set as if the bandwidth was still calculated.

Figure 2 shows the two alternatives that can be used in modifying the costs of the serial links in the topology. The right side of the figure shows the **ip ospf cost** command equivalents of the **bandwidth** commands on the left.

Refer to
Online Course
for Illustration

6.2.4   Verify OSPF

6.2.4.1   Verify OSPF Neighbors

Figure 1 shows the reference topology.

Use the **show ip ospf neighbor** command to verify that the router has formed an adjacency with its neighboring routers. If the router ID of the neighboring router is not displayed, or if it does not show as being in a state of FULL, the two routers have not formed an OSPF adjacency.

If two routers do not establish adjacency, link-state information is not exchanged. Incomplete LSDBs can cause inaccurate SPF trees and routing tables. Routes to destination networks may not exist, or may not be the most optimum path.

Figure 2 displays the neighbor adjacency of R1. For each neighbor, this command displays the following output:

- **Neighbor ID** - The router ID of the neighboring router.

- **Pri** - The OSPF priority of the interface. This value is used in the DR and BDR election.

- **State** - The OSPF state of the interface. FULL state means that the router and its neighbor have identical OSPF LSDBs. On multiaccess networks, such as Ethernet, two routers that are adjacent may have their states displayed as 2WAY. The dash indicates that no DR or BDR is required because of the network type.

- **Dead Time** - The amount of time remaining that the router waits to receive an OSPF Hello packet from the neighbor before declaring the neighbor down. This value is reset when the interface receives a Hello packet.

- **Address** - The IPv4 address of the neighbor's interface to which this router is directly connected.

- **Interface** - The interface on which this router has formed adjacency with the neighbor.

Use the Syntax Checker in Figure 3 to verify the R2 and R3 neighbors using the `show ip ospf neighbor` command.

Two routers may not form an OSPF adjacency if:

- The subnet masks do not match, causing the routers to be on separate networks.

- OSPF Hello or Dead Timers do not match.

- OSPF Network Types do not match.

- There is a missing or incorrect OSPF `network` command.

Refer to
Online Course
for Illustration

6.2.4.2   Verify OSPF Protocol Settings

As shown in Figure 1, the `show ip protocols` command is a quick way to verify vital OSPF configuration information. This includes the OSPF process ID, the router ID, networks the router is advertising, the neighbors the router is receiving updates from, and the default administrative distance, which is 110 for OSPF.

Use the Syntax Checker in Figure 2 to verify the OSPF protocol settings of R2 and R3 using the `show ip protocols` command.

Refer to
Online Course
for Illustration

6.2.4.3   Verify OSPF Process Information

The `show ip ospf` command can also be used to examine the OSPF process ID and router ID, as shown in Figure 1. This command displays the OSPF area information and the last time the SPF algorithm was calculated.

Use the Syntax Checker in Figure 2 to verify the OSPF process of R2 and R3 using the `show ip ospf` command.

Refer to
Online Course
for Illustration

6.2.4.4   Verify OSPF Interface Settings

The quickest way to verify OSPF interface settings is to use the `show ip ospf interface` command. This command provides a detailed list for every OSPF-enabled interface. The command is useful to determine whether the `network` statements were correctly composed.

To get a summary of OSPF-enabled interfaces, use the `show ip ospf interface brief` command, as shown in Figure 1.

Use the Syntax Checker in Figure 2 to retrieve and view a summary of OSPF-enabled interfaces on R2 using the `show ip ospf interface brief` command. Notice that specifying the interface name as done in the `show ip ospf interface serial 0/0/1` command provides detailed OSPF information.

Continue using the Syntax Checker in Figure 2 to get a summary of OSPF-enabled interfaces on R3 using the `show ip ospf interface brief` command. Retrieve and view additional information for the Serial 0/0/0 interface using the `show ip ospf interface serial 0/0/0` command.

Refer to
Lab Activity
for this chapter

6.2.4.5   Lab - Configuring Basic Single-Area OSPFv2

In this lab, you will complete the following objectives:

- Part 1: Build the Network and Configure Basic Device Settings
- Part 2: Configure and Verify OSPF Routing
- Part 3: Change Router ID Assignments
- Part 4: Configure OSPF Passive Interfaces
- Part 5: Change OSPF Metrics

Refer to
Online Course
for Illustration

6.3   Configure Single-Area OSPFv3

6.3.1   OSPFv2 vs. OSPFv3

6.3.1.1   OSPFv3

OSPFv3 is the OSPFv2 equivalent for exchanging IPv6 prefixes. Recall that in IPv6, the network address is referred to as the prefix and the subnet mask is called the prefix-length.

Similar to its IPv4 counterpart, OSPFv3 exchanges routing information to populate the IPv6 routing table with remote prefixes, as shown in the figure.

Note   With the OSPFv3 Address Families feature, OSPFv3 includes support for both IPv4 and IPv6.

OSPFv2 runs over the IPv4 network layer, communicating with other OSPF IPv4 peers, and advertising only IPv4 routes.

OSPFv3 has the same functionality as OSPFv2, but uses IPv6 as the network layer transport, communicating with OSPFv3 peers and advertising IPv6 routes. OSPFv3 also uses the SPF algorithm as the computation engine to determine the best paths throughout the routing domain.

As with all IPv6 routing protocols, OSPFv3 has separate processes from its IPv4 counterpart. The processes and operations are basically the same as in the IPv4 routing protocol, but run independently. OSPFv2 and OSPFv3 each have separate adjacency tables, OSPF topology tables, and IP routing tables, as shown in the figure.

The OSPFv3 configuration and verification commands are similar those used in OSPFv2.

Refer to **Online Course** for Illustration

6.3.1.2 Similarities Between OSPFv2 to OSPFv3

As shown in the figure, the following are similarities between OSPFv2 and OSPFv3:

- **Link-state** - OSPFv2 and OSPFv3 are both classless link-state routing protocols.

- **Routing algorithm** - OSPFv2 and OSPFv3 use the SPF algorithm to make routing decisions.

- **Metric** - The RFCs for both OSPFv2 and OSPFv3 define the metric as the cost of sending packets out the interface. OSPFv2 and OSPFv3 can be modified using the `auto-cost reference-bandwidth` *ref-bw* router configuration mode command. The command only influences the OSPF metric where it was configured. For example, if this command was entered for OSPFv3, it does not affect the OSPFv2 routing metrics.

- **Areas** - The concept of multiple areas in OSPFv3 is the same as in OSPFv2. Multiareas that minimize link-state flooding and provide better stability with the OSPF domain.

- **OSPF packet types** - OSPFv3 uses the same five basic packet types as OSPFv2 (Hello, DBD, LSR, LSU, and LSAck).

- **Neighbor discovery mechanism** - The neighbor state machine, including the list of OSPF neighbor states and events, remains unchanged. OSPFv2 and OSPFv3 use the Hello mechanism to learn about neighboring routers and form adjacencies. However, in OSPFv3, there is no requirement for matching subnets to form neighbor adjacencies. This is because neighbor adjacencies are formed using link-local addresses, not global unicast addresses.

- **DR/BDR election process** - The DR/BDR election process remains unchanged in OSPFv3.

- **Router ID** - Both OSPFv2 and OSPFv3 use a 32-bit number for the router ID represented in dotted-decimal notation. Typically this is an IPv4 address. The OSPF `router-id` command must be used to configure the router ID. The process in determining the 32-bit Router ID is the same in both protocols. Use an explicitly-configured router ID; otherwise, the highest loopback IPv4 address becomes the router ID.

Refer to **Online Course** for Illustration

6.3.1.3 Differences Between OSPFv2 and OSPFv3

The figure shows the differences between OSPFv2 and OSPFv3:

- **Advertises** - OSPFv2 advertises IPv4 routes, whereas OSPFv3 advertises routes for IPv6.

- **Source address** - OSPFv2 messages are sourced from the IPv4 address of the exit interface. In OSPFv3, OSPF messages are sourced using the link-local address of the exit interface.

- **All OSPF router multicast addresses** - OSPFv2 uses 224.0.0.5; whereas, OSPFv3 uses FF02::5.

- **DR/BDR multicast address** - OSPFv2 uses 224.0.0.6; whereas, OSPFv3 uses FF02::6.

- **Advertise networks** - OSPFv2 advertises networks using the `network` router configuration command; whereas, OSPFv3 uses the `ipv6 ospf` *process-id* `area` *area-id* interface configuration command.

- **IP unicast routing** - Enabled, by default, in IPv4; whereas, the `ipv6 unicast-routing` global configuration command must be configured.

- **Authentication** - OSPFv2 uses either plaintext authentication or MD5 authentication. OSPFv3 uses IPv6 authentication.

Refer to
Online Course
for Illustration

6.3.1.4 Link-Local Addresses

Routers running a dynamic routing protocol, such as OSPF, exchange messages between neighbors on the same subnet or link. Routers only need to send and receive routing protocol messages with their directly connected neighbors. These messages are always sent from the source IPv4 address of the router doing the forwarding.

IPv6 link-local addresses are ideal for this purpose. An IPv6 link-local address enables a device to communicate with other IPv6-enabled devices on the same link and only on that link (subnet). Packets with a source or destination link-local address cannot be routed beyond the link from where the packet originated.

As shown in the figure, OSPFv3 messages are sent using:

- **Source IPv6 address** - This is the IPv6 link-local address of the exit interface.

- **Destination IPv6 address** - OSPFv3 packets can be sent to a unicast address using the neighbor IPv6 link-local address. They can also be sent using a multicast address. The FF02::5 address is the all OSPF router address, while the FF02::6 is the DR/BDR multicast address.

Refer to
Interactive Graphic
in online course.

6.3.1.5 Activity - Compare and Contrast OSPFv2 and OSPFv3

Refer to
Online Course
for Illustration

6.3.2 Configuring OSPFv3

6.3.2.1 OSPFv3 Network Topology

Figure 1 displays the network topology that is used to configure OSPFv3.

Figure 2 shows IPv6 unicast routing and the configuration of the global unicast addresses of R1, as identified in the reference topology. Assume that the interfaces of R2 and R3 have also been configured with their global unicast addresses, as identified in the referenced topology.

In this topology, none of the routers have IPv4 addresses configured. A network with router interfaces configured with IPv4 and IPv6 addresses is referred to as dual-stacked. A dual-stacked network can have OSPFv2 and OSPFv3 simultaneously-enabled.

Figure 3 displays the steps to configure basic OSPFv3 in a single area.

Refer to
Online Course
for Illustration

6.3.2.2   Link-Local Addresses

In the figure, the output of the `show ipv6 interface brief` command confirms that the correct global IPv6 addresses have been successfully configured and that the interfaces are enabled. Also, notice that each interface automatically generated a link-local address, as highlighted in the figure.

Link-local addresses are automatically created when an IPv6 global unicast address is assigned to the interface. Global unicast addresses are not required on an interface; however, IPv6 link-local addresses are.

Unless configured manually, Cisco routers create the link-local address using FE80::/10 prefix and the EUI-64 process. EUI-64 involves using the 48-bit Ethernet MAC address, inserting FFFE in the middle and flipping the seventh bit. For serial interfaces, Cisco uses the MAC address of an Ethernet interface. Notice in the figure that all three interfaces are using the same link-local address.

Refer to
Online Course
for Illustration

6.3.2.3   Assigning Link-Local Addresses

Link-local addresses created using the EUI-64 format or in some cases, random interface IDs, make it difficult to recognize and remember those addresses. Because IPv6 routing protocols use IPv6 link-local addresses for unicast addressing and next-hop address information in the routing table, it is common practice to make it an easily recognizable address.

Configuring the link-local address manually provides the ability to create an address that is recognizable and easier to remember. As well, a router with several interfaces can assign the same link-local address to each IPv6 interface. This is because the link-local address is only required for local communications.

Link-local addresses can be configured manually using the same interface command used to create IPv6 global unicast addresses, but appending the `link-local` keyword to the `ipv6 address` command.

A link-local address has a prefix within the range FE80 to FEBF. When an address begins with this hextet (16-bit segment) the `link-local` keyword must follow the address.

The example in Figure 1 configures the same link-local address FE80::1 on the three R1 interfaces. FE80::1 was chosen to make it easy to remember the link-local addresses of R1.

A quick look at the interfaces as shown in Figure 2 confirms that the R1 interface link-local addresses have been changed to FE80::1.

Use the Syntax Checker in Figure 3 to configure and verify link-local address FE80::2 on R2, and the link-local address FE80::3 on R3.

Refer to
Online Course
for Illustration

6.3.2.4   Configuring the OSPFv3 Router ID

Use the `ipv6 router ospf` *process-id* global configuration mode command to enter router configuration mode. The IPv6 router configuration mode prompt is different than the IPv4 router configuration mode prompt. Use the IPv6 router confirmation mode to configure global OSPFv3 parameters, such as a assigning a 32-bit OSPF router ID and reference bandwidth.

IPv6 routing protocols are enabled on an interface, and not from router configuration mode, like their IPv4 counterparts. The **network** IPv4 router configuration mode command does not exist in IPv6.

Like OSPFv2, the *process-id* value is a number between 1 and 65,535 and is chosen by the network administrator. The *process-id* value is locally significant, which means that it does not have to match other OSPF routers to establish adjacencies with those neighbors.

OSPFv3 requires a 32-bit router ID to be assigned before OSPF can be enabled on an interface. The logic diagram in Figure 1 displays how a router ID is chosen. Like OSPFv2, OSPFv3 uses:

- An explicitly configured router ID first.

- If none are configured, then the router uses the highest configured IPv4 address of a loopback interface.

- If none are configured, then the router uses the highest configured IPv4 address of an active interface.

- If there are no sources of IPv4 addresses on a router, then the router displays a console message to configure the router ID manually.

Note   For consistency, all three routers use the process ID of 10.

As shown in the topology in Figure 2, routers R1, R2, and R3 are to be assigned the router IDs indicated. The **router-id** *rid* command used to assign a router ID in OSPFv2 is the same command used in OSPFv3.

The example in Figure 3:

- Enters the router OSPFv3 configuration mode. Notice how the router prompt is different than the default IPv4 routing protocol mode router prompt. Also notice how an informational console message appeared when the OSPFv3 router configuration mode was accessed.

- Assigns the router ID 1.1.1.1.

- Adjusts the reference bandwidth to 1,000,000,000 bps (1 Gb/s), because there are Gigabit Ethernet links in the network. Notice the information console message that this command must be configured on all routers in the routing domain.

- The **show ipv6 protocols** command is used to verify that the OSPFv3 process ID 10 is using the router ID 1.1.1.1.

Use the Syntax Checker in Figure 4 to configure global OSPFv3 settings on R2 and R3.

Refer to
Online Course
for Illustration

6.3.2.5   Modifying an OSPFv3 Router ID

Router IDs sometimes must be changed, for example, if the network administrator has established a new router ID identification scheme. However, after an OSPFv3 router establishes a router ID, that router ID cannot be changed until the router is reloaded or the OSPF process is cleared.

In Figure 1, notice that the current router ID is 10.1.1.1. The OSPFv3 router ID should be 1.1.1.1.

In Figure 2, the router ID 1.1.1.1 is being assigned to R1.

Note   Clearing the OSPF process is the preferred method to reset the router ID.

In Figure 3, the OSPF routing process is cleared using the `clear ipv6 ospf process` privileged EXEC mode command. Doing this forces OSPF on R1 to renegotiate neighbor adjacencies using the new router ID.

The `show ipv6 protocols` command verifies that the router ID has changed.

Use the Syntax Checker in Figure 4 to modify the router ID for R1.

Refer to
Online Course
for Illustration

6.3.2.6   Enabling OSPFv3 on Interfaces

OSPFv3 uses a different method to enable an interface for OSPF. Instead of using the `network` router configuration mode command to specify matching interface addresses, OSPFv3 is configured directly on the interface.

To enable OSPFv3 on an interface, use the `ipv6 ospf` *process-id* `area` *area-id* interface configuration mode command.

The *process-id* value identifies the specific routing process and must be the same as the process ID used to create the routing process in the `ipv6 router ospf` *process-id* command.

The *area-id* value is the area to be associated with the OSPFv3 interface. Although any value could have been configured for the area, 0 was selected, because area 0 is the backbone area to which all other areas must attach, as shown in Figure 1. This helps in the migration to multiarea OSPF, if the need arises.

In Figure 2, OSPFv3 is enabled on the R1 interfaces using the `ipv6 ospf 10 area 0` command. The `show ipv6 ospf interface brief` command displays the active OSPFv3 interfaces.

Use the Syntax Checker in Figure 3 to enable OSPFv3 on the R2 and R3 interfaces.

Refer to
Online Course
for Illustration

6.3.3   Verify OSPFv3

6.3.3.1   Verify OSPFv3 Neighbors

Use the `show ipv6 ospf neighbor` command to verify that the router has formed an adjacency with its neighboring routers. If the router ID of the neighboring router is not displayed, or if it does not show as being in a state of FULL, the two routers have not formed an OSPF adjacency.

If two routers do not establish a neighbor adjacency, link-state information is not exchanged. Incomplete LSDBs can cause inaccurate SPF trees and routing tables. Routes to destination networks may not exist or may not be the most optimum path.

Figure 1 displays the neighbor adjacency of R1. For each neighbor, this command displays the following output:

- **Neighbor ID** - The router ID of the neighboring router.

- **Pri** - The OSPF priority of the interface. Value is used in the DR and BDR election.

- **State** - The OSPF state of the interface. FULL state means that the router and its neighbor have identical OSPF LSDBs. On multiaccess networks such as Ethernet, two routers that are adjacent may have their states displayed as 2WAY. The dash indicates that no DR or BDR is required because of the network type.

- **Dead Time** - The amount of time remaining that the router waits to receive an OSPF Hello packet from the neighbor before declaring the neighbor down. This value is reset when the interface receives a Hello packet.

- **Interface ID** - The interface ID or link ID.

- **Interface** - The interface on which this router has formed adjacency with the neighbor.

Use the Syntax Checker in Figure 2 to verify the R2 and R3 neighbors using the `show ipv6 ospf neighbor` command.

Refer to
Online Course
for Illustration

6.3.3.2   Verify OSPFv3 Protocol Settings

As shown in Figure 1, the `show ipv6 protocols` command is a quick way to verify vital OSPFv3 configuration information, including the OSPF process ID, the router ID, and the interfaces enabled for OSPFv3.

Use the Syntax Checker in Figure 2 to verify the OSPF protocol settings of R2 and R3 using the `show ipv6 protocols` command.

Use the `show ipv6 ospf` command to also examine the OSPFv3 process ID and router ID. This command displays the OSPF area information and the last time the SPF algorithm was calculated.

Refer to
Online Course
for Illustration

6.3.3.3   Verify OSPFv3 Interfaces

The quickest way to verify OSPF interface settings is to use the `show ipv6 ospf interface` command. This command provides a detailed list for every OSPF-enabled interface.

To retrieve and view a summary of OSPFv3-enabled interfaces on R1, use the `show ipv6 ospf interface brief` command, as shown in Figure 1.

Use the Syntax Checker in Figure 2 to view a summary of OSPF-enabled interfaces on R2 using the `show ipv6 ospf interface brief` command. Notice that specifying the interface name as done in the `show ipv6 ospf interface serial 0/0/1` command provides detailed OSPF information.

Continue using the Syntax Checker in Figure 2 to get a summary of OSPF-enabled interfaces on R3 using the `show ipv6 ospf interface brief` command. Retrieve and view additional information for the Serial 0/0/0 interface using the `show ipv6 ospf interface serial 0/0/0` command.

6.3.3.4   Verify the IPv6 Routing Table

In Figure 1, the `show ipv6 route ospf` command provides specifics about OSPF routes in the routing table.

Use the Syntax Checker in Figure 2 to verify the OSPFv3 routing table of R2 and R3, use the `show ipv6 route ospf` command.

6.3.3.5   Packet Tracer - Configuring Basic OSPFv3

In this activity, the IPv6 addressing is already configured. You are responsible for configuring the three router topology with a basic single-area OSPFv3, and then verifying connectivity between end devices.

6.3.3.6   Lab - Configuring Basic Single-Area OSPFv3

In this lab, you will complete the following objectives:

- Part 1: Build the Network and Configure Basic Device Settings

- Part 2: Configure OSPFv3 Routing

- Part 3: Configure OSPFv3 Passive Interfaces

6.4   Summary

6.4.1.1   Class Activity - Stepping Through OSPFv3

Activity - Stepping Through OSPFv3

Scenario

This class activity is designed for groups of three students. The objective is to review the Shortest Path First (SPF) routing process.

You will design and address a network, communicate the network address scheme and operation of network links to your group members, and compute the SPF.

Complete the steps as shown on the PDF for this class activity.

If you have time, share your network design and Open Shortest Path First (OSPF) process with another group.

6.4.1.2   Packet Tracer - Skills Integration Challenge

In this Skills Integration Challenge, your focus is OSPFv2 and OSPFv3 configurations. You will configure IP addressing for all devices. Then you will configure OSPFv2 routing for the IPv4 portion of the network and OSPFv3 routing for the IPv6 portion of the network. One router will be configured with both IPv4 and IPv6 configurations. Finally, you will verify your configurations and test connectivity between end devices.

Refer to
Online Course
for Illustration

6.4.1.3 Summary

The current version of OSPF for IPv4 is OSPFv2 introduced in RFC 1247 and updated in RFC 2328 by John Moy. In 1999, OSPFv3 for IPv6 was published in RFC 2740.

OSPF is a classless, link-state routing protocol with a default administrative distance of 110, and is denoted in the routing table with a route source code of **o**.

OSPF is enabled with the **router ospf** *process-id* global configuration mode command. The *process-id* value is locally significant, which means that it does not need to match other OSPF routers to establish adjacencies with those neighbors.

The **network** command used with OSPF has the same function as when used with other IGP routing protocols, but with slightly different syntax. The *wildcard-mask* value is the inverse of the subnet mask, and the *area-id* value should be set to **0**.

By default, OSPF Hello packets are sent every 10 seconds on multiaccess and point-to-point segments and every 30 seconds on NBMA segments (Frame Relay, X.25, ATM), and are used by OSPF to establish neighbor adjacencies. The Dead interval is four times the Hello interval, by default.

For routers to become adjacent, their Hello interval, Dead interval, network types, and subnet masks must match. Use the **show ip ospf neighbors** command to verify OSPF adjacencies.

OSPF elects a DR to act as collection and distribution point for LSAs sent and received in the multiaccess network. A BDR is elected to assume the role of the DR should the DR fail. All other routers are known as DROTHERs. All routers send their LSAs to the DR, which then floods the LSA to all other routers in the multiaccess network.

The **show ip protocols** command is used to verify important OSPF configuration information, including the OSPF process ID, the router ID, and the networks the router is advertising.

OSPFv3 is enabled on an interface and not under router configuration mode. OSPFv3 needs link-local addresses to be configured. IPv6 Unicast routing must be enabled for OSPFv3. A 32-bit router-ID is required before an interface can be enabled for OSPFv3.

Go to the online course to take the quiz and exam.

Chapter 6 Quiz

This quiz is designed to provide an additional opportunity to practice the skills and knowledge presented in the chapter and to prepare for the chapter exam. You will be allowed multiple attempts and the grade does not appear in the gradebook.

Chapter 6 Exam

The chapter exam assesses your knowledge of the chapter content.

Your Chapter Notes

Adjust and Troubleshoot Single-Area OSPF

7.0 Adjust and Troubleshoot Single-Area OSPF

7.0.1.1 Introduction

OSPF is a popular link state routing protocol that can be fine-tuned in many ways. Some of the most common methods of fine tuning include manipulating the Designated Router/Backup Designated Router (DR/BDR) election process, propagating default routes, fine-tuning the OSPFv2 and OSPFv3 interfaces and authentication.

This chapter of OSPF describes these tuning features, the configuration mode commands to implement these features for both IPv4 and IPv6, and the components and commands used to troubleshoot OSPFv2 and OSPFv3.

Refer to
Lab Activity
for this chapter

7.0.1.2 Class Activity - DR and BDR Election

Activity - DR and BDR Elections

Scenario

You are trying to decide how to influence the selection of the designated router and backup designated router for your OSPF network. This activity simulates that process.

Three separate designated-router election scenarios will be presented. The focus is on electing a DR and BDR for your group. Refer to the PDF for this activity for the remaining instructions.

If additional time is available, two groups can be combined to simulate DR and BDR elections.

Refer to
Online Course
for Illustration

7.1 Advanced Single-Area OSPF Configurations

7.1.1 OSPF in Multiaccess Networks

7.1.1.1 OSPF Network Types

To configure OSPF adjustments, start with a basic implementation of the OSPF routing protocol.

OSPF defines five network types, as shown in Figures 1 to 5:

- **Point-to-point** - Two routers interconnected over a common link. No other routers are on the link. This is often the configuration in WAN links. (Figure 1)

- **Broadcast multiaccess** - Multiple routers interconnected over an Ethernet network. (Figure 2)

- **Nonbroadcast multiaccess (NBMA)** - Multiple routers interconnected over an NBMA network such as Frame Relay. (Figure 3)

- **Point-to-multipoint** - Multiple routers interconnected in a hub-and-spoke topology over an NBMA network. Often used to connect branch sites (spokes) to a central site (hub). (Figure 4)

- **Virtual links** - Special OSPF network used to interconnect distant OSPF areas to the backbone area. (Figure 5)

A multiaccess network is a network with multiple devices on the same shared media, which are sharing communications. Ethernet LANs are the most common example of broadcast multiaccess networks. In broadcast networks, all devices on the network see all broadcast and multicast frames. They are multiaccess networks because there may be numerous hosts, printers, routers, and other devices that are all members of the same network.

Refer to
Online Course
for Illustration

7.1.1.2   Challenges in Multiaccess Networks

Multiaccess networks can create two challenges for OSPF regarding the flooding of LSAs:

- **Creation of multiple adjacencies** - Ethernet networks could potentially interconnect many OSPF routers over a common link. Creating adjacencies with every router is unnecessary and undesirable. This would lead to an excessive number of LSAs exchanged between routers on the same network.

- **Extensive flooding of LSAs** - Link-state routers flood their link-state packets when OSPF is initialized, or when there is a change in the topology. This flooding can become excessive.

The following formula can be used to calculate the number of required adjacencies. The number of adjacencies required for any number of routers (designated as n) on a multiaccess network is:

$n (n - 1) / 2$

Figure 1 shows a simple topology of four routers, all of which are attached to the same multiaccess Ethernet network. Without some type of mechanism to reduce the number of adjacencies, collectively these routers would form six adjacencies: 4 (4 - 1) / 2 = 6, as shown in Figure 2. Figure 3 shows that as routers are added to the network, the number of adjacencies increases dramatically.

Refer to
Online Course
for Illustration

7.1.1.3   OSPF Designated Router

The solution to managing the number of adjacencies and the flooding of LSAs on a multiaccess network is the DR. On multiaccess networks, OSPF elects a DR to be the collection and distribution point for LSAs sent and received. A BDR is also elected in case the DR fails. The BDR listens passively to this exchange and maintains a relationship with all the routers. If the DR stops producing Hello packets, the BDR promotes itself and assumes the role of DR.

All other non-DR or BDR routers become DROTHER (a router that is neither the DR nor the BDR).

In Figure 1, R1 has been elected as the designated router for the Ethernet LAN interconnecting R2, R3, and R4. Notice how the number of adjacencies has been reduced to 3.

Routers on a multiaccess network elect a DR and BDR. DROTHERs only form full adjacencies with the DR and BDR in the network. Instead of flooding LSAs to all routers in the network, DROTHERs only send their LSAs to the DR and BDR using the multicast address 224.0.0.6 (all DR routers).

Click the Play button in Figure 2 to see the animation of the role of DR. In the animation, R1 sends LSAs to the DR. The BDR also listens. The DR is responsible for forwarding the LSAs from R1 to all other routers. The DR uses the multicast address 224.0.0.5 (all OSPF routers). The end result is that there is only one router doing all of the flooding of all LSAs in the multiaccess network.

Note   DR/BDR elections only occur in multiaccess networks and do not occur in point-to-point networks.

Refer to **Online Course** for Illustration

7.1.1.4   Verifying DR/BDR Roles

In the multiaccess topology shown in Figure 1, there are three routers interconnected over a common Ethernet multiaccess network, 192.168.1.0/28. Each router is configured with the indicated IP address on the Gigabit Ethernet 0/0 interface.

Because the routers are connected over a common multiaccess broadcast network, OSPF has automatically elected a DR and BDR. In this example, R3 has been elected as the DR because its router ID is 3.3.3.3, which is the highest in this network. R2 is the BDR because it has the second highest router ID in the network.

To verify the roles of the router, use the `show ip ospf interface` command (Figure 2). The output generated by R1 confirms that:

- R1 is not the DR or BDR, but is a DROTHER with a default priority of 1. (1)

- The DR is R3 with router ID 3.3.3.3 at IP address 192.168.1.3, while the BDR is R2 with router ID 2.2.2.2 at IP address 192.168.1.2. (2)

- R1 has two adjacencies: one with the BDR and one with the DR. (3)

The output generated by R2 in Figure 3 confirms that:

- R2 is the BDR with a default priority of 1. (1)

- The DR is R3 with router ID 3.3.3.3 at IP address 192.168.1.3, while the BDR is R2 with router ID 2.2.2.2 at IP address 192.168.1.2. (2)

- R2 has two adjacencies; one with a neighbor with router ID 1.1.1.1 (R1) and the other with the DR. (3)

The output generated by R3 in Figure 4 confirms that:

- R3 is the DR with a default priority of 1. (1)

- The DR is R3 with router ID 3.3.3.3 at IP address 192.168.1.3, while the BDR is R2 with router ID 2.2.2.2 at IP address 192.168.1.2. (2)

- R3 has two adjacencies: one with a neighbor with router ID 1.1.1.1 (R1) and the other with the BDR. (3)

Refer to
Online Course
for Illustration

7.1.1.5   Verifying DR/BDR Adjacencies

To verify the OSPF adjacencies, use the `show ip ospf neighbor` command as shown in Figure 1.

Unlike serial links that only display a state of FULL/- , the state of neighbors in multi-access networks can be:

- *FULL/DROTHER* - This is a DR or BDR router that is fully adjacent with a non-DR or BDR router. These two neighbors can exchange Hello packets, updates, queries, replies, and acknowledgments.

- *FULL/DR* - The router is fully adjacent with the indicated DR neighbor. These two neighbors can exchange Hello packets, updates, queries, replies, and acknowledgments.

- *FULL/BDR* - The router is fully adjacent with the indicated BDR neighbor. These two neighbors can exchange Hello packets, updates, queries, replies, and acknowledgments.

- *2-WAY/DROTHER* - The non-DR or BDR router has a neighbor relationship with another non-DR or BDR router. These two neighbors exchange Hello packets.

The normal state for an OSPF router is usually FULL. If a router is stuck in another state, it is an indication that there are problems in forming adjacencies. The only exception to this is the 2-WAY state, which is normal in a multiaccess broadcast network.

In multiaccess networks, DROTHERs only form FULL adjacencies with the DR and BDR. However, DROTHERs will still form a 2-WAY neighbor adjacency with any DROTHERs that join the network. This means that all DROTHER routers in the multiaccess network still receive Hello packets from all other DROTHER routers. In this way, they are aware of all routers in the network. When two DROTHER routers form a neighbor adjacency, the neighbor state displays as 2-WAY/DROTHER.

The output generated by R1 confirms that R1 has adjacencies with router:

- R2 with router ID 2.2.2.2 is in a Full state and the role of R2 is BDR. (1)
- R3 with router ID 3.3.3.3 is in a Full state and the role of R3 is DR. (2)

The output generated by R2 in Figure 2 confirms that R2 has adjacencies with router:

- R1 with router ID 1.1.1.1 is in a Full state and R1 is neither the DR nor BDR. (1)
- R3 with router ID 3.3.3.3 is in a Full state and the role of R3 is DR. (2)

The output generated by R3 in Figure 3 confirms that R3 has adjacencies with router:

- R1 with router ID 1.1.1.1 is in a Full state and R1 is neither the DR nor BDR. (1)
- R2 with router ID 2.2.2.2 is in a Full state and the role of R2 is BDR. (2)

Refer to
Online Course
for Illustration

7.1.1.6   Default DR/BDR Election Process

How do the DR and BDR get elected? The OSPF DR and BDR election decision is based on the following criteria, in sequential order:

1. The routers in the network elect the router with the highest interface priority as the DR. The router with the second highest interface priority is elected as the BDR. The

priority can be configured to be any number between 0 – 255. The higher the priority, the likelier the router will be selected as the DR. If the priority is set to 0, the router is not capable of becoming the DR. The default priority of multiaccess broadcast interfaces is 1. Therefore, unless otherwise configured, all routers have an equal priority value and must rely on another tie breaking method during the DR/BDR election.

2. If the interface priorities are equal, then the router with the highest router ID is elected the DR. The router with the second highest router ID is the BDR.

Recall that the router ID is determined in one of three ways:

■ The router ID can be manually configured.

■ If no router IDs are configured, the router ID is determined by the highest loopback IP address.

■ If no loopback interfaces are configured, the router ID is determined by the highest active IPv4 address.

Note   In an IPv6 network, if there are no IPv4 addresses configured on the router, then the router ID must be manually configured with the **router-id** *rid* command; otherwise, OSPFv3 does not start.

In the figure, all Ethernet router interfaces have a default priority of 1. As a result, based on the selection criteria listed above, the OSPF router ID is used to elect the DR and BDR. R3 with the highest router ID becomes the DR; and R2, with the second highest router ID, becomes the BDR.

Note   Serial interfaces have default priorities set to 0; therefore, they do not elect DR and BDRs.

The DR and BDR election process takes place as soon as the first router with an OSPF-enabled interface is active on the multiaccess network. This can happen when the routers are powered on, or when the OSPF **network** command for that interface is configured. The election process only takes a few seconds. If all of the routers on the multiaccess network have not finished booting, it is possible that a router with a lower router ID becomes the DR. (This can be a lower-end router that takes less time to boot.)

Refer to
Online Course
for Illustration

7.1.1.7   DR/BDR Election Process

OSPF DR and BDR elections are not preemptive. If a new router with a higher priority or higher router ID is added to the network after the DR and BDR election, the newly added router does not take over the DR or the BDR role. This is because those roles have already been assigned. The addition of a new router does not initiate a new election process.

After the DR is elected, it remains the DR until one of the following events occurs:

■ The DR fails

■ The OSPF process on the DR fails or is stopped

■ The multiaccess interface on the DR fails or is shutdown

If the DR fails, the BDR is automatically promoted to DR. This is the case even if another DROTHER with a higher priority or router ID is added to the network after the initial DR/BDR election. However, after a BDR is promoted to DR, a new BDR election occurs and the DROTHER with the higher priority or router ID is elected as the new BDR.

Figures 1 to 4 illustrate various scenarios relating to the DR and BDR election process.

In Figure 1, the current DR (R3) fails; therefore, the pre-elected BDR (R2) assumes the role of DR. Subsequently, an election is held to choose a new BDR. Because R1 is the only DROTHER, it is elected as the BDR.

In Figure 2, R3 has re-joined the network after several minutes of being unavailable. Because the DR and BDR already exist, R3 does not take over either role; instead, it becomes a DROTHER.

In Figure 3, a new router (R4) with a higher router ID is added to the network. DR (R2) and BDR (R1) retain the DR and BDR roles. R4 automatically becomes a DROTHER.

In Figure 4, R2 has failed. The BDR (R1) automatically becomes the DR and an election process selects R4 as the BDR because it has the higher router ID.

Refer to
Online Course
for Illustration

7.1.1.8   The OSPF Priority

The DR becomes the focal point for the collection and distribution of LSAs; therefore, this router must have sufficient CPU and memory capacity to handle the workload. It is possible to influence the DR/BDR election process through configurations.

If the interface priorities are equal on all routers, the router with the highest router ID is elected the DR. It is possible to configure the router ID to manipulate the DR/BDR election. However, this process only works if there is a stringent plan for setting the router ID on all routers. In large networks, this can be cumbersome.

Instead of relying on the router ID, it is better to control the election by setting interface priorities. Priorities are an interface-specific value, which means it provides better control on a multiaccess network. This also allows a router to be the DR in one network and a DROTHER in another.

To set the priority of an interface, use the following commands:

- `ip ospf priority` *value* - OSPFv2 interface command
- `ipv6 ospf priority` *value* - OSPFv3 interface command

The *value* can be:

- **0** - Does not become a DR or BDR.
- **1 - 255** - The higher the priority value, the more likely the router becomes the DR or BDR on the interface.

In the figure, all routers have an equal OSPF priority because the priority value defaults to 1 for all router interfaces. Therefore, the router ID is used to determine the DR (R3) and BDR (R2). Changing the priority value on an interface from 1 to a higher value, would enable the router to become a DR or BDR router during the next election.

If the interface priority is configured after OSPF is enabled, the administrator must shut down the OSPF process on all routers, and then re-enable the OSPF process, to force a new DR/BDR election.

Refer to
Online Course
for Illustration

7.1.1.9   Changing the OSPF Priority

In the topology in Figure 1, R3 is the DR and R2 is the BDR. It has been decided that:

- R1 should be the DR and will be configured with a priority of 255.

- R2 should be the BDR and will be left with the default priority of 1.

- R3 should never be a DR or BDR and will be configured with a priority of 0.

Figure 2 changes the R1 interface Gigabit 0/0 priority from 1 to 255.

Figure 3 changes the R3 interface Gigabit 0/0 priority from 1 to 0.

The changes do not automatically take effect because the DR and BDR are already elected. Therefore, the OSPF election must be negotiated using one of the following methods:

- Shutdown the router interfaces and then re-enable them starting with the DR, then the BDR, and then all other routers.

- Reset the OSPF process using the `clear ip ospf process` privileged EXEC mode command on all routers.

Figure 4 displays how to clear the OSPF process on R1. Assume that the `clear ip ospf process` privileged EXEC mode command has been also been configured on R2 and R3. Notice the OSPF state information generated.

The output displayed in Figure 5 confirms that R1 is now the DR with a priority of 255 and identifies the new neighbor adjacencies of R1.

Use the Syntax Checker in Figure 6 to verify the role and adjacencies of R2 and R3.

Refer to
Interactive Graphic
in online course.

7.1.1.10   Activity - Identify OSPF Network Type Terminology

Refer to
Interactive Graphic
in online course.

7.1.1.11   Activity - Select the Designated Router

Refer to **Packet
Tracer Activity**
for this chapter

7.1.1.12   Packet Tracer - Determining the DR and BDR

In this activity, you will examine DR and BDR roles and watch the roles change when there is a change in the network. You will then modify the priority to control the roles and force a new election. Finally, you will verify routers are filling the desired roles.

Refer to
Lab Activity
for this chapter

7.1.1.13   Lab - Configuring OSPFv2 on a Multiaccess Network

In this lab, you will complete the following objectives:

- Part 1: Build the Network and Configure Basic Device Settings

- Part 2: Configure and Verify OSPFv2 on the DR, BDR and DROther

- Part 3: Configure OSPFv2 Interface Priority to Determine the DR and BDR

Refer to
Online Course
for Illustration

7.1.2   Default Route Propagation

7.1.2.1   Propagating a Default Static Route in OSPFv2

Propagating a Default Static Route

As with EIGRP, the router connected to the Internet is used to propagate a default route to other routers in the OSPF routing domain. This router is sometimes called the edge, entrance or gateway router. However, in OSPF terminology, the router located between an OSPF routing domain and a non-OSPF network is also called the autonomous system boundary router (ASBR).

In Figure 1, R2 is single-homed to a service provider. Therefore, all that is required for R2 to reach the Internet is a default static route to the service provider.

Note   In this example, a loopback interface with IP address 209.165.200.225 is used to simulate the connection to the service provider.

To propagate a default route, the edge router (R2) must be configured with:

- A default static route using the `ip route 0.0.0.0 0.0.0.0` {`ip-address | exit-intf`} command.

- The `default-information originate` router configuration mode command. This instructs R2 to be the source of the default route information and propagate the default static route in OSPF updates.

Figure 2 shows how to configure a fully-specified default static route to the service provider.

Refer to
Online Course
for Illustration

7.1.2.2   Verifying the Propagated Default Route

Verify the default route settings on R2 using the `show ip route` command, as shown in Figure 1.

Use the Syntax Checker in Figure 2 to verify that the default route has been propagated to R1 and R3. Notice that the route source is `O*E2`, signifying that it was learned using OSPF. The asterisk identifies this as a good candidate for the default route. The E2 designation identifies that it is an external route.

External routes are either external type 1 or external type 2. The difference between the two is in the way the cost (metric) of the route is being calculated. The cost of a type 2 route is always the external cost, regardless of the interior cost to reach that route. A type 1 cost is the addition of the external cost and the internal cost used to reach that route. A type 1 route is always preferred over a type 2 route for the same destination.

Refer to
Online Course
for Illustration

7.1.2.3   Propagating a Default Static Route in OSPFv3

The process of propagating a default static route in OSPFv3 is almost identical to OSPFv2.

In Figure 1, R2 is single-homed to a service provider. Therefore, all that is required for R2 to reach the Internet is a default static route to the service provider.

Note   In this example, a loopback interface with the IP address of 2001:DB8:FEED:1::1/64 is used to simulate the connection to the service provider.

Figure 2 displays the current IPv6 routing table of R1. Notice that it has no knowledge of the route to the Internet.

To propagate a default route, the edge router (R2) must be configured with:

- A default static route using the `ipv6 route ::/0` {*ipv6-address* | *exit-intf*} command.

- The `default-information originate` router configuration mode command. This instructs R2 to be the source of the default route information and propagate the default static route in OSPF updates.

The example in Figure 3 configures a fully-specified default static route to the service provider.

Refer to
Online Course
for Illustration

7.1.2.4   Verifying the Propagated IPv6 Default Route

Verify the default static route setting on R2 using the `show ipv6 route` command, as shown in Figure 1.

Use the Syntax Checker in Figure 2 to verify that the default route has been propagated to R1 and R3. Notice that the route source is `OE2` signifying that it was learned using OSPFv3. The E2 designation identifies that it is external route.

Unlike the IPv4 routing table, IPv6 does not use the asterisk to signify that the route is a good candidate for the default route.

Refer to **Packet
Tracer Activity**
for this chapter

7.1.2.5   Packet Tracer - Propagating a Default Route in OSPFv2

In this activity, you will configure an IPv4 default route to the Internet and propagate that default route to other OSPF routers. You will then verify the default route is in downstream routing tables and that hosts can now access a web server on the Internet.

Refer to
Online Course
for Illustration

7.1.3   Fine-tuning OSPF Interfaces

7.1.3.1   OSPF Hello and Dead Intervals

Like EIGRP, the OSPF Hello and Dead intervals are configurable on a per-interface basis. Unlike EIGRP, the OSPF intervals must match or a neighbor adjacency does not occur.

To verify the currently configured interface intervals, use the `show ip ospf interface` command, as shown in Figure 1. The Serial 0/0/0 Hello and Dead intervals are set to the default 10 seconds and 40 seconds respectively.

Figure 2 provides an example of using a filtering technique to display the OSPF intervals for the OSPF enabled interface Serial 0/0/0 on R1.

In Figure 3, the `show ip ospf neighbor` command is used on R1 to verify that R1 is adjacent to R2 and R3. Notice in the output that the Dead Time is counting down from 40 seconds. By default, this value is refreshed every 10 seconds when R1 receives a Hello from the neighbor.

Refer to
Online Course
for Illustration

7.1.3.2   Modifying OSPFv2 Intervals

It may be desirable to change the OSPF timers so that routers detect network failures in less time. Doing this increases traffic, but sometimes the need for quick convergence is more important than the extra traffic it creates.

Note   The default Hello and Dead intervals are based on best practices and should only be altered in rare situations.

OSPF Hello and Dead intervals can be modified manually using the following interface configuration mode commands:

- `ip ospf hello-interval` *seconds*

- `ip ospf dead-interval` *seconds*

Use the `no ip ospf hello-interval` and `no ip ospf dead-interval` commands to reset the intervals to their default.

The example in Figure 1 modifies the Hello interval to 5 seconds. Immediately after changing the Hello interval, the Cisco IOS automatically modifies the Dead interval to four times the Hello interval. However, it is always good practice to explicitly modify the timer instead of relying on an automatic IOS feature so that modifications are documented in the configuration. Therefore, the Dead interval is also manually set to 20 seconds on the R1 Serial 0/0/0 interface.

As displayed by the highlighted OSPFv3 adjacency message in the figure, when the Dead Timer on R1 expires, R1 and R2 lose adjacency. The reason is because the values have only been altered on one side of the serial link between R1 and R2. Recall that the OSPF Hello and Dead intervals must match between neighbors.

Use the `show ip ospf neighbor` command on R1 to verify the neighbor adjacencies, as shown in Figure 2. Notice that the only neighbor listed is the 3.3.3.3 (R3) router and that R1 is no longer adjacent with the 2.2.2.2 (R2) neighbor. The timers set on Serial 0/0/0 do not affect the neighbor adjacency with R3.

To restore adjacency between R1 and R2, the R2 Serial 0/0/0 interface Hello interval is set to `5` seconds, as shown in Figure 3. Almost immediately, the IOS displays a message that adjacency has been established with a state of `FULL`.

Verify the interface intervals using the `show ip ospf interface` command, as shown in Figure 4. Notice that the Hello time is 5 seconds and that the Dead Time was automatically set to 20 seconds instead of the default 40 seconds. Remember that the OSPF automatically sets the Dead interval to four times the Hello interval.

Refer to
Online Course
for Illustration

7.1.3.3   Modifying OSPFv3 Intervals

Like OSPFv2, OSPFv3 intervals can also be adjusted.

OSPFv3 Hello and Dead intervals can be modified manually using the following interface configuration mode commands:

- `ipv6 ospf hello-interval` *seconds*

- `ipv6 ospf dead-interval` *seconds*

Note Use the `no ipv6 ospf hello-interval` and `no ipv6 ospf dead-interval` commands to reset the intervals to their default.

Refer to the IPv6 topology in Figure 1. Assume that the network has converged using OSPFv3.

The example in Figure 2 modifies the OSPFv3 Hello interval to 5 seconds. Immediately after changing the Hello interval, the Cisco IOS automatically modifies the Dead interval to four times the Hello interval. However, as with OSPFv2, it is always good practice to explicitly modify the timer instead of relying on an automatic IOS feature so that modifications are documented in the configuration. Therefore, the Dead interval is also manually set to 20 seconds on the R1 Serial 0/0/0 interface.

Once the Dead Timer on R1 expires, R1 and R2 lose adjacency, as displayed by the highlighted OSPFv3 adjacency message in Figure 2, because the values have only been altered on one side of the serial link between R1 and R2. Recall that the OSPFv3 Hello and Dead intervals must be equivalent between neighbors.

Use the `show ipv6 ospf neighbor` command on R1 to verify the neighbor adjacencies (Figure 3). Notice that R1 is no longer adjacent with the 2.2.2.2 (R2) neighbor.

To restore adjacency between R1 and R2, the R2 Serial 0/0/0 interface Hello interval is set to 5 seconds (Figure 4). Almost immediately, the IOS displays a message that adjacency has been established with a state of **FULL**.

Verify the interface intervals using the `show ipv6 ospf interface` command (Figure 5). Notice that the Hello time is 5 seconds and that the Dead Time was automatically set to 20 seconds instead of the default 40 seconds. Remember that the OSPF automatically sets the Dead interval to four times the Hello interval.

Refer to
Online Course
for Illustration

7.1.4 Secure OSPF

7.1.4.1 Routers are Targets

The role of routers in a network is so crucial that they are often the targets of network attacks. Network administrators must be aware that routers are at risk from attack just as much as end-user systems.

In general, routing systems can be attacked by disrupting the routing peers or by falsifying the information carried within the routing protocol. Falsified routing information may generally be used to cause systems to misinform (lie to) each other, cause a denial-of-service (DoS) attack, or cause traffic to follow a path it would not normally follow. The consequences of falsifying routing information are:

- Redirecting traffic to create routing loops
- Redirecting traffic so it can be monitored on an insecure link
- Redirecting traffic to discard it

Click the Play button in the animation to see an example of an attack that creates a routing loop. An attacker has been able to connect directly to the link between routers R1 and R2. The attacker injects false routing information destined to router R1 only, indicating that R3 is the preferred destination to the 192.168.10.10/32 host route. Although R1 has a routing table entry to the directly connected 192.168.10.0/24 network, it adds the injected route to its routing table because of the longer subnet mask. A route with a longer matching subnet mask is considered to be superior to a route with a shorter subnet mask. Consequently, when a router receives a packet, it selects the longer subnet mask, because it is a more precise route to the destination.

When PC3 sends a packet to PC1 (192.168.10.10/24), R1 does not forward the packet to the PC1 host. Instead, it routes the packet to router R3, because the apparent best path to 192.168.10.10/32 is through R3. When R3 gets the packet, it looks in its routing table and forwards the packet back to R1, which creates the loop.

To mitigate against routing protocol attacks, configure OSPF authentication.

Refer to
Online Course
for Illustration

7.1.4.2   Secure Routing Updates

When neighbor authentication has been configured on a router, the router authenticates the source of each routing update packet that it receives. This is accomplished by the exchange of an authenticating key (sometimes referred to as a password) that is known to both the sending and the receiving router.

To exchange routing update information in a secure manner, enable OSPF authentication. OSPF authentication can either be none (or null), simple, or Message Digest 5 (MD5).

OSPF supports 3 types of authentication:

- **Null** - This is the default method and means that no authentication is used for OSPF.

- **Simple password authentication** - This is also referred to as plaintext authentication because the password in the update is sent in plaintext over the network. This is considered to be a legacy method of OSPF authentication.

- **MD5 authentication** - This is the most secure and recommended method of authentication. MD5 authentication provides higher security because the password is never exchanged between peers. Instead it is calculated using the MD5 algorithm. Matching results authenticate the sender.

Click the Play button in the animation to see how MD5 authentication is used to authenticate neighboring peer messages.

Note   RIPv2, EIGRP, OSPF, IS-IS, and BGP all support various forms of MD5 authentication.

Refer to
Online Course
for Illustration

7.1.4.3   MD5 Authentication

The following example illustrates how MD5 authentication is used to authenticate two neighboring OSPF routers.

In Figure 1, R1 combines the routing message with the pre-shared secret key and calculates the signature using the MD5 algorithm. The signature is also known as a hash value.

In Figure 2, R1 adds the signature to the routing message and sends it to R2.

MD5 does not encrypt the message; therefore, the content is easily readable.

In Figure 3, R2 opens the packet, combines the routing message with the pre-shared secret key and calculates the signature using the MD5 algorithm.

- If the signatures match, then R2 accepts the routing update.

- If the signatures do not match, then R2 discards the update.

OSPFv3 (OSPF for IPv6) does not include any authentication capabilities of its own. Instead it relies entirely on IPSec to secure communications between neighbors using the `ipv6 ospf authentication ipsec spi` interface configuration mode command. This is beneficial in simplifying the OSPFv3 protocol and standardizing its authentication mechanism.

Refer to
Online Course
for Illustration

7.1.4.4   Configuring OSPF MD5 Authentication

OSPF supports routing protocol authentication using MD5. MD5 authentication can be enabled globally for all interfaces or on a per-interface basis.

To enable OSPF MD5 authentication globally, configure:

- `ip ospf message-digest-key` *key* `md5` *password* interface configuration mode command.

- `area` *area-id* `authentication` `message-digest` router configuration mode command.

This method forces authentication on all OSPF enabled interfaces. If an interface is not configured with the `ip ospf message-digest-key` command, it will not be able to form adjacencies with other OSPF neighbors.

To provide more flexibility, authentication is now supported on a per-interface basis. To enable MD5 authentication on a per-interface basis, configure:

- `ip ospf message-digest-key` *key* `md5` *password* interface configuration mode command.

- `ip ospf authentication message-digest` interface configuration mode command.

Global and per-interface OSPF MD5 authentication can be used on the same router. However, the interface setting overrides the global setting. MD5 authentication passwords do not have to be the same throughout an area; however, they do need to be the same between neighbors.

For example, assume that all routers in the figure have converged using OSPF and routing is functioning properly. OSPF authentication will be implemented on all routers.

Refer to
Online Course
for Illustration

7.1.4.5   OSPF MD5 Authentication Example

The example in Figure 1 configures R1 to enable OSPF MD5 authentication on all interfaces. Notice the informational messages stating that the OSPF neighbor adjacencies with R2 and R3 have changed to the Down state, because R2 and R3 have not yet been configured to support MD5 authentication.

As an alternative to globally enabling MD5 authentication, the example in Figure 2 demonstrates how to configure R1 to enable OSPF MD5 authentication on a per-interface basis.

Again, notice how the OSPF neighbor adjacencies have changed to the Down state.

Use the Syntax Checker in Figure 3 to enable OSPF MD5 authentication globally on R2 and R3.

Again, informational messages appear. The first message is because the neighbor adjacency with R1 has been re-established. However, the adjacency with R3 has transitioned to the Down state, because R3 is still not configured

After R3 is configured, all neighbor adjacencies have been re-established.

Refer to
Online Course
for Illustration

7.1.4.6   Verifying OSPF MD5 Authentication

To verify that OSPF MD5 authentication is enabled, use the `show ip ospf interface` privileged EXEC mode command. By verifying that the routing table is complete successful authentication can be confirmed.

Figure 1 verifies the OSPF MD5 authentication on R1. Notice how the ISO filter can be used to verify all OSPF-enabled interfaces.

Figure 2 confirms that the authentication is successful.

Refer to **Packet Tracer Activity** for this chapter

Use the Syntax Checker in Figure 3 to verify the OSPF MD5 authentication on R2 and R3.

7.1.4.7   Packet Tracer - Configuring OSPFv2 Advance Features

In this activity, OSPF is already configured and all end devices currently have full connectivity. You will modify the default OSPF routing configuration by changing the Hello and Dead timers, adjusting the bandwidth of a link, and enabling OSPF authentication. Then you will verify that full connectivity is restored for all end devices.

Refer to
Lab Activity
for this chapter

7.1.4.8   Lab - Configuring OSPFv2 Advance Features

In this lab, you will complete the following objectives:

- Part 1: Build the Network and Configure Basic Device Settings
- Part 2: Configure and Verify OSPF Routing
- Part 3: Change OSPF Metrics
- Part 4: Configure and Propagate a Static Default Route
- Part 5: Configure OSPF Authentication

Refer to
Online Course
for Illustration

7.2   Troubleshooting Single-Area OSPF Implementations

7.2.1   Components of Troubleshooting Single-Area OSPF

7.2.1.1   Overview

OSPF is a popularly implemented routing protocol used in large enterprise networks.

Troubleshooting problems related to the exchange of routing information is one of the most essential skills for a network professional that is involved in the implementation and maintenance of large, routed enterprise networks that use OSPF as the IGP.

Issues with forming OSPF adjacencies are listed in the figure.

Refer to
Online Course
for Illustration

7.2.1.2   OSPF States

To troubleshoot OSPF, it is important to understand how OSPF routers traverse different OSPF states when adjacencies are being established.

The figure lists the OSPF states and provides a summary of functions of each state.

When troubleshooting OSPF neighbors, be aware that the FULL or 2WAY states are normal. All other states are transitory; that is, the router should not remain in those states for extended periods of time.

Refer to
Online Course
for Illustration

7.2.1.3   OSPF Troubleshooting Commands

There are many different OSPF commands that can be used to help in the troubleshooting process. The following summarizes the most common of these commands:

- **`show ip protocols`** (Figure 1) - Used to verify vital OSPF configuration information, including the OSPF process ID, the router ID, networks the router is advertising, the neighbors the router is receiving updates from, and the default administrative distance, which is 110 for OSPF.

- **`show ip ospf neighbor`** (Figure 2) - Used to verify that the router has formed an adjacency with its neighboring routers. Displays the neighbor router ID, neighbor priority, OSPF state, Dead timer, neighbor interface IP address, and interface that the neighbor is accessible through. If the router ID of the neighboring router is not displayed, or if it does not show as a state of FULL or 2WAY, the two routers have not formed an OSPF adjacency. If two routers do not establish adjacency, link-state information will not be exchanged. Incomplete link-state databases can cause inaccurate SPF trees and routing tables. Routes to destination networks may not exist or may not be the most optimum path.

- **`show ip ospf interface`** (Figure 3) - Used to display the OSPF parameters configured on an interface, such as the OSPF process ID that the interface is assigned to, the area that the interfaces are in, the cost of the interface, and the Hello and Dead intervals. Adding the interface name and number to the command displays output for a specific interface.

- **`show ip ospf`** (Figure 4) - Used to examine the OSPF process ID and router ID. Additionally, this command displays the OSPF area information, as well as the last time the SPF algorithm was calculated.

- **`show ip route ospf`** (Figure 5) - Used to display only the OSPF learned routes in the routing table. The output shows that R1 has learned about four remote networks through OSPF.

- **`clear ip ospf`** [*process-id*] **`process`** - Used to reset the OSPFv2 neighbor adja-

Refer to
Online Course
for Illustration

cencies.

7.2.1.4 Components of Troubleshooting OSPF

As shown in the figure, OSPF problems usually relate to:

- Neighbor adjacencies

- Missing routes

- Path selection

When troubleshooting neighbor issues, verify if the router has established adjacencies with neighboring routers using the `show ip ospf neighbors` command. If there is no adjacency, then the routers cannot exchange routes. Verify if interfaces are operational and enabled for OSPF using the `show ip interface brief` and the `show ip ospf interface` commands. If the interfaces are operational and enabled for OSPF, ensure that interfaces on both routers are configured for the same OSPF area and the interfaces are not configured as passive interfaces.

If adjacency between two routers is established, verify that there are OSPF routes in the routing table using the `show ip route ospf` command. If there are no OSPF routes, verify that there are no other routing protocols with lower administrative distances running in the network. Verify if all of the required networks are advertised into OSPF. Also verify if an access list is configured on a router that would filter either incoming or outgoing routing updates.

Refer to
Interactive Graphic
in online course.

If all of the required routes are in the routing table, but the path that traffic takes is not correct, verify the OSPF cost on interfaces on the path. Also be careful in cases where the interfaces are faster than 100 Mb/s, because all interfaces above this bandwidth have the same OSPF cost, by default.

Refer to
Online Course
for Illustration

7.2.1.5 Activity - Identify the Troubleshooting Command

7.2.2 Troubleshoot Single-Area OSPFv2 Routing Issues

7.2.2.1 Troubleshooting Neighbor Issues

This example will highlight how to troubleshoot neighbor problems.

In the topology in Figure 1, all of the routers have been configured to support OSPF routing.

A quick look at the R1 routing table, as shown in Figure 2, reveals that it is not adding any OSPF routes. There are multiple reasons why this could be. However, a prerequisite for the neighbor relationship to form between two routers is OSI Layer 3 connectivity.

The output in Figure 3 confirms that the S0/0/0 interface is up and active. The successful ping also confirms that the R2 serial interface is active. A successful ping does not mean an adjacency will form because it is possible to have overlapping subnets. You still have to verify that interfaces on the connected devices share the same subnet. If the ping was not successful, check the cabling and verify that interfaces on connected devices are configured correctly and operational.

For an interface to be enabled for OSPF, a matching `network` command must be configured under the OSPF routing process. Active OSPF interfaces can be verified using the `show ip ospf interface` command. The output in Figure 4 verifies that the Serial 0/0/0 interface is enabled for OSPF. If connected interfaces on two routers are not enabled for OSPF, the neighbors will not form an adjacency.

Verify the OSPF settings using the `show ip protocols` command. The output displayed in Figure 5 verifies that OSPF is enabled and also lists the networks being advertised as enabled by the `network` command. If an IP address on an interface falls within a network that has been enabled for OSPF, the interface will be enabled for OSPF.

However, notice that the Serial 0/0/0 interface is listed as passive. Recall that the `passive-interface` command stops both outgoing and incoming routing updates because the effect of the command causes the router to stop sending and receiving Hello packets over an interface. For this reason, the routers will not become neighbors.

To disable the interface as passive, use the `no passive-interface` router configuration mode command as shown in Figure 6. After you disable the passive interface, the routers become adjacent as indicated by automatically generated information message.

Refer to
Online Course
for Illustration

A quick verification of the routing table as shown in Figure 7 confirms that OSPF is now exchanging routing information.

7.2.2.2   Troubleshooting OSPF Routing Table Issues

In the topology in Figure 1, all of the routers have been configured to support OSPF routing.

A quick look at the R1 routing table (Figure 2) reveals that it receives default route information, the R2 LAN (172.16.2.0/24) and the link between R2 and R3 (192.168.10.8/30). However, it does not receive the R3 LAN OSPF route.

The output in Figure 3 verifies the OSPF settings on R3. Notice that R3 only advertises the link between R3 and R2. It does not advertise the R3 LAN (192.168.1.0/24).

For an interface to be enabled for OSPF, a matching `network` command must be configured under the OSPF routing process. The output in Figure 4 confirms that the R3 LAN is not advertised in OSPF.

Refer to **Packet Tracer Activity**
for this chapter

The example in Figure 5 adds a `network` command for the R3 LAN. R3 should now advertise the R3 LAN to its OSPF neighbors.

The output in Figure 6 verifies that the R3 LAN is now in the routing table of R1.

7.2.2.3   Packet Tracer - Troubleshooting Single-Area OSPFv2

In this activity, you will troubleshoot OSPF routing issues using `ping` and `show` commands to identify errors in the network configuration. Then, you will document the errors you discover and implement an appropriate solution. Finally, you will verify end-to-end connectivity is restored.

Refer to
Online Course
for Illustration

7.2.3   Troubleshoot Single-Area OSPFv3 Routing Issues

7.2.3.1   OSPFv3 Troubleshooting Commands

Refer to Figure 1 for the OSPFv3 reference topology.

Troubleshooting OSPFv3 is almost identical to OSPFv2; therefore, many OSPFv3 commands and troubleshooting criteria also apply to OSPFv3.

For example, the following are the equivalent commands used with OSPFv3:

- **show ipv6 protocols** (Figure 2) - This command is used to verify vital OSPFv3 configuration information, including the OSPFv3 process ID, the router ID, networks the router is advertising, and the neighbors the router is receiving updates from.

- **show ipv6 ospf neighbor** (Figure 3) - Used to verify that the router has formed an adjacency with its neighboring routers. This output displays the neighbor router ID, the neighbor priority, OSPFv3 state, dead timer, neighbor interface ID, and the interface that the neighbor is accessible through. If the router ID of the neighboring router is not displayed, or if it does not show as a state of **FULL** or **2WAY**, the two routers have not formed an OSPFv3 adjacency. If two routers do not establish adjacency, link-state information will not be exchanged. Incomplete link-state databases can cause inaccurate SPF trees and routing tables. Routes to destination networks may not exist, or they may not be the most optimum paths.

- **show ipv6 ospf interface** (Figure 4) - Used to display the OSPFv3 parameters configured on an interface, such as the OSPFv3 process ID that the interface is assigned to, area that the interfaces are in, and cost of the interface, and the Hello and Dead intervals. Adding the interface name and number to the command displays output for a specific interface.

- **show ipv6 ospf** (Figure 5) - Used to examine the OSPF process ID and router ID, as well as information about the LSA transmissions.

- **show ipv6 route ospf** (Figure 6) - Used to display only the OSPFv3 learned routes in the routing table. The output shows that R1 has learned about four remote networks through OSPFv3.

- **clear ipv6 ospf** [*process-id*] **process** - Used to reset the OSPFv3 neighbor adjacencies.

Refer to
Online Course
for Illustration

7.2.3.2   Troubleshooting OSPFv3

In the topology in Figure 1, all of the routers have been configured to support OSPFv3 routing.

A quick look at the R1 IPv6 routing table (Figure 2) reveals that it receives the default route, the R2 LAN (2001:DB8:CAFE:2::/64) and the link between R2 and R3 (2001:DB8:CAFE:A002::/64). However, it does not receive the R3 LAN OSPFv3 route (2001:DB8:CAFE:3::/64).

The output in Figure 3 verifies the OSPFv3 settings on R3. Notice that R3 is only enabled on the Serial 0/0/1 interface. It appears that it is not enabled on the G0/0 R3 interface.

Unlike OSPFv2, OSPFV3 does not use the **network** command. Instead OSPFv3 is enabled directly on the interface. The output in Figure 4 confirms that the R3 interface is not enabled for OSPFv3.

The example in Figure 5 enables OSPFv3 on the R3 Gigabit Ethernet 0/0 interface. R3 should now advertise the R3 LAN to its OSPFv3 neighbors.

The output in Figure 6 verifies that the R3 LAN is now in the routing table of R1.

7.2.3.3   Lab - Troubleshooting Basic Single-Area OSPFv2 and OSPFv3

In this lab, you will complete the following objectives:

- Part 1: Build the Network and Load Device Configurations
- Part 2: Troubleshoot Layer 3 Connectivity
- Part 3: Troubleshoot OSPFv2
- Part 4: Troubleshoot OSPFv3

7.2.3.4   Lab - Troubleshooting Advanced Single-Area OSPFv2

In this lab, you will complete the following objectives:

- Part 1: Build the Network and Load Device Configurations
- Part 2: Troubleshoot OSPF

7.3   Summary

7.3.1.1   Class Activity - OSPF Troubleshooting Mastery

Activity - OSPF Troubleshooting Mastery

Scenario

You have decided to change your routing protocol from RIPv2 to OSPFv2. Your small- to medium-sized business network topology will not change from its original physical settings. Use the diagram on the PDF for this activity as your company's small- to medium-sized business network design.

Your addressing design is complete and you then configure your routers with IPv4 and VLSM. OSPF has been applied as the routing protocol. However, some routers are sharing routing information with each other and some are not.

Open the PDF file that accompanies this modeling activity and follow the directions to complete the activity.

When the steps in the directions are complete, regroup as a class and compare recorded activity correction times. The group taking the shortest time to find and fix the configuration error will be declared the winner only after successfully explaining how they found the error, fixed it, and proved that the topology is now working.

7.3.1.2   Packet Tracer - Skills Integration Challenge

In this Skills Integration Challenge, your focus is OSPFv2 advanced configurations. IP addressing has been configured for all devices. You will configure OSPFv2 routing with

Refer to
Online Course
for Illustration

passive interfaces and default route propagation. You will modify the OSPFv2 configuration by adjusting timers and establishing MD5 authentication. Finally, you will verify your configurations and test connectivity between end devices.

7.3.1.3 Summary

OSPF defines five network types: point-to-point, broadcast multiaccess, nonbroadcast multiaccess, point-to-multipoint, and virtual links.

Multiaccess networks can create two challenges for OSPF regarding the flooding of LSAs: creation of multiple adjacencies and extensive flooding of LSAs. The solution to managing the number of adjacencies and the flooding of LSAs on a multiaccess network is the DR and BDR. If the DR stops producing Hellos, the BDR promotes itself and assumes the role of DR.

The routers in the network elect the router with the highest interface priority as DR. The router with the second highest interface priority is elected the BDR. The higher the priority, the likelier the router will be selected as the DR. If set to 0, the router is not capable of becoming the DR. The default priority of multiaccess broadcast interfaces is 1. Therefore, unless otherwise configured, all routers have an equal priority value and must rely on another tie breaking method during the DR/BDR election. If the interface priorities are equal, then the router with the highest router ID is elected the DR. The router with the second highest router ID is the BDR. The addition of a new router does not initiate a new election process.

To propagate a default route in OSPF, the router must be configured with a default static route and the `default-information originate` command must be added to the configuration. Verify routes with the `show ip route` or `show ipv6 route` command.

To assist OSPF in making the correct path determination, the reference bandwidth must be changed to a higher value to accommodate networks with links faster than 100 Mb/s. To adjust the reference bandwidth, use the `auto-cost reference-bandwidth` *Mbps* router configuration mode command. To adjust the interface bandwidth, use the `bandwidth` *kilobits* interface configuration mode command. The cost can be manually configured on an interface using the `ip ospf cost` *value* interface configuration mode command.

The OSPF Hello and Dead intervals must match or a neighbor adjacency does not occur. To modify these intervals, use the following interface commands:

- `ip ospf hello-interval` *seconds*

- `ip ospf dead-interval` *seconds*

- `ipv6 ospf hello-interval` *seconds*

- `ipv6 ospf dead-interval` *seconds*

OSPF supports 3 types of authentication: null, simple password authentication, and MD5 authentication. OSPF MD5 authentication can be configured globally or per interface. To verify OSPF MD5 implementation is enabled, use the `show ip ospf interface` privileged EXEC mode command.

When troubleshooting OSPF neighbors, be aware that the FULL or 2WAY states are normal. The following commands summarize IPv4 OSPF troubleshooting:

- `show ip protocols`

- `show ip ospf neighbor`

- `show ip ospf interface`

- `show ip ospf`

- `show ip route ospf`

- `clear ip ospf [ process-id ] process`

Troubleshooting OSPFv3 is similar to OSPFv2. The following commands are the equivalent commands used with OSPFv3: `show ipv6 protocols`, `show ipv6 ospf neighbor`, `show ipv6 ospf interface`, `show ipv6 ospf`, `show ipv6 route ospf`, and `clear ipv6 ospf [process-id] process`.

Go to the online course to take the quiz and exam.

Chapter 7 Quiz

This quiz is designed to provide an additional opportunity to practice the skills and knowledge presented in the chapter and to prepare for the chapter exam. You will be allowed multiple attempts and the grade does not appear in the gradebook.

Chapter 7 Exam

The chapter exam assesses your knowledge of the chapter content.

Your Chapter Notes

Multiarea OSPF

8.0 Multiarea OSPF

8.0.1.1 Introduction

Multiarea OSPF is used to divide a large OSPF network. Too many routers in one area increase the load on the CPU and create a large link-state data base. In this chapter, directions are provided to effectively partition a large single area into multiple areas. Area 0 used in a single-area OSPF is known as the backbone area.

Discussion is focused on the LSAs exchanged between areas. In addition, activities for configuring OSPFv2 and OSPFv3 are provided. The chapter concludes with the **show** commands used to verify OSPF configurations.

> Refer to
> **Lab Activity**
> for this chapter

8.0.1.2 Class Activity Leaving on a Jet Plane

Leaving on a Jet Plane

Scenario

You and a classmate are starting a new airline to serve your continent.

In addition to your core area or headquarters airport, you will locate and map four intra-continental airport service areas and one transcontinental airport service area that can be used for additional source and destination travel.

Use the blank world map provided to design your airport locations. Additional instructions for completing this activity can be found in the accompanying PDF.

> Refer to
> **Online Course**
> for Illustration

8.1 Multiarea OSPF Operation

8.1.1 Why Multiarea OSPF?

8.1.1.1 Single-Area OSPF

Single-area OSPF is useful in smaller networks where the web of router links is not complex, and paths to individual destinations are easily deduced.

However, if an area becomes too big, the following issues must be addressed (see the figure for illustration):

- **Large routing table** - OSPF does not perform route summarization by default. If the routes are not summarized, the routing table can become very large, depending on the size of the network.

■ **Large link-state database (LSDB)** - Because the LSDB covers the topology of the entire network, each router must maintain an entry for every network in the area, even if not every route is selected for the routing table.

■ **Frequent SPF algorithm calculations** - In a large network, changes are inevitable, so the routers spend many CPU cycles recalculating the SPF algorithm and updating the routing table.

To make OSPF more efficient and scalable, OSPF supports hierarchical routing using areas. An OSPF area is a group of routers that share the same link-state information in their link-state databases.

Refer to
Online Course
for Illustration

8.1.1.2 Multiarea OSPF

When a large OSPF area is divided into smaller areas, this is called multiarea OSPF. Multiarea OSPF is useful in larger network deployments to reduce processing and memory overhead.

For instance, any time a router receives new information about the topology, as with additions, deletions, or modifications of a link, the router must rerun the SPF algorithm, create a new SPF tree, and update the routing table. The SPF algorithm is CPU-intensive and the time it takes for calculation depends on the size of the area. Too many routers in one area make the LSDB larger and increase the load on the CPU. Therefore, arranging routers into areas effectively partitions one potentially large database into smaller and more manageable databases.

Multiarea OSPF requires a hierarchical network design. The main area is called the backbone area (area 0) and all other areas must connect to the backbone area. With hierarchical routing, routing still occurs between the areas (interarea routing); while many of the tedious routing operations, such as recalculating the database, are kept within an area.

As illustrated in Figure 1, the hierarchical-topology possibilities of multiarea OSPF have these advantages:

■ **Smaller routing tables** - There are fewer routing table entries as network addresses can be summarized between areas. For example, R1 summarizes the routes from area 1 to area 0 and R2 summarizes the routes from area 51 to area 0. R1 and R2 also propagate a default static route to area 1 and area 51.

■ **Reduced link-state update overhead** - Minimizes processing and memory requirements, because there are fewer routers exchanging LSAs.

■ **Reduced frequency of SPF calculations** - Localizes impact of a topology change within an area. For instance, it minimizes routing update impact, because LSA flooding stops at the area boundary.

In Figure 2, assume a link fails between two internal routers in area 51. Only the routers in area 51 exchange LSAs and rerun the SPF algorithm for this event. R1 does not receive LSAs from area 51 and does not recalculate the SPF algorithm.

Refer to
Online Course
for Illustration

8.1.1.3   OSPF Two-Layer Area Hierarchy

Multiarea OSPF is implemented in a two-layer area hierarchy:

- **Backbone (Transit) area** - An OSPF area whose primary function is the fast and efficient movement of IP packets. Backbone areas interconnect with other OSPF area types. Generally, end users are not found within a backbone area. The backbone area is also called OSPF area 0. Hierarchical networking defines area 0 as the core to which all other areas directly connect. (Figure 1)

- **Regular (Non-backbone) area** - Connects users and resources. Regular areas are usually set up along functional or geographical groupings. By default, a regular area does not allow traffic from another area to use its links to reach other areas. All traffic from other areas must cross a transit area. (Figure 2)

Note   A regular area can have a number of subtypes, including a standard area, stub area, totally stubby area, and not-so-stubby area (NSSA). Stub, totally stubby, and NSSAs are beyond the scope of this chapter.

OSPF enforces this rigid two-layer area hierarchy. The underlying physical connectivity of the network must map to the two-layer area structure, with all non-backbone areas attaching directly to area 0. All traffic moving from one area to another area must traverse the backbone area. This traffic is referred to as interarea traffic.

The optimal number of routers per area varies based on factors such as network stability, but Cisco recommends the following guidelines:

- An area should have no more than 50 routers.

- A router should not be in more than three areas.

- Any single router should not have more than 60 neighbors.

Refer to
Online Course
for Illustration

8.1.1.4   Types of OSPF Routers

OSPF routers of different types control the traffic that goes in and out of areas. The OSPF routers are categorized based on the function they perform in the routing domain.

There are four different types of OSPF routers:

- **Internal router** – This is a router that has all of its interfaces in the same area. All internal routers in an area have identical LSDBs. (Figure 1)

- **Backbone router** – This is a router in the backbone area. Generally, the backbone area is set to area 0. (Figure 2)

- **Area Border Router (ABR)** – This is a router that has interfaces attached to multiple areas. It must maintain separate LSDBs for each area it is connected to, and can route between areas. ABRs are exit points for the area, which means that routing information destined for another area can get there only via the ABR of the local area. ABRs can be configured to summarize the routing information from the LSDBs of their attached areas. ABRs distribute the routing information into the backbone. The backbone routers then forward the information to the other ABRs. In a multiarea network, an area can have one or more ABRs. (Figure 3)

■ **Autonomous System Boundary Router (ASBR)** – This is a router that has at least one interface attached to an external internetwork (another autonomous system), such as a non-OSPF network. An ASBR can import non-OSPF network information to the OSPF network, and vice versa, using a process called route redistribution. (Figure 4)

Redistribution in multiarea OSPF occurs when an ASBR connects different routing domains (e.g., EIGRP and OSPF) and configures them to exchange and advertise routing information between those routing domains.

A router can be classified as more than one router type. For example, if a router connects to area 0 and area 1, and in addition, maintains routing information for another, non-OSPF network, it falls under three different classifications: a backbone router, an ABR, and an ASBR.

Refer to
Interactive Graphic
in online course.

8.1.1.5 Activity - Identify the Multiarea OSPF Terminology

Refer to
Online Course
for Illustration

8.1.2 Multiarea OSPF LSA Operation

8.1.2.1 OSPF LSA Types

LSAs are the building blocks of the OSPF LSDB. Individually, they act as database records and provide specific OSPF network details. In combination, they describe the entire topology of an OSPF network or area.

The RFCs for OSPF currently specify up to 11 different LSA types (Figure 1). However, any implementation of multiarea OSPF must support the first five LSAs: LSA 1 to LSA 5 (Figure 2). The focus of this topic is on these first five LSAs.

Each router link is defined as an LSA type. The LSA includes a link ID field that identifies, by network number and mask, the object to which the link connects. Depending on the type, the link ID has different meanings. LSAs differ on how they are generated and propagated within the routing domain.

Note OSPFv3 includes additional LSA types.

Refer to
Online Course
for Illustration

8.1.2.2 OSPF LSA Type 1

As shown in the figure, all routers advertise their directly connected OSPF-enabled links in a type 1 LSA and forward their network information to OSPF neighbors. The LSA contains a list of the directly connected interfaces, link types, and link states.

Type 1 LSAs are also referred to the router link entries.

Type 1 LSAs are flooded only within the area in which they originated. ABRs subsequently advertise the networks learned from the type 1 LSAs to other areas as type 3 LSAs.

The type 1 LSA link ID is identified by the router ID of the originating router.

Refer to
Online Course
for Illustration

8.1.2.3 OSPF LSA Type 2

A type 2 LSA only exists for multiaccess and non-broadcast multiaccess (NBMA) networks where there is a DR elected and at least two routers on the multiaccess segment. The type 2 LSA contains the router ID and IP address of the DR, along with the router ID of all other routers on the multiaccess segment. A type 2 LSA is created for every multiaccess network in the area.

The purpose of an a type 2 LSA is to give other routers information about multiaccess networks within the same area.

The DR floods type 2 LSAs only within the area in which they originated. Type 2 LSAs are not forwarded outside of an area.

Type 2 LSAs are also referred to the network link entries.

As shown in the figure, ABR1 is the DR for the Ethernet network in area 1. It generates the type 2 LSA and forwards it into area 1. ABR2 is the DR for the multiaccess network in area 0. There are no multiaccess networks in area 2 and therefore, no type 2 LSAs are ever propagated in that area.

The link-state ID for a network LSA is the IP interface address of the DR that advertises it.

Refer to
Online Course
for Illustration

8.1.2.4   OSPF LSA Type 3

Type 3 LSAs are used by ABRs to advertise networks from other areas. ABRs collect type 1 LSAs in the LSDB. After an OSPF area has converged, the ABR creates a type 3 LSA for each of its learned OSPF networks. Therefore, an ABR with many OSPF routes must create type 3 LSAs for each network.

As shown in the figure, ABR1 and ABR2 floods type 3 LSAs from one area to other areas. The ABRs propagate the type 3 LSAs into other areas. In a large OSPF deployment with many networks, propagating type 3 LSAs can cause significant flooding problems. For this reason, it is strongly recommended that manual route summarization be configured on the ABR.

The link-state ID is set to the network number and the mask is also advertised.

Receiving a type 3 LSA into its area does not cause a router to run the SPF algorithm. The routes being advertised in the type 3 LSAs are appropriately added to or deleted from the router's routing table, but a full SPF calculation is not necessary.

Refer to
Online Course
for Illustration

8.1.2.5   OSPF LSA Type 4

Type 4 and type 5 LSAs are used collectively to identify an ASBR and advertise external networks into an OSPF routing domain.

A type 4 summary LSA is generated by an ABR only when an ASBR exists within an area. A type 4 LSA identifies the ASBR and provides a route to it. All traffic destined to an external autonomous system requires routing table knowledge of the ASBR that originated the external routes.

As shown in the figure, the ASBR sends a type 1 LSA, identifying itself as an ASBR. The LSA includes a special bit known as the external bit (e bit) that is used to identify the router as an ASBR. When ABR1 receives the type 1 LSA, it notices the e bit, it builds a type 4 LSA, and then floods the type 4 LSA to the backbone (area 0). Subsequent ABRs flood the type 4 LSA into other areas.

The link-state ID is set to the ASBR router ID.

Refer to
Online Course
for Illustration

8.1.2.6   OSPF LSA Type 5

Type 5 external LSAs describe routes to networks outside the OSPF autonomous system. Type 5 LSAs are originated by the ASBR and are flooded to the entire autonomous system.

Type 5 LSAs are also referred to as autonomous system external LSA entries.

In the figure, the ASBR generates type 5 LSAs for each of its external routes and floods it into the area. Subsequent ABRs also flood the type 5 LSA into other areas. Routers in other areas use the information from the type 4 LSA to reach the external routes.

In a large OSPF deployment with many networks, propagating multiple type 5 LSAs can cause significant flooding problems. For this reason, it is strongly recommended that manual route summarization be configured on the ASBR.

The link-state ID is the external network number.

Refer to
Interactive Graphic
in online course.

8.1.2.7   Activity - Identify the OSPF LSA Type

Refer to
Online Course
for Illustration

8.1.3   OSPF Routing Table and Types of Routes

8.1.3.1   OSPF Routing Table Entries

Figure 1 provides a sample routing table for a multiarea OSPF topology with a link to an external non-OSPF network. OSPF routes in an IPv4 routing table are identified using the following descriptors:

- **O** - Router (type 1) and network (type 2) LSAs describe the details within an area. The routing table reflects this link-state information with a designation of O, meaning that the route is intra-area.

- **O IA** - When an ABR receives summary LSAs, it adds them to its LSDB and regenerates them into the local area. When an ABR receives external LSAs, it adds them to its LSDB and floods them into the area. The internal routers then assimilate the information into their databases. Summary LSAs appear in the routing table as IA (interarea routes).

- **O E1** or **O E2** - External LSAs appear in the routing table marked as external type 1 (E1) or external type 2 (E2) routes.

Figure 2 displays an IPv6 routing table with OSPF router, interarea, and external routing table entries.

Refer to
Online Course
for Illustration

8.1.3.2   OSPF Route Calculation

Each router uses the SPF algorithm against the LSDB to build the SPF tree. The SPF tree is used to determine the best paths.

As shown in the figure, the order in which the best paths are calculated is as follows:

1. All routers calculate the best paths to destinations within their area (intra-area) and add these entries to the routing table. These are the type 1 and type 2 LSAs, which are noted in the routing table with a routing designator of O. (1)

2. All routers calculate the best paths to the other areas within the internetwork. These best paths are the interarea route entries, or type 3 and type 4 LSAs, and are noted with a routing designator of O IA. (2)

3. All routers (except those that are in a form of stub area) calculate the best paths to the external autonomous system (type 5) destinations. These are noted with either an O E1 or an O E2 route designator, depending on the configuration. (3)

When converged, a router can communicate with any network within or outside the OSPF autonomous system.

Refer to
Interactive Graphic
in online course.

8.1.3.3   Activity - Order the Steps for OSPF Best Path Calculations

Refer to
Online Course
for Illustration

8.2   Configuring Multiarea OSPF

8.2.1   Configuring Multiarea OSPF

8.2.1.1   Implementing Multiarea OSPF

OSPF can be implemented as single-area or multiarea. The type of OSPF implementation chosen depends on the specific requirements and existing topology.

There are 4 steps to implementing multiarea OSPF, as displayed in the figure.

Steps 1 and 2 are part of the planning process.

Step 1.   **Gather the network requirements and parameters** - This includes determining the number of host and network devices, the IP addressing scheme (if already implemented), the size of the routing domain, the size of the routing tables, the risk of topology changes, and other network characteristics.

Step 2.   **Define the OSPF parameters** - Based on information gathered during Step 1, the network administrator must determine if single-area or multiarea OSPF is the preferred implementation. If multiarea OSPF is selected, there are several considerations the network administrator must take into account while determining the OSPF parameters, to include:

- **IP addressing plan** - This governs how OSPF can be deployed and how well the OSPF deployment might scale. A detailed IP addressing plan, along with the IP subnetting information, must be created. A good IP addressing plan should enable the usage of OSPF multiarea design and summarization. This plan more easily scales the network, as well as optimizes OSPF behavior and the propagation of LSA.

- **OSPF areas** - Dividing an OSPF network into areas decreases the LSDB size and limits the propagation of link-state updates when the topology changes. The routers that are to be ABRs and ASBRs must be identified, as are those that are to perform any summarization or redistribution.

- **Network topology** - This consists of links that connect the network equipment and belong to different OSPF areas in a multiarea OSPF design. Network topology is important to determine primary and backup links.

Primary and backup links are defined by the changing OSPF cost on interfaces. A detailed network topology plan should also be used to determine the different OSPF areas, ABR, and ASBR as well as summarization and redistribution points, if multiarea OSPF is used.

Step 3.   Configure the multiarea OSPF implementation based on the parameters.

Step 4.   Verify the multiarea OSPF implementation based on the parameters.

Refer to
Online Course
for Illustration

8.2.1.2   Configuring Multiarea OSPF

Figure 1 displays the reference multiarea OSPF topology. In this example:

- R1 is an ABR because it has interfaces in area 1 and an interface in area 0.

- R2 is an internal backbone router because all of its interfaces are in area 0.

- R3 is an ABR because it has interfaces in area 2 and an interface in area 0.

There are no special commands required to implement this multiarea OSPF network. A router simply becomes an ABR when it has two **network** statements in different areas.

As shown in Figure 2, R1 is assigned the router ID 1.1.1.1. This example enables OSPF on the two LAN interfaces in area 1. The serial interface is configured as part of OSPF area 0. Because R2 has interfaces connected to two different areas, it is an ABR.

Use the Syntax Checker in Figure 3 to configure multiarea OSPF on R2 and R3. In this Syntax Checker, on R2, use the wildcard mask of the interface network address. On R3, use the 0.0.0.0 wildcard mask for all networks.

Upon completion of the R2 and R3 configuration, notice the informational messages informing of the adjacencies with R1 (1.1.1.1).

Upon completion of the R3 configuration, notice the informational messages informing of an adjacency with R1 (1.1.1.1) and R2 (2.2.2.2). Also notice how the IP addressing scheme used for the router ID makes it easy to identify the neighbor.

Note   The inverse wildcard masks used to configure R2 and R3 purposely differ to demonstrate the two alternatives to entering **network** statements. The method used for R3 is simpler because the wildcard mask is always `0.0.0.0` and does not need to be calculated.

Refer to
Online Course
for Illustration

8.2.1.3   Configuring Multiarea OSPFv3

Like OSPFv2, implementing the multiarea OSPFv3 topology in Figure 1 is simple. There are no special commands required. A router simply becomes an ABR when it has two interfaces in different areas.

For example in Figure 2, R1 is assigned the router ID 1.1.1.1. The example also enables OSPF on the two LAN interfaces in area 1 and the serial interface in area 0. Because R1 has interfaces connected to two different areas, it becomes an ABR.

Use the Syntax Checker in Figure 3 to configure multiarea OSPFv3 on R2 and on R3.

Upon completion of the R2 configuration, notice the message that there is an adjacency with R1 (1.1.1.1).

Upon completion of the R3 configuration, notice the message that there is an adjacency with R2 (2.2.2.2).

Refer to
Online Course
for Illustration

8.2.2   OSPF Route Summarization

8.2.2.1   OSPF Route Summarization

Summarization helps keep routing tables small. It involves consolidating multiple routes into a single advertisement, which can then be propagated into the backbone area.

Normally, type 1 and type 2 LSAs are generated inside each area, translated into type 3 LSAs, and sent to other areas. If area 1 had 30 networks to advertise, then 30 type 3 LSAs would be forwarded into the backbone. With route summarization, the ABR consolidates the 30 networks into one of two advertisements.

In Figure 1, R1 consolidates all of the network advertisements into one summary LSA. Instead of forwarding individual LSAs for each route in area 1, R1 forwards a summary LSA to the core router C1. C1 in turn, forwards the summary LSA to R2 and R3. R2 and R3 then forward it to their respective internal routers.

Summarization also helps increase the network's stability, because it reduces unnecessary LSA flooding. This directly affects the amount of bandwidth, CPU, and memory resources consumed by the OSPF routing process. Without route summarization, every specific-link LSA is propagated into the OSPF backbone and beyond, causing unnecessary network traffic and router overhead.

In Figure 2, a network link on R1a fails. R1a sends an LSA to R1. However, R1 does not propagate the update, because it has a summary route configured. Specific-link LSA flooding outside the area does not occur.

Refer to
Online Course
for Illustration

8.2.2.2   Interarea and External Route Summarization

In OSPF, summarization can only be configured on ABRs or ASBRs. Instead of advertising many specific networks, the ABR routers and ASBR routers advertise a summary route. ABR routers summarize type 3 LSAs and ASBR routers summarize type 5 LSAs.

By default, summary LSAs (type 3 LSAs) and external LSAs (type 5 LSAs) do not contain summarized (aggregated) routes; that is, by default, summary LSAs are not summarized.

As illustrated in Figures 1 and 2, route summarization can be configured as follows:

- **Interarea route summarization** - Interarea route summarization occurs on ABRs and applies to routes from within each area. It does not apply to external routes injected into OSPF via redistribution. To perform effective interarea route summarization, network addresses within areas should be assigned contiguously so that these addresses can be summarized into a minimal number of summary addresses.

- **External route summarization** - External route summarization is specific to external routes that are injected into OSPF via route redistribution. Again, it is important to ensure the contiguity of the external address ranges that are being summarized. Generally, only ASBRs summarize external routes. As shown in Figure 2, EIGRP external routes are summarized by ASBR R2 in a single LSA and sent to R1 and R3.

Note External route summarization is configured on ASBRs using the `summary-address` *address* *mask* router configuration mode command.

Refer to **Online Course** for Illustration

8.2.2.3 Interarea Route Summarization

OSPF does not perform auto-summarization. Interarea summarization must be manually configured on ABRs.

Summarization of internal routes can only be done by ABRs. When summarization is enabled on an ABR, it injects into the backbone a single type 3 LSA describing the summary route. Multiple routes inside the area are summarized by the one LSA.

A summary route is generated if at least one subnet within the area falls in the summary address range. The summarized route metric is equal to the lowest cost of all subnets within the summary address range.

Note An ABR can only summarize routes that are within the areas connected to the ABR.

Figure 1 shows a multiarea OSPF topology. The routing tables of R1 and R3 are examined to see the effect of the summarization.

Figure 2 displays the R1 routing table before summarization is configured, while Figure 3 displays the R3 routing table. Notice how R3 currently has two interarea entries to the R1 area 1 networks.

Refer to **Online Course** for Illustration

8.2.2.4 Calculating the Summary Route

The figure illustrates that summarizing networks into a single address and mask can be done in three steps:

Step 1. List the networks in binary format. In the example the two area 1 networks 10.1.1.0/24 and 10.1.2.0/24 are listed binary format.

Step 2. Count the number of far left matching bits to determine the mask for the summary route. As highlighted, the first 22 far left matching bits match. This results in the prefix /22 or subnet mask **255.255.252.0**.

Step 3. Copy the matching bits and then add zero bits to determine the summarized network address. In this example, the matching bits with zeros at the end result in a network address of 10.1.0.0/22. This summary address summarizes four networks: 10.1.0.0/24, 10.1.1.0/24, 10.1.2.0/24, and 10.1.3.0/24.

In the example the summary address matches four networks although only two networks exist.

Refer to **Online Course** for Illustration

8.2.2.5 Configuring Interarea Route Summarization

In Figure 1, to demonstrate the effect of route summarization, R1 is configured to summarize the internal area 1 routes.

To manually configure interarea route summarization on an ABR, use the `area` *area-id* `range` *address* *mask* router configuration mode command. This instructs the ABR to summarize routes for a specific area before injecting them into a different area, via the backbone as type 3 summary LSAs.

Note   In OSPFv3, the command is identical except for the IPv6 network address. The command syntax for OSPFv3 is **area** *area-id* **range** *prefix/prefix-length*.

Figure 2 summarizes the two internal area 1 routes into one OSPF interarea summary route on R1. The summarized route 10.1.0.0/22 actually summarizes four network addresses, 10.1.0.0/24 to 10.1.3.0/24.

Figure 3 displays the IPv4 routing table of R1. Notice how a new entry has appeared with a `Null0` exit interface. The Cisco IOS automatically creates a bogus summary route to the `Null0` interface when manual summarization is configured to prevent routing loops. A packet sent to a null interface is dropped.

For example, assume R1 received a packet destined for 10.1.0.10. Although it would match the R1 summary route, R1 does not have a valid route in area 1. Therefore, R1 would refer to the routing table for the next longest match, which would be the `Null0` entry. The packet would get forwarded to the `Null0` interface and dropped. This prevents the router from forwarding the packet to a default route and possibly creating a routing loop.

Figure 4 displays the updated R3 routing table. Notice how there is now only one interarea entry going to the summary route 10.1.0.0/22. Although this example only reduced the routing table by one entry, summarization could be implemented to summarize many networks. This would reduce the size of routing tables.

Use the Syntax Checker in Figure 5 to summarize the area 2 routes on R3.

Refer to **Online Course** for Illustration

8.2.3   Verifying Multiarea OSPF

8.2.3.1   Verifying Multiarea OSPF

The same verification commands used to verify single-area OSPF also can be used to verify the multiarea OSPF topology in the figure:

- `show ip ospf neighbor`

- `show ip ospf`

- `show ip ospf interface`

Commands that verify specific multiarea information include:

- `show ip protocols`

- `show ip ospf interface brief`

- `show ip route ospf`

- `show ip ospf database`

Note   For the equivalent OSPFv3 command, simply substitute `ip` with `ipv6`.

Refer to
Online Course
for Illustration

8.2.3.2   Verify General Multiarea OSPF Settings

Use the `show ip protocols` command to verify the OSPF status. The output of the command reveals which routing protocols are configured on a router. It also includes routing protocol specifics such as the router ID, number of areas in the router, and networks included within the routing protocol configuration.

Figure 1 displays the OSPF settings of R1. Notice that the command shows that there are two areas. The `Routing for Networks` section identifies the networks and their respective areas.

Use the `show ip ospf interface brief` command to display concise OSPF-related information of OSPF-enabled interfaces. This command reveals useful information, such as the OSPF process ID that the interface is assigned to, the area that the interfaces are in, and the cost of the interface.

Figure 2 verifies the OSPF-enabled interfaces and the areas to which they belong.

Use the Syntax Checker in Figure 3 to verify general settings on R2 and R3.

Refer to
Online Course
for Illustration

8.2.3.3   Verify the OSPF Routes

The most common command used to verify a multiarea OSPF configuration is the `show ip route` command. Add the `ospf` parameter to display only OSPF-related information.

Figure 1 displays the routing table of R1. Notice how the **O IA** entries in the routing table identify networks learned from other areas. Specifically, **O** represents OSPF routes, and **IA** represents interarea, which means that the route originated from another area. Recall that R1 is in area 0, and the 192.168.1.0 and 192.168.2.0 subnets are connected to R3 in area 2. The [110/1295] entry in the routing table represents the administrative distance that is assigned to OSPF (`110`) and the total cost of the routes (cost of `1295`).

Use the Syntax Checker in Figure 2 to verify the routing table of R2 and R3 using the `show ip route ospf` command.

Refer to
Online Course
for Illustration

8.2.3.4   Verify the Multiarea OSPF LSDB

Use the `show ip ospf database` command to verify the contents of the LSDB.

There are many command options available with the `show ip ospf database` command.

For example, Figure 1 displays the content of the LSDB of R1. Notice R1 has entries for area 0 and area 1, because ABRs must maintain a separate LSDB for each area to which they belong. In the output, `Router Link States` in area 0 identifies three routers. The `Summary Net Link States` section identifies networks learned from other areas and which neighbor advertised the network.

Use the Syntax Checker in Figure 2 to verify the LSDB of R2 and R3 using the `show ip ospf database` command. R2 only has interfaces in area 0; therefore, only one LSDB is required. Like R1, R3 contains two LSDBs.

Refer to
Online Course
for Illustration

8.2.3.5   Verify Multiarea OSPFv3

Like OSPFv2, OSPFv3 provides similar OSPFv3 verification commands. Refer to the reference OSPFv3 topology in Figure 1.

Figure 2 displays the OSPFv3 settings of R1. Notice that the command confirms that there are now two areas. It also identifies each interface enabled for the respective area.

Figure 3 verifies the OSPFv3-enabled interfaces and the area to which they belong.

Figure 4 displays the routing table of R1. Notice how the IPv6 routing table displays **OI** entries in the routing table to identify networks learned from other areas. Specifically, **O** represents OSPF routes, and **I** represents interarea, which means that the route originated from another area. Recall that R1 is in area 0, and the 2001:DB8:CAFE3::/64 subnet is connected to R3 in area 2. The [110/1295] entry in the routing table represents the administrative distance that is assigned to OSPF (110) and the total cost of the routes (cost of 1295).

Figure 5 displays the content of the LSDB of R1. The command offers similar information to its OSPFv2 counterpart. However, the OSPFv3 LSDB contains additional LSA types not available in OSPFv2.

Refer to **Packet Tracer Activity** for this chapter

8.2.3.6   Packet Tracer - Configuring Multiarea OSPFv2

In this activity, you will configure multiarea OSPFv2. The network is already connected and interfaces are configured with IPv4 addressing. Your job is to enable multiarea OSPFv2, verify connectivity, and examine the operation of multiarea OSPFv2.

Refer to **Packet Tracer Activity** for this chapter

8.2.3.7   Packet Tracer - Configuring Multiarea OSPFv3

In this activity, you will configure multiarea OSPFv3. The network is already connected and interfaces are configured with IPv6 addressing. Your job is to enable multiarea OSPFv3, verify connectivity, and examine the operation of multiarea OSPFv3.

Refer to **Lab Activity** for this chapter

8.2.3.8   Lab - Configuring Multiarea OSPFv2

In this lab, you will complete the following objectives:

- Part 1: Build the Network and Configure Basic Device Settings

- Part 2: Configure a Multiarea OSPFv2 Network

- Part 3: Configure Interarea Summary Routes

Refer to **Lab Activity** for this chapter

8.2.3.9   Lab - Configuring Multiarea OSPFv3

In this lab, you will complete the following objectives:

- Part 1: Build the Network and Configure Basic Device Settings

- Part 2: Configure Multiarea OSPFv3 Routing

- Part 3: Configure Interarea Route Summarization

Refer to **Lab Activity** for this chapter

8.2.3.10   Lab - Troubleshooting Multiarea OSPF

In this lab, you will complete the following objectives:

- Part 1: Build the Network and Load Device Configurations

- Part 2: Troubleshoot Layer 3 Connectivity

- Part 3: Troubleshoot OSPFv2

- Part 4: Troubleshoot OSPFv3

Refer to
Online Course
for Illustration

Refer to
Lab Activity
for this chapter

8.3   Summary

8.3.1.1   Class Activity Digital Trolleys

Digital Trolleys

Scenario

Your city has an aging digital trolley system based on a one-area design. All communications within this one area are taking longer to process as trolleys are being added to routes serving the population of your growing city. Trolley departures and arrivals are also taking a little longer, because each trolley must check large routing tables to determine where to pick up and deliver residents from their source and destination streets.

A concerned citizen has come up with the idea of dividing the city into different areas for a more efficient way to determine trolley routing information. It is thought that if the trolley maps are smaller, the system might be improved because of faster and smaller updates to the routing tables.

Your city board approves and implements the new area-based, digital trolley system. But to ensure the new area routes are more efficient, the city board needs data to show the results at the next open board meeting.

Complete the directions found in the PDF for this activity. Share your answers with your class.

Refer to
Online Course
for Illustration

8.3.1.2   Summary

Single-area OSPF is useful in smaller networks but in larger networks multiarea OSPF is a better choice. Multiarea OSPF solves the issues of large routing table, large link-state database, and frequent SPF algorithm calculations.

The main area is called the backbone area (area 0) and all other areas must connect to the backbone area. Routing still occurs between the areas while many of the routing operations, such as recalculating the database, are kept within an area.

There are four different types of OSPF routers: Internal router, Backbone router, Area Border Router (ABR), and Autonomous System Boundary Router (ASBR). A router can be classified as more than one router type.

Link State Advertisements (LSAs) are the building blocks of OSPF. This chapter concentrated on LSA type 1 to LSA type 5. Type 1 LSAs are referred to as the router link entries. Type 2 LSAs are referred to as the network link entries and are flooded by a DR. Type 3 LSAs are referred to as the summary link entries and are created and propagated by ABRs. A type 4 summary LSA is generated by an ABR only when an ASBR exists within an area. Type 5 external LSAs describe routes to networks outside the OSPF autonomous system. Type 5 LSAs are originated by the ASBR and are flooded to the entire autonomous system.

OSPF routes in an IPv4 routing table are identified using the following descriptors: O, O IA, O E1 or O E2. Each router uses the SPF algorithm against the LSDB to build the SPF tree. The SPF tree is used to determine the best paths.

There are no special commands required to implement a multiarea OSPF network. A router simply becomes an ABR when it has two `network` statements in different areas.

An example of multiarea OSPF configuration:

```
R1(config)# router ospf 10
R1(config-router)# router-id 1.1.1.1
R1(config-router)# network 10.1.1.1 0.0.0.0 area 1
R1(config-router)# network 10.1.2.1 0.0.0.0 area 1
R1(config-router)# network 192.168.10.1 0.0.0.0 area 0
```

OSPF does not perform auto summarization. In OSPF, summarization can only be configured on ABRs or ASBRs. Interarea route summarization must be manually configured and occurs on ABRs and applies to routes from within each area. To manually configure interarea route summarization on an ABR, use the **area** *area-id* **range** *address* *mask* router configuration mode command.

External route summarization is specific to external routes that are injected into OSPF via route redistribution. Generally, only ASBRs summarize external routes. External route summarization is configured on ASBRs using the **summary-address** *address* *mask* router configuration mode command.

Commands that are used to verify OSPF configuration consist of the following:

- **show ip ospf neighbor**
- **show ip ospf**
- **show ip ospf interface**
- **show ip protocols**
- **show ip ospf interface brief**
- **show ip route ospf**
- **show ip ospf database**

Go to the online course to take the quiz and exam.

Chapter 8 Quiz

This quiz is designed to provide an additional opportunity to practice the skills and knowledge presented in the chapter and to prepare for the chapter exam. You will be allowed multiple attempts and the grade does not appear in the gradebook.

Chapter 8 Exam

The chapter exam assesses your knowledge of the chapter content.

Your Chapter Notes

Access Control Lists

9.0 Access Control Lists

9.0.1.1 Introduction

Network security is a huge subject, and much of it is far beyond the scope of this course. However, one of the most important skills a network administrator needs is mastery of access control lists (ACLs).

Network designers use firewalls to protect networks from unauthorized use. Firewalls are hardware or software solutions that enforce network security policies. Consider a lock on a door to a room inside a building. The lock allows only authorized users with a key or access card to pass through the door. Similarly, a firewall filters unauthorized or potentially dangerous packets from entering the network. On a Cisco router, you can configure a simple firewall that provides basic traffic filtering capabilities using ACLs. Administrators use ACLs to stop traffic or permit only specified traffic on their networks.

An ACL is a sequential list of permit or deny statements that apply to addresses or upper-layer protocols. ACLs provide a powerful way to control traffic into and out of a network. ACLs can be configured for all routed network protocols.

The most important reason to configure ACLs is to provide security for a network. This chapter explains how to use standard and extended ACLs on a Cisco router as part of a security solution. Included are tips, considerations, recommendations, and general guidelines on how to use ACLs.

This chapter includes an opportunity to develop your mastery of ACLs with a series of lessons, activities, and lab exercises.

Refer to
Lab Activity
for this chapter

9.0.1.2 Class Activity Permit Me to Assist You

Permit Me to Assist You

Scenario

Each individual in the class will record five questions they would ask a candidate who is applying for a security clearance for a network assistant position within a small- to medium-sized business. The list of questions should be listed in order of importance to selecting a good candidate for the job. The preferred answers will also be recorded.

Two interviewers from the class will be selected. The interview process will begin. Candidates will be allowed or denied the opportunity to move to the next level of questions based upon their answers to the interviewer's questions.

Refer to the accompanying PDF for further instructions for this activity.

The entire class will then get together and discuss their observations regarding the process to permit or deny them the opportunity to continue on to the next level of interviews.

Refer to
Online Course
for Illustration

9.1   IP ACL Operation

9.1.1   Purpose of ACLs

9.1.1.1   What is an ACL?

An ACL is a series of IOS commands that control whether a router forwards or drops packets based on information found in the packet header. ACLs are among the most commonly used features of Cisco IOS software.

When configured, ACLs perform the following tasks:

- Limit network traffic to increase network performance. For example, if corporate policy does not allow video traffic on the network, ACLs that block video traffic could be configured and applied. This would greatly reduce the network load and increase network performance.

- Provide traffic flow control. ACLs can restrict the delivery of routing updates. If updates are not required because of network conditions, bandwidth is preserved.

- Provide a basic level of security for network access. ACLs can allow one host to access a part of the network and prevent another host from accessing the same area. For example, access to the Human Resources network can be restricted to authorized users.

- Filter traffic based on traffic type. For example, an ACL can permit email traffic, but block all Telnet traffic.

- Screen hosts to permit or deny access to network services. ACLs can permit or deny a user to access file types, such as FTP or HTTP.

By default, a router does not have ACLs configured; therefore, by default a router does not filter traffic. Traffic that enters the router is routed solely based on information within the routing table. However, when an ACL is applied to an interface, the router performs the additional task of evaluating all network packets as they pass through the interface to determine if the packet can be forwarded.

In addition to either permitting or denying traffic, ACLs can be used for selecting types of traffic to be analyzed, forwarded, or processed in other ways. For example, ACLs can be used to classify traffic to enable priority processing. This capability is similar to having a VIP pass at a concert or sporting event. The VIP pass gives selected guests privileges not offered to general admission ticket holders, such as priority entry or being able to enter a restricted area.

The figure shows a sample topology with ACLs applied.

Refer to
Online Course
for Illustration

9.1.1.2 A TCP Conversation

ACLs enable administrators to control traffic into and out of a network. This control can be as simple as permitting or denying traffic based on network addresses or as complex as controlling network traffic based on the TCP port being requested. It is easier to understand how an ACL filters traffic by examining the dialogue that occurs during a TCP conversation, such as when requesting a webpage.

TCP Communication

When a client requests data from a web server, IP manages the communication between the PC (source) and the server (destination). TCP manages the communication between the web browser (application) and the network server software.

When you send an email, look at a webpage, or download a file, TCP is responsible for breaking data down into segments for IP before they are sent. TCP also manages assembling the data from the segments when they arrive. The TCP process is very much like a conversation in which two nodes on a network agree to pass data between one another.

TCP provides a connection-oriented, reliable, byte stream service. Connection-oriented means that the two applications must establish a TCP connection prior to exchanging data. TCP is a full-duplex protocol, meaning that each TCP connection supports a pair of byte streams, each stream flowing in one direction. TCP includes a flow-control mechanism for each byte stream that allows the receiver to limit how much data the sender can transmit. TCP also implements a congestion-control mechanism.

The animation shown in Figure 1 illustrates how a TCP/IP conversation takes place. TCP segments are marked with flags that denote their purpose: a SYN starts (synchronizes) the session; an ACK is an acknowledgment that an expected segment was received, and a FIN finishes the session. A SYN/ACK acknowledges that the transfer is synchronized. TCP data segments include the higher level protocol needed to direct the application data to the correct application.

The TCP data segment also identifies the port which matches the requested service. For example, HTTP is port 80, SMTP is port 25, and FTP is port 20 and port 21. Figure 2 shows ranges of UDP and TCP ports.

Figures 3 through 5 explore TCP/UDP ports.

Refer to
Online Course
for Illustration

9.1.1.3 Packet Filtering

So how does an ACL use the information passed during a TCP/IP conversation to filter traffic?

Packet filtering, sometimes called static packet filtering, controls access to a network by analyzing the incoming and outgoing packets and passing or dropping them based on given criteria, such as the source IP address, destination IP addresses, and the protocol carried within the packet.

A router acts as a packet filter when it forwards or denies packets according to filtering rules. When a packet arrives at the packet-filtering router, the router extracts certain information from the packet header. Using this information, the router makes decisions, based on configured filter rules, as to whether the packet can pass through or be discarded. As shown in the figure, packet filtering can work at different layers of the OSI model, or at the internet layer of TCP/IP.

A packet-filtering router uses rules to determine whether to permit or deny traffic. A router can also perform packet filtering at Layer 4, the transport layer. The router can filter packets based on the source port and destination port of the TCP or UDP segment. These rules are defined using ACLs.

An ACL is a sequential list of permit or deny statements, known as access control entries (ACEs). ACEs are also commonly called ACL statements. ACEs can be created to filter traffic based on certain criteria such as: the source address, destination address, the protocol, and port numbers. When network traffic passes through an interface configured with an ACL, the router compares the information within the packet against each ACE, in sequential order, to determine if the packet matches one of the statements. If a match is found, the packet is processed accordingly. In this way, ACLs can be configured to control access to a network or subnet.

To evaluate network traffic, the ACL extracts the following information from the Layer 3 packet header:

- Source IP address
- Destination IP address
- ICMP message type

The ACL can also extract upper layer information from the Layer 4 header, including:

- TCP/UDP source port
- TCP/UDP destination port

Refer to
Online Course
for Illustration

9.1.1.4 Packet Filtering (Cont.)

Packet Filtering Example

To understand the concept of how a router uses packet filtering, imagine that a guard has been posted at a locked door. The guard's instructions are to allow only people whose names appear on a list to pass through the door. The guard is filtering people based on the criterion of having their names on the authorized list. An ACL works in a similar manner, making decisions based on set criteria.

For example, an ACL could be configured to logically, "Permit web access to users from network A but deny all other services to network A users. Deny HTTP access to users from network B, but permit network B users to have all other access." Refer to the figure to examine the decision path the packet filter uses to accomplish this task.

For this scenario, the packet filter looks at each packet as follows:

- If the packet is a TCP SYN from Network A using Port 80, it is allowed to pass. All other access is denied to those users.

- If the packet is a TCP SYN from Network B using Port 80, it is blocked. However, all other access is permitted.

This is just a simple example. Multiple rules can be configured to further permit or deny services to specific users.

Refer to
Online Course
for Illustration

9.1.1.5   ACL Operation

ACLs define the set of rules that give added control for packets that enter inbound inter-faces, packets that relay through the router, and packets that exit outbound interfaces of the router. ACLs do not act on packets that originate from the router itself.

ACLs are configured to apply to inbound traffic or to apply to outbound traffic as shown in the figure.

- **Inbound ACLs** - Incoming packets are processed before they are routed to the out-bound interface. An inbound ACL is efficient because it saves the overhead of routing lookups if the packet is discarded. If the packet is permitted by the tests, it is then processed for routing. Inbound ACLs are best used to filter packets when the network attached to an inbound interface is the only source of the packets needed to be exam-ined.

- **Outbound ACLs** - Incoming packets are routed to the outbound interface, and then they are processed through the outbound ACL. Outbound ACLs are best used when the same filter will be applied to packets coming from multiple inbound interfaces before exiting the same outbound interface.

The last statement of an ACL is always an implicit deny. This statement is automatically inserted at the end of each ACL even though it is not physically present. The implicit deny blocks all traffic. Because of this implicit deny, an ACL that does not have at least one per-mit statement will block all traffic.

Refer to **Packet
Tracer Activity**
for this chapter

9.1.1.6   Packet Tracer - ACL Demonstration

In this activity, you will observe how an access control list (ACL) can be used to prevent a ping from reaching hosts on remote networks. After removing the ACL from the configura-tion, the pings will be successful.

Refer to
Online Course
for Illustration

9.1.2   Standard versus Extended IPv4 ACLs

9.1.2.1   Types of Cisco IPv4 ACLs

The two types of Cisco IPv4 ACLs are standard and extended.

Note   Cisco IPv6 ACLs are similar to IPv4 extended ACLs and are discussed in a later sec-tion.

Standard ACLs

Standard ACLs can be used to permit or deny traffic only from source IPv4 addresses. The destination of the packet and the ports involved are not evaluated. The example in Figure 1 allows all traffic from the 192.168.30.0/24 network. Because of the implied "deny any" at the end, all other traffic is blocked with this ACL. Standard ACLs are created in global configuration mode.

Extended ACLs

Extended ACLs filter IPv4 packets based on several attributes:

- Protocol type
- Source IPv4 address
- Destination IPv4 address
- Source TCP or UDP ports
- Destination TCP or UDP ports
- Optional protocol type information for finer control

In Figure 2, ACL 103 permits traffic originating from any address on the 192.168.30.0/24 network to any IPv4 network if the destination host port is 80 (HTTP). Extended ACLs are created in global configuration mode.

The commands for ACLs are explained in the next few topics.

Note   Standard and extended ACLs are discussed in more detail later in this chapter.

Refer to
Online Course
for Illustration

9.1.2.2   Numbering and Naming ACLs

Standard and extended ACLs can be created using either a number or a name to identify the ACL and its list of statements.

Using numbered ACLs is an effective method for determining the ACL type on smaller networks with more homogeneously defined traffic. However, a number does not provide information about the purpose of the ACL. For this reason, starting with Cisco IOS Release 11.2, a name can be used to identify a Cisco ACL.

The figure summarizes the rules to follow to designate numbered ACLs and named ACLs.

Regarding numbered ACLs, numbers 200 to 1299 are skipped because those numbers are used by other protocols, many of which are legacy or obsolete. This course focuses only on IP ACLs. Examples of legacy ACL protocol numbers are 600 to 699 used by AppleTalk, and numbers 800 to 899 used by IPX.

Refer to
Online Course
for Illustration

9.1.3   Wildcard Masks in ACLs

9.1.3.1   Introducing ACL Wildcard Masking

Wildcard Masking

IPv4 ACEs include the use of wildcard masks. A wildcard mask is a string of 32 binary digits used by the router to determine which bits of the address to examine for a match.

Note   Unlike IPv4 ACLs, IPv6 ACLs do not use wildcard masks. Instead, the prefix-length is used to indicate how much of an IPv6 source or destination address should be matched. IPv6 ACLs are discussed later in this chapter.

As with subnet masks, the numbers 1 and 0 in the wildcard mask identify how to treat the corresponding IP address bits. However, in a wildcard mask, these bits are used for different purposes and follow different rules.

Subnet masks use binary 1s and 0s to identify the network, subnet, and host portion of an IP address. Wildcard masks use binary 1s and 0s to filter individual IP addresses or groups of IP addresses to permit or deny access to resources.

Wildcard masks and subnet masks differ in the way they match binary 1s and 0s. Wildcard masks use the following rules to match binary 1s and 0s:

- Wildcard mask bit 0 - Match the corresponding bit value in the address.

- Wildcard mask bit 1 - Ignore the corresponding bit value in the address.

Figure 1 shows how different wildcard masks filter IP addresses. In the example, remember that binary 0 signifies a bit that must match, and binary 1 signifies a bit that can be ignored.

Note Wildcard masks are often referred to as an inverse mask. The reason is that, unlike a subnet mask in which binary 1 is equal to a match and binary 0 is not a match, in a wildcard mask the reverse is true.

Using a Wildcard Mask

The table in Figure 2 shows the results of applying a 0.0.255.255 wildcard mask to a 32-bit IPv4 address. Remember that a binary 0 indicates a value that is matched.

Wildcard masks are also used when configuring some IPv4 routing protocols, such as OSPF, to enable the protocol on specific interfaces.

Refer to
Online Course
for Illustration

9.1.3.2 Wildcard Mask Examples

Wildcard Masks to Match IPv4 Subnets

Calculating the wildcard mask can take some practice. Figure 1 provides three examples of wildcard masks.

In the first example the wildcard mask stipulates that every bit in the IPv4 192.168.1.1 must match exactly.

In the second example, the wildcard mask stipulates that anything will match.

In the third example, the wildcard mask stipulates that any host within the 192.168.1.0/24 network will match.

These examples were fairly simple and straightforward. However, the calculation of wildcard masks can be more complex.

Wildcard Masks to Match Ranges

The two examples in Figure 2 are more complex. In example 1, the first two octets and first four bits of the third octet must match exactly. The last four bits in the third octet and the last octet can be any valid number. This results in a mask that checks for the range of networks 192.168.16.0 to 192.168.31.0.

Example 2 shows a wildcard mask that matches the first two octets, and the least significant bit in the third octet. The last octet and the first seven bits in the third octet can be any valid number. The result is a mask that would permit or deny all hosts from odd subnets from the 192.168.0.0 major network.

Refer to **Online Course** for Illustration

9.1.3.3   Calculating the Wildcard Mask

Calculating wildcard masks can be challenging. One shortcut method is to subtract the subnet mask from 255.255.255.255.

Wildcard Mask Calculation: Example 1

In the first example in the figure, assume you wanted to permit access to all users in the 192.168.3.0 network. Because the subnet mask is 255.255.255.0, you could take the 255.255.255.255 and subtract the subnet mask 255.255.255.0 as is indicated in the figure. The solution produces the wildcard mask 0.0.0.255.

Wildcard Mask Calculation: Example 2

In the second example in the figure, assume you wanted to permit network access for the 14 users in the subnet 192.168.3.32/28. The subnet mask for the IP subnet is 255.255.255.240, therefore take 255.255.255.255 and subtract the subnet mask 255.255.255.240. The solution this time produces the wildcard mask 0.0.0.15.

Wildcard Mask Calculation: Example 3

In the third example in the figure, assume you wanted to match only networks 192.168.10.0 and 192.168.11.0. Again, you take the 255.255.255.255 and subtract the regular subnet mask which in this case would be 255.255.252.0. The result is 0.0.3.255.

You could accomplish the same result with statements like the two shown below:

```
R1(config)# access-list 10 permit 192.168.10.0
R1(config)# access-list 10 permit 192.168.11.0
```

It is far more efficient to configure the wildcard mask in the following way:

```
R1(config)# access-list 10 permit 192.168.10.0 0.0.3.255
```

Consider the configuration below to match networks in the range between 192.168.16.0 to 192.168.31.0:

```
R1(config)# access-list 10 permit 192.168.16.0
R1(config)# access-list 10 permit 192.168.17.0
R1(config)# access-list 10 permit 192.168.18.0
R1(config)# access-list 10 permit 192.168.19.0
R1(config)# access-list 10 permit 192.168.20.0
R1(config)# access-list 10 permit 192.168.21.0
R1(config)# access-list 10 permit 192.168.22.0
R1(config)# access-list 10 permit 192.168.23.0
R1(config)# access-list 10 permit 192.168.24.0
R1(config)# access-list 10 permit 192.168.25.0
R1(config)# access-list 10 permit 192.168.26.0
R1(config)# access-list 10 permit 192.168.27.0
R1(config)# access-list 10 permit 192.168.28.0
R1(config)# access-list 10 permit 192.168.29.0
R1(config)# access-list 10 permit 192.168.30.0
R1(config)# access-list 10 permit 192.168.31.0
```

The previous 16 configuration statements can be reduced to a single statement using the correct wildcard mask as shown below:

```
R1(config)# access-list 10 permit 192.168.16.0 0.0.15.255
```

Refer to
Online Course
for Illustration

9.1.3.4   Wildcard Mask Keywords

Wildcard Bit Mask Keywords

Working with decimal representations of binary wildcard mask bits can be tedious. To simplify this task, the keywords **host** and **any** help identify the most common uses of wildcard masking. These keywords eliminate entering wildcard masks when identifying a specific host or an entire network. These keywords also make it easier to read an ACL by providing visual clues as to the source or destination of the criteria.

The **host** keyword substitutes for the 0.0.0.0 mask. This mask states that all IPv4 address bits must match or only one host is matched.

The **any** option substitutes for the IP address and 255.255.255.255 mask. This mask says to ignore the entire IPv4 address or to accept any addresses.

Example 1: Wildcard Masking Process with a Single IP Address

In Example 1 in the figure, instead of entering `192.168.10.10  0.0.0.0`, you can use `host 192.168.10.10`.

Example 2: Wildcard Masking Process with a Match Any IP Address

In Example 2 in the figure, instead of entering `0.0.0.0  255.255.255.255`, you can use the keyword **any** by itself.

Note   The keywords **host** and **any** can also be used when configuring an IPv6 ACL.

Refer to
Online Course
for Illustration

9.1.3.5   Examples Wildcard Mask Keywords

The any and host Keywords

Example 1 in the figure shows how to use the **any** keyword to substitute for the IPv4 address 0.0.0.0 with a wildcard mask of 255.255.255.255.

Example 2 shows how to use the **host** keyword to substitute for the wildcard mask when identifying a single host.

Refer to
Interactive Graphic
in online course.

9.1.3.6   Activity - Determine the Correct Wildcard Mask

Refer to
Interactive Graphic
in online course.

9.1.3.7   Activity - Determine the Permit or Deny

Refer to
Online Course
for Illustration

9.1.4   Guidelines for ACL creation

9.1.4.1   General Guidelines for Creating ACLs

Writing ACLs can be a complex task. For every interface there may be multiple policies needed to manage the type of traffic allowed to enter or exit that interface. The router in the figure has two interfaces configured for IPv4 and IPv6. If we needed ACLs for both protocols, on both interfaces and in both directions, this would require eight separate ACLs. Each interface would have four ACLs; two ACLs for IPv4 and two ACLs for IPv6. For each protocol, one ACL is for inbound traffic and one for outbound traffic.

Note   ACLs do not have to be configured in both directions. The number of ACLs and their direction applied to the interface will depend on the requirements being implemented.

Here are some guidelines for using ACLs:

■ Use ACLs in firewall routers positioned between your internal network and an external network such as the Internet.

■ Use ACLs on a router positioned between two parts of your network to control traffic entering or exiting a specific part of your internal network.

■ Configure ACLs on border routers, that is, routers situated at the edges of your networks. This provides a very basic buffer from the outside network, or between a less controlled area of your own network and a more sensitive area of your network.

■ Configure ACLs for each network protocol configured on the border router interfaces.

The Three Ps

A general rule for applying ACLs on a router can be recalled by remembering the three Ps. You can configure one ACL per protocol, per direction, per interface:

■ **One ACL per protocol** - To control traffic flow on an interface, an ACL must be defined for each protocol enabled on the interface.

■ **One ACL per direction** - ACLs control traffic in one direction at a time on an interface. Two separate ACLs must be created to control inbound and outbound traffic.

■ **One ACL per interface** - ACLs control traffic for an interface, for example, GigabitEthernet 0/0.

Refer to
Online Course
for Illustration

9.1.4.2   ACL Best Practices

Using ACLs requires attention to detail and great care. Mistakes can be costly in terms of downtime, troubleshooting efforts, and poor network service. Before configuring an ACL, basic planning is required. The figure presents guidelines that form the basis of an ACL best practices list.

Refer to
Interactive Graphic
in online course.

9.1.4.3   Activity - ACL Operation

Refer to
Online Course
for Illustration

9.1.5   Guidelines for ACL Placement

9.1.5.1   Where to Place ACLs

The proper placement of an ACL can make the network operate more efficiently. An ACL can be placed to reduce unnecessary traffic. For example, traffic that will be denied at a remote destination should not be forwarded using network resources along the route to that destination.

Every ACL should be placed where it has the greatest impact on efficiency. As shown in the figure, the basic rules are:

- **Extended ACLs** - Locate extended ACLs as close as possible to the source of the traffic to be filtered. This way, undesirable traffic is denied close to the source network without crossing the network infrastructure.

- **Standard ACLs** - Because standard ACLs do not specify destination addresses, place them as close to the destination as possible. Placing a standard ACL at the source of the traffic will effectively prevent that traffic from reaching any other networks through the interface where the ACL is applied.

Placement of the ACL and therefore the type of ACL used may also depend on:

- **The extent of the network administrator's control** - Placement of the ACL can depend on whether or not the network administrator has control of both the source and destination networks.

- **Bandwidth of the networks involved** - Filtering unwanted traffic at the source prevents transmission of the traffic before it consumes bandwidth on the path to a destination. This is especially important in low bandwidth networks.

- **Ease of configuration** - If a network administrator wants to deny traffic coming from several networks, one option is to use a single standard ACL on the router closest to the destination. The disadvantage is that traffic from these networks will use bandwidth unnecessarily. An extended ACL could be used on each router where the traffic originated. This will save bandwidth by filtering the traffic at the source but requires creating extended ACLs on multiple routers.

Note   For CCNA certification the general rule is that extended ACLs are placed as close as possible to the source and standard ACLs are placed as close as possible to the destination.

9.1.5.2   Standard ACL Placement

Refer to
Online Course
for Illustration

A standard ACL can only filter traffic based on a source address. The basic rule for placement of a standard ACL is to place the ACL as close as possible to the destination network. This allows the traffic to reach all other networks except the network where the packets will be filtered.

In the figure, the administrator wants to prevent traffic originating in the 192.168.10.0/24 network from reaching the 192.168.30.0/24 network.

If the standard ACL is placed on the outbound interface of R1, this would prevent traffic on the 192.168.10.0/24 network from reaching any networks reachable through the Serial 0/0/0 interface of R1.

Following the basic placement guidelines of placing the standard ACL close to the destination, the figure shows two possible interfaces on R3 to apply the standard ACL:

- **R3 S0/0/1 interface** - Applying a standard ACL to prevent traffic from 192.168.10.0/24 from entering the S0/0/1 interface will prevent this traffic from reaching 192.168.30.0/24 and all other networks reachable by R3. This includes the

192.168.31.0/24 network. Because the intent of the ACL is to filter traffic destined only for 192.168.30.0/24, a standard ACL should not be applied to this interface.

■ **R3 G0/0 interface** - Applying the standard ACL to traffic exiting the G0/0 interface will filter packets from 192.168.10.0/24 to 192.168.30.0/24. This will not affect other networks reachable by R3. Packets from 192.16810.0/24 will still be able to reach 192.168.31.0/24.

Refer to
Online Course
for Illustration

9.1.5.3   Extended ACL Placement

Like a standard ACL, an extended ACL can filter traffic based on the source address. However, an extended ACL can also filter traffic based on the destination address, protocol, and port number. This allows network administrators more flexibility in the type of traffic that can be filtered and where to place the ACL. The basic rule for placing an extended ACL is to place it as close to the source as possible. This prevents unwanted traffic from being sent across multiple networks only to be denied when it reaches its destination.

Network administrators can only place ACLs on devices that they control. Therefore, placement must be determined in the context of where the control of the network administrator extends. In the figure, the administrator of Company A, which includes the 192.168.10.0/24 and 192.168.11.0/24 networks (referred to as .10 and .11 in this example) wants to control traffic to Company B. Specifically, the administrator wants to deny Telnet and FTP traffic from the .11 network to Company B's 192.168.30.0/24 (.30, in this example) network. At the same time, all other traffic from the .11 network must be permitted to leave Company A without restriction.

There are several ways to accomplish these goals. An extended ACL on R3 that blocks Telnet and FTP from the .11 network would accomplish the task, but the administrator does not control R3. In addition, this solution also allows unwanted traffic to cross the entire network, only to be blocked at the destination. This affects overall network efficiency.

A better solution is to place an extended ACL on R1 that specifies both source and destination addresses (.11 network and .30 network, respectively), and enforces the rule, "Telnet and FTP traffic from the .11 network is not allowed to go to the .30 network." The figure shows two possible interfaces on R1 to apply the extended ACL:

■ **R1 S0/0/0 interface (outbound)** - One possibility is to apply an extended ACL outbound on the S0/0/0 interface. Because the extended ACL can examine both source and destination addresses, only FTP and Telnet packets from 192.168.11.0/24 will be denied. Other traffic from 192.168.11.0/24 and other networks will be forwarded by R1. The disadvantage of placing the extended ACL on this interface is that all traffic exiting S0/0/0 must be processed by the ACL including packets from 192.168.10.0/24.

■ **R1 G0/1 interface (inbound)** - Applying an extended ACL to traffic entering the G0/1 interface means that only packets from the 192.168.11.0/24 network are subject to ACL processing on R1. Because the filter is to be limited to only those packets leaving the 192.168.11.0/24 network, applying the extended ACL to G0/1 is the best solution.

Refer to
Interactive Graphic
in online course.

9.1.5.4   Activity - Placing Standard and Extended ACLs

Refer to
Online Course
for Illustration

9.2   Standard IPv4 ACLs

9.2.1   Configure Standard IPv4 ACLs

9.2.1.1   Entering Criteria Statements

When traffic enters the router, the traffic is compared to all ACEs in the order that the entries occur in the ACL. The router continues to process the ACEs until it finds a match. The router will process the packet based on the first match found and no other ACEs will be examined.

If no matches are found when the router reaches the end of the list, the traffic is denied. This is because, by default, there is an implied deny at the end of all ACLs for traffic that was not matched to a configured entry. A single-entry ACL with only one deny entry has the effect of denying all traffic. At least one permit ACE must be configured in an ACL or all traffic is blocked.

For the network in the figure, applying either ACL 1 or ACL 2 to the S0/0/0 interface of R1 in the outbound direction will have the same effect. Network 192.168.10.0 will be permitted to access the networks reachable through S0/0/0 while 192.168.11.0 will not be allowed to access those networks.

Refer to
Online Course
for Illustration

9.2.1.2   Configuring a Standard ACL

Standard ACL Logic

In the figure, packets that enter the router through interface G0/0 are checked for their source addresses based on the following entries:

```
access-list 2 deny 192.168.10.10
access-list 2 permit 192.168.10.0 0.0.0.255
access-list 2 deny 192.168.0.0 0.0.255.255
access-list 2 permit 192.0.0.0 0.255.255.255
```

If packets are permitted, they are routed through the router to an output interface. If packets are denied, they are dropped at the incoming interface.

Refer to
Online Course
for Illustration

9.2.1.3   Configuring a Standard ACL (Cont.)

Configuring Standard ACLs

To use numbered standard ACLs on a Cisco router, you must first create the standard ACL and then activate the ACL on an interface.

The **access-list** global configuration command defines a standard ACL with a number in the range of 1 through 99. Cisco IOS Software Release 12.0.1 extended these numbers by allowing 1300 to 1999 to be used for standard ACLs. This allows for a maximum of 798 possible standard ACLs. These additional numbers are referred to as expanded IP ACLs.

The full syntax of the standard ACL command is as follows:

```
Router(config)# access-list access-list-number { deny | permit | remark } source [
source-wildcard ] [ log ]
```

Figure 1 provides a detailed explanation of the syntax for a standard ACL.

ACEs can deny or permit an individual host or a range of host addresses. To create a host statement in numbered ACL 10 that permits a specific host with the IP address 192.168.10.0, you would enter:

```
R1(config)# access-list 10 permit host 192.168.10.10
```

As shown in Figure 2, to create a statement that will permit a range of IPv4 addresses in a numbered ACL 10 that permits all IPv4 addresses in the network 192.168.10.0/24, you would enter:

```
R1(config)# access-list 10 permit 192.168.10.0 0.0.0.255
```

To remove the ACL, the global configuration **no access-list** command is used. Issuing the **show access-list** command confirms that access list 10 has been removed.

Typically, when an administrator creates an ACL, the purpose of each statement is known and understood. However, to ensure that the administrator and others recall the purpose of a statement, remarks should be included. The **remark** keyword is used for documentation and makes access lists a great deal easier to understand. Each remark is limited to 100 characters. The ACL in Figure 3, although fairly simple, is used to provide an example. When reviewing the ACL in the configuration using the **show running-config** command, the remark is also displayed.

Refer to
Online Course
for Illustration

9.2.1.4   Internal Logic

Cisco IOS applies an internal logic when accepting and processing standard ACEs. As discussed previously, ACEs are processed sequentially. Therefore, the order in which ACEs are entered is important.

For example, in Figure 1 ACL 3 contains two ACEs. The first ACE uses a wildcard mask to deny a range of addresses, which includes all hosts in the 192.168.10.0/24 network. The second ACE is a host statement that examines a specific host: 192.168.10.10. This is a host within the range of hosts that was configured in the previous statement. In other words, 192.168.10.10 is a host in the 192.168.10.0/24 network. The IOS internal logic for standard access lists rejects the second statement and returns an error message because it is a subset of the previous statement. Notice in the figure that the router automatically assigns sequence num 10 as the sequence number assigned to the first statement entered in this example. The router output includes the message that the rule is "part of the existing rule at sequence num 10" and does not accept the statement.

Note   Currently, extended ACLs do not produce a similar error.

The configuration in Figure 2 of ACL 4 has the same two statements but in reverse order. This is a valid sequence of statements because the first statement refers a specific host, not a range of hosts.

In Figure 3, ACL 5 shows that a host statement can be configured after a statement that denotes a range of hosts. The host must not be within the range covered by a previous statement. The 192.168.11.10 host address is not a member of the 192.168.10.0/24 network so this is a valid statement.

Note The order in which standard ACEs are entered may not be the order that they are stored, displayed, or processed by the router. This will be discussed in a later section.

Refer to
Online Course
for Illustration

9.2.1.5 Applying Standard ACLs to Interfaces

Standard ACL Configuration Procedures

After a standard ACL is configured, it is linked to an interface using the **ip access-group** command in interface configuration mode:

```
Router(config-if)# ip access-group { access-list-number | access-list-name } { in
| out }
```

To remove an ACL from an interface, first enter the **no ip access-group** command on the interface, and then enter the global **no access-list** command to remove the entire ACL.

Figure 1 lists the steps and syntax to configure and apply a numbered standard ACL on a router.

Figure 2 shows an example of an ACL to permit a single network.

This ACL allows only traffic from source network 192.168.10.0 to be forwarded out of interface S0/0/0. Traffic from networks other than 192.168.10.0 is blocked.

The first line identifies the ACL as access list 1. It permits traffic that matches the selected parameters. In this case, the IPv4 address and wildcard mask identifying the source network is 192.168.10.0 0.0.0.255. Recall that there is an implicit deny all statement that is equivalent to adding the line **access-list 1 deny 0.0.0.0 255.255.255.255**.

The **ip access-group 1 out** interface configuration command links and ties ACL 1 to the Serial 0/0/0 interface as an outbound filter.

Therefore, ACL 1 only permits hosts from the 192.168.10.0/24 network to exit router R1. It denies any other network including the 192.168.11.0 network.

Refer to
Online Course
for Illustration

9.2.1.6 Applying Standard ACLs to Interfaces (Cont.)

Figure 1 shows an example of an ACL that permits a specific subnet except for a specific host on that subnet.

This ACL replaces the previous example, but also blocks traffic from a specific address. The first command deletes the previous version of ACL 1. The next ACL statement, denies the PC1 host located at 192.168.10.10. Every other host on the 192.168.10.0/24 network is permitted. Again the implicit deny statement matches every other network.

The ACL is reapplied to interface S0/0/0 in an outbound direction.

Figure 2 an example of an ACL that denies a specific host. This ACL replaces the previous example. This example still blocks traffic from host PC1 but permits all other traffic.

The first two commands are the same as the previous example. The first command deletes the previous version of ACL 1 and the next ACL statement denies the PC1 host that is located at 192.168.10.10.

The third line is new and permits all other hosts. This means that all hosts from the 192.168.10.0/24 network will be permitted except for PC1 which was denied in the previous statement.

This ACL is applied to interface G0/0 in the inbound direction. Because the filter only affects the 192.168.10.0/24 LAN on G0/0 it is more efficient to apply the ACL to the inbound interface. The ACL could be applied to s0/0/0 in the outbound direction but then R1 would have to examine packets from all networks including 192.168.11.0/24.

Refer to
Online Course
for Illustration

9.2.1.7 Creating Named Standard ACLs

Naming an ACL makes it easier to understand its function. For example, an ACL configured to deny FTP could be called NO_FTP. When you identify your ACL with a name instead of with a number, the configuration mode and command syntax are slightly different.

Figure 1 shows the steps required to create a standard named ACL.

Step 1.   Starting from the global configuration mode, use the `ip access-list` command to create a named ACL. ACL names are alphanumeric, case sensitive, and must be unique. The `ip access-list standard` *name* is used to create a standard named ACL, whereas the command `ip access-list extended` *name* is for an extended access list. After entering the command, the router is in named standard ACL configuration mode as indicated by the prompt.

Note   Numbered ACLs use the global configuration command `access-list` whereas named IPv4 ACLs use the `ip access-list` command.

Step 2.   From the named ACL configuration mode, use `permit` or `deny` statements to specify one or more conditions for determining whether a packet is forwarded or dropped.

Step 3.   Apply the ACL to an interface using the `ip access-group` command. Specify if the ACL should be applied to packets as they enter into the interface (`in`) or applied to packets as they exit the interface (`out`).

Figure 2 shows the commands used to configure a standard named ACL on router R1, interface G0/0 that denies host 192.168.11.10 access to the 192.168.10.0 network. The ACL is named NO_ACCESS.

Capitalizing ACL names is not required, but makes them stand out when viewing the running-config output. It also makes it less likely that you will accidentally create two different ACLs with the same name but with different uses of capitalization.

Refer to
Online Course
for Illustration

9.2.1.8 Commenting ACLs

You can use the `remark` keyword to include comments (remarks) about entries in any IP standard or extended ACL. The remarks make the ACL easier for you to understand and scan. Each remark line is limited to 100 characters.

The remark can go before or after a `permit` or `deny` statement. You should be consistent about where you put the remark so that it is clear which remark describes which `permit` or `deny` statement. For example, it would be confusing to have some remarks before the associated `permit` or `deny` statements and some remarks after the statements.

To include a comment for IPv4 numbered standard or extended ACLs, use the **access-list** *access-list_number* **remark** *remark* global configuration command. To remove the remark, use the **no** form of this command.

In the first example, the numbered ACL denies the 192.168.10.10 guest workstation from exiting S0/0/0 but permits all other devices from 192.168.0.0/16.

For an entry in a named standard or extended ACL, use the **remark** access-list configuration command. To remove the remark, use the **no** form of this command. Example 2 shows a standard named ACL. In this example, the remark statements indicate that the lab workstation with the host address 192.168.11.10 is denied but devices from all other networks are permitted.

Refer to
Interactive Graphic
in online course.

9.2.1.9   Activity - Configuring Standard ACLs

Refer to **Packet Tracer Activity** for this chapter

9.2.1.10   Packet Tracer - Configuring Standard ACLs

Standard access control lists (ACLs) are router configuration scripts that control whether a router permits or denies packets based on the source address. This activity focuses on defining filtering criteria, configuring standard ACLs, applying ACLs to router interfaces, and verifying and testing the ACL implementation. The routers are already configured, including IP addresses and EIGRP routing.

Refer to **Packet Tracer Activity** for this chapter

9.2.1.11   Packet Tracer - Configuring Named Standard ACLs

The senior network administrator has tasked you to create a standard named ACL to prevent access to a file server. All clients from one network and one specific workstation from a different network should be denied access.

Refer to
Online Course
for Illustration

9.2.2   Modify IPv4 ACLs

9.2.2.1   Editing Standard Numbered ACLs

Editing Numbered ACLs

When configuring a standard ACL, the statements are added to the running-config. However, there is no built-in editing feature that allows you to edit a change in an ACL.

There are two ways that a standard numbered ACL can be edited.

Method 1: Using a Text Editor

After someone is familiar with creating and editing ACLs, it may be easier to construct the ACL using a text editor such as Microsoft Notepad. This allows you to create or edit the ACL and then paste it into the router. For an existing ACL, you can use the **show running-config** command to display the ACL, copy and paste it into the text editor, make the necessary changes, and paste it back in.

Configuration: For example, assume that the host IPv4 address in the figure was incorrectly entered. Instead of the 192.168.10.99 host, it should have been the 192.168.10.10 host. Here are the steps to edit and correct ACL 1:

Step 1.   Display the ACL using the **show running-config** command. The example in the figure uses the **include** keyword to display only the ACEs.

Step 2. Highlight the ACL, copy it, and then paste it into Microsoft Notepad. Edit the list as required. After the ACL is correctly displayed in Microsoft Notepad, highlight it and copy it.

Step 3. In global configuration mode, remove the access list using the `no access-list 1` command. Otherwise, the new statements would be appended to the existing ACL. Then paste the new ACL into the configuration of the router.

Step 4. Using the `show running-config` command, verify the changes

It should be mentioned that when using the `no access-list` command, different IOS software releases act differently. If the ACL that has been deleted is still applied to an interface, some IOS versions act as if no ACL is protecting your network while others deny all traffic. For this reason it is good practice to remove the reference to the access list from the interface before modifying the access list. Also, be aware that if there is an error in the new list, disable it and troubleshoot the problem. In that instance, again, the network has no ACL during the correction process.

Refer to **Online Course** for Illustration

9.2.2.2   Editing Standard Numbered ACLs (Cont.)

Method 2: Using the Sequence Number

As shown in the figure the initial configuration of ACL 1 included a host statement for host 192.168.10.99. This was in error. The host should have been configured as 192.168.10.10. To edit the ACL using sequence numbers follow these steps:

Step 1. Display the current ACL using the `show access-lists 1` command. The output from this command will be discussed in more detail later in this section. The sequence number is displayed at the beginning of each statement. The sequence number was automatically assigned when the access list statement was entered. Notice that the misconfigured statement has the sequence number 10.

Step 2. Enter the `ip access-lists standard` command that is used to configure named ACLs. The ACL number, 1, is used as the name. First the misconfigured statement needs to be deleted using the `no 10` command with 10 referring to the sequence number. Next, a new sequence number 10 statement is added using the command, `10 deny host 192.168.10.10`.

Note   Statements cannot be overwritten using the same sequence number as an existing statement. The current statement must be deleted first, and then the new one can be added.

Step 3. Verify the changes using the `show access-lists` command.

As discussed previously, Cisco IOS implements an internal logic to standard access lists. The order in which standard ACEs are entered may not be the order in which they are stored, displayed or processed by the router. The `show access-lists` command displays the ACEs with their sequence numbers.

Refer to
Online Course
for Illustration

9.2.2.3   Editing Standard Named ACLs

In a previous example, sequence numbers were used to edit a standard numbered ACL. By referring to the statement sequence numbers, individual statements can easily be inserted or deleted. This method can also be used to edit standard named ACLs.

The figure shows an example of inserting a line to a named ACL.

- In the first **show** command output, you can see that the ACL named NO_ACCESS has two numbered lines indicating access rules for a workstation with the IPv4 address 192.168.11.10.

- The **ip access-list standard** command used to configure named ACLs. From named access list configuration mode statements can be inserted or removed. The **no** *sequence-number* command is used to delete individual statements.

- To add a statement to deny another workstation requires inserting a numbered line. In the example, the workstation with the IPv4 address 192.168.11.11 is being added using a new sequence number of 15.

- The final **show** command output verifies that the new workstation is now denied access.

Refer to
Online Course
for Illustration

9.2.2.4   Verifying ACLs

As shown in Figure 1, the **show ip interface** command is used to verify the ACL on the interface. The output from this command includes the number or name of the access list and the direction in which the ACL was applied. The output shows router R1 has the access list 1 applied to its S0/0/0 outbound interface and the access list NO_ACCESS applied to its g0/0 interface also in the outbound direction.

The example in Figure 2 shows the result of issuing the **show access-lists** command on router R1. To view an individual access list use the **show access-lists** command followed by the access list number or name. The NO_ACCESS statements may look strange. Notice that sequence number 15 is displayed prior to sequence number 10. This is a result of the router internal process and will be discussed later in this section.

Refer to
Online Course
for Illustration

9.2.2.5   ACL Statistics

Once the ACL has been applied to an interface and some testing has occurred, the **show access-lists** command will show statistics for each statement that has been matched. In the output in Figure 1, note that some of the statements have been matched. When traffic is generated that should match an ACL statement, the matches shown in the **show access-lists** command output should increase. For instance in this example, if a ping is issued from PC1 to PC3 or PC4, the output will show an increase in the matches for the deny statement of ACL 1.

Both permit and deny statements will track statistics for matches; however, recall that every ACL has an implied deny any as the last statement. This statement will not appear in the **show access-lists** command, therefore, statistics for that statement will not appear. To view statistics for the implied deny any statement, the statement can be configured manually and will appear in the output. Extreme caution should be taken when manually configuring the deny any statement, as it will match all traffic. If this statement is not configured as the last statement in the ACL, it could cause unexpected results.

During testing of an ACL, the counters can be cleared using the `clear access-list counters` command. This command can be used alone or with the number or name of a specific ACL. As shown in Figure 2 this command clears the statistic counters for an ACL.

Refer to
Online Course
for Illustration

9.2.2.6   Standard ACL Sequence Numbers

Cisco IOS implements an internal logic to standard ACLs. As discussed previously, part of this logic prevents host statements from being configured after a range statement if the host is a member of that range, as shown in Figure 1.

Another part of the IOS internal logic involves the internal sequencing of standard ACEs. Figure 2 shows the configuration of a standard access list. Range statements that deny three networks are configured first followed by five host statements. The host statements are all valid statements because their host IP addresses are not part of the previously entered range statements.

The `show running-config` command is used to verify the ACL configuration. Notice that the statements are listed in a different order than they were entered. We will use the `show access-lists` command to understand the logic behind this.

As shown in Figure 3, the `show access-lists` command displays ACEs along with their sequence numbers. We might expect the order of the statements in the output to reflect the order in which they were entered. However, the `show access-lists` output shows that this is not the case.

The order in which the standard ACEs are listed is the sequence used by the IOS to process the list. Notice that the statements are grouped into two sections, host statements followed by range statements. The sequence number indicates the order that the statement was entered, not the order the statement will be processed.

The host statements are listed first but not necessarily in the order that they were entered. The IOS puts host statements in an order using a special hashing function. The resulting order optimizes the search for a host ACL entry.

The range statements are displayed after the host statements. These statements are listed in the order in which they were entered.

Recall that standard and numbered ACLs can be editing using sequence numbers. The sequence number shown in the `show access-lists` command output is the number used when deleting an individual statement from the list. When inserting a new ACL statement, the sequence number will only affect the location of a range statement in the list. Host statements will always be put in order using the hashing function.

Continuing with the example, after saving the running-configuration the router is reloaded (rebooted). As shown in Figure 3, the `show access-lists` command displays the ACL in the same order, however the statements have been renumbered. The sequence numbers are now in numerical order.

Note   The hashing function is only applied to host statements in an IPv4 standard access list. The algorithm is not used for IPv4 extended ACLs or IPv6 ACLs. This is because extended and IPv6 ACLs filter on more than just a single source address. The details of the hashing function are beyond the scope of this course.

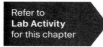

Refer to
Lab Activity
for this chapter

9.2.2.7   Lab - Configuring and Verifying Standard ACLs

In this lab, you will complete the following objectives:

- Part 1: Set Up the Topology and Initialize Devices
- Part 2: Configure Devices and Verify Connectivity
- Part 3: Configure and Verify Standard Numbered and Named ACLs
- Part 4: Modify a Standard ACL

Refer to
Online Course
for Illustration

9.2.3   Securing VTY ports with a Standard IPv4 ACL

9.2.3.1   Configuring a Standard ACL to Secure a VTY Port

Using an ACL to Control VTY Access

Cisco recommends using SSH for administrative connections to routers and switches. If the Cisco IOS software image on your router does not support SSH, you can improve the security of administrative lines by restricting VTY access. Restricting VTY access is a technique that allows you to define which IP addresses are allowed Telnet access to the router EXEC process. You can control which administrative workstation or network manages your router with an ACL and an **access-class** statement configured on your VTY lines. You can also use this technique with SSH to further improve administrative access security.

The **access-class** command configured in line configuration mode restricts incoming and outgoing connections between a particular VTY (into a Cisco device) and the addresses in an access list.

Standard and extended access lists apply to packets that travel through a router. They are not designed to block packets that originate within the router. An outbound Telnet extended ACL does not prevent router-initiated Telnet sessions, by default.

Filtering Telnet or SSH traffic is typically considered an extended IP ACL function because it filters a higher level protocol. However, because the **access-class** command is used to filter incoming or outgoing Telnet/SSH sessions by source address, a standard ACL can be used.

The command syntax of the **access-class** command is:

```
Router(config-line)# access-class access-list-number { in [ vrf-also ] | out }
```

The parameter **in** restricts incoming connections between the addresses in the access list and the Cisco device, while the parameter **out** restricts outgoing connections between a particular Cisco device and the addresses in the access list.

An example allowing a range of addresses to access VTY lines 0 - 4 is shown in Figure 1. The ACL in the figure is configured to permit network 192.168.10.0 to access VTY lines 0 - 4 but deny all other networks.

The following should be considered when configuring access lists on VTYs:

- Only numbered access lists can be applied to VTYs.
- Identical restrictions should be set on all the VTYs, because a user can attempt to connect to any of them.

Use the Syntax Checker in Figure 2 to practice securing VTY access.

Refer to
Online Course
for Illustration

9.2.3.2   Verifying a Standard ACL used to Secure a VTY Port

After the ACL to restrict access to the VTY lines is configured, it is important to verify that it is working as expected. The figure shows two devices attempting to connect to R1 using SSH. Access list 21 has been configured on the VTY lines on R1. PC1 is successful while PC2 fails to establish a SSH connection. This is the expected behavior, as the configured access list permits VTY access from the 192.168.10.0/24 network while denying all other devices.

The output for R1 shows the result of issuing the `show access-lists` command after the SSH attempts by PC1 and PC2. The match in the permit line of the output is a result of a successful SSH connection by PC1. The match in the deny statement is due to the failed attempt to create an SSH connection by PC2, a device on the 192.168.11.0/24 network.

Refer to **Packet
Tracer Activity**
for this chapter

9.2.3.3   Packet Tracer - Configuring an ACL on VTY Lines

As administrator of a network, you need to have remote access to your router. This access should not be available to other users of the network. Therefore, you will configure and apply an ACL that allows PC access to the Telnet lines, but denies all other source IP addresses.

Refer to
Lab Activity
for this chapter

9.2.3.4   Lab - Configuring and Verifying VTY Restrictions

In this lab, you will complete the following objectives :

■ Part 1: Configure Basic Device Settings

■ Part 2: Configure and Apply the Access Control List on R1

■ Part 3: Verify the Access Control List Using Telnet

■ Part 4: Challenge - Configure and Apply the Access Control List on S1

Refer to
Online Course
for Illustration

9.3   Extended IPv4 ACLs

9.3.1   Structure of an Extended IPv4 ACL

9.3.1.1   Extended ACLs

Testing Packets with Extended ACLs

For more precise traffic-filtering control, extended IPv4 ACLs can be created. Extended ACLs are numbered 100 to 199 and 2000 to 2699, providing a total of 799 possible extended numbered ACLs. Extended ACLs can also be named.

Extended ACLs are used more often than standard ACLs because they provide a greater degree of control. As shown in the figure, like standard ACLs, extended ACLs check source addresses of packets, but they also check the destination address, protocols, and port numbers (or services). This provides a greater range of criteria on which to base the ACL. For example, an extended ACL can simultaneously allow email traffic from a network to a specific destination while denying file transfers and web browsing.

Refer to
Online Course
for Illustration

9.3.1.2   Extended ACLs (Cont.)

Testing for Ports and Services

The ability to filter on protocol and port number allows network administrators to build very specific extended ACLs. An application can be specified by configuring either the port number or the name of a well-known port.

Figure 1 shows some examples of how an administrator specifies a TCP or UDP port number by placing it at the end of the extended ACL statement. Logical operations can be used, such as equal (eq), not equal (neq), greater than (gt), and less than (lt).

Figure 2 shows how to display a list of port numbers and keywords that can be used when building an ACL using the command:

```
R1(config)# access-list 101 permit tcp any any eq ?
```

Refer to
Online Course
for Illustration

9.3.2   Configure Extended IPv4 ACLs

9.3.2.1   Configuring Extended ACLs

The procedural steps for configuring extended ACLs are the same as for standard ACLs. The extended ACL is first configured, and then it is activated on an interface. However, the command syntax and parameters are more complex to support the additional features provided by extended ACLs.

Note   The internal logic applied to the ordering of standard ACL statement does not apply to extended ACLs. The order in which the statements are entered during configuration is the order they are displayed and processed.

Figure 1 shows the common command syntax for extended IPv4 ACLs. Note that there are many keywords and parameters for extended ACLs. It is not necessary to use all of the keywords and parameters when configuring an extended ACL. Recall that the ? can be used to get help when entering complex commands.

Figure 2 shows an example of an extended ACL. In this example, the network administrator has configured ACLs to restrict network access to allow website browsing only from the LAN attached to interface G0/0 to any external network. ACL 103 allows traffic coming from any address on the 192.168.10.0 network to go to any destination, subject to the limitation that the traffic is using ports 80 (HTTP) and 443 (HTTPS) only.

The nature of HTTP requires that traffic flow back into the network from websites accessed from internal clients. The network administrator wants to restrict that return traffic to HTTP exchanges from requested websites, while denying all other traffic. ACL 104 does that by blocking all incoming traffic, except for previously established connections. The permit statement in ACL 104 allows inbound traffic using the **established** parameter.

The **established** parameter allows only responses to traffic that originates from the 192.168.10.0/24 network to return to that network. A match occurs if the returning TCP segment has the ACK or reset (RST) bits set, which indicates that the packet belongs to an existing connection. Without the **established** parameter in the ACL statement, clients could send traffic to a web server, but not receive traffic returning from the web server.

Refer to
Online Course
for Illustration

9.3.2.2   Applying Extended ACLs to Interfaces

In the previous example, the network administrator configured an ACL to allow users from the 192.168.10.0/24 network to browse both insecure and secure websites. Even though it has been configured, the ACL will not filter traffic until it is applied to an interface. To apply an ACL to an interface, first consider whether the traffic to be filtered is going in or out. When a user on the internal LAN accesses a website on the Internet, traffic is traffic going out to the Internet. When an internal user receives an email from the Internet, traffic is coming into the local router. However, when applying an ACL to an interface, in and out take on different meanings. From an ACL consideration, in and out are in reference to the router interface.

In the topology in the figure, R1 has three interfaces. It has a serial interface, S0/0/0, and two Gigabit Ethernet interfaces, G0/0 and G0/1. Recall that an extended ACL should typically be applied close to the source. In this topology the interface closest to the source of the target traffic is the G0/0 interface.

Web request traffic from users on the 192.168.10.0/24 LAN is inbound to the G0/0 interface. Return traffic from established connections to users on the LAN is outbound from the G0/0 interface. The example applies the ACL to the G0/0 interface in both directions. The inbound ACL, 103, checks for the type of traffic. The outbound ACL, 104, checks for return traffic from established connections. This will restrict 192.168.10.0 Internet access to allow only website browsing.

Note   The access lists could have been applied to the S0/0/0 interface but in that case, the router's ACL process would have to examine all packets entering the router, not only traffic to and from 192.168.11.0. This would cause unnecessary processing by the router.

Refer to
Online Course
for Illustration

9.3.2.3   Filtering Traffic with Extended ACLs

The example shown in Figure 1 denies FTP traffic from subnet 192.168.11.0 that is going to subnet 192.168.10.0, but permits all other traffic. Note the use of wildcard masks and the explicit deny any statement. Remember that FTP uses TCP ports 20 and 21; therefore the ACL requires both port name keywords **ftp** and **ftp-data** or **eq 20** and **eq 21** to deny FTP.

If using port numbers instead of port names, the commands would be written as:

```
access-list 114 permit tcp 192.168.20.0 0.0.0.255 any eq 20
access-list 114 permit tcp 192.168.20.0 0.0.0.255 any eq 21
```

To prevent the implied deny any statement at the end of the ACL from blocking all traffic, the **permit ip any any** statement is added. Without at least one **permit** statement in an ACL, all traffic on the interface where that ACL was applied would be dropped. The ACL should be applied inbound on the G0/1 interface so that traffic from the 192.168.11.0/24 LAN is filtered as it enters the router interface.

The example shown in Figure 2, denies Telnet traffic from any source to the 192.168.11.0/24 LAN, but allows all other IP traffic. Because traffic destined for the 192.168.11.0/24 LAN is outbound on interface G0/1, the ACL would be applied to G0/1 using the **out** keyword. Note the use of the **any** keywords in the permit statement. This permit statement is added to ensure that no other traffic is blocked.

Note The examples in Figures 1 and 2 both use the `permit ip any any` statement at the end of the ACL. For greater security the `permit 192.168.11.0 0.0.0.255 any` command may be used.

Refer to
Online Course
for Illustration

9.3.2.4 Creating Named Extended ACLs

Named extended ACLs are created in essentially the same way that named standard ACLs are created. Follow these steps to create an extended ACL, using names:

Step 1. From global configuration mode, use the `ip access-list extended` *name* command to define a name for the extended ACL.

Step 2. In named ACL configuration mode, specify the conditions to `permit` or `deny`.

Step 3. Return to privileged EXEC mode and verify the ACL with the `show access-lists` *name* command.

Step 4. Save the entries in the configuration file with the `copy running-config startup-config` command.

To remove a named extended ACL, use the `no ip access-list extended` *name* global configuration command.

The figure shows the named versions of the ACLs created in the previous examples. The named ACL, SURFING, permits the users on the 192.168.10.0/24 LAN to access web sites. The named ACL, BROWSING, allows the return traffic from established connections. Using the ACL names, the rules are applied inbound and outbound on the G0/0 interface.

Refer to
Online Course
for Illustration

9.3.2.5 Verifying Extended ACLs

After an ACL has been configured and applied to an interface, use Cisco IOS `show` commands to verify the configuration. In the figure, the top example shows the Cisco IOS command used to display the contents of all ACLs. The bottom example shows the result of issuing the `show ip interface g0/0` command on router R1.

Unlike standard ACLs, extended ACLs do not implement the same internal logic and hashing function. The output and sequence numbers displayed in the `show access-lists` command output is the order in which the statements were entered. Host entries are not automatically listed prior to range entries.

The `show ip interface` command is used to verify the ACL on the interface and the direction in which it was applied. The output from this command includes the number or name of the access list and the direction in which the ACL was applied. The capitalized ACL names BROWSING and SURFING stand out in the screen output.

After an ACL configuration has been verified, the next step is to confirm that the ACLs work as planned; blocking and permitting traffic as expected.

The guidelines discussed earlier in this section, suggest that ACLs should be configured on a test network and then implemented on the production network.

Refer to
Online Course
for Illustration

9.3.2.6   Editing Extended ACLs

Editing an extended ACL can be accomplished using the same process as editing a standard ACL as discussed in a previous section. An extended ACL can be modified using:

- **Method 1 Text editor** - Using this method, the ACL is copied and pasted into the text editor where the changes are made. The current access list is removed using the **no access-list** command. The modified ACL is then pasted back into the configuration.

- **Method 2 Sequence numbers** - Sequence numbers can be used to delete or insert an ACL statement. The **ip access-list extended** *name* command is used to enter named-ACL configuration mode. If the ACL is numbered instead of named, the ACL number is used in the *name* parameter. ACEs can be inserted or removed.

In the figure the administrator needs to edit the ACL named SURFING to correct a typo in the source network statement. To view the current sequence numbers, the **show access-lists** command is used. The statement to be edited is identified as statement 10. The original statement is removed with the **no** *sequence_#* command. The corrected statement is added replacing the original statement.

Refer to
Interactive Graphic
in online course.

9.3.2.7   Activity - Creating an Extended ACL Statement

Refer to
Interactive Graphic
in online course.

9.3.2.8   Activity - Evaluating Extended ACEs

Refer to
Interactive Graphic
in online course.

9.3.2.9   Activity - ACL Testlet

Refer to **Packet Tracer Activity** for this chapter

9.3.2.10   Packet Tracer - Configuring Extended ACLs - Scenario 1

Scenario

Two employees need access to services provided by the server. PC1 only needs FTP access while PC2 only needs web access. Both computers will be able to ping the server, but not each other.

Refer to **Packet Tracer Activity** for this chapter

9.3.2.11   Packet Tracer - Configuring Extended ACLs - Scenario 2

Scenario

In this scenario, devices on one LAN are allowed to remotely access devices in another LAN using the Telnet protocol. Besides ICMP, all traffic from other networks is denied.

Refer to **Packet Tracer Activity** for this chapter

9.3.2.12   Packet Tracer - Configuring Extended ACLs - Scenario 3

Background / Scenario

In this scenario, specific devices on the LAN are allowed to various services on servers located on the Internet.

9.3.2.13   Lab - Configuring and Verifying Extended ACLs

In this lab, you will complete the following objectives :

- Part 1: Set Up the Topology and Initialize Devices

- Part 2: Configure Devices and Verify Connectivity

- Part 3: Configure and Verify Extended Numbered and Named ACLs

- Part 4: Modify and Verify Extended ACLs

Refer to
Online Course
for Illustration

9.4   Troubleshoot ACLs

9.4.1   Processing Packets with ACLs

9.4.1.1   Inbound and Outbound ACL Logic

Inbound ACL Logic

Figure 1 shows the logic for an inbound ACL. If the information in a packet header and an ACL statement match, the rest of the statements in the list are skipped, and the packet is permitted or denied as specified by the matched statement. If a packet header does not match an ACL statement, the packet is tested against the next statement in the list. This matching process continues until the end of the list is reached.

At the end of every ACL is a statement is an implicit deny any statement. This statement is not shown in output. This final implied statement applied to all packets for which conditions did not test true. This final test condition matches all other packets and results in a "deny" action. Instead of proceeding into or out of an interface, the router drops all of these remaining packets. This final statement is often referred to as the "implicit deny any statement" or the "deny all traffic" statement. Because of this statement, an ACL should have at least one permit statement in it; otherwise, the ACL blocks all traffic.

Outbound ACL Logic

Figure 2 shows the logic for an outbound ACL. Before a packet is forwarded to an outbound interface, the router checks the routing table to see if the packet is routable. If the packet is not routable, it is dropped and is not tested against the ACEs. Next, the router checks to see whether the outbound interface is grouped to an ACL. If the outbound interface is not grouped to an ACL, the packet can be sent to the output buffer. Examples of outbound ACL operation are as follows:

- **No ACL applied to the interface:** If the outbound interface is not grouped to an outbound ACL, the packet is sent directly to the outbound interface.

- **ACL applied to the interface:** If the outbound interface is grouped to an outbound ACL, the packet is not sent out on the outbound interface until it is tested by the combination of ACEs that are associated with that interface. Based on the ACL tests, the packet is permitted or denied.

For outbound lists, "permit" means to send the packet to the output buffer, and "deny" means to discard the packet.

Refer to
Online Course
for Illustration

9.4.1.2   ACL Logic Operations

ACL and Routing and ACL Processes on a Router

The figure shows the logic of routing and ACL processes. When a packet arrives at a router interface, the router process is the same, whether ACLs are used or not. As a frame enters an interface, the router checks to see whether the destination Layer 2 address matches its interface Layer 2 address, or whether the frame is a broadcast frame.

If the frame address is accepted, the frame information is stripped off and the router checks for an ACL on the inbound interface. If an ACL exists, the packet is tested against the statements in the list.

If the packet matches a statement, the packet is either permitted or denied. If the packet is accepted, it is then checked against routing table entries to determine the destination interface. If a routing table entry exists for the destination, the packet is then switched to the outgoing interface, otherwise the packet is dropped.

Next, the router checks whether the outgoing interface has an ACL. If an ACL exists, the packet is tested against the statements in the list.

If the packet matches a statement, it is either permitted or denied.

If there is no ACL or the packet is permitted, the packet is encapsulated in the new Layer 2 protocol and forwarded out the interface to the next device.

Refer to
Online Course
for Illustration

9.4.1.3   Standard ACL Decision Process

Standard ACLs only examine the source IPv4 address. The destination of the packet and the ports involved are not considered.

The decision process for a standard ACL is mapped in the figure. Cisco IOS software tests addresses against the conditions in the ACL one by one. The first match determines whether the software accepts or rejects the address. Because the software stops testing conditions after the first match, the order of the conditions is critical. If no conditions match, the address is rejected.

Refer to
Online Course
for Illustration

9.4.1.4   Extended ACL Decision Process

The figure shows the logical decision path used by an extended ACL built to filter on source and destination addresses, and protocol and port numbers. In this example, the ACL first filters on the source address, then on the port and protocol of the source. It then filters on the destination address, then on the port and protocol of the destination, and makes a final permit or deny decision.

Recall that entries in ACLs are processed one after the other, so a 'No' decision does not necessarily equal a 'Deny'. As you go through the logical decision path, note that a 'No' means go to the next entry until a condition is matched.

Refer to
Interactive Graphic
in online course.

9.4.1.5 Activity - Place in Order the Steps of the ACL Decision Making Process

Refer to
Online Course
for Illustration

9.4.2 Common ACLs Errors

9.4.2.1 Troubleshooting Common ACL Errors - Example 1

Using the `show` commands described earlier reveals most of the more common ACL errors. The most common errors are entering ACEs in the wrong order and not applying adequate criteria to the ACL rules.

Error Example 1

In the figure, host 192.168.10.10 has no connectivity with 192.168.30.12. When viewing the output of the `show access-lists` command, matches are shown for the first deny statement. This is an indicator that this statement has been matched by traffic.

Solution - Look at the order of the ACEs. Host 192.168.10.10 has no connectivity with 192.168.30.12 because of the order of rule 10 in the access list. Because the router processes ACLs from the top down, statement 10 denies host 192.168.10.10, so statement 20 can never be matched. Statements 10 and 20 should be reversed. The last line allows all other non-TCP traffic that falls under IP (ICMP, UDP, etc.).

Refer to
Online Course
for Illustration

9.4.2.2 Troubleshooting Common ACL Errors - Example 2

Error Example 2

In the figure, the 192.168.10.0/24 network cannot use TFTP to connect to the 192.168.30.0/24 network.

Solution - The 192.168.10.0/24 network cannot use TFTP to connect to the 192.168.30.0/24 network because TFTP uses the transport protocol UDP. Statement 30 in access list 120 allows all other TCP traffic. However, because TFTP uses UDP instead of TCP, it is implicitly denied. Recall that the implied deny any statement does not appear in `show access-lists` output and therefore matches are not shown.

Statement 30 should be `ip any any`.

This ACL works whether it is applied to G0/0 of R1, or S0/0/1 of R3, or S0/0/0 of R2 in the incoming direction. However, based on the rule about placing extended ACLs closest to the source, the best option is to place it inbound on G0/0 of R1 because it allows undesirable traffic to be filtered without crossing the network infrastructure.

Refer to
Online Course
for Illustration

9.4.2.3 Troubleshooting Common ACL Errors - Example 3

Error Example 3

In the figure, the 192.168.11.0/24 network can use Telnet to connect to 192.168.30.0/24, but according to company policy, this connection should not be allowed. The results of the `show access-lists 130` command indicate that the permit statement has been matched.

Solution - The 192.168.11.0/24 network can use Telnet to connect to the 192.168.30.0/24 network, because the Telnet port number in statement 10 of access list 130 is listed in the wrong position in the ACL statement. Statement 10 currently denies any source packet with a port number that is equal to Telnet. To deny Telnet traffic inbound on G0/1, deny the destination port number that is equal to Telnet, for example, `deny tcp any any eq telnet`.

Refer to
Online Course
for Illustration

9.4.2.4   Troubleshooting Common ACL Errors - Example 4

Error Example 4

In the figure, host 192.168.30.12 is able to Telnet to connect to 192.168.31.12, but company policy states that this connection should not be allowed. Output from the `show access-lists 140` command indicate that the permit statement has been matched.

Solution - Host 192.168.30.12 can use Telnet to connect to 192.168.31.12 because there are no rules that deny host 192.168.30.12 or its network as the source. Statement 10 of access list 140 denies the router interface on which traffic enters the router. The host IPv4 address in statement 10 should be 192.168.30.12.

Refer to
Online Course
for Illustration

9.4.2.5   Troubleshooting Common ACL Errors - Example 5

Error Example 5

In the figure, host 192.168.30.12 can use Telnet to connect to 192.168.31.12, but according to the security policy, this connection should not be allowed. Output from the `show access-lists 150` command indicate that no matches have occurred for the deny statement as expected.

Solution - Host 192.168.30.12 can use Telnet to connect to 192.168.31.12 because of the direction in which access list 150 is applied to the G0/1 interface. Statement 10 denies any source address to connect to host 192.168.31.12 using telnet. However, this filter should be applied outbound on G0/1 to filter correctly.

Refer to **Packet
Tracer Activity**
for this chapter

9.4.2.6   Packet Tracer - Troubleshooting ACLs

Scenario

Create a network that has the following three policies implemented:

- Hosts from the 192.168.0.0/24 network are unable to access any TCP service of Server3.

- Hosts from the 10.0.0.0/8 network are unable to access the HTTP service of Server1.

- Hosts from the 172.16.0.0/16 network are unable to access the FTP service of Server2.

Refer to
Lab Activity
for this chapter

9.4.2.7   Lab - Troubleshooting ACL Configuration and Placement

In this lab, you will complete the following objectives:

- Part 1: Build the Network and Configure Basic Device Settings

- Part 2: Troubleshoot Internal Access

- Part 3: Troubleshoot Remote Access

Refer to **Packet Tracer Activity** for this chapter

9.4.2.8   Packet Tracer - Skills Integration Challenge

In this challenge activity, you will finish the addressing scheme, configure routing, and implement named access control lists.

Refer to **Online Course** for Illustration

9.5   IPv6 ACLs

9.5.1   IPv6 ACL Creation

9.5.1.1   Type of IPv6 ACLs

IPv6 ACLs are very similar to IPv4 ACLs in both operation and configuration. Being familiar with IPv4 access lists makes IPv6 ACLs easy to understand and configure.

In IPv4 there are two types of ACLs, standard and extended. Both types of ACLs can be either numbered or named ACLs.

With IPv6, there is only one type of ACL, which is equivalent to an IPv4 extended named ACL. There are no numbered ACLs in IPv6. To summarize, IPv6 ACLs are:

■ Named ACLs only

■ Equivalent to the functionality of an IPv4 Extended ACL

An IPv4 ACL and an IPv6 ACL cannot share the same name.

Refer to **Online Course** for Illustration

9.5.1.2   Comparing IPv4 and IPv6 ACLs

Although IPv4 and IPv6 ACLs are very similar, there are three significant differences between them.

■ **Applying an IPv6 ACL**

The first difference is the command used to apply an IPv6 ACL to an interface. IPv4 uses the command `ip access-group` to apply an IPv4 ACL to an IPv4 interface. IPv6 uses the `ipv6 traffic-filter` command to perform the same function for IPv6 interfaces.

■ **No Wildcard Masks**

Unlike IPv4 ACLs, IPv6 ACLs do not use wildcard masks. Instead, the prefix-length is used to indicate how much of an IPv6 source or destination address should be matched.

■ **Additional Default Statements**

The last major difference has to with the addition of two implicit permit statements at the end of each IPv6 access list. At the end of every IPv4 standard or extended ACL is an implicit `deny any` or `deny any any`. IPv6 includes a similar `deny ipv6 any any` statement at the end of each IPv6 ACL. The difference is IPv6 also includes two other implicit statements by default:

■ `permit icmp any any nd-na`

■ `permit icmp any any nd-ns`

These two statements allow the router to participate in the IPv6 equivalent of ARP for IPv4. Recall that ARP is used in IPv4 to resolve Layer 3 addresses to Layer 2 MAC addresses. As shown in the figure, IPv6 uses ICMP Neighbor Discovery (ND) messages to accomplish the same thing. ND uses Neighbor Solicitation (NS) and Neighbor Advertisement (NA) messages.

ND messages are encapsulated in IPv6 packets and require the services of the IPv6 network layer while ARP for IPv4 does not use Layer 3. Because IPv6 uses the Layer 3 service for neighbor discovery, IPv6 ACLs need to implicitly permit ND packets to be sent and received on an interface. Specifically, both Neighbor Discovery - Neighbor Advertisement (nd-na) and Neighbor Discovery - Neighbor Solicitation (nd-ns) messages are permitted.

9.5.2   Configuring IPv6 ACLs

Refer to Online Course for Illustration

9.5.2.1   Configuring IPv6 Topology

Figure 1 shows the topology that will be used for configuring IPv6 ACLs. The topology is similar to the previous IPv4 topology except for the IPv6 addressing scheme. There are three 2001:DB8:CAFE::/64 subnets: 2001:DB8:CAFE:10::/64, 2001:DB8:CAFE:11::/64 and 2001:DB8:CAFE:30::/64. Two serial networks connect the three routers: 2001:DB8:FEED:1::/64 and 2001:DB8:FEED:2::/64.

Figures 2, 3, and 4 show the IPv6 address configuration for each router. The `show ipv6 interface brief` command is used to verify the address and the state of the interface.

Note   The `no shutdown` command and the `clock rate` command are not shown.

Refer to Online Course for Illustration

9.5.2.2   Configuring IPv6 ACLs

In IPv6 there are only named ACLs. The configuration is similar to that of an IPv4 extended named ACL.

Figure 1 shows the command syntax for IPv6 ACLs. The syntax is similar to the syntax used for an IPv4 extended ACL. One significant difference is the use of the IPv6 prefix-length instead of an IPv4 wildcard mask.

There are three basic steps to configure an IPv6 ACL:

Step 1.   From global configuration mode, use the `ipv6 access-list` *name* command to create an IPv6 ACL. Like IPv4 named ACLs, IPv6 names are alphanumeric, case sensitive, and must be unique. Unlike IPv4, there is no need for a standard or extended option.

Step 2.   From the named ACL configuration mode, use the `permit` or `deny` statements to specify one or more conditions to determine if a packet is forwarded or dropped.

Step 3.   Return to privileged EXEC mode with the `end` command.

Figure 2 demonstrates the steps to create an IPv6 ACL with a simple example based on the previous topology. The first statement names the IPv6 access list NO-R3-LAN-ACCESS. Similar to IPv4 named ACLs, capitalizing IPv6 ACL names is not required, but makes them stand out when viewing the running-config output.

The second statement denies all IPv6 packets from the 2001:DB8:CAFE:30::/64 destined for any IPv6 network. The third statement allows all other IPv6 packets.

Figure 3 shows the ACL in context with the topology.

Refer to **Online Course** for Illustration

9.5.2.3   Applying an IPv6 ACL to an Interface

After an IPv6 ACL is configured, it is linked to an interface using the **ipv6 traffic-filter** command:

```
Router(config-if)# ipv6 traffic-filter access-list-name { in | out }
```

The figure shows the NO-R3-LAN-ACCESS ACL configured previously and the commands used to apply the IPv6 ACL inbound to the S0/0/0 interface. Applying the ACL to the inbound S0/0/0 interface will deny packets from 2001:DB8:CAFE:30::/64 to both of the LANs on R1.

To remove an ACL from an interface, first enter the **no ipv6 traffic-filter** command on the interface, and then enter the global **no ipv6 access-list** command to remove the access list.

Note   IPv4 and IPv6 both use the **ip access-class** command to apply an access list to VTY ports.

Refer to **Online Course** for Illustration

9.5.2.4   IPv6 ACL Examples

Deny FTP

The topology for the examples is shown in Figure 1.

In the first example shown in Figure 2, router R1 is configured with an IPv6 access list to deny FTP traffic to 2001:DB8:CAFE:11::/64. Ports for both FTP data (port 20) and FTP control (port 21) need to be blocked. Because he filter is applied inbound on the G0/0 interface on R1 only traffic from the 2001:DB8:CAFE:10::/64 network will be denied.

Restricted Access

In the second example shown in Figure 3, an IPv6 ACL is configured to give the LAN on R3 limited access to the LANs on R1. Comments are added in the configuration to document the ACL. The following features have been labelled in the ACL:

1. The first two permit statements allow access from any device to the web server at 2001:DB8:CAFE:10::10.

2. All other devices are denied access to the 2001:DB8:CAFE:10::/64 network.

3. PC3 at 2001:DB8:CAFE:30::12 is permitted Telnet access to PC2 which has the IPv6 address 2001:DB8:CAFE:11::11.

4. All other devices are denied Telnet access to PC2.

5. All other IPv6 traffic is permitted to all other destinations.

6. The IPv6 access list is applied to interface G0/0 in the inbound direction, so only the 2001:DB8:CAFE:30::/64 network is affected.

Refer to
Online Course
for Illustration

9.5.2.5   Verifying IPv6 ACLs

The commands used to verify an IPv6 access list are similar to those used for IPv4 ACLs. Using these commands, the IPv6 access list RESTRICTED-ACCESS that was configured previously can be verified. Figure 1 shows the output of the `show ipv6 interface` command. The output confirms that RESTRICTED-ACCESS ACL is configured inbound on the G0/0 interface.

As shown in Figure 2, the `show access-lists` command displays all access lists on the router including both IPv4 and IPv6 ACLs. Notice that with IPv6 ACLs the sequence numbers occur at the end of the statement and not the beginning as with IPv4 access lists. Although the statements appear in the order they were entered, they are not always incremented by 10. This is because the remark statements that were entered use a sequence number but are not displayed in the output of the `show access-lists` command.

Similar to extended ACLs for IPv4, IPv6 access lists are displayed and processed in the order the statements are entered. Remember, IPv4 standard ACLs use an internal logic which changes their order and processing sequence.

As shown in Figure 3, the output from the `show running-config` command includes all of the ACEs and remark statements. Remark statements can come before or after `permit` or `deny` statements but should be consistent in their placement.

Refer to Packet
Tracer Activity
for this chapter

9.5.2.6   Packet Tracer - Configuring IPv6 ACLs
Objectives

- Part 1: Configure, Apply, and Verify an IPv6 ACL
- Part 2: Configure, Apply, and Verify a Second IPv6 ACL

Refer to
Lab Activity
for this chapter

9.5.2.7   Lab - Configuring and Verifying IPv6 ACLs
In this lab, you will complete the following objectives :

- Part 1: Set Up the Topology and Initialize Devices
- Part 2: Configure Devices and Verify Connectivity
- Part 3: Configure and Verify IPv6 ACLs
- Part 4: Edit IPv6 ACLs

Refer to
Online Course
for Illustration

9.6   Summary

Refer to
Lab Activity
for this chapter

9.6.1.1   Class Activity FTP Denied

FTP Denied

Scenario

It was recently reported that viruses are on the rise within your small- to medium-sized business network. Your network administrator has been tracking network performance and has determined that one particular host is constantly downloading files from a remote FTP server. This host just may be the virus source perpetuating throughout the network!

Use Packet Tracer to complete this activity. Write a named ACL to deny the host access to the FTP server. Apply the ACL to the most effective interface on the router.

To complete the physical topology, you must use:

- One PC host station
- Two switches
- One Cisco 1941 series Integrated Services Router
- One server

Using the Packet Tracer text tool, record the ACL you prepared. Validate that the ACL works to deny access to the FTP server by trying to access the FTP server's address. Observe what happens while in simulation mode.

Save your file and be prepared to share it with another student, or with the entire class.

Refer to **Online Course** for Illustration

9.6.1.2 Summary

By default a router does not filter traffic. Traffic that enters the router is routed solely based on information within the routing table.

Packet filtering controls access to a network by analyzing the incoming and outgoing packets and passing or dropping them based on criteria such as the source IP address, destination IP addresses, and the protocol carried within the packet. A packet-filtering router uses rules to determine whether to permit or deny traffic. A router can also perform packet filtering at Layer 4, the transport layer.

An ACL is a sequential list of permit or deny statements. The last statement of an ACL is always an implicit deny which blocks all traffic. To prevent the implied deny any statement at the end of the ACL from blocking all traffic, the **permit ip any any** statement can be added.

When network traffic passes through an interface configured with an ACL, the router compares the information within the packet against each entry, in sequential order, to determine if the packet matches one of the statements. If a match is found, the packet is processed accordingly.

ACLs are configured to apply to inbound traffic or to apply to outbound traffic.

Standard ACLs can be used to permit or deny traffic only from a source IPv4 addresses. The destination of the packet and the ports involved are not evaluated. The basic rule for placing a standard ACL is to place it close to the destination.

Extended ACLs filter packets based on several attributes: protocol type, source or destination IPv4 address, and source or destination ports. The basic rule for placing an extended ACL is to place it as close to the source as possible.

The **access-list** global configuration command defines a standard ACL with a number in the range of 1 through 99 or an extended ACL with numbers in the range of 100 to 199 and 2000 to 2699. Both standard and extended ACLs can also be named. The **ip access-list standard** *name* is used to create a standard named ACL, whereas the command **ip** `access-list extended` *name* is for an extended access list. IPv4 ACEs include the use of wildcard masks.

After an ACL is configured, it is linked to an interface using the `ip access-group` command in interface configuration mode. Remember the three Ps, one ACL per protocol, per direction, per interface.

To remove an ACL from an interface, first enter the `no ip access-group` command on the interface, and then enter the global `no access-list` command to remove the entire ACL.

The `show running-config` and `show access-lists` commands are used to verify ACL configuration. The `show ip interface` command is used to verify the ACL on the interface and the direction in which it was applied.

The `access-class` command configured in line configuration mode restricts incoming and outgoing connections between a particular VTY and the addresses in an access list.

Like IPv4 named ACLs, IPv6 names are alphanumeric, case sensitive, and must be unique. Unlike IPv4, there is no need for a standard or extended option.

From global configuration mode, use the `ipv6 access-list` *name* command to create an IPv6 ACL. Unlike IPv4 ACLs, IPv6 ACLs do not use wildcard masks. Instead, the prefix-length is used to indicate how much of an IPv6 source or destination address should be matched.

After an IPv6 ACL is configured, it is linked to an interface using the `ipv6 traffic-filter` command.

Go to the online course to take the quiz and exam.

Chapter 9 Quiz

This quiz is designed to provide an additional opportunity to practice the skills and knowledge presented in the chapter and to prepare for the chapter exam. You will be allowed multiple attempts and the grade does not appear in the gradebook.

Chapter 9 Exam

The chapter exam assesses your knowledge of the chapter content.

Your Chapter Notes

IOS Images and Licensing

10.0 IOS Images and Licensing

10.0.1.1 Introduction

Cisco IOS (originally Internetwork Operating System) is software used on most Cisco routers and switches. IOS is a package of routing, switching, security, and other internetworking technologies integrated into a single multitasking operating system.

The Cisco IOS portfolio supports a broad range of technologies and features. Customers choose an IOS based on a set of protocols and features supported by a particular image. Understanding the Cisco portfolio of feature sets is helpful in selecting the proper IOS to meet the needs of an organization.

Cisco made significant changes in the packaging and licensing of its IOS when transitioning from IOS 12.4 to 15.0. This chapter explains the naming conventions and packaging of IOS 12.4 and 15. Beginning with IOS 15, Cisco also implemented a new packaging format and licensing process for IOS. This chapter discusses the process of obtaining, installing, and managing Cisco IOS 15 software licenses.

Note   The release of IOS after 12.4 is 15.0. There is no IOS software release 13 or 14.

Refer to
Lab Activity
for this chapter

10.0.1.2 Class Activity IOS Detection

Activity - IOS Detection

Your school or university has just received a donation of Cisco routers and switches. You transport them from your shipping and receiving department to your Cisco networking lab and start sorting them into switch and router groups.

Refer to the accompanying PDF for directions on how to proceed with this modeling activity. Save your work and share the data you found with another group or the entire class.

Refer to
Online Course
for Illustration

10.1 Managing IOS System Files

10.1.1 Naming Conventions

10.1.1.1 Cisco IOS Software Release Families and Trains

Cisco IOS Software has evolved from a single platform operating system for routing, to a sophisticated operating system that supports a large array of features and technologies such as VoIP, NetFlow, and IPsec. To better meet the requirements of the different market segments, the software is organized into software release families and software trains.

A software release family is comprised of multiple IOS software release versions that:

- Share a code base

- Apply to related hardware platforms

- Overlap in support coverage (as one OS comes to end-of-life, another OS is introduced and supported)

Examples of IOS software releases, within a software release family, include 12.3, 12.4, 15.0, and 15.1.

Along with each software release, there are new versions of the software created to implement bug fixes and new features. IOS refers to these versions as trains.

A Cisco IOS train is used to deliver releases with a common code base to a specific set of platforms and features. A train may contain several releases, each release being a snapshot of the code base of the train at the moment of the release. Because different software release families can apply to different platforms or market segments, several trains can be current at any point in time.

This chapter examines the trains of both IOS 12.4 and 15.

Refer to
Online Course
for Illustration

10.1.1.2   Cisco IOS 12.4 Mainline and T Trains

12.4 Trains

The figure shows the migration from software release 12.3 to 12.4. Within a software release family there may be two or more closely related and active trains. For example, the Cisco IOS Software 12.4 release family has two trains, the 12.4 mainline and the 12.4T trains.

The Cisco IOS Software 12.4 train is considered the mainline train. The mainline train receives mostly software (bug) fixes with the goal of increasing software quality. The mainline train releases are also designated as Maintenance Deployment releases (MD).

A mainline train is always associated with a technology train (T train). A T train, such as 12.4T, receives the same software bug fixes as the mainline train. The T train also receives new software and hardware support features. Releases in the Cisco IOS Software 12.4T train are considered Early Deployment (ED) releases.

There may be other trains, depending on the software release family. For example, another train available is the service provider train (S train). An S train will contain specific features designed to meet service provider requirements.

All child trains of the mainline train (T, S, etc.) typically contain an uppercase letter designating the train type.

Mainline train = 12.4

T train = 12.4T (12.4 + new software and hardware support features)

Up to and including the Cisco IOS Software 12.4 release family, the mainline and T trains were separated. In other words, from the mainline train, a T train would branch out and become a separate code base that received new features and hardware support. Eventually, a new mainline train would evolve from an established T train and the cycle would start again. This use of multiple trains was changed with the software release, Cisco IOS 15.

The figure illustrates the relationships between the release of the Cisco IOS Software 12.4 mainline train and the 12.4T train.

Refer to **Online Course** for Illustration

10.1.1.3   Cisco IOS 12.4 Mainline and T Numbering

The IOS release numbering convention is used to identify the release of the IOS software, including any bug fixes and new software features. An example of the numbering scheme is shown in the figure for both the mainline and T trains:

- The software release numbering scheme for a mainline train is composed of a train number, a maintenance identifier, and a rebuild identifier. For example, the Cisco IOS Software Release 12.4(21a) is a mainline train. The release for a T train is composed of a train number, a maintenance identifier, a train identifier, and a rebuild identifier. For example, Cisco IOS Software Release 12.4(20)T1 belongs to the Cisco IOS Software 12.4T train.

- Each maintenance identifier of Cisco IOS Software 12.4 mainline, such as 12.4(7), includes additional software and maintenance fixes. This change is indicated with the number within the parentheses. Each maintenance release of Cisco IOS Software 12.4T, such as 12.4(20)T, includes these same software fixes, along with additional software features, and hardware support.

- Cisco uses rebuilds of an individual release to integrate fixes for significant issues. This reduces the possible impact on customers who have already deployed and certified an individual release. A rebuild typically includes fixes to a limited number of software defects, which are known as caveats. It is indicated by a lowercase letter inside the parenthesis of mainline trains, or by a final number in other trains. For example, Cisco IOS Software Release 12.4(21) received a few caveat fixes and the resulting rebuild was named 12.4(21a). Similarly, 12.4(15)T8 is the eighth rebuild of 12.4(15)T. Each new rebuild increments the rebuild identifier and delivers additional software fixes on an accelerated schedule, prior to the next planned individual release. The criteria for making changes in a rebuild are strict.

A single set of individual release numbers are used for all Cisco IOS Software 12.4 trains. Cisco IOS Software Maintenance Release 12.4 and Cisco IOS Software Release 12.4T use a pool of individual release numbers that are shared across the entire Cisco IOS Software 12.4 release family. Cisco IOS Software Release 12.4(6)T was followed by 12.4(7)T and 12.4(8)T. This permits the administrator to track changes introduced in the code.

Note   Any caveat that is fixed in a T train release should be implemented in the next mainline release.

Refer to **Online Course** for Illustration

10.1.1.4   Cisco IOS 12.4 System Image Packaging

Pre Cisco IOS Software Release 15.0, Cisco IOS Software Packaging consisted of eight packages for Cisco routers, as shown in the figure. This packaging scheme was introduced with the Cisco IOS Software 12.3 mainline train and was later used in other trains. The image packaging consists of eight IOS images, three of which are considered premium packages.

The five non-premium packages are:

- **IP Base** - IP Base is the entry level Cisco IOS Software Image

- **IP Voice** - Converged voice and data, VoIP, VoFR, and IP Telephony

- **Advanced Security** - Security and VPN features including Cisco IOS Firewall, IDS/IPS, IPsec, 3DES, and VPN

- **SP (Service Provider) Services** - Adds SSH/SSL, ATM, VoATM, and MPLS to IP Voice

- **Enterprise Base** - Enterprise protocols: Appletalk, IPX, and IBM Support

Note Starting with the Cisco IOS Software 12.4 release family SSH is available in all images.

Three other premium packages offer additional IOS software feature combinations that address more complex network requirements. All features merge in the Advanced Enterprise Services package. This package integrates support for all routing protocols with Voice, Security, and VPN capabilities:

- **Advanced Enterprise Services** - Full Cisco IOS Software features

- **Enterprise Services** - Enterprise Base and Service Provider Services

- **Advanced IP Services** - Advanced Security, Service Provider Services, and support for IPv6

Note The Cisco Feature Navigator is a tool used to find the right Cisco operating system depending on the features and technologies needed.

Refer to
Online Course
for Illustration

10.1.1.5   Cisco IOS 15.0 M and T Trains

Following the Cisco IOS 12.4(24)T release, the next release of Cisco IOS Software was 15.0.

IOS 15.0 provides several enhancements to the operating system including:

- New feature and hardware support

- Broadened feature consistency with other major IOS releases

- More predictable new feature release and rebuild schedules

- Proactive individual release support policies

- Simplified release numbering

- Clearer software deployment and migration guidelines

As shown in the figure, Cisco IOS 15.0 uses a different release model from the traditional separate mainline and T trains of 12.4. Instead of diverging into separate trains, Cisco IOS Software 15 mainline and T will have extended maintenance release (EM release) and standard maintenance release (T release). With the new IOS release model, Cisco IOS 15 mainline releases are referred to as M trains.

Beginning with 15.0, new releases in the form of a T train are available approximately two to three times per year. EM releases are available approximately every 16 to 20 months. T releases enable faster Cisco feature delivery before the next EM release becomes available.

An EM release incorporates the features and hardware support of all the previous T releases. This makes newer EM releases available that contain the full functionality of the train at the time of release.

In summary, the benefits of the new Cisco IOS release model include:

■ Feature inheritance from Cisco IOS Software Releases 12.4T and 12.4 mainline

■ New feature releases approximately two to three times a year delivered sequentially from a single train

■ EM releases approximately every 16 to 20 months and includes new features

■ T releases for the very latest features and hardware support before next EM release becomes available on Cisco.com

■ Maintenance rebuilds of M and T releases contain bug fixes only

Refer to
Online Course
for Illustration

10.1.1.6   Cisco IOS 15 Train Numbering

The release numbering convention for IOS 15 identifies the specific IOS release, including bug fixes and new software features, similar to previous IOS release families. The figure shows examples of this convention for both the EM release and T release.

Extended Maintenance Release

The EM release is ideal for long-term maintenance, enabling customers to qualify, deploy, and remain on the release for an extended period. The mainline train incorporates features delivered in previous releases plus incremental new feature enhancements and hardware support.

The first maintenance rebuild (for bug fixes only, not new features or new hardware support) of Release 15.0(1)M is numbered 15.0(1)M1. Subsequent maintenance releases are defined by an increment of the maintenance rebuild number (i.e., M2, M3, etc.).

Standard Maintenance Release

The T release is used for short deployment releases ideal for the latest new features and hardware support before the next EM release becomes available. The T release provides regular bug fix maintenance rebuilds, plus critical fix support for network affecting bugs such as Product Security Incident Report Team (PSIRT) issues.

The first planned 15 T new feature release is numbered Release 15.1(1)T. The first maintenance rebuild (for bug fixes only, not new features or new hardware support) of Release 15.1(1)T will be numbered 15.1(1)T1. Subsequent releases are defined by an increment of the maintenance rebuild number (i.e., T2, T3, etc.).

Refer to
Online Course
for Illustration

10.1.1.7   IOS 15 System Image Packaging

Cisco Integrated Services Routers Generation Two (ISR G2) 1900, 2900, and 3900 Series support services on demand through the use of software licensing. The Services on Demand process enables customers to realize operational savings through ease of software ordering and management. When an order is placed for a new ISR G2 platform, the router is shipped with a single universal Cisco IOS Software image and a license is used to enable the specific feature set packages, as shown in Figure 1.

There are two types of universal images supported in ISR G2:

- **Universal images with the "universalk9" designation in the image name** - This universal image offers all of the Cisco IOS Software features, including strong payload cryptography features, such as IPsec VPN, SSL VPN, and Secure Unified Communications.

- **Universal images with the "universalk9_npe" designation in the image name** - The strong enforcement of encryption capabilities provided by Cisco Software Activation satisfies requirements for the export of encryption capabilities. However, some countries have import requirements that require that the platform does not support any strong cryptography functionality, such as payload cryptography. To satisfy the import requirements of those countries, the npe universal image does not support any strong payload encryption.

With Cisco IOS Software release 15.0, the cross-platform feature sets simplify the image selection process by providing similar functions across platform boundaries. Each device ships with Universal image. The technology packages IP Base, Data, UC (Unified Communications), and SEC (Security), are enabled in the universal image using Cisco Software Activation licensing keys. Each licensing key is unique to a particular device and is obtained from Cisco by providing the product ID and serial number of the router and a Product Activation Key (PAK). The PAK is provided by Cisco at the time of software purchase. The IP Base is installed by default.

Figure 2 shows the suggested migration for the next generation ISRs from the IOS 12 (IOS Reformation Packaging) to IOS 15 (Simplified Packaging).

10.1.1.8   IOS Image Filenames

Refer to
Online Course
for Illustration

When selecting or upgrading a Cisco IOS router, it is important to choose the proper IOS image with the correct feature set and version. The Cisco IOS image file is based on a special naming convention. The name for the Cisco IOS image file contains multiple parts, each with a specific meaning. It is important to understand this naming convention when upgrading and selecting a Cisco IOS Software.

As shown in Figure 1, the `show flash` command displays the files stored in flash memory, including the system image files.

An example of an IOS 12.4 software image name is shown in Figure 2.

- **Image Name (c2800nm)** - Identifies the platform on which the image runs. In this example, the platform is a Cisco 2800 router with a network module.

- **advipservicesk9** - Specifies the feature set. In this example, advipservicesk9 refers to the advanced IP services feature set which includes both the advanced security and service provider packages, along with IPv6.

- **mz** - Indicates where the image runs and if the file is compressed. In this example, mz indicates that the file runs from RAM and is compressed.

- **124-6.T** - The filename format for image 12.4(6)T. This is the train number, maintenance release number, and the train identifier.

■ **bin** - The file extension. This extension indicates that this file is a binary executable file.

Figure 3 illustrates the different parts of an IOS 15 system image file displayed with the **show flash** command:

■ **Image Name (c1900)** - Identifies the platform on which the image runs. In this example, the platform is a Cisco 1900 router.

■ **universalk9** - Specifies the feature set. In this case, universal refers to the universal, single image set, which includes IP Base, Security, Unified Communication, and Data feature sets. Each router is activated for IP Base feature set. However, for other feature sets, software activation is needed.

■ **mz** - Indicates where the image runs and if the file is compressed. In this example, mz indicates that the file runs from RAM and is compressed.

■ **SPA** - Designates that file is digitally signed by Cisco.

■ **152-4.M3** - Specifies the filename format for the image 15.2(4)M3. This is the version of IOS, which includes the major release, minor release, maintenance release, and maintenance rebuild numbers. The M indicates this is an extended maintenance release.

■ **bin** - The file extension. This extension indicates that this file is a binary executable file.

The most common designation for memory location and compression format is mz. The first letter indicates the location where the image is executed on the router. The locations can include:

■ **f** - flash

■ **m** - RAM

■ **r** - ROM

■ **l** - relocatable

The compression format can be either z for zip or x for mzip. Zipping is a method Cisco uses to compress some run-from-RAM images that is effective in reducing the size of the image. It is self-unzipping, so when the image is loaded into RAM for execution, the first action is to unzip.

Note The Cisco IOS Software naming conventions, field meaning, image content, and other details are subject to change.

Memory Requirements

On most Cisco routers including the integrated services routers, the IOS is stored in compact flash as a compressed image and loaded into DRAM during boot-up. The Cisco IOS Software Release 15.0 feature sets available for the Cisco 1900 and 2900 ISR require 256MB of flash and 512MB of RAM. The 3900 ISR requires 256MB of flash and 1GB of RAM. This does not include additional management tools such as Cisco Configuration Professional (Cisco CP). For complete details, refer to the product data sheet for the specific router.

Refer to **Packet Tracer Activity** for this chapter

10.1.1.9   Packet Tracer - Decode IOS Image Names

As a network technician, it is important that you are familiar with the IOS image naming convention so that you can, at a glance, determine important information about operating systems currently running on a device. In this scenario, Company A has merged with Company B. Company A has inherited network equipment from Company B. You have been assigned to document the features for the IOS images on these devices.

Refer to **Online Course** for Illustration

10.1.2   Managing Cisco IOS Images

10.1.2.1   TFTP Servers as a Backup Location

As a network grows, Cisco IOS Software images and configuration files can be stored on a central TFTP server. This helps to control the number of IOS images and the revisions to those IOS images, as well as the configuration files that must be maintained.

Production internetworks usually span wide areas and contain multiple routers. For any network, it is good practice to keep a backup copy of the Cisco IOS Software image in case the system image in the router becomes corrupted or accidentally erased.

Widely distributed routers need a source or backup location for Cisco IOS Software images. Using a network TFTP server allows image and configuration uploads and downloads over the network. The network TFTP server can be another router, a workstation, or a host system.

Refer to **Online Course** for Illustration

10.1.2.2   Creating Cisco IOS Image Backup

To maintain network operations with minimum down time, it is necessary to have procedures in place for backing up Cisco IOS images. This allows the network administrator to quickly copy an image back to a router in case of a corrupted or erased image.

In Figure 1, the network administrator wants to create a backup of the current image file on the router (c1900-universalk9-mz.SPA.152-4.M3.bin) to the TFTP server at 172.16.1.100.

To create a backup of the Cisco IOS image to a TFTP server, perform the following three steps:

Step 1.   Ensure that there is access to the network TFTP server. Ping the TFTP server to test connectivity, as shown in Figure 2.

Step 2.   Verify that the TFTP server has sufficient disk space to accommodate the Cisco IOS Software image. Use the **show flash0:** command on the router to determine the size of the Cisco IOS image file. The file in the example is 68831808 bytes long.

Step 3.   Copy the image to the TFTP server using the **copy** *source-url destination-url* command, as shown in Figure 3.

After issuing the command using the specified source and destination URLs, the user is prompted for the source file name, IP address of the remote host, and destination file name. The transfer will then begin.

Use the Syntax Checker in Figure 4 on R2 to copy the IOS to a TFTP server.

Refer to
Online Course
for Illustration

10.1.2.3   Copying a Cisco IOS Image

Cisco consistently releases new Cisco IOS software versions to resolve caveats and provide new features. This example uses IPv6 for the transfer to show that TFTP can also be used across IPv6 networks.

Figure 1 illustrates copying a Cisco IOS router image from a TFTP server. A new image file (c1900-universalk9-mz.SPA.152-4.M3.bin) will be copied from the TFTP server at 2001:DB8:CAFE:100::99 to the router.

Follow these steps to upgrade the software on the Cisco router:

Step 1.   Select a Cisco IOS image file that meets the requirements in terms of platform, features and software. Download the file from cisco.com and transfer it to the TFTP server.

Step 2.   Verify connectivity to the TFTP server. Ping the TFTP server from the router. The output in Figure 2 shows the TFTP server is accessible from the router.

Step 3.   Ensure that there is sufficient flash space on the router that is being upgraded. The amount of free flash can be verified using the `show flash0:` command. Compare the free flash space with the new image file size. The `show flash0:` command in Figure 3 is used to verify free flash size. Free flash space in the example is 182,394,880 bytes.

Step 4.   Copy the IOS image file from the TFTP server to the router using the `copy` command shown in Figure 4. After issuing this command with specified source and destination URLs, the user will be prompted for IP address of the remote host, source file name, and destination file name. The transfer of the file will begin.

Refer to
Online Course
for Illustration

10.1.2.4   Boot System

Boot system command

To upgrade to the copied IOS image after that image is saved on the router's flash memory, configure the router to load the new image during bootup using the `boot system` command. Save the configuration. Reload the router to boot the router with new image. After the router has booted, to verify the new image has loaded, use the `show version` command.

During startup, the bootstrap code parses the startup configuration file in NVRAM for the `boot system` commands that specify the name and location of the Cisco IOS Software image to load. Several `boot system` commands can be entered in sequence to provide a fault-tolerant boot plan.

Shown in Figure 1, the `boot system` command is a global configuration command that allows the user to specify the source for the Cisco IOS Software image to load. Some of the syntax options available include:

- Specify the flash device as the source of the Cisco IOS image.

    ```
    Router(config)# boot system flash0://c1900-universalk9-mz.SPA.152-4.M3.bin
    ```

- Specify the TFTP server as a source of Cisco IOS image, with ROMmon as backup.

    ```
    Router(config)# boot system tftp://c1900-universalk9-mz.SPA.152-4.M3.bin
    Router(config)# boot system rom
    ```

If there are no **boot system** commands in the configuration, the router defaults to loading the first valid Cisco IOS image in flash memory and running it.

As shown in Figure 2, the **show version** command can be used to verify the software image file.

Refer to **Packet Tracer Activity** for this chapter

10.1.2.5 Packet Tracer - Using a TFTP Server to Upgrade a Cisco IOS Image

A TFTP server can help manage the storage of IOS images and revisions to IOS images. For any network, it is good practice to keep a backup copy of the Cisco IOS Software image in case the system image in the router becomes corrupted or accidentally erased. A TFTP server can also be used to store new upgrades to the IOS and then deployed throughout the network where it is needed. In this activity, you will upgrade the IOS images on Cisco devices by using a TFTP server. You will also backup an IOS image with the use of a TFTP server.

Refer to **Interactive Graphic** in online course.

10.1.2.6 Video Demonstration - Managing Cisco IOS Images

Refer to **Online Course** for Illustration

10.2   IOS Licensing

10.2.1   Software Licensing

10.2.1.1 Licensing Overview

Beginning with Cisco IOS Software release 15.0, Cisco modified the process to enable new technologies within the IOS feature sets. Cisco IOS Software release 15.0 incorporates cross-platform feature sets to simplify the image selection process. It does this by providing similar functions across platform boundaries. Each device ships with the same universal image. Technology packages are enabled in the universal image via Cisco Software Activation licensing keys. The Cisco IOS Software Activation feature allows the user to enable licensed features and register licenses. The Cisco IOS Software Activation feature is a collection of processes and components used to activate Cisco IOS software feature sets by obtaining and validating Cisco software licenses.

Figure 1 shows the technology packages that are available:

- IP Base

- Data

- Unified Communications (UC)

- Security (SEC)

Note   The IP Base license is a prerequisite for installing the Data, Security, and Unified Communications licenses. For earlier router platforms that can support Cisco IOS Software release 15.0, a universal image is not available. It is necessary to download a separate image that contains the desired features.

Technology Package Licenses

Technology package licenses are supported on Cisco ISR G2 platforms (Cisco 1900, 2900, and 3900 Series routers). The Cisco IOS universal image contains all packages and features in one image. Each package is a grouping of technology-specific features. Multiple technology package licenses can be activated on the Cisco 1900, 2900, and 3900 series ISR platforms.

Note   Use the `show license feature` command to view the technology package licenses and feature licenses supported on the router.

Refer to
Online Course
for Illustration

10.2.1.2   Licensing Process

When a new router is shipped, it comes preinstalled with the software image and the corresponding permanent licenses for the customer-specified packages and features.

The router also comes with the evaluation license, known as a temporary license, for most packages and features supported on the specified router. This allows customers to try a new software package or feature by activating a specific evaluation license. If customers want to permanently activate a software package or feature on the router, they must get a new software license.

The figure shows the three steps to permanently activate a new software package or feature on the router.

Refer to
Online Course
for Illustration

10.2.1.3   Step 1. Purchase the Software Package or Feature to Install

Step 1. Purchase the software package or feature to install.

The first step is to purchase the software package or feature needed. This may be the IP Base license for a specific software release or adding a package to IP Base, such as Security.

Software Claim Certificates are used for licenses that require software activation. The claim certificate provides the Product Activation Key (PAK) for the license and important information regarding the Cisco End User License Agreement (EULA). In most instances, Cisco or the Cisco channel partner will have already activated the licenses ordered at the time of purchase and no Software Claim Certificate is provided.

In either instance, customers receive a product activation key (PAK) with their purchase. The PAK serves as a receipt and is used to obtain a license. A PAK is an 11 digit alpha numeric key created by Cisco manufacturing. It defines the Feature Set associated with the PAK. A PAK is not tied to a specific device until the license is created. A PAK can be purchased that generates any specified number of licenses. As shown in the figure, a separate license is required for each package, IP Base, Data, UC, and SEC.

Refer to
Online Course
for Illustration

10.2.1.4   Step 2. Obtain a License

Step 2. Obtain a license.

The next step is to obtain the license, which is actually a license file. A license file, also known as a Software Activation License, is obtained using one of the following options:

- **Cisco License Manager (CLM)** - This is a free software application available at http://www.cisco.com/go/clm. Cisco License Manager is a standalone application from Cisco that helps network administrators rapidly deploy multiple Cisco software licenses across their networks. Cisco License Manager can discover network devices, view their license information, and acquire and deploy licenses from Cisco. The application provides a GUI that simplifies installation and helps automate license acquisition, as well as perform multiple licensing tasks from a central location. CLM is free of charge and can be downloaded from CCO.

- **Cisco License Registration Portal** - This is the web-based portal for getting and registering individual software licenses, available at http://www.cisco.com/go/license.

Both of these processes require a PAK number and a Unique Device Identifier (UDI).

The PAK is received during purchase.

The UDI is a combination of the Product ID (PID), the Serial Number (SN), and the hardware version. The SN is an 11 digit number which uniquely identifies a device. The PID identifies the type of device. Only the PID and SN are used for license creation. This UDI can be displayed using the `show license udi` command shown in Figure 1. This information is also available on a pull-out label tray found on the device. Figure 2 shows an example of the pull-out label on a Cisco 1941 router.

After entering the appropriate information, the customer receives an email containing the license information to install the license file. The license file is an XML text file with a .lic extension.

Use the Syntax Checker in Figure 3 to determine the UDI on router R2.

Refer to
Online Course
for Illustration

10.2.1.5   Step 3. Install the License

Step 3. Install the License

After the license has been purchased, the customer receives a license file, which is an XML text file with a .lic extension. Installing a permanent license requires two steps:

a. Use the `license install` *stored-location-url* privileged exec mode commandto install a license file.

b. Reload the router using the privileged exec command `reload`. A reload is not required if an evaluation license is active.

Figure 1 shows the configuration for installing the permanent license for the Security package on the router.

Note   Unified Communications is not supported on 1941 routers.

A permanent license is a license that never expires. After a permanent license is installed on a router, it is good for that particular feature set for the life of the router, even across IOS versions. For example, when a UC, SEC, or Data license is installed on a router, the subsequent features for that license are activated even if the router is upgraded to a new IOS release. A permanent license is the most common license type used when a feature set is purchased for a device.

Note Cisco manufacturing preinstalls the appropriate permanent license on the ordered device for the purchased feature set. No customer interaction with the Cisco IOS Software Activation processes is required to enable that license on new hardware.

Use the Syntax Checker in Figure 2 to install a permanent license file on router R2.

Refer to
Online Course
for Illustration

10.2.2 License Verification and Management

10.2.2.1 License Verification

After a new license has been installed the router must be rebooted using the `reload` command. As shown in Figure 1, the `show version` command is used after the router is reloaded to verify that license has been installed.

The `show license` command in Figure 2 is used to display additional information about Cisco IOS software licenses. This command displays license information used to help with troubleshooting issues related to Cisco IOS software licenses. This command displays all the licenses installed in the system. In this example, both the IP Base and Security licenses have been installed. This command also displays the features that are available, but not licensed to execute, such as the Data feature set. Output is grouped according to how the features are stored in license storage.

The following is a brief description of the output:

- **Feature** - Name of the feature

- **License Type** - Type of license; such as Permanent or Evaluation

- **License State** - Status of the license; such as Active or In Use

- **License Count** - Number of licenses available and in use, if counted. If non-counted is indicated, the license is unrestricted.

- **License Priority** - Priority of the license; such as high or low

Note Refer to the Cisco IOS 15 command reference guide for complete details on the information displayed in the `show license` command.

Refer to
Online Course
for Illustration

10.2.2.2 Activate an Evaluation Right-To-Use License

The Evaluation license process has gone through three revisions on the ISR G2 devices. The latest revision, starting with Cisco IOS Releases 15.0(1)M6, 15.1(1)T4, 15.1(2)T4, 15.1(3) T2, and 15.1(4)M Evaluation licenses are replaced with Evaluation Right-To-Use licenses (RTU) after 60 days. An Evaluation License is good for a 60 day evaluation period. After the 60 days, this license automatically transitions into an RTU license. These licenses are available on the honor system and require the customer's acceptance of the EULA. The EULA is automatically applied to all Cisco IOS software licenses.

The `license accept end user agreement` global configuration mode command is used to configure a one-time acceptance of the EULA for all Cisco IOS software packages and features. After the command is issued and the EULA accepted, the EULA is automatically applied to all Cisco IOS software licenses and the user is not prompted to accept the EULA during license installation.

Figure 1 shows how to configure a one-time acceptance of the EULA:

```
Router(config)# license accept end user agreement
```

In addition, Figure 1 shows the command to activate an Evaluation RTU license:

```
Router# license boot module module-name technology-package package-name
```

Use the ? in place of the arguments to determine which module names and supported software packages are available on the router. Technology package names for Cisco ISR G2 platforms are:

- *ipbasek9* - IP Base technology package

- *securityk9* - Security technology package

- *datak9* - Data technology package

- *uck9* - Unified Communications package (not available on 1900 series)

Note   A reload using the `reload` command is required to activate the software package.

Evaluation licenses are temporary, and are used to evaluate a feature set on new hardware. Temporary licenses are limited to a specific usage period (for example, 60 days).

Reload the router after a license is successfully installed using the `reload` command. The `show license` command in Figure 2 verifies that the license has been installed.

Use the Syntax Checker in Figure 3 to save all license files on router R2 to accept the EULA and activate an Evaluation RTU data package license on the 1900 router.

Refer to
Online Course
for Illustration

10.2.2.3 Back up the License

The `license save` command is used to copy all licenses in a device and store them in a format required by the specified storage location. Saved licenses are restored by using the `license install` command.

The command to back up a copy of the licenses on a device is:

```
Router# license save file-sys://lic-location
```

Use the `show flash0:` command to verify that the licenses have been saved (Figure 1).

The license storage location can be a directory or a URL that points to a file system. Use the ? command to see the storage locations supported by a device.

Use the Syntax Checker in Figure 2 to save all license files on router R2.

Refer to
Online Course
for Illustration

10.2.2.4   Uninstall the License

To clear an active permanent license from the Cisco 1900 series, 2900 series, and 3900 series routers, perform the following steps:

Step 1.   **Disable the technology package.**

  ■ Disable the active license with the command:

```
Router(config)# license boot module module-name technology-package
package-name disable
```

  ■ Reload the router using the **reload** command. A reload is required to make the software package inactive.

Step 2.   **Clear the license.**

  ■ Clear the technology package license from license storage.

```
Router# license clear feature-name
```

  ■ Clear the **license boot module** module-name **technology-package** package-name **disable** command used for disabling the active license:

```
Router(config)# no license boot module module-name technology-package
package-name disable
```

Note   Some licenses, such as built-in licenses, cannot be cleared. Only licenses that have been added by using the **license install** command are removed. Evaluation licenses are not removed.

Figure 1 shows an example of clearing an active license.

Use the Syntax Checker in Figure 2 to uninstall the security license on router R2.

Refer to
Interactive Graphic
in online course.

10.2.2.5   Video Demonstration - Working with IOS 15 Image Licenses

Refer to
Online Course
for Illustration

10.3   Summary

Refer to
Lab Activity
for this chapter

10.3.1.1   Class Activity Powerful Protocols

Powerful Protocols

Scenario

At the end of this course, you are asked to complete two Capstone Projects where you will create, configure, and verify two network topologies using the two main routing protocols taught in this course, EIGRP and OSPF.

To make things easier, you decide to create a chart of configuration and verification commands to use for these two design projects. To help devise the protocol charts, ask another student in the class to help you.

Refer to the PDF for this chapter for directions on how to create a design for this modeling project. When complete, share your work with another group or with the class. You may also want to save the files created for this project in a network portfolio for future reference.

Refer to **Packet Tracer Activity** for this chapter

10.3.1.2   Packet Tracer - EIGRP Capstone

In this Capstone Project activity, you will demonstrate your ability to:

- Design, configure, verify, and secure EIGRP, IPv4, or IPv6 on a network

- Design a VLSM addressing scheme for the devices connected to the LANs

- Present your design using network documentation from your Capstone Project network

Refer to **Packet Tracer Activity** for this chapter

10.3.1.3   Packet Tracer - OSPF Capstone

In this Capstone Project activity, you will demonstrate your ability to:

- Configure basic OSPFv2 to enable internetwork communications in a small- to medium-sized IPv4 business network.

- Implement advanced OSPF features to enhance operation in a small- to medium-sized business network.

- Implement multiarea OSPF for IPv4 to enable internetwork communications in a small- to medium-sized business network.

- Configure basic OSPFv3 to enable internetwork communications in a small- to medium-sized IPv6 business network.

Refer to **Packet Tracer Activity** for this chapter

10.3.1.4   Packet Tracer - Skills Integration Challenge

As network technician familiar with IPv4 addressing, routing, and network security, you are now ready to apply your knowledge and skills to a network infrastructure. Your task is to finish designing the VLSM IPv4 addressing scheme, implement multi-area OSPF, and secure access to the VTY lines using access control lists.

Refer to **Online Course** for Illustration

10.3.1.5   Summary

Examples of Cisco IOS software releases include 12.3, 12.4, 15.0, and 15.1. Along with each software release there are new versions of the software used to implement bug fixes and new features.

Cisco IOS software 12.4 incorporates new software features and hardware support that was introduced in the Cisco IOS Software 12.3T train and additional software fixes. Mainline releases (also called maintenance releases) contain no uppercase letter in their release designation and inherit new Cisco IOS Software functionality and hardware from lower numbered T releases. Prior to and including 12.4, the mainline "M" train received bug fixes only. The technology "T" train includes fixes as well as new feature and platforms. The 12.4T train provides Cisco IOS software functionality and hardware adoption that introduces new technology, functionality, and hardware advances that are not available in the Cisco IOS Software 12.4 mainline train.

In the Cisco IOS Software 15.0 release family a new strategy is in place. Cisco IOS 15.0 release family does not diverge into separate M and T trains but into M and T releases in the same train. For example, the first release in the Cisco IOS Software 15.0 release family is 15.0(1)M, where M indicates it is an extended maintenance release. An extended maintenance release is ideal for long-term maintenance. Not all releases in the Cisco IOS Software 15.0 release family will be extended maintenance releases; there will also be standard maintenance releases that receive the latest features and hardware support. The standard maintenance releases will have an uppercase T in their designation.

When selecting or upgrading a Cisco IOS router, it is important to choose the proper IOS image with the correct feature set and version. The Cisco IOS image file is based on a special naming convention. The name for the Cisco IOS image file contains multiple parts, each with a specific meaning. Example: c1900-universalk9-mz.SPA.152-4.M3.bin

Commands are available for upgrading and verification of flash. The `show flash` command displays the files store in flash memory including the system image files. This command can also be used to verify free flash size. The `boot system` command is a global configuration command which allows the user to specify the source for the Cisco IOS.

Using a network TFTP server allows image and configuration uploads and downloads over the network. The network TFTP server can be another router, a workstation, or a host system.

Beginning with Cisco IOS Software release 15.0, Cisco modified the process to enable new technologies within the IOS feature sets. Each device ships with the same universal image. Technology packages such as IP Base, Data, UC, and SEC are enabled in the universal image via Cisco software activation licensing keys. Each licensing key is unique to a particular device and is obtained from Cisco by providing the product ID and serial number of the router and a Product Activation Key (PAK).

License activation is not necessary for factory ordered preconfigured licenses prior to use. IP Base comes shipped as a permanent license on all ISR-G2 devices. The other three technology packages: Data, Security, and Unified Communications come with an Evaluation license as the default, but a permanent license may be purchased.

A Permanent License is a license that never expires. For example, once a UC (Unified Communications), Security or Data license is installed on a router, the subsequent features for that license will be activated even if the router is upgraded to a new IOS release.

Installing a License

Prerequisites:

- Obtain the necessary PAK, which is an 11 digit ID that can be delivered by mail or electronically

- Need to have a valid Cisco username/password

- Retrieve serial number and PID with the `show license udi` command or from the router label tray

The `show version` command is used after the router is reloaded to verify that license has been installed.

The `show license` command is used to display additional information about Cisco IOS software licenses.

The `license accept end user agreement` global configuration command is used to configure a one-time acceptance of the EULA for all Cisco IOS software packages and features.

Use the cisco.com web site to research other benefits and information on IOS 15.

Go to the online course to take the quiz and exam.

Chapter 10 Quiz

This quiz is designed to provide an additional opportunity to practice the skills and knowledge presented in the chapter and to prepare for the chapter exam. You will be allowed multiple attempts and the grade does not appear in the gradebook.

Chapter 10 Exam

The chapter exam assesses your knowledge of the chapter content.

Your Chapter Notes

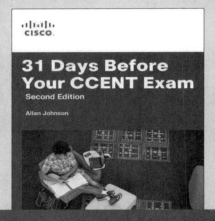